Creating
Born Criminals

Creating
Born Criminals

Nicole Hahn Rafter

University of Illinois Press

Urbana and Chicago

© 1997 by Nicole Hahn Rafter
Manufactured in the United States of America
C 5 4 3 2 1

This book is printed on acid-free paper.

Library of Congress Cataloging-in-Publication Data
Rafter, Nicole Hahn, 1939–
Creating born criminals / Nicole Hahn Rafter.
p.   cm.
Includes bibliographical references and index.
ISBN 0–252–02237–8 (acid-free paper)
1. Criminal behavior—United States—
Genetic aspects. 2. Eugenics—United States.
I. Title.
HV6047.R33   1997
364.2'4—dc20   96–35672
                              CIP

For my accomplice,

Robert Hahn,

with thanks

for leading me astray

Contents

Preface   ix

Introduction: Born Criminals, Eugenics,
and Biological Theories of Crime   1

1. Before Eugenics: Idiots and Idiocy
   in the Mid-Nineteenth Century   17

2. Feebleminded Women and the Advent
   of Eugenic Criminology   35

3. Criminalizing the Mentally Retarded   55

4. The Rise of the Moral Imbecile   73

5. Degenerates Appear in the Prison System   93

6. The Anthropological Born Criminal   110

7. The Criminal Imbecile   133

8. Defective Delinquents   149

9. Psychopaths and the Decline of Eugenic
   Criminology   167

10. Defective Delinquent Legislation   188

11. The Aftermath of Eugenic Criminology   210

Afterword   237
References Cited   241
Index   271

Illustrations follow pages 92 and 148

Preface

This book began at a precise moment: the day in the mid-1970s when I opened Mark Haller's delightful study of eugenics and first read the words *defective delinquent*. The term transfixed me. Who had invented this horrific phrase? Who were they trying to scare, and to whom had the term been applied? I discovered that *defective delinquent* was but one of many terms coined over time to denote "born" criminals—offenders who seemed doomed from birth to commit crime. I also discovered that in the late nineteenth and early twentieth centuries, some states had established eugenic institutions, places where defective delinquents and others considered to be innately criminalistic could be incarcerated to prevent them from reproducing. Astonishingly some of these institutions had survived into the 1960s. Nonetheless, I could discover nothing about them in books about eugenics—the "science" of human breeding—or in histories of criminal justice. Americans, it seemed, did not want to know about their past efforts to exterminate "inferiors."

A grant from the National Science Foundation enabled me to travel to institutions that had generated eugenics doctrine. I visited the Syracuse Developmental Center, founded in the 1850s, the first asylum for mentally retarded people and the point of origin for an entire system of institutions that produced eugenic information about "the unfit." The recent destruction of this institution's oldest building proved advantageous, for under its cornerstone the dismantlers had found a document, placed there more than a century earlier, listing the Syracuse citizens who had helped to bring the asylum to their town. Rummaging in local records, I uncovered information about these sponsors that, by throwing light on the much-debated issue of the reasons residential institutions were founded in the nineteenth century, helped me to understand the context in which eugenic ideas about criminality took root. Interest in eugenic criminology also led me to the institutions that the doctrine produced, including the gloomy Napanoch prison where, beginning in 1921 and continuing for decades, New York incarcerated male defective delinquents.

The more information I gathered, however, the more I realized that I could not single-handedly produce a history of biological theories of crime and eugenics, a work that would require familiarity with not only the evolution of criminological thought but also the development of a number of institutional systems, professions, and social movements. I continued to investigate related issues while other scholars also produced works that in time helped to create the foundation for this one.

Haller's pioneering study of eugenics was followed by others that, although they too paid little attention to criminology, demonstrated that eugenics had been a respectable and powerful movement in turn-of-the-century America, attracting liberals and radicals as well as right-wing extremists. Institutional historians published studies that facilitated my investigations of the evolution of the prison and mental retardation systems. The growing body of literature on professionalization enabled me to understand why members of emerging social control occupations became the warhorses of the eugenics movement. Most important, I became familiar with work by Michel Foucault that enabled me to conceptualize interrelationships among knowledge production, criminal bodies, and social control.

My decision to return to biological theories of crime was prompted once again by a fortuitous encounter with defective delinquents. In the late 1980s a grant from the New York State Archives enabled me to examine the case files of the Napanoch Institution for Male Defective Delinquents. I ploughed through these documents until I came to a six-inch-thick file for the prisoner I call Fenix Whipple. At last I had found details on the life of an "actual" born criminal, someone who fit nearly all definitions of the type. Fenix's story opens and closes this book.

■ ■ ■

In the twenty years I have been working (off and on) on this study, I have been helped by more people than I can possibly thank here, but in particular I want to acknowledge the assistance of many friends at the New York State Archives, especially Richard Andress, who spent many hours guiding me through the collection and arranging for the illustrations; Kathleen Roe, who provided documents, citations, and good cheer; and James D. Folts, who gave me permission to use Fenix Whipple's mug shots. Ann Aronson photographed the illustrations. JoAnne Edwards, Linda Kramer, and Peter Spitzform at Dewey Library, Johnson State College in Vermont, together with Salvatore Genovese, Amy Kautzman, Jeanne Siraco, Yves Yacinthe, and other librarians at Northeastern University, provided a lifeline to obscure sources. Mary Ann Hawkes interrupted her own work to give me invaluable information on eugenic sterilizations at the New Jersey Reformatory for Women, and Ellen Dwyer enabled me to spend several months in the library of Indiana University at Bloomington.

Portions of this book first appeared in "Criminal Anthropology in the United States," *Criminology* 30 (Nov. 1992): 525–45, used here with the permission of the American Society of Criminology; and "Claims-making and Socio-cultural Context in the First U.S. Eugenics Campaign," *Social Problems* 39 (Feb. 1992): 17–34, © 1992 by the Society for the Study of Social Problems, used here by permission of the Society.

The many people who read the manuscript in part or in whole, offering valuable suggestions, include Piers Beirne, Pam Block, Dorothy Chunn, Ellen Dwyer, Robert Hahn, Ken Jacobson, Robert Menzies, James Messerschmidt, Steven Noll, April Pattavina, Alexander Pisciotta, Neal Shover, Alan Stoskopf, Alexandra Todd, and Diane Vaughan. James W. Trent Jr. responded generously to my many calls for advice. Anne and Steve Turner have supported me through faith in my work since graduate school, Alexander Pisciotta and Steve Noll picked me up when I fell down, and Kathleen Daly helped me to track down the work of the bloodthirsty W. Duncan McKim. When I thought the manuscript was completed, I sent a copy to Neal Shover, who disabused me of my illusion; his meticulous editing and thoughtful suggestions did much to strengthen the (next) final version. Pamela Allara, Mary Campbell, and Lisa Cuklanz, who were my fellow instructors in the Graduate Consortium in Women's Studies at Radcliffe, and the students in our seminars stimulated my thinking about gender, representation, and social control. Others who helped include Kevin Dann; Lou Ferliger; my mother (and favorite clipping service), Elizabeth Wilson Fischer; Laura Frader; Dr. Bernard Glueck Jr.; Mary Gibson; my children, Sarah Rachel Hahn and Charles Alexander Hahn; Frances Heidensohn; Nancy Reichman; and my editors, Richard Martin and Bruce Bethell. As usual, I owe my greatest debt to my partner, Robert Hahn. Insofar as this book is defective or delinquent, I am solely to blame.

Creating
Born Criminals

Introduction:

Born Criminals, Eugenics, and Biological Theories of Crime

> Not until comparatively lately has much attention been given to the way in which criminals are produced. . . . It is certain, however, that lunatics and criminals are as much manufactured articles as are steam-engines and calico-printing machines.
>
> Henry Maudsley, *Responsibility in Mental Disease*

How are born criminals made? At first that question may seem absurd ("There's no such thing as a born criminal") or simpleminded ("Genes, naturally"). Nonetheless, the question of the factors responsible for people who seem to be criminalistic from birth or an early age has intrigued thinkers for thousands of years. Ultimately it is a question about the origins of evil. There are three ways to answer it. One way is religious: according to some theologians, God predestines certain people to sin. A second is biological: since about 1800, physicians and other scientists have contended that in some cases biological defects determine who will commit crimes. The third type of answer is definitional: according to such explanations, no matter what the theological or biological circumstances may be, born criminals are produced through social processes and do not—in fact cannot—exist independent of them.

This book focuses on the second, biological type of answer to the question of the way in which born criminals come into being. It concentrates on a series of biological explanations for criminal behavior framed in terms of *eugenics,* the theory that socially problematic behaviors are inherited and can be reduced or eliminated by preventing the carriers of bad seeds from reproducing. Eugenics theory flourished in the United States between 1870 and 1920, a period during which eugenic explanations of and solutions to crime achieved extraordinary influence. To study these explanations, I take the third, definitional approach to the issue of the production of born criminals, examining the social processes through which eugenicists came to define and apply their hereditarian theories of crime.

Thus I simultaneously present two different answers to the fundamental question, How are born criminals made? I take theories that in effect attribute the creation of born criminals to biological events and investigate how these theories themselves brought criminal bodies into being.

The Making of a Born Criminal

To illustrate what I mean by the social definition or creation of born criminals, let me re-create a seemingly innocuous event that took place in late October 1921, when an inmate was transferred from one prison to another. The inmate—whose records I discovered in the New York State Archives, long after his death—was transferred from New York's Elmira Reformatory to Napanoch, a prison recently designated as an institution for defective delinquents. Officials probably did not inform the twenty-two-year-old inmate, whom I will call Fenix Whipple, that his transfer had been triggered by his diagnosis as a "defective delinquent," the then-current synonym for "born criminal." Nor in all likelihood did they tell Fenix that the transfer automatically extended his sentence into an indefinite term— potentially a life sentence. The Napanoch Institution for Defective Delinquents, established to hold offenders until they recovered from the disease of criminality, was the first eugenic prison in the United States. It was also the ultimate custodial institution, since those who operated it, while dedicated to the rehabilitative "medical" model of crime control, were certain that defective delinquents such as Fenix could never be cured.[1]

The Elmira officials who transferred Fenix to Napanoch believed that he had amply demonstrated himself to be a delinquent in the sense that we today call "genetic." Fenix's criminal career had begun about 1915 with an arrest for assault and rape. His behavior in this case may have been less serious than these charges suggest, or officials may have already decided that he was too abnormal to be held fully responsible. At any rate, although sixteen years old, he was not prosecuted but rather committed to Letchworth Village, a civil institution for the feebleminded and epileptic. Fenix escaped from Letchworth Village, however, and over the next three years he was rearrested at least five times and found guilty of simple assault (hitting a fellow worker with a pitchfork), petty larceny (stealing coonskins on one occasion and old coins on another), and robbery (breaking into a safe in Poughkeepsie). Court officers reacted in measured fashion to the youth's offenses, sending him first to the civil institution, then to jails for short terms, and later to Elmira, a prison designed to reform young men. Fenix was paroled from Elmira several times, only to be rearrested and returned.

Mental testing at Elmira showed Fenix to be "defective" as well as delinquent. The prison's physician, measuring Fenix's IQ at 47 and his "Binet age" at ten, concluded that he was "feeble-minded": "Unable to read simple sentences—is unteachable—is strongly sexed and inclined toward licentious activities—is very ignorant of the most ordinary facts and unfit to be at large." This was precisely the type of offender that the institution at Napanoch had been designed to hold. Napanoch aimed at incapacitating men like Fenix in two ways: it would prevent them from committing further crimes (the traditional goal of incapacitation), and it would immobilize them reproductively, making it impossible for them to pass on their hereditary unfitness to the next generation.

Fenix's family background seemed to confirm prison officials' assumption—a commonplace of eugenics theory—that weak intelligence indicates bad heredity. Of Polish ancestry, the Whipples were extremely poor, deriving their sole income from seasonal labor on Upper New York State farms. Fenix's father, an alcoholic, had an arrest record and may have been as peculiar as his son—he "once stole a cow, dehorned her, and painted her black." Moreover, Fenix's records continue, "both parents are reputed feebleminded." All four of Fenix's brothers had criminal records, which apparently constituted further evidence of the family's bad heredity and the close connection between feeblemindedness[2] and criminality. One of these brothers was also committed to Napanoch, where he died after a tonsillectomy. Another died at Sing Sing while serving a twenty-five-year sentence for rape. A niece was committed to Napanoch's sister prison, an institution for feebleminded, criminalistic women at Albion, New York. To prison officials, it seemed clear that Fenix was an offender of the "typical hereditary type."

Despite their problems, members of the Whipple family remained concerned about Fenix's fate. His file includes letters from relatives to prison officials inquiring as to when they might expect his release. His indefinite sentence baffled them, as it did Fenix himself.[3] Not long after he was sent to Napanoch, his father wrote to the institution's superintendent: "Now Dr I would like to know how he is getting a long and if you could tell me about how long he has to stay here[.] Frank L. Christian [superintendent of Elmira] says he was sent Back for defective delinquents I don't understand what he means by that name." Later his father wrote another official to say that Fenix expected to return home only "in a ruff Box."

Even among Napanoch's inmates, many of whom were transferred to the institution because prison officials elsewhere found them offensive, Fenix stood out as exceptionally difficult. Soon after arriving he was caught with a container of petrolatum "practicing bestiality" on Libbie, the female airedale who had the run of the prison yard. Subsequent sexual misconduct, together with Fenix's inability "to employ himself except under continuous and stern discipline," led one officer to conclude that "he should never be considered" for the parole that had by that time become an option for Napanoch prisoners.

His troublesomeness notwithstanding, Fenix was paroled twice. After seven months of liberty in 1927, he had his parole revoked because he jumped at some women along a country road and said, with characteristic clumsiness, "Come here girls I want to fuck you." Reparoled thirty years later, he managed to stay out of prison for a year and a half, living with a farm couple. But when Fenix threatened the husband, stole the wife's church money, and demonstrated an "over-affectionate attitude or desire to become involved with children," his parole was revoked again.

Ironically, at the time when Napanoch was turned into an institution for defective delinquents, geneticists were already questioning whether criminality could be inherited, and psychologists had begun to doubt the supposed causal connection between feeblemindedness and crime. The concept of defective delinquency, popular for the past decade, was being eclipsed by a less hereditarian form of born-criminal theory, the psychiatric concept of psychopathy. Nevertheless, even though the scientific ground for a defective delinquent diagnosis was crumbling, Napanoch held Fenix for over five decades, until his death in 1962, first on the eugenic ground that he carried the bad seed of hereditary criminality and later because he proved to be impossible to reform.

Fenix Whipple presents an undeniably difficult case. Damaged biologically (although not necessarily genetically), Fenix was a person whom almost anyone might label "incorrigibly criminalistic." His biography, to which I return in the last chapter, brings us as close as we are likely to get to an "actual" born criminal.

Fenix's commitment as a defective delinquent was in a sense the goal toward which born-criminal theorists had been working for over a century. The process that Michel Foucault describes as the "psychiatrization of criminal danger" began about 1800 with efforts to determine what made the most notorious criminals commit their atrocities; by 1900 it had led to the putative discovery of morbid states in even petty offenders. Fenix, with his weak intelligence and perpetual misbehavior, literally constituted what Foucault calls a criminal "without reason," one of the pathetic recidivists with whom discussions of dangerousness culminated early in the twentieth century.[4]

As summarized by Foucault, the ongoing psychiatric search for the essence of dangerousness posed three questions: "Are there individuals who are intrinsically dangerous? By what signs can they be recognized, and how can one react to their presence?" In this book I show how Fenix Whipple and eugenic institutions such as Napanoch became answers to these questions—responses formulated by not only psychiatrists but an entire phalanx of social control experts. I tell the tale of the "pathologi-fication" of crime and of the criminal body, the momentous shift from the eighteenth-century preoccupation with illegal actions to the twentieth-century obsession with individuals whose biological conditions seem to disease society.[5] Despite the dreariness of his offenses, Fenix became his period's born criminal, a defective delinquent whose dangerousness resided in his body itself—in his abnormal brain, his sperm, and his degenerate heredity.

Until he was transferred to Napanoch, Fenix was but one Elmira prisoner among many. His diagnosis as a "defective delinquent" changed that, reconstructing him as a born criminal. The diagnosis gave him what sociologist Harold Garfinkel calls a new "total identity." This identity was "total" in that it referred not to what Fenix had done or might do but to "the ultimate 'grounds' or 'reasons' for his performance."[6] In short it was an identity based not on his actions but on what people defined as his condition. Fenix never managed to escape it.

Fenix's designation as a defective delinquent required a series of eugenic suppositions about his condition. Officials first had to assume that he had been born feebleminded, which they did despite evidence that in childhood he had been beaten unconscious by his father and had injured his head falling from a moving train. Next they had to assume that he had inherited his feeblemindedness, a supposition they justified with the vague report that "both parents are reputed feebleminded." They also had to assume that there was a causal connection between his "hereditary" feeblemindedness and his criminal activities and that, if allowed to reproduce, he would father feebleminded, criminalistic children. Why the officials made these assumptions and concluded that Fenix Whipple had to be a defective delinquent is one of the questions I address in this study. The following chapters show how, during the nineteenth and early twentieth centuries, *criminality, feeblemindedness,* and related terms were interpreted and reinterpreted so as to make the officials' readings seem not merely plausible but scientific and hence compelling.

Rediscovering Eugenic Criminology

In the United States biological theories of crime have developed in three stages. During the first stage, which ran from the late eighteenth century until after the Civil War (ca. 1785–1875), physicians tried to explain seemingly innate depravity in terms of biologically based mental disorders. Their biological explanations had little hereditarian content, however, and only slightly affected the treatment of convicted criminals. During the third stage, which began about 1925 and continues into the present, biological explanations have again tended to avoid hereditarianism and have had little impact (at least so far) on criminal justice policies. During the second of these three stages, however, from about 1875 into the 1920s, born-criminal theories incorporated popular hereditarian explanations of social problems and significantly affected public policy. Because second-stage versions of born-criminal theories all built to some degree on eugenics principles, it seems useful to group them under the general heading of *eugenic criminology*.

Previous studies have traced the evolution of biological theories of crime in terms of the development of particular sciences (phrenology, criminology, psychology, psychiatry) or concepts (degeneration, feeblemindedness, insanity, psychopathy). These studies include Norman Dain's *Concepts of Insanity in the United States, 1789–1865* (1964); John D. Davies's *Phrenology: Fad and Science* (1955); Arthur E. Fink's *Causes of Crime: Biological Theories in the United States, 1800–1915* (1938); Foucault's "Dangerous Individual" (1988); Stephen Jay Gould's *Mismeasure of Man* (1981); Sydney Maughs's (1941) dense survey of psychopathy theory; Ysabel Rennie's *Search for Criminal Man* (1978); and—the most comprehensive source—a Swedish dissertation, Henry Werlinder's *Psychopathy: A History of the Concept* (1978). But none of these works has recognized the general phenomenon of eugenic criminology.[7] That is, none has recognized the eugenic themes that permeate and tie together such apparently diverse notions as criminal anthropology, defective delinquency, degeneration, and moral imbecility.

Several obstacles have blocked conceptualization of the category of *eugenic criminology*. The term *eugenics* was not coined till 1883[8] and did not enter the American vocabulary until after the turn of the century. As a result, it has been difficult to perceive that eugenic ideas began shaping U.S. social policies a good deal earlier, even though they did not yet bear the "eugenics" label. Then too, important revisions in eugenics doctrine just after 1900 have obscured equally important continuities in late nineteenth- and early twentieth-century thinking about the origins of criminals and other "degenerates." Focusing on the differences, historians have missed the themes that unite various forms of eugenic criminology.[9] Another obstacle to recognizing eugenic criminology as a distinct type of theory has been the fact that many Americans, knowing what horrors the Nazis committed in the name of eugenics, have shut their eyes to their own country's eugenic experiments. Finally, historians of the U.S. eugenics movement have simply not investigated its influence on criminology and criminal justice in sufficient detail to realize that eugenic criminology constitutes a distinctive set of criminological discourses.[10]

For somewhat different reasons, historians of mental disorder have sidestepped the sizable literature on inherent criminality. Eugenicists pictured inherent criminality as not a loss but a lack, not an acquired condition but an innate one, a form not of insanity but of mental retardation. Historians have long been fascinated by insanity and the crime-associated disorder of "moral insanity," but they have shown little interest in mental retardation and *its* crime-associated disorder of "moral idiocy," or "moral imbecility." In the hierarchy of mental abnormalities, insanity has higher status than retardation and attracts more sympathy from public, scholars, and physicians alike. (In theory we are all susceptible to mental disease, but no one can "become" mentally retarded.) Thus historians have overlooked ways in which definitions of mental retardation intersected with definitions of inborn criminality. They have for the most part ignored the rich literature on moral idiocy and moral imbecility.

Likewise legal scholars and the law itself have slighted the legal ramifications of mental retardation and eugenic criminology. Legal theorists have written volumes about the criminal (ir)responsibility of the mentally diseased but almost nothing about the criminal culpability of the mentally retarded. Because eugenicists associated criminality with feeblemindedness, not insanity, their theories of crime, together with the social science they produced and legal reforms they achieved, have sunk with few traces.

My central goal in this book is to reconstruct eugenic theories of crime and assess their impact on criminal justice practices. Second, I document the history of born criminals themselves—those offenders (and even potential offenders) whom eugenicists identified as incurably criminalistic. Thus I investigate who was affected by these theories and how. Third, I show how eugenic criminology represented criminal bodies and discursively brought them into being. The biological abnormalities attributed to born criminals changed from generation to generation as theorists encoded offenders' bodies with new signs of evil. These hieroglyphics became most spectacular in the late nineteenth century with the appearance of the criminal anthropologists' apelike born criminal, a monstrosity who manifested wickedness from coarse head hair to prehensile toe. At other times the abnormalities grew inward, receding into offenders' brains and germ plasm. Such variations reflected and at the same time promoted new definitions of what it meant to be average, normal, and a good citizen. Thus, following the lead of biologist Anne Fausto-Sterling, I conceptualize born criminals' bodies as "politicized bodies,"[11] asking such questions as the following: Whose bodies are we discussing? How are they pictured? How do they differ by gender?

This study is national in scope but concentrates on New York, the state that led all others in formulating and applying eugenic criminology. In the late nineteenth century New York established the first civil institution for persons deemed hereditarily criminalistic; in the early twentieth century it established the first penal unit for defective delinquents. The founding of these two institutions constituted milestones in the application of eugenic criminology. Moreover, because both were institutions for females, created to prevent reproduction by criminalistic women, they enable us to explore gender differences in the articulation and consequences of born-criminal theory. In addition, New York is ideal for in-depth study because it developed the most elaborate state institutional system for officially labeled defective delinquents.[12]

Early in my work on this book, I found myself hamstrung by a vocabulary problem: the English language has no general term for offenders considered to be biological criminals. I discovered a multitude of entrancing specific terms, such as *congenital criminal, constitutional psychopath, degenerate, moral imbecile,* and *moral lunatic.*[13] Biological theorists, despite their ability to invent these evocative synonyms, nevertheless failed to coin an all-encompassing term for their subject. Working without reference to their predecessors' ideas and often in different professions, they had little sense of mutual tradition or of a common project. Moreover, as I came to realize, the born-criminal idea is a chameleon-like concept that adapts easily to new social-historical circumstances. It frequently serves as a metaphor for otherness, and as science historian JoAnne Brown explains, metaphors owe their social effectiveness to their flexibility, their "very vagueness and multiplicity of . . . meanings." "Metaphor, through its familiar literal referent, appears to offer self-evident, socially shared meaning to the unfamiliar. Yet it invites each listener to interpret its meaning personally, even privately. . . . Thus each listener is likely to interpret a given metaphor differently, yet also perceive that interpretation to be widely shared, without ever realizing that the consensus is created by the vagueness of the metaphor itself."[14] This malleability contributed to the ongoing vitality of the born-criminal concept, but at the same time it fed the illusion that an umbrella term for born criminals was unnecessary.

Lacking a general term but unable to write this study without one, I chose the most familiar of the concept's many synonyms, the criminal anthropologists' phrase *born criminal*. I use *born criminal*, then, to denote generically those to whom over time biological theorists have attributed the condition of innate criminality.

My definitional approach, which treats born criminals as cultural artifacts, is in most respects the antithesis of that used by born-criminal theorists themselves. Born-criminal theorists aim at establishing scientific truths. In contrast and opposition, I assume that there is no unmediated, hard scientific truth about born criminals as such. In the epigraph to this introduction, English psychiatrist Henry Maudsley, an influential born-criminal theorist of the late nineteenth century, speaks of criminals as biologically "manufactured"; I argue that they were socially manufactured, brought into being by the discourses of scientists and social-control specialists. We would agree, however, that the nature of their production is an empirical issue, one that can and indeed must be decided by carefully evaluating the data.[15]

From the viewpoint of modern genetics, eugenic criminologists misunderstood the mechanisms of heredity. Thus their born criminals are a bit like witches: once perceived as immense social threats, today they are not perceived at all. There are nevertheless sound reasons for studying the constructs of eugenic criminology. Notions that may today seem ludicrous have nonetheless changed the course of human history, as the thousands who burned at the stake or (like Fenix Whipple) were imprisoned as defective delinquents might testify. The way in which born criminals of the past were defined and hunted down illuminates the dynamics of social problems movements in general. Moreover, by following the steps through which eugenicists defined born criminals, we can observe the processes through which the science of eugenics itself came into being; that is, we can observe a science (albeit a now-discredited one) in the making. And we can trace, with considerable specificity, the production of criminological knowledge, examining how born-criminal theories were shaped by and in turn affected their social contexts. Although definitional or constructionist studies are now common in other social and physical sciences, they remain unusual in criminology.[16] Their growth has been stunted partly by the success of born-criminal theories. These theories obscure definitional processes by claiming direct access to a reality "out there." In the absence of a critical, definitional tradition, criminology continues to lack accounts of its own epistemological and disciplinary history.

I thus approach born-criminal discourses as a series of texts that created social truths. Whether one regards eugenic criminology as scientific or pseudoscientific is, in the final analysis, irrelevant, for (to borrow words that cultural theorist Zillah Eisenstein uses in a related context) it helped to "establish how people think about what is real." I am concerned not with digging down to a supposed bedrock of truths but with scientific knowledge as an enormously important stratum and resource in the structuring of power and social organization. I want to show how scientific discourses about inherent criminality emerged and gained authority, only to be disconfirmed eventually by other, more powerful streams of thought. To treat truth as relative in this manner does not bar one from forming judgments about the accuracy of truth claims, as I do here about the theories of eugenic criminology. "Plurality does not mean that all truths are equal," Eisenstein explains; "it merely uncovers the role of power in defining truth." [17]

The Organization of This Study

This book is organized around stages in the evolution of eugenic criminology and of the two most closely related institutional systems, asylums for the retarded and prisons for criminals. The next three chapters trace the origins and early development of the mental retardation system. Chapter 1 establishes mid-nineteenth-century baselines against which this system's subsequent involvement in the production of eugenic criminology may be measured. It describes the founding and early operation of the first independent state institution for the retarded, New York's Syracuse Asylum for Idiots. Acting in sharp contrast to later policy, New York established this residential school to shield mentally backward children from abuse, train them for self-sufficiency, and return them, healed, to the community.

Twenty-five years later New York established a second institution, the Newark Custodial Asylum for Feeble-minded Women, to protect society against the retarded, a group now conceptualized as criminalistic degenerates. Chapter 2 discusses the founding of this first eugenic institution and the theory of degeneration that lay behind it. By the century's end, as chapter 3 shows, nearly every American superintendent of an institution for the feebleminded had rejected Syracuse's curative philosophy in favor of Newark's degenerationist creed and custodial principles. Following the lead of Pennsylvania superintendent Isaac N. Kerlin, the system's other superintendents identified eugenics as the route to professionalization. They became experts in the diseases of society, afflictions that, they taught, flowed from their inmates' inborn and inherited criminality.

Chapter 4 makes a transition between the early chapters on asylums for the retarded and later chapters on prisons. Unlike other chapters, it is not tied to a particular institutional setting but rather ranges freely across time and space to examine the evolution of born-criminal theory up to 1900. It concludes with a section on born criminals as metaphors that analyzes the social meanings of the born-criminal idea. This section shows how these meanings contributed to the distribution of authority and power in American society—to the emergence of what Richard Herrnstein and Charles Murray, in *The Bell Curve,* call "a cognitive elite."[18] The born-criminal idea, I argue, works to divide the world into two camps, the fit versus the unfit, the intelligent versus the mentally subnormal, the worthy versus the undeserving, Us versus Them. It justifies the existence of a cognitive elite that then produces Herrnsteins and Murrays who then produce more born-criminal theory—and round we go again.

Chapter 5 shows how the professionalization of penology and the newly adopted goal of rehabilitation turned prison officials down the path that led, paradoxically, to eugenic criminology. Rehabilitation was first systematically attempted at New York's Elmira Reformatory, where in the 1880s superintendent Zebulon Brockway introduced indeterminate sentencing and intensive education in highly publicized efforts to reform inmates. The publicity put Brockway in a quandary, however, for despite his efforts some inmates simply would not behave within the institution or remain law-abiding after release. In despair the superintendent concluded that such prisoners must be "incorrigibles," mental and physical degenerates incapable of obedience. Brockway himself remained more interested in reforming the majority of prisoners than in eugenic control of the degenerate minority, but his widely cited experiments with Elmira's incorrigibles prepared other Americans for the next stage in eugenic criminology, criminal anthropology.

As propounded by the Italian Cesare Lombroso, criminal anthropology merely teetered on the brink of hereditarianism. Lombroso did write of heredity as "the principal organic cause of criminal tendencies,"[19] but he hesitated to predict that born criminals would invariably produce criminalistic children. Moreover, when he recommended that born criminals be imprisoned for life or executed, his goal was to prevent crime in the current generation, not in the next. In the United States at the end of the nineteenth century, however, Lombroso's research gave rise to a new social control specialty, that of criminologist (chap. 6). American criminal anthropologists reformulated born-criminal theory in hereditarian terms, merging it with the doctrine of eugenics. Eugenical criminal anthropologists believed that they had discovered both the cause of and a cure for biological criminality: the cause was an inherited "taint"; the solution, to prevent born criminals from bearing more of their kind. They took a second significant step by recognizing (far more clearly than Lombroso had) a central implication of Lombroso's work: the criminal, if primitive morally and biologically, must also be backward intellectually. Their work "imbecilized" the criminal, producing a theory almost identical to the mental retardation system's doctrine of the criminalistic imbecile. By 1900 notions nourished separately in the two institutional systems were converging.

Whereas Lombroso and his followers taught that criminality manifests itself throughout the body, the next generation of born-criminal theorists, the topic of chapter 7, sited the law-breaking propensity within the head. They could close in on the head—more precisely, on the brain—because Alfred Binet had recently devised an instrument to measure intelligence. Criminal anthropologists had been limited to crudely measuring the head's circumference or weighing beheaded criminals' brains. Binet's pen-and-paper tests provided an apparently simpler means to gauge mental capacity.

Psychologist Henry H. Goddard introduced Binet's tests in the United States in 1910, when policymakers were stressing the need for efficiency, scientific management of populations, and rational decision making and when it seemed clearer than ever before that society itself is an organism, a body that like the human body requires close attention to hygiene. In this context intelligence testing became a way of mapping biological worthiness across social groups and a technology for cleansing society. It also became a means of legitimating the new science of psychology, of which Goddard was an early practitioner. Deliberately moving in on criminal anthropologists' professional territory, Goddard maintained that psychologists could do a better job at detecting born criminals.

Chapter 8 follows the transmutation of Goddard's criminal imbecile into the defective delinquent by tracing events during 1910–20 at New York's Bedford Hills Reformatory for Women. There, with funds from John D. Rockefeller Jr. and other wealthy eugenicists, superintendent Katharine Bement Davis determined through intelligence testing that large proportions of her inmates fell into the defective delinquent category. This finding led to the establishment at Bedford Hills of the first penal unit that could hold biological offenders for life.

Just as the defective delinquency scare reached its peak, however, psychiatrists usurped psychologists' authority over inherent criminality. Chapter 9 shows how, about 1915, psychiatrists began translating the psychological concept of defective delinquency into their own theory of psychopathy. In doing so psychiatrists broke with the view that intellectual and moral weakness must go hand in hand in born criminals. Returning to a pre-eugenic position on innate depravity, they portrayed the psychopath as "constitutionally inferior" but not necessarily feebleminded. Moreover, although many of these psychiatrists sympathized with eugenics, few claimed that psychopathy is heritable. In other ways, too, their writings diluted the idea of innate criminality. Whereas Lombroso's born criminal had been a ferocious, masculine monster, the psychiatrists' psychopath was a puny, homosexual boy, girlish and ineffectual, or (in the female case) an unnaturally rebellious woman.

Psychiatrists slowed the hunt for defective delinquents, but the eugenics movement retained sufficient vigor to make a final push for defective delinquent legislation. Chapter 10 follows New York's campaign for defective delinquent laws, the Progressive effort that in 1921 created the Napanoch Institution for Defective Delinquents. Chapter 11 examines the institutional consequences of eugenic criminology in New York and other states.

In recent decades born-criminal theory has reemerged in various guises: the XYY, or extra male chromosome, explanation of criminal behavior; research on hereditary factors in aggression; family studies that attempt to isolate a genetic component in illegal activity; and other studies that, like *The Bell Curve*, find a relationship between low intelligence and criminal offending. These versions exhibit some differences from earlier ones, however. Contemporary theorists insist on more rigorous evidence than that used by their forerunners. Sensitive to what the Nazis perpetrated in the name of "race betterment," they try to avoid eugenic implications. And they sometimes recognize (as their predecessors did not) interactive effects between heredity and environment.

Nonetheless, despite these differences, contemporary researchers often seek to explain the same characteristics that eugenic criminologists attributed to born criminals. They too are intrigued by behaviors that seem inexplicable in terms of mere environmental factors—criminal activities that, while not necessarily serious, appear to be motiveless, impulsive, and uncontrollable. Born criminals, we are still told, are unable to identify with others. Impervious to deterrent sanctions, some actually relish punishment. That they start demonstrating antisocial behavior in early childhood indicates that they may be abnormal from birth; that their parents or other close relatives have exhibited similar characteristics (another frequent finding) suggests heredity may be at work. In the following pages I investigate the origins and consequences of such ideas.

Notes

1. All information on the inmate I call Fenix Whipple comes from case file 298 of the New York State Institution for Male Defective Delinquents at Napanoch (New York State Archives, series 14610-88B, inmate case files, 1920–56).

2. Terms referring to those today called "mentally retarded" or "mentally handicapped" changed frequently over the period covered in this study; indeed, those changes are part of my subject. I use the terms in vogue at various points (*idiots* when I discuss the 1850s, *feebleminded* for the 1880s, and so on), exploring their denotations while trying to avoid their derogatory connotations. I also use *mentally retarded* to mean "those who at that time constituted the group today defined as mentally retarded."

Mentally handicapped is a less negative term than *mentally retarded*, but I have found it to be insufficiently clear to prevent readers from confusing the intellectually impaired with the mentally ill. *Persons with mental retardation* avoids the categorization inherent in *mentally retarded*, but it is an awkward term. Thus I continue to use *mentally retarded* or simply *retarded*.

3. In 1938, when he had in fact been at Napanoch for seventeen years, Fenix wrote New York's commissioner of correction, complaining, "I have been hear 5 years and I have pay for my crame that I have done 5 year a Go and I thank you should Give me a fair chance to Go out a Gain."

4. Foucault 1988:128, 136.

5. Ibid., 1988:149, 133.

6. Garfinkel 1956:420.

7. Jenkins 1984 comes close; also see Jenkins 1982.

8. Sir Francis Galton coined the term *eugenics* in 1883 (Galton [1883] 1973:17 n. 1), suggesting that it be used to indicate "the science of improving stock."

9. But see Jenkins 1984.

10. Historians of eugenics have not been entirely blind in this respect. For example, Haller (1963) and Kevles (1985) deal with criminology in the course of their general surveys of the eugenics movement, as does Degler (1991) in his study of the recent revival of interest in biological explanations for social phenomena. The problem is that specialized studies of eugenics have focused elsewhere: Bannister 1979, on social Darwinism's impact on American thinking; Cravens 1978, on the heredity-environment controversy among American scientists; Ludmerer 1972, on genetics; Larson 1991 and 1995 and Noll 1991, 1995a, and 1995b, on eugenics in the South; Pickens 1968, on the interrelations between the eugenics and Progressive movements; Stepan 1991, on Latin American eugenics; Zenderland 1987, on the psychologist H. H. Goddard; and so on. No one has tackled the issue of how U.S. eugenics affected criminology. However, criminal justice historians have begun to cover the eugenics movement's impact on specific prison practices; see Pisciotta 1994 and Rafter 1990a.

11. Fausto-Sterling 1992:vii.

12. Schneider and Deutsch's 1941 history of public welfare in New York State continues to provide a useful foundation; I relied on it throughout.

13. Other terms for the condition include *constitutional inferior, criminal imbecile, defective delinquent, delinquents of congenital tendency, feebleminded criminal, habitual criminal* (in some usages), *imbecile with criminal instincts, incorrigible* or *instinctive criminal, mental defective, moral idiot, psychopath, psychopathic inferior, segregable delinquent,* and *sociopath*. For more, see Werlinder 1978:191–92.

14. J. Brown 1992:13–14.

15. Maudsley 1876:28. On the definitional or constructionist approach, see Best 1989; Holstein and Miller 1993; Schneider 1985; and Spector and Kituse 1987. My position is close to what Best (1989) calls "contextual constructionism"; indeed this position seems to me to be a prerequisite for social histories of social problems (Rafter 1992c). I assume we can know about the historical circumstances under which social problems such as mental retardation and crime are defined. I also assume that in any situation, the constructionist processes of claims making, efforts

to validate those claims, and so on are at work, selecting—from the wide range of conditions that might be defined as problematic—specific conditions that become the target of concern and determining *how* those specific conditions are defined and addressed.

Woolgar and Pawluch (1985) fault constructionists for using a double standard when such theorists allege that those who "discovered" or "invented" a new sort of social problem made a mistake but exempt themselves from the same possibility of error. My analysis may seem vulnerable to this objection because I suggest that various theorists inaccurately defined certain individuals as born criminals. However, an analysis such as the one I present here resorts to a double standard only if it claims a monopoly on truth. A growing body of literature indicates that historical context shapes the physical as well as the social sciences (see, for example, Harding 1986; Kaye 1986; Kuhn 1970; Longino 1990). Rather than claim to have discovered "the truth" behind the errors of born-criminal theorists, I proceed on the assumption that historical realities can be known only through successive and partial approximations, of which this study is one.

16. Rafter 1990b; but see Jenkins 1994.

17. Eisenstein 1988:25, 23; also see Lorber 1993.

18. Herrnstein and Murray 1994.

19. Lombroso-Ferrero [1911] 1972:137.

1

Before Eugenics:

Idiots and Idiocy
in the Mid-Nineteenth Century

Every movement creates precursors.

William Vaughan, *Romantic Art*

Mid-nineteenth-century attitudes toward the intellectually impaired and institutionalization contrasted starkly with the eugenic thinking that soon followed. During this precursor phase, sympathizers rescued the retarded from the poorhouses, jails, and homes where they had been squirreled away, uneducated because no one knew how to help them and mocked because they seemed to be more brutish than human. These sympathizers redefined the retarded as innocent victims and gathered them into institutions to be trained and then released as near-normal adults. Institutionalization was driven not by horror stories about the inhumanity of idiots but by tales of success and an optimistic benevolence.

"An Onward Step in Civilization": The First Institutions

Most institutional systems have blurry origins, but the mental retardation system began clearly and precisely on July 1, 1848, when Hervey Backus Wilbur first took a retarded pupil into his home in Barre, Massachusetts. Unprecedented in the United States, Wilbur's decision to attempt systematic education of the mentally retarded flew in the face of the ancient belief that idiots are unteachable, no more capable than brutes of improvement. A resident of the rural village of Barre later recalled that Wilbur's neighbors were "annoyed and chagrined."[1] Even had they welcomed idiots into their midst, they probably would have considered Wilbur to be poorly qualified to conduct such an experiment. Twenty-seven years old, recently married, and father of an infant daughter, Wilbur did have a medical degree, but physicians had little professional authority at the time.[2] Neighbors considered Wilbur to be financially irresponsible and nearly as foolish as his pupil.[3] Yet within three years he had proved them wrong. With fifteen pupils, his Institution for the Education of Idiots, Imbeciles and Children of Retarded Mental Development of Mind was a success.[4] He had moved from his cottage to a mansion that accommodated both students and his family; most important, he had shown that idiots could be taught.

Need and ambition no doubt contributed to Wilbur's odd decision to educate idiots, but he was probably also searching for a challenge and a cause. All his life he was quick to do combat for principle's sake. The records of Amherst College include an apology Wilbur was forced to write after participating in an undergraduate protest. In maturity he fought with the country's most powerful psychiatrists over policies he considered to be detrimental to inmates of their insane asylums. At a memorial for Wilbur a colleague remembered him as "ready to accept everything . . . that was in his judgment wise," testimony further supported by one of Wilbur's own last letters in which he described himself as "a zealous advocate of anything in the line of my convictions."[5] Despite his isolated circumstances, when he opened his innovative school, Wilbur had ferreted out information that made him one of the few Americans aware of European advances in the new humanitarian cause of idiot education. Most of his information came from a book by Edward Seguin, leader of European efforts to start training schools for idiots.

Wilbur described the events that led to his life's work at the funeral of Seguin, who, after moving to the United States, had become Wilbur's mentor and friend:

> In the year 1847, I saw, in a number of Chambers's Journal, an account of a visit . . . to a school for training idiots, in Paris, in charge of Edouard Seguin. . . . Not long after, as I now remember, I met in one or more numbers of a British medical journal a very glowing account of a professional visit to the same [Seguin's] class. . . .
>
> These papers were my first inspiration in what has proved to be with me a life occupation. . . . When my purpose, thus originating, had ripened into a definite plan for starting a similar institution in America, I sent abroad an order for any books treating upon the subject of the training and education of idiots. In reply to this unlimited order, I got only a single book; namely, the volume published in 1846 by my deceased friend.[6]

Thus equipped, the country doctor founded the first North American institution for the retarded.

Albany: The Public Experiment

As Wilbur made plans to open his private institution, he became aware that several other Americans were working to establish public asylums for retarded children. Samuel Gridley Howe, head of Boston's Perkins Institution for the Blind, was conducting a survey of idiots to persuade the Massachusetts legislature that it needed to establish an experimental public school for this class. Three months after Wilbur opened his private school in Barre, Howe became head of the first publicly funded school for idiots, a unit operated under his supervision at the Perkins Institution.[7] New York state senator Frederick F. Backus had been pressing for public education of idiots in his state since January 1846. After two defeats Backus's bill won approval in 1851.[8]

Vying for honors, New York and Massachusetts later quarreled about which had been first—first to recommend an asylum for idiots, first to establish an experimental asylum, and first to establish its asylum on a permanent basis. The debate obscured the far more significant fact that by 1850 reformers in both states were showing considerable interest in educating the retarded. Instead of dueling, they had in fact collaborated: Howe's Massachusetts research seems to have been stimulated by the initial investigation of New York's Senator Backus, and New York's legislature finally decided to fund an experimental asylum after a visit from Howe, who brought along retarded pupils to demonstrate the benefits of their education.[9] Clearly the time was ripe for the systematic training Hervey Wilbur initiated at Barre. He won a race that, until the last moment, he did not realize was underway.

Details of the quarrel also obscure Wilbur's significance to the evolution of the mental retardation system as a whole. Although Howe was indeed first to superintend idiots in a publicly funded institution, his idiot school was initially only an experiment, a tenuous trial. Even after becoming permanent, it remained under the wing of the Perkins Institution. Moreover, after launching public institutional care of the retarded in Massachusetts, Howe took almost no part in the system's development. It was Wilbur who, through example and lobbying, encouraged other states to found asylums for idiots and who carved out a new area of professional work in superintending such institutions.

Wilbur emerged as the system's leader after accepting an invitation to head New York's first school for idiots. When New York founded this institution in 1851, it appointed trustees who were supposed to locate a suitable site and hire a superintendent. The trustees were irritated by their appointments and skeptical about what they saw as "a visionary and impracticable project." [10] Nonetheless, several of them set out for Boston to consult with Samuel Gridley Howe. On the way they stopped by Barre, where, after two days of observing Wilbur's work, they shed their skepticism and offered him the job. Wilbur may in fact have been eyeing the New York position for some time. [11] He accepted the offer and, after selling his private school, prepared to move to Albany.

Everyone connected with the New-York State Asylum for Idiots during its trial period proceeded warily, anxious to see the experiment succeed but reminded daily that others viewed idiot education as a contradiction in terms. The institution was located in Albany to permit close supervision by the trustees, four of whom, as state officials, were tied to the capitol area. Because New York had not yet committed itself to permanent support, the trustees leased quarters for the institution, renting a large residence where Wilbur, his family, and pupils lived together; as at Barre, the asylum combined the models of family and school. Within six months it had sixteen pupils, seven of whose families contributed to their support.

Wilbur used his annual reports to educate legislators about idiocy and tactfully promote his venture. His central message was that idiots could be taught: afflicted with an absence of "harmonious development of the mental, active and moral powers," usually due to "some defect or infirmity of nervous organization," idiots "are yet human beings." "At the basis of all our efforts lies the principle that the human attributes of intelligence, sensitivity and will are not absolutely wanting in an idiot, but dormant and undeveloped." [12] Describing his training methods, Wilbur insisted that idiots are as entitled to education as is any other group, including the deaf and dumb and the blind, for whom the state had already provided. To train idiots, moreover, is cost-effective, for they "must be supported somewhere at public expense, if not in a State institution." Without education, he added, using a scare tactic he himself probably did not take seriously, they might commit "crimes . . . of a serious character." [13] Wilbur pointed out that in its second year of operation the temporary asylum was already full, that he had been forced to turn away more applicants than he could accept, and that New York had hundreds of idiotic children in need of training.

Such arguments were good politics for a superintendent hoping for permanent appointment, but it was Wilbur's success with pupils that persuaded the legislators to move beyond the experimental stage. Following Seguin's physiological approach, which held that physical training should precede efforts to awaken the intellect, Wilbur began by using gymnastic equipment to strengthen the children's bodies. From there he proceeded to develop his pupils' senses, moving from touch, taste, and smell to hearing and sight. Advanced pupils learned rudimentary reading, writing, geography, and "the simple relations of numbers." [14] To illustrate his progress, Wilbur described specific pupils:

> A boy of 10 years old, idiotic from birth; . . . inattentive to the calls of nature; came October 29th, 1852; could not speak a word; had no idea of language, not even knowing his own name when called; would not hold anything in his hands except food; . . . he now feeds himself very well with a fork; knows his own name; will obey some simple commands; holds anything in his hands; will sit or stand still when required; can assist himself more in dressing or undressing; . . . will go up and down ladders when told, and takes pleasure in marching.[15]

At this early stage in the system's development, Wilbur and his trustees were vehemently anticustodial and anti-institutional. The asylum's purpose, they stressed, was educational and restorative—to return "a class of human beings, now a burden to community, . . . to their friends and to society." Recognizing that the small Albany institution could not begin to educate all backward children in the state, but convinced that "more than 150 pupils cannot be properly attended to by one Superintendent, however numerous his assistants," the board hoped that the asylum might become a center for the training of "practiced teachers" who would then fan out to work in small, local schools for idiots. Although even the optimistic Dr. Wilbur admitted that some idiots of "the lowest class" might require lifelong care, he anticipated only "well-conducted public industrial institutions" where adult idiots would work under supervision.[16] The idea of involuntary commitment to a closed institution would have horrified him.

Syracuse: The Experiment Made Permanent

In 1853 New York's legislature voted to make the New-York State Asylum for Idiots a permanent institution. Land had already been purchased in Albany when the trustees received an intriguing offer from some citizens of Syracuse: they would contribute ten acres or $7,500 toward the site if the institution were located in their town. The benefactors kept their identities secret, burying a list of their names and contributions under the asylum's cornerstone when it was laid in Syracuse in 1854. This list was recovered, however, when the building was demolished in the 1970s, and together with other evidence it enables one to reconstruct the motives behind the effort to attract the idiot asylum to Syracuse.[17]

Prime mover in this campaign was Elias W. Leavenworth, New York's secretary of state and the central figure in a group of wealthy Syracuse citizens who owned extensive property in the rapidly developing town, controlled its banks and utilities, and ran its government. Leavenworth headed the committee that persuaded over 150 Syracusians to donate $7,500 toward the land-or-cash offer. In fact, it was he who owned the proffered ten acres. The trustees opted for the money, purchasing the land and adjoining parcels for $10,300. Although Leavenworth had contributed $500 to the fund, and although he protested that he would have preferred not to sell part of his farm, he nevertheless profited from the transaction. Like Leavenworth, other donors became trustees of the new institution; like Leavenworth, they too were enterprising capitalists who gained from an institution's presence in their town.[18]

This genial combination of altruism and self-interest meshed well with the civic pride and generally expansive mood that prevailed in Syracuse (as elsewhere) at midcentury. Syracuse was not incorporated as a city until 1848; previously some of the asylum's new trustees had served as overseers of the village (with Leavenworth for a long period as their president), and they were ardent Syracusians. When the Erie Canal opened in 1825, they had identified Syracuse as likely to become one of the state's most important commercial centers. Like the city fathers of Utica, New York, who a few years earlier had offered the state $6,000 to locate an insane asylum in their town,[19] the Syracuse leaders recognized that an institution would bring jobs and business. The city's first mayor expressed their ambitions in a speech described as "the most sanguine, hopeful, [and] confident, regarding the future of Syracuse that was ever delivered."[20]

The tone of the idiot asylum's dedication ceremonies was also one of soaring aspiration and self-congratulation. "Complete this institution," one state official prophesied, "and in a few years you may see the little boy and girl—children of misfortune—with their countenances beaming with intelligence." This "new effort to alleviate the calamities of mankind," former governor Hunt observed at the asylum's dedication, marked "an onward step in civilization."[21] These celebrants thought of idiots as deserving victims, not oversexed menaces to the nation's health.

The asylum to which Wilbur and ninety pupils moved in 1855 was situated grandly on a hill above the city. The Italianate building was too large to be mistaken for a house; although the asylum continued to combine the family model with that of a residential school, the latter now predominated. Training techniques, influenced by Seguin from the start, were now guided by the Frenchman himself. Wilbur's successor at Syracuse told the Wilbur family's story of how "about 1854 or 5" the expatriated Frenchman and his American disciple "accidentally met each other in R. R. Station at Albany—the former waiting for a train to N.Y. & the latter waiting for one to Syracuse. They happened to take a seat in the Station one by the side of the other, and naturally fell into conversation, became in that way acquainted. Dr. W. invited Dr. S. to visit him in S., which he did quite frequently ever afterwards until [his] death."[22] Befriended by Wilbur, Seguin attended Syracuse's dedication ceremonies and thereafter paid extensive visits to the institution.

Wilbur embraced not only Seguin's physiological method but also his precepts about "moral treatment," according to which the mentally disabled should be given therapeutic tasks, supervised by concerned attendants, and trained in an atmosphere of serenity, trust, and love.[23] Moral treatment originated in the flowering of medicine that followed the French Revolution and was associated in particular with the French psychiatrist Philippe Pinel, who was said to have freed the insane from their chains. It had already taken root in U.S. insane asylums, and Wilbur would have adopted the approach had he never met Seguin. But Seguin, who had worked with Pinel's associates, formed a direct link between the French champion of moral treatment and Wilbur.[24]

Wilbur continued to work closely with his charges, as illustrated by his account of training E. P., an eight-year-old girl: "There were but few external impressions (if any) that would produce a reflex motion in her. . . . She would allow the ball of her eye to be touched, without winking. . . . She did not stand or sit alone, or even hold up her head. . . . Of course she had no idea of language." Wilbur discovered that E. P. enjoyed sponge cake and tea. "With a piece of sponge cake on a fork, I drew gradually, and in successive lessons, the sensation of taste forward on the tongue; then to the lips. . . . Soon I was able, by touching the lips, the mouth, at its sides and above and below, to make her reach her head forward, to turn it a little from side to side, and up and down, in pursuit of the desired morsel."[25] He taught E. P. to stand, walk, and follow the other children. This example helps to explain why Wilbur (in contrast to later eugenicists) conceived of intelligence as elastic and capable of expansion. His purpose was to help pupils to develop dormant abilities and become self-determining. In the early years at Syracuse, while he could still devote attention to individuals, he frequently succeeded. Similarly, superintendents of the early mental hospitals, also working closely with patients in benign environments, seem to have achieved considerable success.[26]

"Children of Misfortune": Midcentury Attitudes toward the Retarded

At midcentury, attitudes toward the mentally retarded were on the cusp of a radical reorientation that entailed both distinguishing between idiots and the insane and defining the former group as victims, deserving state care. Common law had long differentiated between the idiot ("a person who has been without understanding from his nativity") and the lunatic ("one who has had understanding, which he has lost").[27] Medically, however, the distinction was often hazy. Even the leading theorist of mental disease, Isaac Ray, classified idiocy and imbecility as subtypes of insanity.[28]

In practice, too, it was difficult to separate the retarded from the mad. Noting flaws in New York's census of 1845, which had attempted to enumerate the insane and idiotic separately, Amariah Brigham, head of the Utica Lunatic Asylum, observed that the idiot category included "demented insane persons": "Strictly speaking, idiocy is not like insanity, a disease, or the result of disease, but the consequence of the malformation of the brain, and exists from birth or from very early life. This distinction, however, is not generally made, as those who, from long continued insanity, have become demented and exhibit but little mind, are considered, though incorrectly, to have become idiots. Hence we suppose that many enumerated [by the census] as idiots should have been classed with the insane."[29] Samuel Gridley Howe identified similar problems with Massachusetts's first survey of idiots.[30] From personal experience Howe knew that abused children, too, were sometimes misclassified as idiots.[31]

Such criticisms eventually led to more precise diagnoses. Moreover, as states began undertaking censuses of special groups, they became more adept at assessing the prevalence of idiocy and understanding its nature and causes. For example, Connecticut's survey analyzed idiots along a host of dimensions including condition (age, health, temperament), habits (gluttony, intemperance, filthiness), and causes ("Were the parents . . . related by blood?" "Mental ability of parents?"). Defining and counting were reciprocal processes. Starting in the 1840s, statistics played a vital role in the social construction of mental retardation.[32]

As understanding of idiocy improved, pressure built to develop a more precise vocabulary through which to describe this condition. Wilbur insisted on using the old-fashioned term *idiocy;* he refused to prettify the problem.[33] Howe, too, used *idiocy,* while acknowledging problems with the term that soon led it to be discarded in favor of *feebleminded:* "Evil may arise from the misuse of the term **Idiot**, as the name of a class, if it causes them to be considered as a distinct order of persons, and different from other men in being utterly devoid of mind, for it will be considered useless to try to teach those who have no mind at all; but if they are considered as differing from others not in kind, but in degree only,—as merely having **feeble** minds, then their very feebleness, like that of little children, will commend them to our hearts."[34] In addition to using *feebleminded,* specialists introduced yet other terms: *fatuity, imbecility, mental deficiency,* and even *retarded.*[35] Howe became even more precise when he classified idiots by degrees of ability, "SIMPLETONS being the highest, FOOLS the next, and IDIOTS proper, the lowest."[36]

The treatment of idiocy, like its definition, changed dramatically about

1850. In colonial times idiots had been chained, hidden, abused, jailed, and chased out of town. Their situation improved slightly when, during the first half of the nineteenth century, they were moved into local poorhouses. The principles of moral treatment had filtered down to some poorhouse keepers, producing better care for idiots and other inmates of these county institutions. As Howe remarked, however, even in the best poorhouses idiots might be "terribly abused by the pauper inmates,"[37] and in no case could keepers provide specialized care. Dorothea Dix, the indefatigable poorhouse reformer, condemned the way these establishments mixed the "infirm, aged, and imbecile poor." In New York's Broome County institution, she reported, "several idiots occupied together a portion of one building; *one gibbering, senseless creature, was the mother of a young infant.*" Most county institutions, Dix chided, isolated "incurables" in *"close, unventilated rooms; narrow dark cells; cheerless dungeons, cold and damp."*[38] Idiots not consigned to poorhouses sometimes ended up in local jails or insane asylums.

Distinguishing idiots from the insane and exposing their maltreatment, reformers began to identify a new social problem. Mental retardation itself was not new, but it was being "discovered" and radically redefined. The discovery involved conceptually separating idiocy from insanity, reinterpreting idiots as worthy and improvable, and demonstrating the inadequacy of current measures. "These helpless and degraded fellow creatures are on our hands," Connecticut's commissioners on idiocy concluded in their 1856 report, "and we must provide for their instruction and improvement; if we can remove, in part, the blighting, withering results of violated physical laws, let us do so; for they are the victims, not the offenders."[39]

Supporters of idiot education drew on two rhetorical strategies that, Joel Best has shown, are utilized frequently during campaigns to identify social problems: they argued that it would be immoral to further ignore members of this class (what Best calls "the rhetoric of rectitude") and that it was socially beneficial to help them (Best's "rhetoric of rationality").[40] Eugenic criminologists later used the same strategies to define the retarded as deviant and socially dangerous. In this first instance, however, Wilbur and his allies aimed at empowering idiots and reducing their deviance. As they saw it, the social problem lay less in idiots themselves than in society's failure to train them. Moreover, in contrast to later eugenicists, these midcentury reformers showed little interest in medicalizing mental retardation, even though many of them were physicians. Far from assigning idiots to a sick role, Seguin's physiological method and the moral treatment approach stressed their capacity for responsibility and independence. The reformers did utilize the concept of cure, but their emphasis fell on not malady but restoration.[41]

Nonetheless, there were obstacles to defining mental retardation as an important social problem. The nature of these obstacles becomes clear if we compare midcentury attitudes toward idiocy and insanity. Idiots never attracted the attention bestowed on the insane. Specialized insane asylums were founded earlier and always had more status. The difference was a function of the lesser status of idiots themselves. The mad had more prestige, as they still do. Idiocy carried strong connotations of infancy and animality. Citizens, legislators, and physicians identified more easily with the insane. "It should never be forgotten," reminded Thomas Story Kirkbride, head of the Pennsylvania Hospital for the Insane, "that every individual who has a brain is liable to insanity." [42] No one, the public was realizing, need fear becoming an idiot.

Several developments helped reformers to surmount these impediments and establish schools for idiots. One bit of good fortune lay in the encouraging reports flowing in from Europe. Idiot instruction had commenced somewhat earlier in Europe, starting with attempts to train Victor, the famous "wild boy" of Aveyron.[43] News of European progress began trickling into the United States in the 1840s in journal articles (such as the one that originally inspired Wilbur), in letters that U.S. advocates solicited from European experts in the field, and in firsthand accounts by American visitors to the European schools.[44] American proponents could now relate success stories to prove that idiots can be taught.

These success stories made idiot education appear to be not just possible but rather easy, an impression American reformers were delighted to pass on to their legislatures. Advocates slyly goaded legislators into competition. "Why should we be backward," New York's Senator Backus demanded, "in adopting and applying the means of alleviating . . . misery . . . that have been so successfully used in despotic governments of Europe[?]" In Howe's view, "It would be an insult to Massachusetts to suppose that she will not be among the first to make those efforts for her idiot population, which many European states are already commencing." [45] European reports thus provided authority and both practical and patriotic inspiration. Without them state legislatures would have been slower to invest in idiot asylums.

Once in place the first institutions attracted new allies, supporters who, like the original advocates, believed that the retarded could be restored nearly to normalcy. Their enthusiasm formed an aspect of what Albert Deutsch calls the "cult of curability"—expectations for high rates of recovery that insane asylum superintendents encouraged to spur institutional growth. Deutsch attributes the cult to conscious deception by superintendents who doctored statistics in an escalating competition for cures of the insane. Backers of idiot asylums, as Deutsch observes, were swept up by the same "high wave of optimism." [46] Deutsch does not recognize, however, that when the latter stressed idiots' capacity for improvement, they did so not to compete professionally but to counter the prevailing view that idiocy was incurable. For them, curability was less cult than cause. Bolstered by the generally expansive midcentury mood, the cause could be magnetic, as when the New York asylum trustees experienced overnight conversion during their Barre visit and when Syracuse citizens, mingling humanitarianism with self-interest, decided to entice the idiot asylum to their town.

Like Howe, Wilbur was careful not to promise total success ("We do not propose to create or supply faculties absolutely wanting"). Also like Howe, however, he was confident that he could "restore" to the community idiots "educated in some simple occupations and industry, capable of self-support."[47] At midcentury neither the superintendents of idiot asylums nor their supporters doubted that this was possible.

Campaigns for idiot asylums were further reinforced by efforts to force states to assume responsibility for poorhouse dependents. From one perspective the nineteenth century's proliferation of institutions was little more than the result of attempts to replace poorhouses with specialized asylums. Some poorhouses had themselves embarked on rudimentary specialization by holding different groups—the insane, imbeciles, the elderly —in separate buildings. But even these poorhouses could merely classify, never treat. Efforts to transfer poorhouse populations to specialized treatment institutions concentrated on the insane; Dorothea Dix, in particular, crusaded for states to rescue the insane from deplorable poorhouse conditions. The campaign for state institutions was joined by idiot asylum advocates, however, as when Connecticut officials pointed out that of their state's idiots, "nearly, or quite, one-half of the whole number are tenants of our alms houses or houses of correction," establishments offering little hope "that they can be materially elevated from their present condition."[48]

A final factor favoring the establishment of idiot asylums was the public school movement. By 1850 the principle of universal education had produced specialized state institutions for blind, deaf, and mute children; why, some asked, should the principle not be extended to idiots? "We regard it as the duty of the State," Connecticut officials advised, "to require that all of its children shall have the opportunity of mental culture, the weak as well as the strong." The bylaws of the Syracuse Asylum explained that its "design and object . . . are . . . to furnish the means of education to that portion of the youth of the State, not provided for in any of its other educational institutions."[49] With local teachers unprepared to work with the mentally and physically impaired, special education naturally began in state institutions.

Defining the New Profession

Like other social problems movements aimed at rescuing a neglected group, the campaign on behalf of idiots produced a new profession to deal with the problem. To follow the formation of idiot training as a recognized profession, we might trace the steps that Wilbur and other early superintendents took to establish a workplace organization, develop expertise, and promote their work—a route I follow in chapter 3. Here, however, it is more fruitful to focus on the concept of professional jurisdiction,[50] asking how the new area of work was originally conceived. Eugenics is a story of widening jurisdictional claims. Whereas Wilbur defined the superintendent's jurisdiction narrowly, restricting it to supervising those whose idiocy was obvious, the next generation of superintendents defined it more generously, including criminals, tramps, and other "incapables" among the feebleminded. Because Wilbur's successors used eugenics to broaden jurisdictional boundaries and because "broaden" is a relative term, we must look at how the jurisdiction was initially construed.

"Every profession," Andrew Abbott maintains in *The System of Professions,* aims at "full jurisdiction," a "heartland of work over which it has complete, legally established control."[51] To define itself, however, a new profession must delimit its territory and get rid of work it is not able to handle. This sort of self-definition occurred when insane asylum superintendents worked to have idiots housed in separate asylums. Amariah Brigham, for instance, emphasized the difference between the insane, for whom his lunatic asylum was designed, and idiots, for whom it was not. Defining his own territory, he indicated another, "empty" jurisdiction into which the retarded would (he hoped) fall.[52] Superintendents of lunatic and idiot asylums arrived at an understanding over jurisdictional boundaries of the type Abbott calls "settlement by division of labor."[53] The result was two separate jurisdictions, one headed by psychiatrists[54] and the other headed by idiot asylum superintendents.

Wilbur, as the first head of an empty and uncontested jurisdiction, was initially free to define his clients and the nature of the new profession. He identified the client group straightforwardly and unambiguously as idiotic children. Wilbur was also clear that work in this new field entailed using moral treatment and Seguin's methods in a small, residential setting.

These definitions were soon challenged by others with different conceptions of the jurisdiction and its work, ideas more compatible with eugenics. The next generation's superintendents prized distance from clients and freedom from the "dirty" work of individual treatment. Some advised that the feebleminded should not be educated at all, only trained for institutional maintenance. Members of this second generation, as later chapters show, found a new "client" in society itself, which seemed to need eugenic cleansing. Unlike Wilbur, they valued institutional expansion.

As Wilbur's original ideals came increasingly under fire in his home jurisdiction, he carried the issues into the neighboring jurisdiction of the psychiatrists. During the last decade of his life, Wilbur engaged in a fierce dispute with the leading superintendents of insane asylums, including John P. Gray, Brigham's successor as head of the Utica Lunatic Asylum and editor of the *American Journal of Insanity*. Wilbur's refusal to remain within his own territory—his insistence on speaking authoritatively about conditions in the adjacent jurisdiction—reflects the unsettled understanding of what it meant to be a professional in this period. Although he was more of a specialist than was Samuel Gridley Howe, Wilbur shared Howe's view that a man might be an expert in several fields.[55] Unlike Howe, Wilbur was punished for presuming multicompetence. Work with the disabled was moving toward the principle of one jurisdiction to a profession—a lesson Wilbur learned the hard way at the psychiatrists' hands.[56]

The issue over which Wilbur and the psychiatrists quarreled—the issue of custodial care—indicates yet another dimension of the dispute's professional significance. Mental hospitals had grown large and custodial by the 1870s. Having abandoned moral treatment, their superintendents provided patients with few opportunities for employment, and they increasingly relied on physical and chemical restraints. Wilbur decried these custodial trends. His extensive reading on insanity, his familiarity with U.S. insane asylums, and his tours of European institutions led him to demand nonrestraint: "What is called the 'system of non-restraint,' in its broadest sense, means not only the disuse of mechanical appliances, the muffs and camisoles, etc., in the treatment of the insane, but the absence of all prison-like arrangements of structure, and the substitution for both of a constant and never-tiring personal supervision of the patients."[57] Wilbur advocated small insane asylums, separation of custodial and curable cases, and more state supervision of psychiatrists, so that abuses could be detected and corrected.[58]

Not surprisingly Wilbur's criticisms infuriated the psychiatrists, one of the more tolerant of whom, W. W. Godding, remarked after Wilbur's death that "he knew how to smite unsparingly . . . ; . . . his pamphlets and articles flew thick as arrows, and they were always aggressive and vigorous. We felt that his criticisms of our methods were certainly not generous, hardly just, but the trouble was, there was too much truth in them. . . . The Association of Medical Superintendents of Institutions for the Insane had become too much of a mutual admiration society for healthy growth."[59] Wilbur, previously welcomed at meetings of the psychiatrists' professional association, was now ostracized. Joining with other leaders in social science and mental disability, he formed a rival professional organization, the National Association for the Protection of the Insane and Prevention of Insanity, dedicated to patient rights and treatment reforms. It elected Wilbur its first president. Although this breakaway organization survived him by only two years, its formation posed a rare challenge to the autocratic methods of John Gray and other powerful psychiatrists. Wilbur's "protest against . . . medical *expertness*" led him to become, as he himself put it, " 'almost an outlaw.' " [60]

Why did Wilbur engage in this painful jurisdictional dispute? Dr. Godding, superintendent of the Government Insane Asylum in Washington, D.C., believed that Wilbur had been deeply offended by his exclusion from the psychiatric association meetings ("We unwisely and rudely . . . drove the superintendent of idiot asylums out of our synagogue. Was it to be expected that he would be very indulgent to our methods after that?"). The slight did indeed wound Wilbur. He tried to exculpate himself in a letter to Dorothea Dix, confiding that although "I have no feeling in the matter personally, . . . in point of interest in the general subject of Social Science and perhaps in reading on the subject of Insanity, I am the equal of most of the present race of Supt's." [61] Yet pride could not have been the only factor, for by all accounts Wilbur was a modest and self-effacing man, if a feisty one. [62]

An additional explanation for the dispute, and one that relates it to the rise of eugenics, lies with its timing: it occurred just as Wilbur was being forced to introduce custodialism at Syracuse. By the 1870s he was having to abandon his original professional ideals. Syracuse was expanding, he could no longer work closely with individual pupils, and some adult graduates remained dependent on the asylum. Losing control over his initial self-concept as a professional, Wilbur attempted to assert himself as a "true" professional—concerned with cure, patient rights, and nonrestraint—in the adjacent jurisdiction. [63] He displaced a quarrel that was in part a quarrel with himself.

Wilbur was also having to make a painful decision about one of his own children. Previous biographers have not realized that Wilbur had fathered a retarded son, Harry Aguiro Wilbur. According to Mary Hicks Brown, who knew him, [64] Harry could manage many tasks, such as reading and churchgoing. Nevertheless, when Wilbur wrote his final will in 1880 (Harry was about nineteen years old then), he left $6,000 in trust to maintain the young man at not Syracuse but Barre, which had remained a small, private institution. [65] He had lost faith in education's potential for restoring the retarded to the community and in his own asylum's potential for providing humane long-term care.

Wilbur's disillusionment was all the more poignant because, as the next chapter shows, he himself played a decisive role in negating the work he initiated at Barre. Near the end of his life, and against his better judgment, he helped to establish the nation's first eugenic institution.

Notes

1. C. Brown 1897:134.
2. Starr 1982.
3. C. Brown 1897.
4. Graney (1979:42) gives fifteen as the total number of Wilbur's Barre pupils.
5. Amherst College Archives, s.v. "Hervey Backus Wilbur"; William P. Letchworth, in National Conference of Charities and Corrections, *Proceedings, 1883*, p. xxx (memorial remarks during annual business meeting). Godding (1883:662), quotes one of Wilbur's last letters.
6. Wilbur [1881] 1964:27–28. The book was doubtless Seguin's *Traitement* (1846); see Trent 1994:14.
7. Howe had undertaken the training of "an idiotic blind child" at Perkins as early as 1839 (Massachussetts School for Idiotic and Feeble-Minded Youth, *Annual Report, 1875*, p. 26). Similarly, a few retarded children were educated at Hartford's American Asylum for the Education and Instruction of the Deaf and Dumb before the first institutions for idiots were opened. For accounts of these and other early efforts at idiot education, see Graney 1979; Kanner 1964; Trent 1994; and Tyor and Bell 1984.
8. Backus 1846 and 1847. Senator Backus was apparently no relation to Hervey Backus Wilbur, despite the similarity in names. For a history of the New York legislation, see New York State Asylum for Idiots, *Annual Report, 1851*, pp. 10–12.
9. Wilbur claims that Backus's research inspired Howe in New York State Asylum for Idiots, *Annual Report, 1854*, 57–58. On Howe's demonstration to New York's legislature, see New York State Asylum for Idiots, *Annual Report, 1854*, p. 32.
The order of events was as follows: New York was the first state to consider a bill for an idiot asylum, which it did on January 13, 1846; ten days later Massachusetts appointed commissioners to investigate the condition of idiots in the commonwealth. On May 8, 1848, Massachusetts established the experimental institution that opened at Perkins in October 1848, three months after Wilbur had opened his Barre school. New York established its experimental idiot school in July of 1851; this opened in Albany later the same year. The Massachusetts institution became permanent several years before New York's asylum achieved the same status, but the former remained dependent on Howe until he retired in 1875. See W. Fernald 1893; New York State Asylum for Idiots, *Annual Report, 1854*, pp.57–61; and Tyor and Bell 1984.
10. Board member James H. Titus as quoted in Graney 1979:52; also see C. Brown 1897:139.
11. Graney 1979:45.
12. New York State Asylum for Idiots, *Annual Report, 1851*, pp. 14, 16.
13. New York State Asylum for Idiots, *Annual Report, 1852*, p. 16.

14. Ibid., 24.

15. Ibid., 27–28.

16. New York State Asylum for Idiots, *Annual Report, 1851*, pp. 19, 5, 20.

17. In the late 1970s, when I examined it, the list of donors was held by the institution, then called the Syracuse Developmental Center.

18. The list of donors contains 153 names, each followed by the amount given. The land purchase is recorded in the Onondaga county clerk's office (1854). Leavenworth's protest is mentioned in New York State Asylum for Idiots, *Annual Report, 1854*, p. 4.

Information on the donors can be found in local histories such as Clayton n.d. and Strong 1894. Leavenworth was president of the Syracuse Savings Institution, the Water Works Company, and the Gas Light Company. George F. Comstock was a law partner of Leavenworth, director of the gas and water companies, and an important property owner. Allen Munroe headed the Syracuse Company, which managed the group's real estate interests; he was also an official of the water and gas companies, a banker, and involved in railroads. Lyman Clary was a bank vice president, physician, and large-scale dealer in real estate. After making a fortune in drugs, Hiram Putnam became involved in banking and real estate. Yet another donor, Hamilton White, was a banker, founder of the water works, and railroad director. They evidently constituted what a later generation would call an interlocking directorate.

19. Dwyer 1987:35.

20. Strong 1894:22.

21. New York State Asylum for Idiots, *Annual Report, 1854*, pp. 45, 35.

22. James C. Carson, Wilbur's successor at Syracuse, mentions the figure of ninety pupils in an undated letter that, when I saw it in the late 1970s, was held by the Syracuse Developmental Center (Carson to Charles H. Johnson; a note at the top of this letter says it was "written from Dr. Carson's home after he left the Syracuse State School"). The letter also describes the first encounter between Wilbur and Seguin. Carson's source was Wilbur's second wife; see Carson 1915:171.

23. Seguin [1866] 1971; Kraft 1961.

24. For more on the origins of moral treatment and its early application in the U.S., see Seguin in Connecticut Commissioners on Idiocy 1856:61–62; Deutsch 1949: chap. 6; and Grob 1973.

25. New York State Asylum for Idiots, *Annual Report, 1865*, pp. 15–16.

26. Grob 1973:184–85.

27. Collinson 1812:3, 5.

28. Ray [1838] 1983:71.

29. New York State Lunatic Asylum, *Annual Report, 1845*, p. 47.

30. Howe 1848:21.

31. Howe 1850:38–42.

32. Connecticut Commissioners on Idiocy 1856: appendix A. On the social significance of statistics, see Starr 1987.

33. "Dr. Wilbur's motive in giving the title 'Asylum for Idiots' to the New York institution," his Barre friend Catharine Brown explained, "was to face the full op-

probrium of the condition he proposed to treat" ("Discussion," Association of Medical Officers of American Institutions for Idiotic and Feeble-Minded Persons, *Proceedings, 1891*, p. 160).

34. Howe 1850:34 (capitalization and emphases as in original).

35. Wilbur himself introduced "retarded" in the title of his Barre private school, probably following Seguin's usage of "*retardés*" in his 1846 *Traitement,* but thereafter Wilbur let this term lapse.

36. Howe 1850:33 (capitalization as in original).

37. Ibid., 9. Howe here describes the treatment of idiots in almshouses, the township's equivalent of the county poorhouse; I use *poorhouse* to refer generally to both types of local institution.

38. Dix [1844] 1971:27, 54 (emphases in original).

39. Connecticut Commissioners on Idiocy 1856:53.

40. Best 1987.

41. The early, educational model of institutions for the retarded was so far removed from the medical model that, in the view of Tyor and Bell (1984:xv), it "frustrated medical intervention. The professional concern for teaching, testing, and training inadvertently downgraded the biomedical approach to mental retardation." For a historical overview of the medicalization of deviance, see Conrad and Schneider 1980.

42. Kirkbride as quoted in Deutsch 1949:207.

43. Captured in 1801, Victor, the "wild boy" of Aveyron, was taken to Paris, where he was examined by Pinel (who considered him an idiot and thus unteachable) and by Itard (who considered him merely untaught). Itard worked with Victor, using physiological methods, but finally reversed his opinion and gave up. Thus like Pinel (and in contrast to Seguin), Itard believed that idiots were not worth instructing. Toward the end of his life, however, having heard of Seguin's work with idiots, Itard asked Seguin to help with the education of another retarded child. Through Itard, Seguin was linked to Pinel and the wild boy. See H. Lane 1976; Scheerenberger 1983; and Seguin 1866.

44. See for example Backus 1847; Howe 1848; Connecticut Commissioners on Idiocy 1856.

45. Backus 1847:12; Howe 1848:39.

46. Deutsch 1949:347 and chap. 8, passim.

47. New York State Asylum for Idiots, *Annual Report, 1851*, pp. 15, 19, 20.

48. Connecticut Commissioners on Idiocy 1856:53.

49. Ibid., appendix D; New York State Asylum for Idiots, *Annual Report, 1855*, p. 15.

50. Abbott (1988:20) defines "jurisdiction" as "the link between a profession and its work." I follow Abbott's lead in using the notion of jurisdiction as a key unit of analysis in the study of professions, also borrowing related terms from his study.

51. Ibid., 71.

52. New York State Lunatic Asylum, *Annual Report, 1845.*

53. Abbott (1988:73, 77) distinguishes settlement by division of labor from settlement by client differentiation; in the latter, professionals within a single work-

place informally agree to handle different layers of clients. In settlement by division of labor, formally separate jurisdictions are the result, as in the case of lunatic asylums and idiot asylums.

54. The nineteenth-century term for superintendents of lunatic asylums or hospitals for the mentally ill was *alienists*. In the early twentieth century, *alienists* became *psychiatrists*, a transformation that becomes important in chapter 9. For clarity and simplicity, I use *psychiatrists* throughout.

55. Abbott (1988:74) observes that "maintenance of a [jurisdictional] settlement by division of labor is difficult. The degree of assimilation between the two groups is normally great, and boundaries correspondingly obscure." If Wilbur "poached" on the neighboring jurisdiction, he did so with a sense of entitlement.

56. On the concept of one jurisdiction to a profession, see Abbott 1988:88.

57. Wilbur 1877:143.

58. Wilbur 1872, 1876, 1877, and 1881b.

59. Godding 1883:660.

60. Ibid., 662. The phrase "medical *expertness*" is Godding's own (emphasis in original); Godding quotes Wilbur's description of himself ("almost an outlaw") from a letter that Wilbur wrote one week before his death. On the National Association for the Protection of the Insane and Prevention of Insanity, see Deutsch 1949; Dwyer 1987; Graney 1979; and Grob 1973.

61. Godding 1883:661; H. B. Wilbur to Dorothea Dix, June 28, 1873 (Harvard University, Houghton Library).

62. Wilbur's modesty is reflected in a form he filled out around 1873 for Amherst College, which was soliciting information for an alumni history: "About myself personally," Wilbur wrote, "there is nothing that will redound to the credit of the college. I have not written upon Idiocy as I should have done before this time" (Amherst College Archives, s.v. "Hervey Backus Wilbur"). Here Wilbur mentions not the institutions and the profession he had founded but the book he had not managed to produce. He is similarly critical of himself in a letter to Dix in the Syracuse Development Center's museum (H. B. Wilbur to D. Dix, May 8, 1876); also see G. Brown 1884.

63. Wilbur did advocate custodial institutions for the incurably insane, but he did so to promote the cure of others and in the context of demanding improvements in all insane asylums.

64. Brown and Brown 1976 (interview). Mrs. Brown had married G. Percy Brown, the third generation Brown to manage the Barre institution that Wilbur founded in 1848.

65. Onondaga County Surrogate Court (Syracuse, New York), book Y:196–97 (Wilbur's will). Wilbur died May 1, 1883.

2

Feebleminded Women and the Advent of Eugenic Criminology

Foolish, drunken, or haire-braine women, most part
bring forth children like unto themselves.
Robert Burton, *The Anatomy of Melancholy*

The founding of the Newark Custodial Asylum
for Feeble-minded Women in 1878 marked the
beginning of eugenic criminology, the notion
that criminality is caused by an inherited biological defect and can be curbed by reproductive
controls. The Newark Custodial Asylum singled
out one segment of the mentally retarded population, feebleminded women of childbearing age,
and redefined them as a eugenic problem. According to the asylum's founders, such women
are problematic in two ways: they are inherently promiscuous, and thus crime problems in
and of themselves, and they inevitably give birth
to crime-prone offspring. On Newark's opening,
eugenics doctrine became the basis for public
policy.

The standard-bearer of New York's campaign
against feebleminded women was Josephine
Shaw Lowell, one of the towering figures in
nineteenth-century philanthropy. Lowell was still
in her early thirties when, in 1876, New York's
governor appointed her to the State Board of
Charities (SBC), the agency responsible for cop-
ing with the state's welfare problems. Lowell was
already well known in welfare work; now she
became the charity board's first female commissioner.

Lowell's personal history made her a heroic figure. During the Civil War her brother, Robert Gould Shaw, died in battle at Fort Wagner, commanding the Union army's first black regiment. Not long afterward the war claimed Lowell's young husband, Colonel Charles Russell Lowell, leaving her pregnant with the daughter she bore a month later. Personal fortitude, a family tradition of social activism, and a comfortable income enabled Lowell to transcend these blows and become a pivotal figure in philanthropy, which she helped to transform from the unsystematic benevolence of the mid-nineteenth century into the professionalized charity of the early twentieth century. Lowell aimed at streamlining social control systems and tightening their control over deviants. Under her guidance charity management began to incorporate the findings of the new social sciences, thus becoming more "scientific."[1] Lowell's first major accomplishment on the charity board was to define feebleminded women as a biological threat to society—what the next generation would call "born" criminals.

Lowell's biographers have minimized or entirely ignored her involvement with eugenics, perhaps because eugenics did not become an organized social movement until just before her death in 1905. Lowell nevertheless did help to validate eugenics reasoning by sowing fears of the promiscuous feebleminded woman, a stereotype that became the propaganda centerpiece of subsequent eugenics campaigns. In addition, by founding the Newark Custodial Asylum to prevent such women from reproducing, Lowell established the first eugenic institution in the United States.

The Genealogy of Degeneration

Lowell's view of the feebleminded woman as "depraved in body and mind"[2] built on the concept of degeneracy, a set of ideas that, although nearly forgotten today, nonetheless tremendously influenced turn-of-the-century thinking about the nature of social problems.[3] (Indeed, if we do not understand what *degeneracy* meant to nineteenth- and early twentieth-century writers, including born-criminal theorists, their commentaries on social problems seem silly or incomprehensible. Once the concept is grasped, however, the meaning of those observations becomes clear and logical.) Roughly synonymous with *bad heredity* and conceived as an invisible attribute of the "germ plasm" or "blood," degeneracy was pictured as a tendency to devolve to a lower, simpler, less civilized state. Nineteenth-century theorists taught that the downward spiral into degeneracy could be brought on by immorality (e.g., drinking, gluttony, or sexual excess) and that, if sustained, it could damage the germ plasm. Thus future generations could inherit the degenerative tendency. Whereas bad living could induce degeneracy, however, clean living might reverse the process: in a few generations a family that carefully avoided vice might restore itself to normality.

This nineteenth-century view of degeneracy as protean and mutable, heritable but nonetheless susceptible to environmental influences, encouraged theorists to conceive of social problems such as insanity, poverty, intemperance, and criminality as interrelated and interchangeable, mere symptoms of the underlying degeneracy. For example, one of Lowell's contemporaries wrote that intemperance and poor heredity were "so inextricably mixed, so interdependent," that intemperance could lead to "vice, crime, insanity, idiocy, pauperism, not confined to the one intemperate generation, but handed down to children and children's children, perhaps in an inverse order,—pauperism, idiocy, insanity, crime, intemperance."[4] Conceiving social problems to be heritable and interchangeable, Lowell and other degenerationists naturally looked for connections among the feeble-minded and other problem groups such as criminals and paupers.

The nineteenth-century preoccupation with the process of evolution reinforced the degenerationist association of socially problematic behaviors with reversion to a lower form of life. Charles Darwin's *Origin of Species* (1859) seemed to depict a titanic, ubiquitous struggle between primitive and complex organisms. In *The Descent of Man* (1871) Darwin explained that evolution creates hierarchies of intelligence, morality, and other human characteristics. "The several mental and moral faculties of man have been gradually evolved," he wrote, so that "we may trace a perfect gradation from the mind of an utter idiot, lower than that of an animal low in the scale, to the mind of a Newton."[5] Herbert Spencer and other so-called social Darwinists advised that socially problematic groups should be left to die out, like inferior species. "Under the natural order of things," Spencer wrote, "society is constantly excreting its unhealthy, imbecile, slow, vacillating, faithless members"; to aid the unfit would merely thwart this "purifying process" of extinction.[6] Lowell did not go so far as to suggest abandoning the unfit to die, but her view of feebleminded women as social refuse echoed the teachings of Spencer and other prominent evolutionists.

Lowell's eugenicism also drew on a reputable scientific tradition. As early as 1621, in *The Anatomy of Melancholy*, the English scholar Robert Burton wrote that parents could cause insanity "by Propagation." Citing biblical and classical sources for the idea that "like begets like," Burton states that melancholy "is an hereditary disease," a madness passed from parent to child. Anticipating nineteenth-century degenerationists, Burton holds that environmental influences can affect heredity and that bad heredity can manifest itself in a variety of weaknesses. "If a drunken man get a childe, it will never likely have a good braine," Burton explains, also predicting that "foolish, drunken, or haire-braine women, most part bring forth children like unto themselves." Burton concludes this passage of his famous treatise on a eugenical note, remarking that "it werre happy for humane kinde, if onely such parents as are sound of body and minde, should be suffered to marry."[7] Darwin gave similar eugenic advice in *The Descent of Man,* recommending that "both sexes ought to refrain from marriage if they are in any marked degree inferior in body or mind."[8] Lowell was one of the first Americans openly to support involuntary eugenic measures, but she was not alone. At a meeting where she advocated reproductive controls on feebleminded women, an Iowa physician argued that "the state should prohibit the marriage of all persons who had, at any time after arriving at the age of eighteen years, been supported in any penal or charitable institution, or who are suffering from any incurable bodily infirmity or deformity."[9] Degenerationists had reached the sobering conclusion that society was a kind of body, a network in which a diseased member could infect the whole. Eugenics—what Lowell called "extinction of the line"[10]—seemed to be the best way to deal with those who were biologically, morally, and socially diseased.

By far the most influential American degenerationist was Richard L. Dugdale, author of *"The Jukes": A Study in Crime, Pauperism, Disease and Heredity* (1877). A New York City businessman, Dugdale was keenly interested in social welfare problems, a concern that led him to become one of the nation's first social scientists. He published the initial version of his *"Jukes"* masterpiece just before Lowell joined New York's charity board.[11] This horrific study of a rural clan that, over seven generations, had produced 1,200 bastards, beggars, murderers, prostitutes, thieves, and syphilitics became an immediate best-seller, and *Jukes* became a synonym for degeneracy on both sides of the Atlantic.

"The Jukes" gave the nascent eugenics movement a central, confirmational image, that of the inbreeding, rural family dwelling in "log huts and hovels, . . . hot beds where human maggots are spawned."[12] Dugdale's tract became famous partly because its complex charts and statistics seemed scientific and partly because its language is evocative and vaguely titillating. Above all, however, it succeeded because it provided reformers like Lowell with genealogical proof of what they had come to suspect about bad heredity.[13]

Although Dugdale cautioned against hasty conclusions,[14] his book was widely read as proof of heredity's dominance over environment. This interpretation was fostered by Dugdale's use of hereditarian terminology ("criminal stock," "Juke blood," "reversion"). Nor was it entirely a misinterpretation, for Dugdale's genealogical method *assumed* that the various Juke sins might be at least partially hereditary, symptoms of the more fundamental malaise of "degeneration."[15] Conceptualizing criminality, idiocy, and so on as signs of a shared, underlying affliction, he considered them to be interchangeable: thus "disease in the parent will produce idiocy in the child"; thus "prostitution in the women is the analogue of crime and pauperism in the males"; thus "the crime of one generation may lay the foundation for the pauperism of the next." Dugdale's methodology—the questions he asked about the Jukes—drew on degeneration theory ("Does this person represent a family or near kinsfolk who have been accused of the same or similar offenses? . . . Is epilepsy . . . or any mark of hereditary insanity, known to exist . . . in . . . the father, mother, sister, brother, uncles, aunts, grandfather, or grandmother?"). Predictably his methodology also confirmed degeneration theory, providing apparent proof that, for example, a feebleminded woman could produce criminals and paupers.[16]

"The Jukes" profoundly impressed Lowell and her fellow commissioners. When it appeared, the SBC was in the midst of a poverty crisis. In retrospect one can see that social factors such as the demobilization of Civil War soldiers and a severe financial depression were escalating poverty in the 1870s. Policymakers who had to cope with the spread of poverty tended to blame the poor themselves, however, as their term *pauperism* suggests. Unlike *poverty, pauperism* refers to an ingrained condition, that of being impoverished. It connotes blameworthiness and something close to somatic inferiority. Midcentury hopes of restoring deviants to normalcy, such as the flowery sentiments expressed at the founding of the Syracuse Asylum for Idiots, had withered; "heredity" was becoming a way to explain both the ailments of the poor and policymakers' failures to cure them. Better recordkeeping and the centralization of deviant populations, moreover, now made it easier to investigate family backgrounds, increasing the probability of detecting deviant ancestors.

In a massive study entitled "The Causes of Pauperism," released just as Lowell joined the SBC, board secretary Charles S. Hoyt concluded that "the number of persons in our poor-houses who have been reduced to poverty by causes outside of their own acts is . . . surprisingly small." Like Dugdale, Hoyt began with hereditarian assumptions and reached hereditarian conclusions: "The element of heredity enters so largely in the problem of pauperism that it should receive special attention. . . . There is a large number of families throughout the State . . . the sole end of whose existence seems to be the rearing of children like themselves." Hoyt, too, assumed that the various forms of degeneracy were interrelated; paupers, for example, were "feeble minded."[17]

Lowell thus joined an agency deeply troubled by pauperism and primed to accept the proposition that feebleminded women could be one of its sources.

The Campaign

Receptive though other charity board members might have been, the legislature and general public were unlikely to embrace a proposal for something as radical and untried as a eugenic institution. Moreover, even though

Lowell's SBC associates worried about the apparent fecundity of feeble-minded women, these men originally planned to provide *noncoercive* custodial care for mentally retarded adults of *both* sexes, with no age limit.[18] Lowell had to persuade them to focus more narrowly on fertile women and to establish for this group an asylum combining the noncoercive models of sheltering home and hospital with that of the prison.

Defining the Problem

For decades poorhouse inspectors had complained that some poorhouse inmates were weak-minded women with numerous children. They depicted these women as doubly deviant: defective (mentally retarded) and dependent (unable to support themselves). Adding a third measure of deviance, Lowell further defined feebleminded women as "depraved" or criminalistic, a step she accomplished in a series of papers presented in 1878 and 1879.[19] She called for two new women's institutions, a reformatory prison for those who might be salvageable and a custodial asylum for the feeble-minded who by definition were not. But she did not in fact clearly distinguish among the forms of degeneracy:

> Reformatories are needed for women who are now almost constantly inmates of public institutions, whether jails, penitentiaries or poor-houses, and who perpetuate the classes of criminals and paupers, themselves belonging alternatively to both. . . . They are constantly sinking deeper and deeper into the abyss of vice and crime . . . and are, moreover, . . . producing children who are almost sure to inherit their evil tendencies. These women are the same individuals whether they be committed to jails and penitentiaries as criminals or to poor-houses as vagrants and paupers.[20]

Criminality, pauperism, and "evil" heredity could not be separated.

To launch her campaign, Lowell used many of the rhetorical strategies that Hervey Backus Wilbur and others had employed twenty-five years earlier in lobbying for the first idiot asylums. For instance, she narrated little dramas to galvanize her audience; hers were not success tales but horror stories, however.[21] For example, from Hoyt's pauperism report she quoted passages that seemed to prove that "one of the most important and most dangerous causes of the increase of crime, pauperism, and insanity, is the unrestrained liberty allowed to vagrant and degraded women":[22]

> "In the Albany County poorhouse, a single woman, forty years old, . . . the mother of seven illegitimate children; the woman degraded and debased, and soon again to become a mother. . . .
> "In the Essex County poorhouse, a . . . widowed woman, twenty-four years old, and two children aged respectively four and five years, both illegitimate and feeble-minded and born in the poorhouse, the latter being a mulatto."[23]

For another horror story Lowell turned to *"The Jukes"*: "Mr. Dugdale has computed that in seventy-five years the descendants of five vicious pauper sisters amounted to twelve hundred persons, and had cost the State of New York more than one million and a quarter dollars."[24] In Dugdale's version the Juke family tree is headed by a sire, Max Juke; in Lowell's version degeneracy flows from Max's five daughters.

Twenty-five years earlier New York had been persuaded to establish the Syracuse Asylum by a campaign that identified the mentally retarded as victims of an indifferent and hence villainous society. Lowell's campaign inverted this argument, identifying the retarded as villains and society as their innocent victim. Thus did Lowell alarm her audience and supply them with justifications for rethinking their attitudes toward feebleminded women.

To make her institutional solution to the problem seem to be inevitable, Lowell employed two verbal tactics also used in the earlier campaigns, the "rhetoric of rectitude" and the "rhetoric of rationality."[25] She simultaneously argued that helpless women must be protected against wickedness (her appeal to rectitude) and that society must protect itself against such wicked women (her appeal to rationality). This double-pronged appeal enabled Lowell's audience to rationalize eugenic institutionalization as an act of kindness, and it led directly to Lowell's conclusion that an asylum was necessary:

> What right have we to-day to allow men and women who are diseased and vicious to reproduce their kind, and bring into the world beings whose existence must be one long misery to themselves and others?[26]

> Shall the State of New York suffer a moral leprosy to spread and taint her future generations, because she lacks the courage to set apart those [feebleminded women] who have inherited the deadly poison and who will hand it down to their children, even to the third and fourth generations?[27]

Linking dependency, defectiveness, delinquency, and degenerate heredity, Lowell fashioned the image of the weak-minded mother of criminals.

Establishing the Institution

To establish the asylum permanently, Lowell needed the support of four groups: the SBC, officials of the state's older asylum for the retarded at Syracuse, New York's legislature, and leaders in the town of Newark. The first group, the charities board, seems to have approved her proposal immediately, for by January 7, 1878—just four days after Lowell made her initial presentation on the problem[28]—SBC secretary Hoyt was arranging for her to meet with officials of the Syracuse Asylum for Idiots to work out details for establishing a second state institution for the retarded.[29]

Lowell formed an unlikely alliance with Hervey B. Wilbur, the Syracuse

Asylum's superintendent. Lowell turned to Wilbur for help when he, his institution, and the fledgling mental retardation system as a whole were at a point of painful transition, shifting their mission from cure to custody. As Wilbur was well aware, a decade earlier New York had opened a second institution for the insane, a custodial asylum for chronic cases to supplement the more treatment-oriented Utica Asylum. Now Wilbur had to admit that his system, too, needed a second, custodial asylum, this one to shelter Syracuse's "graduates" and other homeless adult idiots. Thus he agreed to support Lowell's plan.[30]

Wilbur and his trustees—the second group whose support Lowell needed to proceed—nevertheless disputed every aspect of her proposal aside from its custodial thrust. They projected a noncoercive institution combining the models of hospital and home where relatively able idiots could care for invalids, they wanted the institution to hold inmates of both sexes and all ages, and they opposed Lowell's eugenic motives. As a result, when an SBC delegation led by Lowell met with Wilbur and his trustees to formulate plans, they jointly decided that the new asylum should open only on an experimental basis and under the supervision of the Syracuse institution.[31]

Lowell dealt next with the legislature, from which she needed funding. Making the best of the Syracuse officials' resistance, she found a way to avoid confrontation with this third group: an experimental institution could be established without legislation and therefore without discussion of its eugenic purpose. Lowell arranged for an appropriation of $18,000 to be inserted in the state's 1878 supply bill.[32] The Newark Custodial Asylum was founded in one sentence as a line item.[33] The Syracuse subcommittee members maintained silence about the institution's eugenic goal, tersely noting only that "the motives which prompted the conference [with Lowell's delegation] need not here be mentioned."[34] Resisting pressure from the charity board, they refused to make the asylum permanent immediately because they were not convinced that it would defeat "the evil [feeblemindedness] it was designed to meet" and because "the public" (like themselves) did not yet "appreciate" its necessity.[35]

Property owners in the village of Newark, fifty miles west of Syracuse, contacted Wilbur with an attractive offer: he could locate the new asylum in their uninhabited religious academy, rent-free, if the state would refurbish the building. In haste to lease what he thought would be temporary quarters, Wilbur disregarded the site's small size and inadequate water supply. A former poorhouse superintendent was hired to manage daily operations, and thus opened, in 1878, the Custodial Asylum for Feebleminded Women.

Wilbur and his board continued to resist Lowell's "partial and narrow" definition of the feebleminded woman as a eugenic menace.[36] Describing himself as "not very zealous" about the new asylum, Wilbur argued that idiots seldom reproduce, that there were in fact "few imbecile and idiotic females in the county poor-houses," and that the asylum "offer[ed] a sort of premium upon the mismanagement of county poor-houses" that permitted sexual contact among residents.[37] His trustees, unenthusiastic about managing an institution located two counties away on an unsuitable site, refused opportunities to buy the property cheaply. After Wilbur's death in 1883, they decided to terminate the trial program by transferring Newark's inmates to a new Syracuse dormitory built specially for them.[38]

The eugenic experiment would have collapsed at that point had the 1885 legislature not suddenly made Newark an independent, permanent institution with its own board. Although the local residents who ensured the institution's survival repeated Lowell's eugenical claims, it is not clear that this fourth group of supporters cared much one way or the other about eugenics. It *is* clear that they profited from the institution's presence in their town and from its expansion, which they actively promoted.[39]

Learning of the plan to close Newark, two local state assemblymen, Silas S. Peirson and Edwin K. Burnham, led Wayne County (pro-Newark) in a legislative battle with Onondaga County (pro-Syracuse) over the institution's location.[40] After calling for Lowell's help in lobbying the state senate, Wayne County's forces triumphed. Ties with the Syracuse Asylum were severed, and for the next eight years Newark was run as a fiefdom by Peirson (president of its board), Burnham (its secretary), and Eliza C. Perkins, the wife of Peirson's banking partner (treasurer).[41]

Peirson and the Perkinses sold land to the institution; the deeds were authorized by Burnham, Wayne County's notary public.[42] Treasurer Perkins disbursed funds to the firm of Peirson and Perkins[43] and to her husband, hired to landscape the asylum. Other town residents also sold property to the expanding institution, worked at it, and received contracts to provision it; they would have been indebted to the officials who had secured the asylum for their village and who were closely involved in its management. Indeed, the asylum may have been the small town's most profitable venture. Peirson and Perkins resigned when investigations of 1893 and 1894 uncovered their financial misdoings and other officials' cruelty to inmates;[44] Burnham stayed on, however, replacing Perkins as treasurer and, as the institution's receipts show, continuing to write checks to Peirson's relatives.[45]

The Custodial Asylum in Operation

To drum up business for "the Custodial" (as the asylum was locally known), trustees attended the annual conventions of poorhouse superintendents, warning of the dangers of feebleminded women and soliciting transfers. Peirson, for example, assured the poorhouse managers that each had the "right to a certain amount of room" at the Custodial, which, having expanded to forty acres, could accommodate another 1,000 to 1,200 women.[46] Such public relations efforts produced a steady flow of inmates, stimulating growth.

During the years of life that remained to him after Newark opened, Dr. Wilbur, too, dutifully funneled inmates into it. Sensible as always to his responsibilities, however unpleasant, he sent every poorhouse superintendent a brochure outlining the new institution's twofold purpose: Newark would provide custodial care for "unteachable idiots" and Syracuse graduates (his own aim), and it would prevent "imbecile and idiotic females" from giving "birth to illegitimate children" by providing protection "from the dangers to which their want of intelligence exposes them" (Lowell's goal). "Young and healthy" women, the brochure announced, would receive preference.[47] Lowell joined the search for commitments. Making sure her SBC colleagues had copies of Wilbur's circular, she asked that each, "when he visits poorhouses . . . [,] enquire especially if there are any young girls or women who should go to the Asylum and if he finds any, . . . have them transferred." She herself wrote numerous letters to ensure action on potential commitments.[48]

What sorts of women were committed to the Custodial? As of September 30, 1900, the asylum held 414 inmates, nearly all of whom had been delivered directly from poorhouses; thus they indeed were the paupers whose reproduction Lowell hope to staunch. Most were also, as the rules required, "of a child-bearing age,"[49] usually defined as years fifteen to forty-five, although often stretched at both ends of the scale. Some suffered from severe mental defects, but the majority seem to have been only mildly retarded. Many worked within the institution, some operating sewing machines on which they produced clothing and other institutional supplies. A few were probably not retarded at all by today's standards but considered so at the time because of the equation of female sexuality with mental subnormality.[50] Other inmates were the insane or otherwise difficult women whom poorhouse superintendents sometimes managed to dump at Newark.[51]

Even by the loose criteria of the time, few Custodial inmates lived up to their reputation as fountainheads of vice and illegitimacy. According to the highest estimate given in an annual report, no more than half had ever borne children, in or out of wedlock; other reports set the figure at 25 percent. Judging from an 1898 study of 500 evidently consecutive commitments, the actual rate may have been under 5 percent. The author of this study, the physical anthropologist Alešander Hrdlička, was not without his biases (he writes that "the adult female imbecile is almost, as a rule, more or less of a sexual libertine"), yet he found that only 18 of the 500 "had children, 5 as married and 13 as unmarried." Of these children, only 4 were reported feebleminded. But Hrdlička felt that his data sorely underreported the problem and concluded that "society . . . should make most strenuous efforts to hinder similar untoward production." [52] His report reinforced the feebleminded woman's sluttish image.

Reports on the Custodial regularly include a paragraph or two of official language on the dangers of feebleminded women. For example, one claims that "most" of the inmates are "of depraved origin . . . with a hereditary bias to go astray." [53] Other asylum records stress the inmates' "monster evil" and "abnormal animal passions." Its trustees boasted that by 1890 it "had already prevented the illegitimate birth of from one to two thousand feeble-minded children." [54]

Because the Custodial's bylaws did not provide for involuntary commitments, one might ask why inmates did not simply leave. Probably many remained because they had no alternative place to live and no one on the outside to rescue them. Mentally disabled to some degree, the majority lacked the personal resources to make other arrangements and perhaps mistrusted their own ability to cope in the outside world. In addition, officials made departure difficult. The Custodial was fenced, and until the turn of the century, inmates were seldom allowed to leave their buildings even under supervision. Thus for some, commitment was unquestionably involuntary. [55] For others, Newark may have provided a relatively good home.

That the asylum provided a much-needed service for some inmates is suggested by a letter of 1894 from Mrs. Elizabeth Goodings to SBC secretary Charles Hoyt begging him not to discharge her daughter. Mrs. Goodings dictated this letter to explain that Emily, placed at Newark many years earlier by Dr. Wilbur, was now about to be released, "as she had passed the child-bearing age."

> The facts of the case are these: I am totally without income (77 years of age) and dependent upon my soninlaw [sic]. . . . He will not be willing to receive Emily into his home. . . . It would break my heart if my oldest child should be obliged to go to a county house or insane asylum. . . . Does it not seem cruel to throw these children back into the condition from which you have taken them . . . [?] With the exception that they cannot propogate [sic] their kind, will not their last condition be as sad as their first[?] [56]

This letter shows that relatives were aware of the Custodial's eugenic purpose, that Emily was mentally disabled in her family's estimation, and that Newark provided help to impoverished but caring parents who simply could not cope with feebleminded offspring. Studies of other nineteenth-century institutions have similarly found that impoverished families committed relatives because they had no alternatives. [57] For the destitute and desperate, even repressive institutions might provide havens.

The Custodial's eugenical purpose shaped admission and discharge policies in at least three ways. The asylum apparently received a few women who were normal or nearly so solely because they were sexually active. At the same time it resisted the commitment of "unteachable" cases—the most obvious candidates for custodial care—perhaps because they appeared to be infertile. In addition, the asylum often discharged those who, like Emily, had "passed the child-bearing age," ejecting older women who no longer posed a eugenic threat.

We do in fact have a "control" group to help us further gauge the impact of Lowell's eugenic mission. As noted previously, in the early 1880s Syracuse's trustees erected a building for inmates of the Custodial, which they hoped to shut. When Newark gained independence, the Syracuse building became a residence for young female graduates of the training school, comparable to Newark's commitments. Although Syracuse became more custodial at this time, it never operated as cheaply as Newark, and its inmates received a higher level of care. They were not abruptly discharged at menopause, nor is there any evidence that they experienced the punitive treatment to which Custodial inmates were sometimes subjected. And they were not closely confined. In a letter of 1885 Wilbur's successor described his strenuous efforts to find a new home for a woman of twenty, committed "7 or 8 years ago as a private pupil" but now deserted by her family.[58] Syracuse was attempting to discharge a member of the very group that Newark wanted to lock up for eugenic reasons.

Conditions at the Custodial were worse than those of some poorhouses. Impure water and inadequate sewage were constant problems and, according to Newark's physician, a cause of illness. Inmates sickened and died from typhoid, cholera, and malaria. Lacking a separate hospital, the asylum could not isolate these patients or others stricken by epidemics of flu and measles. C. C. Warner, the first overseer, performed some minor surgery himself.[59] The local resident who succeeded him, Langdon Willett, was eventually fired for cruelty to inmates. The state's miserliness toward these women, and the managers' determination to hold operating costs to poorhouse levels, meant that overcrowding and fire hazards were addressed at a dangerously slow pace. Until 1894 there were no pictures on the walls and no opportunities whatsoever for outdoor exercise. Existence must have been monotonous and bleak at this institution, where already unfortunate women were denied liberty on the theory that they might commit sex offenses.

Some improvements occurred after 1893, when Custodial mismanagement prompted two SBC investigations. The first inquiry "fully and clearly showed that the superintendent, matron and first assistant matron had each of them repeatedly inflicted corporal punishment upon the defenseless inmates under their care, and that such punishments had frequently been of grossly cruel and inhuman character."[60] Two inmates so punished "were patients in the hospital with acute diseases, both of whom died soon thereafter, and . . . a number thus punished were insane." The superintendent, it came out, "practiced a unique form of punishment upon the patients, by tripping them from behind and letting them fall on their backs."[61] On one occasion the matron and her assistant, before beating a Mary Moore "with a ferule," had put the inmate in a straitjacket, tied her feet together, and stuffed her mouth with a towel.[62] The three principals in this scandal were dismissed. The doctor was retained, however, even though she, too, came under a cloud for having punished sick inmates.

The second investigation, triggered late in 1893 by "some charges made to the Governor against the . . . Custodial Asylum,"[63] led to the shakeup of the board mentioned earlier. Insane women were shipped elsewhere, as were "a number of helpless bed-ridden cases and cases of advanced age, no longer needing its [the asylum's] protecting care"; the new superintendent reported that he "rarely" needed to resort to restraints.[64] By the century's end the water was drinkable, although still inadequate to quell a fire. Inmates were occasionally taken on outings. For better or worse, they were now encouraged to celebrate Children's Day.

Why Women?

The Newark Custodial Asylum criminalized a condition, that of carrying bad heredity. This was evidently the first time in U.S. history that the body itself was criminalized. Previously only prohibited acts could be punished; now the category of punishable phenomena expanded to include a condition, the state of degeneracy. A new concept of dangerousness was emerging in which the thing to be feared was not harms but individuals.[65]

Why was the first stage of eugenic criminology marked by new iconography of the Bad Woman, not the Bad Man (or both), and by the establishment of an institution to prevent female but not male reproduction? Answers to this question lie in the social context in which the asylum at Newark was founded and in Lowell's personal situation.[66]

The Social Context

Women's roles underwent dramatic shifts in the late nineteenth century. Middle-class women like Lowell entered the public sphere to work for reforms in the treatment of disfranchised groups such as other women, children, and the feebleminded. Simultaneously working-class women moved into the paid labor force and grew socially independent.[67] These transformations set off a punitive reaction to female independence and sexuality, much as they precipitated slightly later clampdowns on prostitution.[68]

New York's charity board commissioners and other middle-class reformers struggled against the erosion of traditional standards of propriety. The nineteenth-century trend toward sexual repressiveness accelerated about 1870, moving from what historian Charles Rosenberg calls "the level of individual exhortation to that of organized efforts to enforce chastity upon the unwilling."[69] Although the purity crusades against abortion, illegitimacy, masturbation, prostitution, and so on did not ignore men, they stressed control of women's sexuality.[70] Moreover, women who did not fit the mold of the True Woman were now castigated as sexually and morally unnatural.[71] Middle-class women who undertook charity work did not escape such charges, but working-class women were at even greater risk. And women who ended up in poorhouses, especially if they had children of indeterminate origin, were particularly likely to become lightening rods for turn-of-the-century sexual and gender anxieties.[72]

Lowell's campaign, conducted in this context of role disturbances, reaffirmed traditional, biological beliefs about gender. Her call for an institution that would protect infirm women against "degrading influences"[73] flowed from the tenet that women are naturally weaker than men. Mentally retarded women, according to this line of reasoning, are especially weak, an extreme version of the biologically helpless female. Lowell's call for the protection of society against feebleminded women followed from the conviction that women are more responsible than men for the health of progeny. This conviction was partly an artifact of hereditarian methodologies: genealogists of degeneration found it easier to identify their subjects' mothers than fathers—thus women headed most branches of the Juke family tree.[74] In addition, the belief that women determine future generations' biological well-being was deeply rooted in nineteenth-century culture and reiterated in many contexts other than that in which Lowell worked.[75] Eugenic imagery of degenerate women was congruent with and actually close to familiar beliefs about the nature of all women. The stereotype of the feebleminded woman came into focus before that of the feebleminded man because it was nearer to hand.

Lowell's campaign paralleled other purity crusades of its day. Middle-class women participated heavily in these crusades, which often also aimed at sexual purity. Moreover, interest in eugenics was widespread among late nineteenth-century feminists, who drew on the doctrine to exalt women and justify female control of conception.[76] Whereas other feminists used eugenics arguments to emancipate "worthy" women, however, Lowell used them to incapacitate the unfit.

In a period when poor women were gaining some economic and sexual autonomy, Lowell's campaign extended state control over such women on the ground that their bodies posed a moral, medical, and social danger. The possibility that poor women might use their bodies unconventionally threatened the biological understanding of gender as fixed and immutable. Newark's creation signified a new stage in governmental management of bodies that, becoming independent, appeared to be problematic and "chaotic."[77] It affirmed the view of the unregulated female body as immoral, diseased, irrational, or mindless.[78]

In addition, Lowell's campaign quasi-legally confirmed the double standard of sexual morality. The double standard, in Frances Olsen's analysis, consists of two ideas: the notion that "non-marital sex . . . separated from emotional commitment . . . is . . . desirable for men but devaluing for women" and the categorization of women as "moral or immoral, good girls or bad girls, virgins or whores."[79] The Custodial Asylum, founded amid challenges to the double standard, punished women (only) for extramarital sex and reinforced the virgin/whore dichotomy. It also legitimated a correlate of the double standard, the belief that women need special protection, by picturing these particular bad women as incapable of informed sexual consent, driven to fornication by degenerate biology or tricked into it by predatory men. Out-of-wedlock pregnancy in poor women (or even its possibility) became synonymous with feeblemindedness.[80]

Lowell's Personal Situation

Lowell's own circumstances probably contributed to the gender specificity of her campaign. Her charity board colleagues would have assumed that, like other middle-class women engaged in philanthropic endeavors, Lowell would concentrate on the problems of women, children, and other groups associated with the female "sphere." To be an effective commissioner, however, Lowell would have had not only to confirm this assumption but also to establish herself as her male colleagues' equal in other areas. Furthermore, Lowell herself was something of a deviant. Like the feebleminded woman whom she sought to control, Lowell was a single mother. Moreover, instead of withdrawing into widowhood, she entered the male world of social reform. Her power did not derive from a man, and she was neither subservient nor accommodating. (Indeed, her correspondence as an SBC commissioner shows that she issued orders with regal authority.)[81] A public figure, she risked the charges of "unnaturalness" to which independent women were exposed.

Lowell's campaign—one of her first acts as commissioner—accomplished several ends. Designating feebleminded women as unfit, it confirmed her own membership among the fit and thus among "true" women.

There could be no doubt that, despite her unorthodox personal circumstances, she was normal and good. The campaign established her authority on women's issues, and it showed the other commissioners a hard-headed way to cope with their most pressing problem, hereditary pauperism.

The White Other

Late nineteenth-century diatribes against the feebleminded introduced a discourse on the dangers of what Ruth Frankenberg, in a different context, calls the "white Other."[82] Lowell's degenerate was neither black nor foreign-born; she was native-born, rural, impoverished, and white. This is not what the secondary literature on the U.S. eugenics movement, which emphasizes campaigns against native blacks and swarthy Europeans, would lead us to expect.[83] But then, eugenic criminology often gives us unexpected new perspectives on the eugenics movement. In the criminological context, what eugenicists spoke of with greatest alarm was the degeneracy of poor whites.

These particular eugenicists—eugenic criminologists—focused on the culture of rural poverty, defining it as marginal, inferior to their own. In so doing they established themselves as a group entitled to scrutinize others, evaluate them, and if necessary imprison them.[84] Much as the white authors of racial and colonial discourses are what Frankenberg calls "the nondefined definers," so too those who produced eugenic criminology assumed and demonstrated their own normalcy by portraying the white Other as different.

The distinction between good and bad whites formed one of the many binarisms of eugenic criminology. From one perspective eugenics was primarily a way of organizing social control around a set of opposites. "Intelligence," for example, became a caste mark, with "good" intelligence signifying the law-abiding middle class and weak-mindedness indicating the degenerate. Previously the cultural field had not been so deeply cleft by dualisms.[85] After 1880, however, criminological tracts devoted themselves to establishing polarities. In this cosmography the polar opposite of all that was civic-minded and socially valuable was the feebleminded woman.

Notes

1. On Lowell's role in the development of state welfare, see Beatty 1986; de Forest et al. 1905; J. Lane 1973; Saveth 1980; Stewart 1911; and Taylor 1963.
2. Lowell 1879a: 193.
3. European versions of degeneration theory have attracted more attention

than have those of the United States. On the concept, see Chamberlin and Gilman 1985; Dowbiggin 1991; Nye 1984; Pick 1989; Rafter 1988; Rafter 1992b; Sarason and Doris 1969; and Walter 1956.

4. Reynolds 1879:211. For other examples, see Henderson 1893; U.S. Dept. of the Interior 1883; and F. Wines 1888.

5. Darwin [1871] 1986:495.

6. Spencer, *Social Statistics* (1851), 323-24, as quoted and cited in Sarason and Doris 1969:225.

7. Burton [1621] 1989:207, 209.

8. Darwin [1871] 1986:918. On the next page Darwin approvingly refers to the view of his cousin, eugenicist Francis Galton, that "if the prudent avoid marriage, whilst the reckless marry, the inferior members tend to supplant the better members of society."

9. Reynolds 1879:214. Reynolds presented this paper at the same conference where Lowell's paper "One Means of Preventing Pauperism" (1879a) was read.

10. Lowell 1879a:199.

11. Dugdale 1874.

12. Dugdale 1877:54.

13. For a more detailed account of the appeal and impact of *"The Jukes,"* see Rafter 1988: introduction. Dugdale's genealogical methodology may have been inspired by *Hereditary Genius,* in which Galton ([1869] 1952:v) devised a family-tree type of notation to trace the offspring of "four hundred illustrious men." Dugdale's genius lay in applying this method to bad families. The charting of bad families became one of the major techniques of eugenics research.

14. Also see E. A. Carlson 1980.

15. In addition to employing the term *degeneration,* Dugdale (1877) uses various synonyms such as *blood, constitutional disease, hereditary tendencies,* and *physical exhaustion.*

16. Dugdale 1877:50, 24, 45. Dugdale's schedule of "Points of Inquiry" appears in Dugdale 1874:127-28.

17. Hoyt 1876:288, 289; for his "Schedule of Inquiries," see pp. 294-95.

18. New York State Board of Charities, *Annual Report, 1876,* p. 15.

19. For more detail on the sequence of papers, see Rafter 1992a, n. 5.

20. Lowell 1879b:173.

21. On horror stories as a rhetorical device, see Johnson 1989.

22. Lowell 1879a:189.

23. Ibid., 189-90.

24. Ibid., 196-97.

25. Again, I draw the terms from Best 1987:116.

26. Lowell 1879a:193.

27. Ibid., 199-200.

28. The sequence of steps in Lowell's campaign can be pieced together from information in Stewart 1911 and Devine 1905.

29. New York State Archives, State Board of Charities, correspondence 1867-1902: vol. 8, pp. 14, 21.

30. New York State Asylum for Idiots, *Annual Report, 1878,* pp. 2–3, 6.

31. Ibid., 7.

32. New York State Board of Charities, *Annual Report, 1878,* p. 283; New York State Board of Charities, *Annual Report, 1879,* p. 122. Correspondence makes it clear that Lowell arranged the appropriation; see New York State Archives, State Board of Charities, correspondence 1867–1902: vol. 8, pp. 120, 121, 137.

33. The hint of sneakiness suggests a lack of support for eugenic measures at this time.

34. New York State Board of Charities, *Annual Report, 1878,* p. 283.

35. New York Asylum for Idiots, *Annual Report, 1879,* p. 13.

36. Wilbur in Association of Medical Officers of American Institutions for Idiotic and Feeble-Minded Persons [1878] 1964:100.

37. Wilbur in Association of Medical Officers of American Institutions for Idiotic and Feeble-Minded Persons [1879] 1964:165; also see Wilbur 1880.

38. New York Asylum for Idiots, *Annual Report, 1884,* pp. 7–8.

39. New York County Superintendents of Poor, *Proceedings, 1888,* pp. 29–31; New York County Superintendents of Poor, *Proceedings, 1890,* p. 78.

40. New York State Custodial Asylum for Feeble-Minded Women 1893:13–16. Peirson's name is also spelled "Pierson" in the institution's documents.

41. Mrs. Perkins is invariably listed as "Mrs. E. C. Perkins" in the institution's reports. I was finally able to confirm her relationship to Peirson's partner through New York State Office of General Services, n.d.: deed 70, which lists "Charles H. Perkins and Eliza C. his wife."

42. New York State Office of General Services, n.d.: deeds 66 and 70.

43. New York State Custodial Asylum for Feeble-Minded Women, *Annual Report, 1890,* p. 11.

44. New York State Custodial Asylum for Feeble-Minded Women, *Annual Report, 1893,* p. 6; New York State Custodial Asylum for Feeble-Minded Women, *Annual Report, 1894,* p. 9; New York State Board of Charities, *Annual Report, 1893,* pp. xli–xliv, 142–44.

45. In the late 1970s, when I saw these receipts, they were in the Historical Museum of the Newark Developmental Center.

46. New York County Superintendents of Poor, *Proceedings, 1890,* p. 79. Peirson anticipates 1,000 or more inmates in New York State Custodial Asylum for Feeble-Minded Women 1893:18–19.

47. A copy of the original circular can be found in New York State Archives, State Board of Charities, correspondence 1867–1902: vol. 18, p. 53, on the reverse of a letter from J. S. Lowell to James O. Fanning, assistant secretary of the SBC, Nov. 1, 1881. Wilbur quotes the circular in New York Asylum for Idiots, *Annual Report, 1880,* p. 16, and reports mailing it to every poorhouse superintendent in the state in a letter of Nov. 10, 1878, to James O. Fanning (New York State Archives, State Board of Charities, correspondence 1867–1902: vol. 9, p. 226).

48. New York State Archives, State Board of Charities, correspondence 1867–1902: vol. 9, p. 238, Lowell to James O. Fanning, Nov. 14, 1878 (quoted letter), vol. 11, p. 12, vol. 14, pp. 30, 39, vol. 18, pp. 16, 53.

49. New York State Custodial Asylum for Feeble-Minded Women, *Annual Report, 1887*, p. 6 ("rules and regulations" state that Newark is for "feeble-minded women of a child-bearing age").

50. See, e.g., New York Asylum for Idiots, *Annual Report, 1882*, p. 14 ("a few of the cases sent, were committed because they were wanton in their habits rather than lacking in intelligence"). Also see Bragar 1977; Noll 1994; Rafter 1992a; Simmons 1978; and Tyor 1977.

51. E.g., New York State Custodial Asylum for Feeble-Minded Women, *Annual Report, 1896*, p. 13.

52. Hrdlička 1898:74–75.

53. New York Asylum for Idiots, *Annual Report, 1880*, p. 9. Curiously in the same paragraph this report states that "only two or three of them were of wanton propensities": one had been impregnated by a poorhouse superintendent; another, by a member of her employer's family (10). Bragar (1977) finds the same sort of contradiction in the Syracuse Asylum's records for 1890–1920. She distinguishes between two contrasting strands of commentary about adult feebleminded females. The "official perspective," voiced by the superintendent to the outside world, repeated the usual cliches about the eugenic dangers of feebleminded women. But line staff portrayed the women as relatively normal. Thus there were "not one but two institutional perspectives" (Bragar 1977:66).

54. New York Asylum for Idiots, *Annual Report, 1896*, p. 13; New York State Custodial Asylum for Feeble-Minded Women, *Annual Report, 1890*, p. 5, citing an unnamed authority, perhaps a member of the SBC or perhaps nonexistent.

55. In a letter of Feb. 8, 1884, Newark's new superintendent, C. C. Warner, wrote Charles Hoyt of the SBC about a poorhouse inmate delivered clandestinely by "two strong men." "She was violent and one of the most Profane Persons that was ever in any Institution that I ever had charge of—More than one attendant carries marks where she has scratched or bit them and many are afrid [*sic*] of her" (New York State Archives, State Board of Charities, correspondence 1867–1902: vol. 23, p. 79).

56. New York State Archives, State Board of Charities, correspondence 1867–1902: vol. 42, p. 199 (letter dated June 19, 1894). I have changed the names of both mother and daughter.

57. Brenzel 1983; Dwyer 1987, 1992.

58. James C. Carson to Charles C. Hoyt, August 1, 1885 (New York State Archives, State Board of Charities, correspondence 1867–1902: vol. 26, p. 85).

59. C. C. Warner to Charles Hoyt, Feb. 1, 1884 (New York State Archives, State Board of Charities, correspondence 1867–1902: vol. 23, p. 62), reports that a Newark inmate who had been "in the hospital for 3 months" could now take some nourishment since he had "removed three badly decayed teeth."

60. New York State Board of Charities, *Annual Report, 1893*, p. xlii.

61. Ibid., 143.

62. Ibid., 142.

63. Charles McLouth (a Newark board member) to Charles Hoyt, December 26, 1893 (New York State Archives, State Board of Charities, correspondence 1867–1902: vol. 40, p. 129).

64. New York State Board of Charities, *Annual Report, 1893*, pp. xliii, xliv.

65. On the emergence of "the dangerous individual," see Foucault 1988.

66. A third answer, an apparent tendency to test social control innovations on women, children, and other groups that are vulnerable to infantilization and unable to resist, is discussed in Rafter 1992a:26.

67. Peiss 1986.

68. Rafter 1990a: esp. chap. 7; Connelly 1980; Rosen 1982.

69. Rosenberg 1976:73.

70. D'Emilio and Freedman 1988; Pivar 1973.

71. Gallagher and Laqueur 1987; Haller and Haller 1974. On the True Woman, see Welter 1966.

72. Also see Groneman 1994 on nineteenth-century attributions of nymphomania, another female somatic disorder.

73. Lowell 1879a:197.

74. Also see Neff, Laughlin, and Cornell 1910; Hahn 1980.

75. See, e.g., Rosenberg 1976: chaps. 2 and 3.

76. Gordon 1977:112.

77. Smart 1989:103.

78. Much has been made of nineteenth-century male physicians' leadership in the diseasing of women's bodies (see, e.g., Mitchinson 1985, 1991). In Newark's case, however, the key physician, Hervey Backus Wilbur, *fought* efforts to biologize deviance. It was Lowell, the feminist, who rejected Wilbur's expertise and defined feebleminded women as triply deviant degenerates.

79. Olsen 1984:402, n. 70.

80. Also see Rosen 1982; Simmons 1978; Tyor 1977.

81. New York State Archives, State Board of Charities, correspondence 1867–1902.

82. In her study of "the social construction of whiteness," Frankenberg (1993: 196) speaks of "Western colonial discourses on the white self, the non-white Other, and the white Other too."

83. But see Larson 1991, according to which "reactionary racism did not underlie passage of Georgia's sterilization law" (63), and Noll 1995b, arguing that white racist and elitist attitudes caused eugenicists to exclude African Americans with mental retardation from institutions.

84. Rafter 1994.

85. Mid-nineteenth century writings about the mentally retarded, for instance, did not exclusively define this group as sick, bad, oversexed, and criminalistic.

3

Criminalizing the Mentally Retarded

> There is free in the community a great host of crime-
> doers who are not so much criminals as mental and
> moral imbeciles. . . . A movement has been inaugu-
> rated . . . toward life confinement of the incorrigible,
> morally insane and the imbecile classes, that their
> propagation shall cease, and thus crime be measurably
> diminished by the partial extinction of criminals.
>
> Isaac N. Kerlin, "Provision for Idiotic
> and Feeble-minded Children"

Josephine Shaw Lowell criminalized but one
group among the feebleminded: women of child-
bearing age. When she and her charities board
founded the Newark Custodial Asylum, moreover, they imposed their eugenic solution on
the mental retardation system from the outside,
while the insider, superintendent Hervey Wilbur,
did what he could to resist it. Within twenty
years, however, nearly every superintendent in
the country had abandoned Wilbur's compassion
for the retarded in favor of Lowell's condemnation. At every opportunity they proclaimed not
only that feebleminded women breed degenerates
but that every feebleminded person is a potential
criminal and eugenic threat to American society.

By the late nineteenth century mental retardation officials were settling on the term *moral
imbecility* to indicate the innate criminality of
the feebleminded.[1] Every mentally backward person, they warned, is afflicted with moral imbecility, a congenital and inherited inability to tell
right from wrong. In addition, there is a particularly criminalistic subgroup of the feebleminded,

moral imbeciles, whose intellectual defects can be discerned only by experts. Cloaked in deceptive normality or even in seeming precocity, moral imbeciles stalk our streets and sit beside our children in schools, their hereditary flaw "doubly dangerous"[2] because of its invisibility. "Here we confront the worst class of criminals," advised Dr. Martin W. Barr, chief physician at the Pennsylvania Training School, equating the moral imbecile with "the murderer; the harlot; the lier-in-wait-to-deceive."[3]

None of these superintendents—not even those who railed most virulently against the feebleminded at the century's end—began his career as a eugenicist. In the 1870s most of them still spoke sympathetically about their charges, seldom referring to heredity or crime. Nevertheless, two decades later they were vying with one another to detect moral imbeciles among their inmate populations and cautioning the nation against the "crime of procreation among the notoriously unfit."[4]

To be sure, other Americans preached the same sermon. Institutionalization of the feebleminded became a fashionable cause in the late nineteenth century. In California a coalition of "prominent and philanthropic ladies and gentlemen" established that state's first institution for the feebleminded in the mid-1880s.[5] About the same time "benevolent ladies"[6] founded at Vineland, New Jersey, an institution for feebleminded women analogous to New York's Newark Custodial Asylum, while similar lobbies formed in other states. Some reformers may simply have wanted to help the feebleminded, but most, like Josephine Shaw Lowell before them, also aimed at controlling reproduction. Isabel Barrows, a well-known activist in charitable causes, explained that "there is not a shadow of doubt as to the immense gain to a commonwealth to have every imbecile and feeble-minded child within its border brought under the control of wise and kind teachers and attendants; for, even were the sadly needed laws passed to-day which should as far as possible prevent the birth and reproduction of these imperfect creatures, there would still be for years the existing multitude to care for."[7] This was eugenic reasoning, although Barrows, like other nineteenth-century Americans, had not yet heard the term *eugenics.*

For the superintendents who worked within the mental retardation system as for the charity reformers who worked outside it, interest in eugenic institutionalization was stimulated by the nineteenth-century fascination with science in general and evolution in particular. Science, Charles Rosenberg observes, "for the first time assumed a significant place in the hierarchy of American values,"[8] displacing the older values and worldviews of traditional religions. Proto-eugenical discourses such as phrenology reflected science's growing hold on the public imagination, as did psychiatrists' debates over the condition they called "moral insanity." That hold tightened with the 1859 publication of Darwin's *Origin of Species,* which fired speculation about speeding up evolutionary processes through selective breeding. Darwinian ideas were also used to explain the presence of the uncivilized in a civilized world: the poor, criminal, and feebleminded were perhaps less well evolved than the law-abiding middle class. Perhaps science could identify a biological factor differentiating the deviant from the normal, the primitive from the civilized, the inferior from the fit. Indeed, theorists believed that they already had identified that factor in degeneracy, the inborn tendency to decay.

Changing relations among social classes also encouraged the development of eugenics doctrine. By the 1880s the Anglo-Saxon elite could no longer count on the advantages and deference it had traditionally enjoyed. Urbanization had transformed towns into slum-ridden cities, immigration had introduced hordes of foreigners who did not recognize their "betters," and industrialization had widened social-class gradations into unbridgeable rifts. The new working class and its shadow, the degenerating underclass, appeared dangerously restive, infected by socialist ideas. Middle-class people also found it difficult to sympathize with the plutocrats who were gobbling up the country's wealth. Caught in between, middle-class reformers addressed problems caused by the two extremes.[9] Although they frowned on the acquisitiveness of robber barons and other nouveaux riches, however, these reformers felt closer to the wealthy than to those they now termed "the dependent, defective, and delinquent classes."[10] They started articulating a worldview in which "higher" meant better and "lower" was synonymous with all that was undeveloped, childlike, and unworthy.

Enthusiasm for science, the widening of social-class divisions, and the popularity of degeneration theory may help to explain why reformers inside and outside the mental retardation system turned toward eugenics, but in the superintendents' case an additional factor—professionalization—came into play. To understand why the superintendents turned on their charges, vilifying backward children as menaces to the nation's health, we need to examine how professionalization gave them motives, over and above those they shared with outsiders, for criminalizing the retarded.

This chapter focuses on the first formal phase in the superintendents' professional development, which began in 1876 with the founding of their professional organization, the Association of Medical Officers of American Institutions for Idiotic and Feeble-Minded Persons (AMO). Using the AMO's *Proceedings* as my main source, I concentrate on the association's first two decades, 1876 through 1895, after which the organization undertook a major professional overhaul.[11] To illustrate the interdependence of the professionalization of the work on the one hand and the development of eugenic criminology on the other, I focus on the career of Isaac N.

Kerlin, superintendent of the Pennsylvania Training School. The AMO's first phase of professionalization coincided almost exactly with Kerlin's reign as the organization's secretary-treasurer and, finally, president.

Professionalizing Care of the Mentally Retarded

In 1875 there were only eight public institutions for the mentally retarded in the United States,[12] all located in the Northeast or Midwest. Small, isolated asylums, most retained their original mission of special education for children who could not be taught by ordinary methods. But their functions were changing. Expectations for what education could accomplish with retarded children had dimmed. Commitment remained voluntary at all the institutions except Newark, but (as at Syracuse) custodial cases accumulated and the average inmate age crept upward.

Superintendents of these training schools faced professional dilemmas on two fronts, institutional and occupational. On the institution front, they had to ensure their schools' survival and growth. They also needed to link the institutions to some sort of national network that could coordinate and systematize their efforts and to reduce per capita costs so that state governments would fund institutional expansion. On the occupational front, the superintendents had to establish their work as a distinct and socially useful specialty. They had to structure this work as a career, with a clear pattern of stages from entry through success, and to establish themselves as experts whose work involved skills and specialized knowledge.[13]

The superintendents took the first step toward solving these institutional and occupational problems in 1876 by founding the Association of Medical Officers of American Institutions for Idiotic and Feeble-Minded Persons. Established at a time when workplace organizations were forming in many fields, the AMO modeled itself specifically on the psychiatrists' professional society, the Association of Medical Superintendents of American Institutions for the Insane, founded in 1844. For the rest of the century, members of the two organizations encountered similar problems, the most critical of which was a widening gulf between their medical and managerial roles.[14] The AMO's founders were all physicians, and physicians continued to constitute the association's core membership during its first two decades. Like the psychiatrists' association, however, the AMO became preoccupied with managerial issues that isolated it from mainstream medicine and scientific research. As the years passed, the relevance of medical training to the work of superintending an institution for the feebleminded became less and less apparent.[15]

This uncertainty in professional role was particularly problematic for

AMO superintendents because, as heads of a newer, smaller, and less prestigious jurisdiction, they also had to define how their work differed from that of the insane asylum superintendents. Was their field merely what one observer called a "special branch of psychiatry"?[16] If not, how was it distinctive? What sorts of knowledge claims could the AMO superintendents make, and where was the literature that set forth these claims?

In the papers they prepared for annual meetings, AMO superintendents tried to create a body of information on the nature and treatment of feeblemindedness. In fact, however, their annual meetings served less as opportunities for developing specialized knowledge than as occasions for exhausted superintendents ("worn-out excursionists," one member described them)[17] to vacation while swapping war stories and administrative lore. The AMO's *Proceedings,* its sole publication during this period, sometimes read like a management manual. In truth, the superintendents knew little about the causes of feeblemindedness. A paper read at the 1892 meeting claimed that "adenoids play a potent role in the cause of feeblemindedness in some children,"[18] and three years later Martin Barr, the chief physician at the Pennsylvania Training School, warned that pregnant women who read the horrific novels of Emile Zola should expect mentally crippled children.[19] Still searching for basic information themselves, the superintendents could hardly impress others with their fund of knowledge.

The AMO gave the superintendents a sense of professional identity,[20] but it remained a small organization. Twelve people, including Edward Seguin's widow and a local minister, spoke at the 1886 annual meeting at Syracuse; seventeen, including two visitors, contributed to the 1895 meeting in New Haven. Unaffiliated with other workplace associations, the AMO remained parochial. Small size and intellectual isolation created a situation in which one particularly energetic member could dominate the association's development. Pennsylvania superintendent Isaac Kerlin, who had organized the AMO's first meeting in conjunction with Philadelphia's 1876 centennial celebration, seized the reins of the association. Kerlin was "essentially a strong man," California superintendent A. E. Osborne observed; "the Association became largely what he made it."[21]

Isaac N. Kerlin

A carpenter's son, Isaac Kerlin (1834–93) studied medicine at the University of Pennsylvania and became assistant to Dr. Joseph Parrish, head of the Pennsylvania Training School at Germantown, one of the earliest idiot asylums.[22] After serving in the Union Army during the Civil War, Kerlin returned to superintend the school, now relocated to Elwyn (Media), near

Philadelphia. As founders of the first institutions died off, Kerlin became the AMO's senior member and its yoke to the past. He presided at Elywn until his death and, with his wife, was buried on its grounds.

Kerlin combined zeal with an inflexible will, administrative brilliance with a need to control, and sentimentality with shrewdness. His assistant and protégé, Dr. Martin Barr, recalled that Kerlin "disliked to see anyone relax" and that, although "genial and kindly by nature . . . [,] when roused he had a most violent temper."[23] Like many of his contemporaries, Kerlin believed that self-indulgence could induce degeneracy; as a result he avoided hiring people who used alcohol or tobacco and also disapproved of "unlawful and excessive use of the organs . . . of procreation."[24] According to Barr, "Dr. Kerlin brought to the work . . . a power that was almost mesmeric, and that controlled absolutely all who came within its influence. Children, attendants, officers, friends, visitors, the most careless, the most indifferent, testified to this undefined 'something' to which all yielded and that made itself felt equally within institution walls as in legislative halls."[25] Aspects of Kerlin's personality may have predisposed him to eugenics: his desire for purity, his perfectionism (he kept a notebook in which to record his secretary's spelling errors),[26] and his sense of entitlement and absolute self-confidence. The same traits probably inclined him to become an apostle of eugenics, preaching the doctrine to others.

In the sole dispute recorded in AMO minutes from this period, Kerlin clashed with Hervey Backus Wilbur, the Syracuse superintendent. At the AMO's second meeting Kerlin spoke in favor of institutions that could become "life-homes" for idiots and imbeciles. Wilbur tried to block publication of the final section of Kerlin's paper, which recommended large, custodial institutions.[27] Kerlin amended the paper, published it, and rankled for years over Wilbur's challenge to his vision.[28] The two men differed markedly in other ways, too; Wilbur's modesty, self-critical bent, and opposition to eugenics may have made Kerlin impatient. At any rate, when Wilbur died in 1883, Kerlin became the system's leader, carrying treatment of the feebleminded in directions that Wilbur had dreaded.

Kerlin devoted more personal and institutional resources to the AMO than did any other superintendent. As secretary-treasurer he controlled the association's agenda and publications. He remained in this office while other superintendents came and went as president. Distance and institutional emergencies occasionally forced other superintendents to skip annual meetings, but Kerlin was an abiding presence, stabilizing the AMO. Sometimes he brought along assistants to deliver research papers; on such occasions the Elwyn contingent dominated annual meetings, numerically and intellectually. Moreover, because Kerlin as secretary contacted professionals in related fields, his AMO colleagues came to depend on him for news of policy developments at home and abroad.

Kerlin's assistants strengthened his power base. He attracted capable young physicians to Elwyn, giving them genuine opportunities for professional advancement. Administrative duties limited Kerlin's time for research, but he nonetheless took the lead in studying the pathology of mental defect by assigning an assistant, Dr. Alfred W. Wilmarth, to dissect the brains of deceased Elwyn inmates.[29] Wilmarth's autopsies, part of a broader search for anatomical anomalies that might reveal how defectives and delinquents differ from normal people, formed a counterpart to criminal anthropology.[30] By 1888 Wilmarth had preserved, dissected, and photographed the brains of fifty feebleminded children.[31] (One hopes he did not ask Elwyn inmates to clean the laboratory, where they might have glimpsed their own fate in pickled form.) Kerlin also encouraged research by his other key assistant, Martin Barr, and helped several subordinates to move on to administrative posts.[32] They in turn elaborated their mentor's eugenic ideas. Barr, Kerlin's successor at Elwyn, published an important eugenical textbook on feeblemindedness.[33]

In an age that equated science with progress, Kerlin, far more than other superintendents, emphasized scientific aspects of work with the feebleminded. His own reports, heavy with statistics and medical terminology, seemed to be more scientific than the educationist and managerial tracts of other superintendents.[34] Kerlin admired the work of Zebulon R. Brockway and J. Bruce Thomson, two early criminal anthropologists, and above all that of social scientist Richard Dugdale, whose *"Jukes"* study Kerlin used as a model for his own statistical work.[35] In keeping with his own background, however, Kerlin insisted that medicine was the science most relevant to work with the feebleminded: "Our work is . . . a medical philanthropy. . . . Medical science . . . is . . . its divinist mission."[36] He investigated the relationship between epilepsy and feeblemindedness and, in his 1892 presidential address, endorsed surgical treatments, recommending both craniectomy (removal of part of the brain) and sterilization.[37] In fact, with funds from "a benevolent lady," Kerlin arranged what was evidently the first sterilization performed in an institution for the feebleminded. For him as for superintendents in other types of institutions, sterilization offered not an alternative to incarceration but a useful supplement, a way to calm hypersexual inmates and maintain order.[38]

Kerlin's earliest AMO remarks were hereditarian but not yet eugenical. In his first AMO speech (1877) he traced mental retardation to bad heredity: "Idiocy and imbecility are dependent *generally* on hereditary or prenatal causes." This view followed logically from Kerlin's degenerationist premises. "Tendencies to congenital cerebral disease of offspring," he explained, "are established through practices and vices which lower the morale, impair the strength, and vitiate the blood of ancestors and parents." At this point Kerlin still viewed feeblemindedness as an "avertible" condition, one that future generations could avoid through moral living.[39] By 1879, however, Kerlin had begun to reason eugenically. He apparently turned this corner through reading the work of J. Bruce Thompson, a Scottish prison physician who as early as 1870 was producing explicitly eugenic recommendations.[40] After 1879 science and eugenics flowed together in Kerlin's thought. He came to regard eugenics as the chief weapon in the war against mental defect and institutionalization as the best method of achieving reproductive control. The large institution that could detain the feebleminded for life would treat them and society simultaneously, "protecting the weak, and exterminating the evil."[41]

Scientific Custodialism

Professionalization and eugenics converged around the concept of custodial care of the feebleminded. A large institution with a thousand or more inmates and multiple buildings on extensive acreage became the superintendents' symbol of professional success. At the same time, it became the eugenic solution to the problem of feeblemindedness.

Some of the superintendents' professional concerns surface in a paper that Dr. A. E. Osborne, the superintendent of California's asylum for the feebleminded, delivered at the 1891 AMO meeting. Osborne heralds a "new era" in professionalization marked by states' willingness to skip the experimental stage in institution building and leap "with one bound to the erection of a plant that from the beginning is designed to accommodate . . . one thousand patients."

> If there should exist in the minds of any one a doubt that we are in a new era, let him compare the humble beginnings of the work at Barre, at Syracuse, or at Germantown, — all less than fifty years ago, — noting their respective early struggle for public recognition and for legislative aid, and their weary years of doubtful hold upon the public purse, with the career of our own plant in California, which in less than five years has secured over six hundred thousand dollars of State aid, thousands of dollars of private aid . . . , an ideal site, and splendidly-equipped buildings.[42]

In earlier years, Osborne continues, the superintendent had been "little else than the general utility man of the place," but the "superintendent of the future" will confer with multiple department heads "much as a college president confers with his faculty, and . . . he will have more time to devote to the study of the brain and mind."[43]

Thus summarizing the superintendents' desire for higher professional status, Osborne associates that improvement with eugenics. States are now willing to fund large institutions, he says, because "society is organizing everywhere for self-protection." The large, preventive institution has become thinkable thanks to the cost efficiencies of the "colonial system" championed by Pennsylvania's superintendent Kerlin.[44]

Kerlin's colonial system, or colony plan, called for separate housing units in which a heterogeneous population could be classified—one dormitory for epileptics, another for able adult women, a third for hospital cases, and so on.[45] The colony concept rejected the model of a series of independent, specialized institutions such as those that New York State had established at Syracuse and Newark.[46] Instead, it called for gathering all an area's feebleminded persons, regardless of age, sex, and degree of disability, under a single institutional roof. So closely was the colony system associated with Kerlin that some called it "the Pennsylvania plan."[47]

The colony concept emphasized farming and other inmate labor that would hold down expenses.[48] California superintendent Osborne estimated that in 1892 his "fruit detail" had produced ten tons of dried fruit and thousands of gallons of canned goods and preserves, much of which he sold to other state institutions. The superintendent of Nebraska's institution hoped that by making profits at a rented farm, he could persuade his legislature to "provide the additional land which we so much need."[49] By reducing costs, farms helped superintendents to meet the constant demand for expansion without exceeding their state appropriation. Yet another advantage lay in the colony plan's ability to provide work for trained inmates. Asylums for the insane, too, expected patients to work when they could, and they too sometimes held useful patients longer than necessary out of institutional convenience.[50] In institutions for the feebleminded, however, custodialism was more explicitly eugenic in aim.

The colony plan induced imperialistic visions. Calling Elwyn an "asylum village," Kerlin claimed that such a colony, with its extensive acreage and multiple buildings linked by narrow-gauge railway, could be "to its wards and employés as cosmopolitan as a city."[51] He predicted that as colonies expanded, jails, criminal courts, and grog shops would dwindle in number, until "scattered over the country, may be 'villages of the simple,' made up of the warped, twisted, and incorrigible, happily contributing to their own and the support of those more lowly,—'cities of refuge,' in truth; havens in which all shall live contentedly, because no longer misunderstood nor taxed . . . beyond their mental or moral capacity. They 'shall go out no more' and 'they shall neither marry nor be given in marriage' in those havens dedicated to incompetency."[52] Farming reminded pathologist A. W. Wilmarth of a more idyllic, paternalistic past; in his opinion there is "no better occupation for our simple minded charges than to return to the most primitive of all industries. . . . It is the most free from temptation. It conflicts with no labor unions. It has been demonstrated to be profitable."[53] For Kerlin and Wilmarth, farm colonies provided simple but profitable environments for the anthropologically backward, American counterparts to the "primitive" societies that imperialists were colonizing in more exotic corners of the globe. Looking closer to home for analogues, Martin Barr compared institutions for the feebleminded to American Indian reservations and southern plantations, other colonies where self-designated superiors regulated the backward.[54]

Initially the colony plan appealed to superintendents because it was practical. It solved the problem of finding jobs for trained inmates, and if the feebleminded could be kept at the institutions after they reached adulthood, they could " 'relieve the State of a portion of the cost of maintenance.' "[55] Using these arguments superintendents lobbied for laws to retain tutored adolescents and to receive feebleminded adults who had never been trained. Imperceptibly, however, such practical arguments took on a eugenic edge: life detention would also prevent the feebleminded from reproducing themselves. In 1887 a correspondent advised the AMO that pending legislation would enable Minnesota to "keep those whom we cannot cure and equip for life in custody until they are past the reproducing age, and stamp out hereditary imbecility and epilepsy right here and now."[56] The colony plan, with its potential for institutionalizing inmates of all ages, nurtured the principle of no release. Protection of the feebleminded became protection against them.

Superintendents who ran their institutions as colonies created two broad divisions, school departments where youngsters of the "improvable class" received training and custodial departments for "unteachables" and older inmates.[57] As custodialism took root, school departments declined in importance. Superintendents redefined education as preparing inmates to perform useful work. They insisted that "there is no abandonment anywhere of the school idea of the earlier superintendents," but increasingly they agreed with superintendent Osborne that " 'a little learning is a dangerous thing.' Instead of books they [the feebleminded] need tools."[58] By the century's close few superintendents trained inmates for release.

State institutions became refuges of last resort for the poor. Families of means sent retarded relatives to private asylums or to the quarters that semiprivate institutions reserved for the wealthy. In contrast, Dr. Fish of Illinois, like other state superintendents, found that the majority of his inmates were committed by "families too poor to furnish clothing and transportation."[59] Poor families lacked resources to object to the indefinite commitment of their relatives and to eugenic denunciations of the feebleminded. Moreover, the impoverished background of most inmates made it easier for superintendents to infantilize them. Whereas several early graduates of the Syracuse Asylum had enlisted in the Union Army, fighting and dying in the Civil War, superintendents now viewed the feebleminded person as "a child, whether he be four or seventy years of age."[60] Inmate demographics made custodialism seem sensible and eugenics appear plausible.

Institutional size, not inmate improvement, became the currency of professional success. Officials competed over the size of their populations, total acreage, and institutional efficiency. Kerlin impressed others by expanding Elwyn while reducing annual per capita costs from $300 to $100.[61] When superintendent Osborne of California was unable to attend a meeting, he cabled a one-sentence message bound to rouse his colleagues' envy: "California, with new site of seventeen hundred acres and appropriation of two hundred and eighty-one thousand dollars, sends greeting to the Association."[62] The new criteria for professional success—growth and cost-effectiveness—meshed easily with eugenics, which also demanded extensive institutionalization at the lowest possible cost.

Superintendents stretched the definition of those who fell within their jurisdiction. They decided that *idiocy,* the mid-nineteenth-century term for mental retardation, had "a bad effect upon those who contemplate placing children in an institution."[63] Moreover, *idiocy* was too narrow a term to cover all those now perceived as mentally backward. Thus the superintendents replaced the generic label *idiot* with *feeble-minded* (a "less harsh expression," Massachusetts superintendent Walter E. Fernald explained),[64] reserving *idiot* to refer to the severely disabled. At the same time they began using *imbecile* and (again) *feeble-minded* to indicate those who fell into the middle and high grades of mental defect, respectively.[65]

Kerlin readily admitted that these changes involved "a broadening of definitions."[66] Detecting feeblemindedness among the apparently normal had in fact become a sign of expertise. When a Stanford University professor suggested that 10 percent of California's public schoolchildren might better be educated in institutions for the feebleminded, superintendent Osborne professed to be "astonished"; as a "specialist," Osborne knew the professor had underestimated the proportion of dullards.[67]

Definitions of "the feebleminded" now included not only the mildly backward but also moral imbeciles: people in whom the impairment was ethical rather than intellectual. Kerlin explained that "*congenital moral imbeciles . . . ,* although often precocious in the power to acquire school learning," were so apt to become criminals that they "should be withdrawn from the community before they reach crime age, and . . . cared for under the discipline of institutions for the idiotic and feeble-minded."[68] Other superintendents repeated this claim, stressing (in the words of Connecticut's George H. Knight) "that a large proportion of the criminal class are recruited from a type which, when we find them in our institutions, we designate as moral imbeciles."[69]

The concept of moral imbecility promoted eugenic thinking. It linked feeblemindedness to criminality, demonstrating the need for eugenic measures against both groups. George Knight followed his definition of moral imbecility with this eugenic prediction: "The time will come when the recognition of these as distinct and dangerous types among the defective classes will result in such timely and thorough preventive measures as shall give them custodial care for life, . . . thus arresting the tendency to crime instead of attempting to reform the fullfledged criminal."[70] The moral imbecility concept also encouraged custodialism. Of moral imbeciles at his Massachusetts School for the Feeble-minded, Walter E. Fernald explained that the "daily routine work of a large institution furnishes these trained adults with abundant opportunities for doing simple manual labor, which otherwise would have to be done by paid employees."[71] The superintendent of Minnesota's institution declared, only half-facetiously, that "moral imbeciles . . . make first-class foremen!"[72] Troublesome but capable, moral imbeciles enabled superintendents to achieve the cost efficiencies that custodialism required.

Institutional Confirmations of Deviance

As institutions swelled in size and adopted custodial goals, individual differences among inmates became increasingly problematic. The larger the institution, the greater the emphasis on uniformity. More rules meant less leeway for individual variation and more punishments. Superintendents absorbed by managerial duties had fewer occasions for direct contact with the feebleminded than had their forerunners in Wilbur's generation, and unfamiliarity bred contempt. As custodialism became the norm, moreover, variations among institutions decreased, narrowing the possibility for alternative management models that might have disconfirmed suspicions about the immorality of the feebleminded. In short, the institutions themselves promoted perceptions of deviance, perceptions that seemed to prove the equation of mental with moral imbecility.

In contrast to Seguin, who had treasured liveliness in his pupils, second-generation superintendents valued conformity. Kerlin, for example, required inmates to "speak seldom" and "repress . . . emotion"; he discovered that military drills brought his boys "into complete subjection."[73] Some degree of regimentation was inevitable in large institutions, and most late nineteenth-century state schools for the feebleminded were an improvement over local poorhouses. But routinization objectified inmates, magnifying their disabilities. Just as Seguin had predicted, large institutions, "by shutting the idiots among themselves," left them "stamped, as in a compressed mold, with a general character of *polished idiocy*."[74]

The disciplinary requirements of large institutions made even minor transgressions irksome. Superintendents now punished behaviors—deceitfulness, sexual exploration, bullying—that less regimented institutions might have tolerated. To prevent masturbation and insubordination, Minnesota's A. C. Rogers transferred inmates from the school to the custodial department. To cure bad tempers, Dr. Fish recommended the medicalized "Elwyn treatment . . .—viz., 'a pint of hot water,' with the advice, 'to lie on [the] left side.'" Some superintendents whipped unruly inmates.[75] The need to correct misbehavior strengthened the degenerationist association of mental backwardness with moral unfitness.

Work with the feebleminded became hierarchical, facilitating eugenic equations of upper with good, lower with bad. Superintendents separated themselves from inmates, delegating work to male assistants who in turn assigned direct care to female staff.[76] Superintendents with sufficient funds built residences where they could live apart from the rest of the colony. In stratified institutions those at the top became estranged from those at the bottom. They now compared the feebleminded to animals and savages. With fond contempt Kerlin described some inmates as "our household pets."[77] Dr. Wilmarth argued for sterilizing female inmates on the ground that in such cases, the operation's eugenic benefits outweighed the risk of death: "It is difficult to understand why these women should retain a function which will only bring the transmission of this great misfortune [feeblemindedness], multiplied, entailing as it does suffering, unhappiness, helplessness or crime. Are these not worse than the possible suppression of a life which has little of what makes life truly valuable?"[78] The institutions came to embody what one AMO speaker called "the aristocracy of intellect."[79]

Custodialism steamrolled across the system, flattening institutional idiosyncrasies and burying diversity. The training schools lost individuality. Variant methods of management that might have contradicted eugenic thinking about the retarded were marginalized or suppressed by the colony plan. There was, to be sure, some resistance to large impersonal institutions. Kentucky's commissioners angrily rejected their superintendent's attempt to expand from a training school to a "custodial home" for 4,500, and Kentucky's remained one of the few noncustodial establishments.[80] Private institutions did not develop farms. "Grass is the largest crop we have," announced Catharine Brown, who with her husband ran the Barre, Massachusetts, school they had purchased from Dr. Wilbur. "As ours is a private school, there is no material for farm-work."[81] Mrs. Brown questioned the value of the colony plan, wondering aloud whether a large institution could "be like a home."[82] But Brown's colleagues ignored her concerns. In time custodialism's opponents fell silent.

An Emperor with No Clothes

By the century's end the mental retardation system consisted of almost thirty institutions, the majority of them public. The institutions as well as the system had grown: Elwyn, the most populous, held about 1,000 inmates; the California School for the Feeble-minded, the most extensive, covered 3,000 acres. In all, the national population of institutionalized feebleminded approached 10,000—impressive enlargement for a system that had struggled into existence only fifty years earlier.[83]

Prodded by the need for institutional survival and growth, searching for professional legitimation, beleaguered by long waiting lists for admission, the superintendents gladly followed Kerlin's lead into custodialism. They built a system of institutions that reinforced and was in turn reinforced by eugenic concepts.

But the superintendents had failed to solve a crucial professional dilemma. They still lacked specialized knowledge, the basic ingredient of professionalism. Relative to their psychiatric counterparts, AMO superintendents had developed even less information about the condition in which they claimed expertise. Nor could they develop treatments for a condition they deemed incurable. In the early twentieth century, psychiatrists overcame their reputation as mere custodians of insane asylums by carrying their work into communities, where they identified new client groups such as the mildly mentally ill and troubled families. But the AMO superintendents, who had been teaching that the feebleminded are criminalistic and likely to reproduce themselves, could hardly advocate community treatment. Trapped by their own arguments, they had only one figleaf to cover their lack of professional knowledge: eugenics doctrine. In this area they would become the nation's experts.

Specialists in mental retardation sought *their* new client groups in other members of the dependent, defective, and delinquent classes, whom they proposed to add to the populations of their asylums. Criminals, tramps, the poor, inebriates—all, according to the superintendents, are fundamentally feebleminded.[84] This argument fell on receptive ears, for other welfare workers were familiar with the degenerationist belief in an organic interconnection among the dependent, defective, and delinquent classes. Few were surprised when superintendents began explaining that feeblemindedness is nearly synonymous with other social ills.

Superintendents stressed in particular the fundamental identity of feeble-mindedness with criminality. The idea of moral imbecility became central to their thinking. The moral imbecile formed a bridge, the crucial conceptual link between the feebleminded and the criminal. Essays on moral imbecility, as the next chapter shows, became the main form of specialized knowledge produced by AMO superintendents in the late nineteenth century. And in these writings the superintendents identified yet another new client: society itself. Using eugenics, they would cure the nation of its evils and restore it to health.

Notes

1. Terminology remained in flux through the 1890s, with Martin Barr, for example, using the term *moral paranoia* synonymously with *moral imbecility* (Barr 1895). By 1904, however, Barr, like most other mental retardation specialists, had settled on *moral imbecility* (Barr [1904] 1973: chap. 16).

2. Barr 1895:525.

3. Ibid., with Barr using the terms *moral paranoia* and *moral imbecility* interchangeably.

4. Osborne 1894:393.

5. Association of Medical Officers of American Institutions for Idiotic and Feeble-Minded Persons (hereafter AMO), *Proceedings, 1886*, pp. 442–43, 354–55.

6. AMO, *Proceedings, 1891*, p. 243.

7. I. Barrows 1894:448. As Larson 1995 shows, this same reasoning later prevailed in eugenics campaigns in the Deep South.

8. Rosenberg 1976:2.

9. Rafter 1994.

10. E.g., Henderson 1893; F. Wines 1888.

11. In his presidential address to the AMO, California superintendent A. E. Osborne outlined the need for professional renewal: "It really seems as though the original organization had served its purpose and outlived its day. We cannot longer hope to retain the organization as a strictly medical one" (Osborne 1894:389). The AMO renamed itself the Association of American Institutions for the Feebleminded and began publishing the *Journal of Psycho-Asthenics* (weak minds).

12. W. Fernald 1893:214.

13. On a profession's need for specialized knowledge, see Abbott 1988.

14. On the Association of Medical Superintendents of American Institutions for the Insane, see Dwyer 1987; Grob 1973, 1983.

15. Kerlin was "unwilling to admit that our work is any other than a medical philanthropy," a specialty that should not "yield this trust to other than medical men" (Kerlin 1892:281). The year after Kerlin's death, however, Alexander Johnson, a layman with a background in charity work, joined the AMO as superintendent of Indiana's School for Feeble-Minded Youth. Vigorous and forward-looking, Johnson soon got even those who shared Kerlin's view to change their minds (see, e.g., AMO, *Proceedings, 1894*, p. 501).

16. Blake 1892:313.

17. Osborne 1894:388, quoting another, unnamed member's concern about professional development.

18. Halstead 1892:287.

19. Barr 1895:530.

20. Tyor and Bell 1984:52.

21. Osborne 1894:386.

22. Established in 1852, the Pennsylvania institution was the third state training school in the United States, after Massachusetts's School for Idiotic and Feeble-Minded Youth and New York's Asylum for Idiots. See W. Fernald 1893:207.

23. Barr 1934:146, 149.

24. Kraft 1961:409-10; Tyor and Bell 1984:34-35. On Kerlin, also see Barr [1904] 1973:67-69; G.E.S. 1894; Osborne 1894; Trent 1982; and the eulogies that appear in the 1894 issue of AMO, *Proceedings* (493-98).

25. Barr [1904] 1973:67.

26. Barr 1934:148.

27. Kerlin 1877:22; AMO, *Proceedings, 1877*, p. 9.

28. Kerlin 1892:280-81. Kerlin here quotes from the passage that offended Dr. Wilbur, stating in conclusion that "after a long experience I am not disposed to abate one jot or tittle, or to amend in any single expression, the language of these paragraphs."

29. AMO, *Proceedings, 1888*, pp. 81-82; Wilmarth 1885, 1886, 1888, and 1890.

30. On the criminal's brain, see Benedikt 1881. On postmortem examinations of the mentally ill and the reasoning behind them, see Burnham 1960:459; and, more generally, Grob 1983: chap. 2.

31. AMO, *Proceedings, 1888*, p. 82.

32. Barr succeeded Kerlin as Elwyn's superintendent (Trent 1982: 77-78). Dr. W. B. Fish, Kerlin's assistant superintendent for three years, became head of the Illinois institution for the feebleminded. Dr. S. J. Fort of Maryland knew Kerlin from boyhood, worked under him at Elwyn, and received assistance from him later in his career (AMO, *Proceedings, 1894*, pp. 497-98). Wilmarth became head of the Wisconsin Home for the Feeble-minded. A. E. Osborne, who originally lived in Media, Pennsylvania (AMO, *Proceedings, 1886*, p. 445), and became head of the first California institution, may also have owed professional debts to Kerlin.

33. Barr [1904] 1973.

34. E.g., Kerlin 1879, 1880.

35. Kerlin 1880:150.

36. Kerlin 1892:281.

37. Kerlin 1881; Kerlin 1892:277.

38. Kerlin 1892:277-278; also see Trent 1993; Radford 1991; and, on English attitudes, Barker 1983. Elwyn's board quickly halted such experimentation, but Kerlin felt the operation had justified itself. The young woman experienced an "entire arrest of an epileptic tendency as well as the removal of inordinate desires which made her an offence to the community" (Kerlin 1892:278). On the late nineteenth-century fear of female sexuality, and the linkages of it with social disorder and bad heredity, see Groneman 1994.

39. Kerlin 1877:20 (emphasis in original).

40. Kerlin 1879:94; Thomson 1870.

41. Kerlin 1892:275.

42. Osborne 1891:177.

43. Ibid., 178.

44. Ibid., 176, 178.

45. On the colony plan, see Fish 1891, 1892; Hurd 1887; Kerlin 1884; Knight 1892; and Osborne 1891.

During the Civil War, Kerlin was appointed to "colonize" escaped slaves at an island settlement (Barr 1934:145–46). Although this plan never materialized, it may have given Kerlin the idea of isolating a large problem population under circumstances where they could contribute to their own support.

46. Illinois superintendent William Fish explicitly rejects the New York State model in Fish 1891:206, as does Kerlin in AMO, *Proceedings, 1891*, p. 244.

47. Dr. Carson of Syracuse in AMO, *Proceedings, 1891*, p. 244.

48. Hervey B. Wilbur founded a farm colony as a branch of the Syracuse asylum, hoping "that this agricultural annex may develop into a large custodial department for males" (AMO, *Proceedings, 1882*, p. 275). In this case, however, the colony was separate from the main institution and not eugenic in design. It was moreover created primarily to provide inmates with useful work, not to exploit their labor.

49. Osborne in AMO, *Proceedings, 1892*, p. 368; Dr. J. T. Armstrong in AMO, *Proceedings, 1892*, p. 377.

50. Dwyer 1987:154.

51. Kerlin 1884:259, 262.

52. Kerlin 1885:174.

53. Wilmarth 1895:517.

54. Trent (1982:107) quotes a remark of Martin Barr about the "feeble-minded reservation," noting that the model here is that of the American Indian reservation. Barr (1895:529) also compared the institutions to "Southern plantations[,] which were neither more nor less than training schools for feeble-minded folk."

55. Kerlin 1885:167, quoting an 1884 Illinois report.

56. AMO, *Proceedings, 1888*, pp. 76–77, quoting the Hon. R. A. Mott, "a veteran in legislation for the defective classes in Minnesota" (76).

57. Moral imbeciles, a group discussed separately later, were also held in the custodial departments.

58. Kerlin 1886:295; Osborne 1891:180.

59. Fish in AMO, *Proceedings, 1894*, p. 478. Of the approximately 17,000 feebleminded people institutionalized in 1904, nearly 14,000 were supported entirely by public funds (U.S. Department of Commerce and Labor 1906:230).

60. Dechert 1892:364.

61. W. Fernald 1893:219. Such facts and figures constituted what Abbott (1988:156) calls "professional capital."

62. Osborne in AMO, *Proceedings, 1889*, p. 86.

63. Dr. Fish in AMO, *Proceedings, 1891*, p. 159.

64. W. Fernald 1893:213.

65. On terminology, see W. Fernald 1893 and Salisbury 1891.

66. Kerlin 1884:258. Kerlin acknowledged that "it may seem strange" to find outwardly normal boys and girls in the institutions. But, he explained, "the imperfection" may involve "only the power to form a judgment of values, or . . . of social proprieties, or . . . of moral risk" (251).

Grob (1983:74) notes that the gradual transfer of responsibility for socially problematic groups from local almshouses to state institutions contributed to definitional expansion in the case of the mentally ill: "When states assumed full responsibility for the care and treatment of the mentally ill, . . . local officials saw advantages in redefining insanity to include aged and senile patients, thereby making possible their transfer from almshouses to hospitals and shifting the fiscal burden to the state. The result was a rapid increase in the size of mental hospitals and a change in their function." The concurrent shift of mentally retarded persons from almshouses to state institutions contributed to definitional expansion and the custodial trend in the case of that population, too.

67. Monroe 1894, reporting Osborne's reaction on p. 433.

68. Kerlin 1886:296 (emphases in original).

69. Knight 1894:562.

70. Ibid., 562-63.

71. W. Fernald (1893:218), speaking of the work of "moral imbeciles" and other "trained adults."

72. Dr. Rogers in AMO, *Proceedings, 1894,* p. 477.

73. Kerlin 1885:162; Kerlin in AMO, *Proceedings, 1892,* p. 382.

74. Seguin, *Report on Education* 1875: 94-95, as quoted and cited by Trent (1982:70; my emphases).

75. Rogers 1892:321; Fish 1887:47. On the same page Fish sets guidelines for corporal punishment. On discipline in the nineteenth-century institutions, also see Kraft 1961.

76. Alexander Johnson, the lay superintendent of the Indiana School for Feeble-Minded Youth, hired a female physician to assist him, as did the uncredentialed men who headed the Newark Custodial Asylum; these cases formed partial exceptions to the rule of gender hierarchy.

77. Kerlin [1858] 1975.

78. Wilmarth 1895:518-19.

79. Miller 1895:535.

80. Kentucky Institution for the Education and Training of Feeble-Minded Children 1897:9. Also see AMO, *Proceedings, 1891,* p. 183, where Iowa's Dr. Powell objects to the principle of life detention.

81. C. Brown in AMO, *Proceedings, 1891,* p. 240.

82. Ibid., 216.

83. This overview is based on Tyor and Bell 1984:169-70; W. Fernald 1893; and Barr [1904] 1973:76-77. Also see U. S. Department of Commerce and Labor 1906.

84. See, e.g., Kerlin 1884.

4

The Rise of the Moral Imbecile

> At the bottom of this whole discussion of moral insanity
> there rest the questions of accountability and the nature
> of sin.
>
> Isaac N. Kerlin, "Moral Imbecility"

The Revolutionary War was hardly over before
Americans began to investigate one of the dark-
est mysteries of human nature: why is it that
some people cannot resist committing crimes?
Nineteenth-century writers solemnly explained
this mystery in terms of now unrecognizable conditions like "moral insanity," "moral imbecility,"
and "constitutional depravity." Although today
these explanations sometimes seem as obscure
as medieval debates over the number of angels
that can dance on a pin, they in fact continue
to raise profound questions about the meaning of criminal behavior and, ultimately, about
human nature itself. The fundamental question
remains this: are there are some people—the
morally insane (or "morally imbecilic," "degenerate," "psychopathic," etc.)—who so utterly
lack moral capacity that they cannot tell right
from wrong? Moreover, are there others who,
although capable of telling right from wrong, are
nonetheless unable to choose what is right?

Some nineteenth-century theorists flatly rejected the concept of moral insanity, but others
embraced it, and the quarrels between these two
groups raised additional questions that remain
central in medico-legal discussions. Is criminality
a disease, and if so, can criminals be treated?
Can future offending be predicted? Do criminals

have free will, or is their behavior somehow predetermined? Does criminal behavior originate in the mind, and if so, how does this mental deviance relate to the brain and body? Who should make final judgments about the criminal responsibility of mentally disabled offenders: lawyers or psychiatrists?

This chapter traces the evolution of the born-criminal concept in nineteenth-century thought. In it I aim at establishing the intellectual background from which, about 1870, eugenic criminology began to emerge and at identifying how superintendents of institutions for the feebleminded contributed to this discourse. The first step, outlined in the next section, involved defining compulsive immorality as a mental disease. The second step (as the following section shows) involved linking this disease, often called "moral insanity," to the intellectual maladies of idiocy and imbecility. This linkage produced a new concept, that of "moral idiocy" or "moral imbecility," and a new discourse, "eugenic criminology," according to which crime can be controlled by preventing the feebleminded from reproducing. The mystery of inborn criminality seemed to have been solved: its cause is feeblemindedness. This discovery inspired an outpouring of tracts on eugenic criminology, including (as the third section of this chapter shows) some by superintendents of institutions for the feebleminded. These writings (I argue in conclusion) contributed significantly to the moral structuring of late nineteenth-century society and to the distribution of power within it.

Step One: Diagnosing Moral Insanity

For centuries the idea of innate wickedness was a theological rather than a scientific concept. The Old Testament opens with the Fall of Adam and Eve, a story that accounts for the transmission of original sin. The New Testament, particularly in sections by St. Paul, elaborates on the concept of original sin, explaining that it decays the body, mind, and will. John Calvin, the sixteenth-century theologian, refined the notion of original sin with his doctrine of predestination, according to which some people are damned from birth to disobey God's laws. Scientists began moving into this theological territory in the late eighteenth century, when physicians who specialized in mental disease translated the idea of inherent evil into medical terms: inborn incorrigibility, they asserted, is in fact a mental illness. Armed with this claim, early psychiatrists displaced theologians and established themselves as authorities on the "alienated," or abnormal, mind.

Psychiatrists (or "alienists," as they were then called) used empirical methods to study abnormal behaviors that church and law had long regarded as evil or wrong and therefore punishable. Redefining badness as madness and depravity as disease, psychiatrists formulated the first scientific versions of born-criminal theory. The French psychiatrist Philippe Pinel laid the conceptual groundwork for the new understanding of crime as mental disease, and the English psychiatrist James Cowles Prichard named the disease "moral insanity." Pritchard's definition meshed well with the popular nineteenth-century doctrine of phrenology, a congruence that made the idea of moral insanity more comprehensible. In the United States the concept was first propounded by Benjamin Rush, the father figure of American psychiatry, and later refined by Samuel Gridley Howe, who reiterated early nineteenth-century notions of moral insanity while pointing ahead to hereditarianism.

European Pioneers: Pinel and Pritchard

In *A Treatise on Insanity* (1801) Philippe Pinel (1745–1826), the director of a Parisian hospital for the mentally ill, took the crucial step of identifying "manie sans délire," insanity without delirium or confusion. This step enabled psychiatry to distinguish between mental maladies in which the entire intellect is deranged and those in which only the ethical capacity is disturbed. Pinel's recognition of partial mental disease prepared the ground for theories of "moral" insanity, explanations of what we today would call emotional, psychological, or ethical disturbances.[1]

Pinel exemplifies manie sans délire with the case of a rich and spoiled youth who could not bear "opposition or resistance." "He assaulted his adversary with the audacity of a savage; sought to reign by force, and was perpetually embroiled in disputes and quarrels. If a dog, a horse, or any other animal offended him, he instantly put it to death."[2] The young man was nevertheless fully capable of managing his estate and, when not in a temper, "even distinguished himself by acts of beneficence and compassion." Pinel says little about the cause of manie sans délire in this case. He mentions that the youth had "a mind naturally perverse and unruly," but he is more interested in the fact that the subject was the "only son of a weak and indulgent mother" who gratified his "every caprice and passion."[3] Pinel's causational emphasis, in other words, falls on not heredity but environment. Moral disease has not yet been biologized.

In his 1835 *Treatise on Insanity* James Cowles Prichard (1786–1848) gave the English-speaking world the term *moral insanity*. Drawing on Pinel's concept of manie sans délire, Prichard describes moral insanity as a "morbid" condition of "the moral constitution or feelings . . . independent of any corresponding affection of the understanding." Moral insanity afflicts only the ethical capacity and the feelings, not the intellect or understanding. According to Prichard, moral insanity is characterized by neither hallucinations nor physical injury; rather, it is an "immediate impulse arising spontaneously in the mind, which is diseased only in its moral constitution."[4]

Crime plays but a small role in Prichard's first series of examples, which describe individuals who retain some reasoning power and self-awareness while sliding into moral insanity. When he considers legal implications, however, Prichard introduces examples of morally insane persons who committed homicides and other violent acts. People who suffer from moral insanity, Prichard argues, should be exempt from the death penalty; like those who suffer from total insanity, the morally insane are not fully responsible.[5] He is vague as to the cause of moral insanity but carefully distinguishes it from imbecility and other grades of idiocy. For Prichard, then, moral insanity is a mental disease totally distinct from intellectual backwardness.

The Influence of Phrenology

Well before Prichard introduced the concept of moral insanity, the Austrian physician Franz Joseph Gall (1758–1828) published the foundational texts of the science of phrenology.[6] According to Gall and other phrenologists, each of our mental abilities is localized in a separate part of the brain and functions independently, in relative isolation from the others. One of the brain's "faculties" or "organs" can be normal while another lies dormant or atrophies. Phrenologists differed over the number and names of the faculties but agreed that crime results when faculties such as acquisitiveness and combativeness become disordered.[7] Because phrenologists were unable to study the brain directly, they drew conclusions about it from the contours of the skull; that is, they assumed that the development of the brain's various faculties or organs is reflected in the skull's bumps and hollows.

Medical enthusiasm for phrenology peaked before 1850, but some physicians and many members of the general public continued to subscribe to the doctrine. Indeed, phrenology exerted tremendous influence on thinking about crime and punishment throughout the nineteenth century.[8] In particular, phrenological ideas nurtured the concept of moral insanity and encouraged the association of moral insanity with brain malfunction. Although some proponents of the moral insanity concept rejected phrenology,[9] this idea of partial insanity was clearly compatible with the phrenological notion of independently functioning faculties.[10] The phrenological picture of the brain made it easy to think of morality as a faculty or organ of the brain that could go bad while other parts operated normally. In the United States those who advanced theory about moral disease tended to be strong advocates of phrenology.

In other ways, too, phrenology contributed to mid- and late nineteenth-century thinking about criminality as a mental illness. Phrenology was the first science systematically to spell out the meaning of crime as disease.[11] Advocated most forcefully by physicians, phrenology encouraged articulation of the so-called medical model of criminality, which portrays criminality as a sickness and hence properly part of medicine's jurisdiction. It encouraged the belief that criminals, because sick, are not responsible for their behavior. The phrenological belief in a malleable, improvable brain set the stage for degeneration theory, the somatic underpinning of later hereditarian doctrines. Moreover, if one heeds historian Roger Cooter's reminder that "this was a doctrine about the *head*,"[12] one can see that phrenology was a forerunner of eugenic theories that also located criminal propensities in the head and associated them with mental deficiency. Finally, phrenology provided a biological (and often hereditarian) explanation for crime. For example, the immensely popular phrenologist Johann Gaspar Spurzheim argued that criminality is heritable and thus preventable through reproductive controls.[13] Whereas Pinel and Pritchard had described manie sans délire and moral insanity as afflictions with no physical causes or consequences, phrenologists tied offending to brain matter itself.

American Pioneers: Rush and Howe

Pinel is usually credited with laying the conceptual foundation for moral insanity, but his manie sans délire was in fact anticipated by Dr. Benjamin Rush's diagnosis of "moral derangement."[14] Rush (1745/46–1813), a signer of the Declaration of Independence and author of the first American texts on mental disease, delivered an oration in 1786 entitled "The Influence of Physical Causes upon the Moral Faculty," a very early attempt to explain wicked behavior as the result of physical disease. Foreshadowing phrenology, Rush here defines the moral faculty as the "capacity in the human mind of distinguishing and choosing good and evil."[15] He explains that "in all these cases of innate, preternatural moral depravity, there is probably an original defective organization in those parts of the body, which are occupied by the moral faculties of the mind."[16] Rush chides other physicians for overlooking cases of moral derangement: the affliction is similar to bodily disease, and those who suffer from it are "very properly . . . subjects of medicine."[17] Rush makes this point time and again as he extends medicine into the realms of religion and law.

To illustrate moral derangement, Rush describes a Frenchman named Servin who was brilliant in philosophy, mathematics, and languages but "treacherous, cruel, cowardly, deceitful, a liar, a cheat." Fittingly Servin "expired with the glass in his hand, cursing and denying God."[18] Notwithstanding his highly developed intellect, Servin lacked moral capacity. In another example Rush reports "an instance of a woman, who was exemplary in her obedience to every command of the moral law, except one. She could not refrain from stealing. . . . As a proof that her judgment was not affected by this defect in her moral faculty, she would both confess and lament her crime, when detected in it."[19] Intellectually this woman knew that stealing was wrong, but her moral derangement made theft irresistible.

Rush distinguishes between total and partial moral derangement. In his experience total moral derangement is extremely rare, "innate," and "probably" caused by an inborn defect. Partial moral derangement, on the other hand, is "induced" by poor nutrition and drink.[20] (Here Rush anticipates degeneration theory.) It is more common than total moral derangement and can be cured by improving one's diet and renouncing vice.

Rush tends to use moral derangement as a vehicle for his own views of immoral behavior and to intermix its scientific content with religious ideas. (For example, he suggests that the "infernal spirits" may suffer from moral derangement.)[21] His conceptualization of moral derangement, still rooted in theology, was overshadowed by Pinel's more scientized manie sans délire.[22] Rush's essays on moral derangement are nonetheless historically important because—decades before phrenology's formal emergence—they drew on a notion of the "moral faculty" and an explanation of vicious behavior similar to those of phrenology.[23] Rush's writings are also significant because they inaugurated speculation about moral disease in the first days of the American republic. Thanks to them, we can trace the pedigree of American born-criminal theory back to the days when the nation itself was born.

Rush staked out one of the two positions that have dominated all subsequent debates about the nature of inborn criminality. In his view the intellectual and ethical abilities vary independently. A person can be smart yet wicked; conversely, a mental imbecile is not necessarily immoral. After the Civil War, scientists abandoned this view in favor of a second position according to which intellectual and ethical abilities vary together. A person cannot be mentally weak and ethically strong; a mental imbecile is by definition a moral imbecile. The transition between these two views can be seen in the work of Samuel Gridley Howe, founder of the Massachusetts School for Idiotic and Feeble-Minded Youth (later renamed the "School for the Feeble-minded").

In an 1848 report on his survey of Massachusetts idiots, Howe distinguishes between "*intellectual* idiocy" and "*moral* idiocy," defining the latter as a "condition in which the sentiments, the conscience, the religious feeling, the love of neighbor, the sense of beauty, and the like, are so far dormant or undeveloped, as to incapacitate the person from being a law unto himself [i.e., self-governing and responsible]. . . . This, it is evident, may,

and often does, exist, while the intellectual faculties are quite active. . . .
Idiots of this character are . . . often found in our prisons."[24] Howe, a
phrenologist, thus pictures moral idiocy as a crime-causing condition that
affects part but not all of the brain. His *moral idiocy* is equivalent to Rush's
moral derangement and close to Prichard's *moral insanity*. Howe does not
associate moral with mental idiocy, although his terminology points in that
direction.

What is new in Howe's report is an empirical argument that intellectual
idiocy is inherited. Preparatory to requesting state funds to educate idiots
at his asylum, Howe studied the condition of 574 idiots and concluded
that idiocy is caused by both predisposing and immediate factors. Predisposing factors, which make it likely but not certain that offspring will be
idiots, include intemperance, intermarriage, troublesome pregnancies, and
difficult births. Immediate factors include poverty, hunger, masturbation,
and other factors that induce "degeneration."[25] In this report Howe formu-
lates an early version of the degeneracy doctrine that eventually blossomed
into eugenic thinking: "The moral to be drawn from the prevalent existence of idiocy in society, is, that a very large class of persons . . . overlook
the hereditary transmission of certain morbid tendencies, or they pervert
the natural appetites of the body into lusts of divers kinds . . . and thus
bring down the awful consequences of their own ignorance and sin upon
the heads of their unoffending children."[26] Through violating natural laws,
people deteriorate, acquiring a degenerate condition that is passed on to
the next generation, causing idiocy.

Howe views degeneration as a self-extinguishing tendency, one that produces sterility in the third or fourth generation; nature "refuses to continue
a race so monstrous upon the earth." Anticipating eugenic policies, however, Howe advises that idiots should not be allowed to marry. Such a
prohibition would "lessen the number of idiots in the next generation, and
possibly . . . hasten the period at which the grievous calamity shall be removed."[27]

Howe's report bridges early and late nineteenth-century thinking about
innate criminality. When it discusses moral idiocy, it is phrenological, portraying the condition, as Prichard and Rush did, as an affliction of only one
mental faculty, not all of them. When the report turns to mental idiocy,
however, it becomes degenerationist and hereditarian, forecasting eugenic
criminology.

Step Two: Linking Moral Insanity to Mental Idiocy

Innate immorality became a magnetic topic in the mid-nineteenth century.
Some commentators, such as the American psychiatrist Isaac Ray, asso-

ciated the condition with idiocy and imbecility, while others, such as the English psychiatrist Henry Maudsley, traced it to degeneracy, arguing that degenerate offenders should not be held fully responsible for crime. Meanwhile, from his office in Scotland's Perth prison, Dr. J. Bruce Thomson demonstrated the existence of born criminals.

Isaac Ray

Isaac Ray (1807–81), the most prominent American psychiatrist in the generation after Rush, was the first born-criminal theorist to detect close connections between mental retardation and immorality. In his *Treatise on the Medical Jurisprudence of Insanity* (1838), which remained an authoritative text until the century's end, Ray speaks at length about moral imbecility, defining it much as Howe defined moral idiocy and analyzing it in standard phrenological terms.[28] Ray contributed more distinctively to the literature on inborn criminality through his observations on the condition today known as "mental retardation," which he subdivides into idiocy and imbecility. In contrast to Rush, who reported an idiot with moral genius, Ray considered idiots to be inherently criminalistic ("sexual feelings, cunning, and destructiveness, they often manifest in an inordinate degree of vigor and activity").[29] Imbeciles, the next grade up in ability, are even more dangerous: thievish, undeterrable, inclined to drunkenness and rape, imbeciles become more criminalistic as they approach normal mentality. Because of their apparent rationality, imbeciles are often misdiagnosed and sentenced to prison, but their mental defect should spare them the full force of law. Ray's condemnation of the mentally retarded presages the flood of late nineteenth-century works equating mental with moral imbecility.

During the rest of the century American psychiatrists produced numerous essays on moral insanity/idiocy/imbecility. Some debated whether the condition could exist apart from intellectual defects; others, whether the notion would undermine the whole idea of criminal responsibility. Increasingly they associated moral with mental deficiencies and both with bad heredity.[30] These associations became commonplace as degeneration theory took hold. Americans absorbed degeneration theory from such a variety of sources that it becomes impossible to trace specific genealogies of ideas. Nevertheless, citations make it clear that Richard Dugdale's *"Jukes"* study was of paramount importance, along with the writings of two British physicians: Henry Maudsley, a professor of medical jurisprudence at London's University College, and J. Bruce Thomson, the resident surgeon at Perth prison.

Maudsley and Thomson

"There is a borderland between crime and insanity," Henry Maudsley (1835–1918) writes in *Responsibility in Mental Disease* (1876), a borderland inhabited by mental and moral imbeciles. Just as some people are color-blind or tone-deaf, "so there are some few who are congenitally deprived of moral sense." Moral imbeciles are usually mentally deficient as well, "but not always; it sometimes happens that there is a remarkably acute intellect with no trace of moral feeling."[31] Even experts can find it "a very difficult matter to decide whether there is actual imbecility or not." Moral imbeciles, lacking "self-control against crime," become habitual criminals.[32] Their "moral degeneracy" is a heritable condition. "Not that the failing of the father shall necessarily show in the children," writes Maudsley in language close to that of Dugdale's *"Jukes"*: "it may undergo transformation in the second generation, or may be entirely latent in it, not coming to the surface in any form until the third or fourth generation. But it will run on in the stream of family descent . . . until . . . it is either neutralized by the beneficial influences of wise intermarriages, or . . . entails the decay and extinction of the family."[33] Convinced that "crime is often hereditary," Maudsley speaks of "the true thief" as "born not made." Nonetheless, like Dugdale, he holds that degeneracy and the "moral sense" are acquired characteristics. As the "last acquired faculty in the progress of human evolution," the moral sense is the most delicate and precarious, "the first to suffer when disease invades the mental organization."[34]

Maudsley identifies "a distinct criminal class . . . propagating a criminal population of degenerate beings," but he is concerned less with reproductive control than with criminal responsibility. Those who lurk in the borderland, he argues, are not fully responsible because they suffer from a brain disorder. Thus, when convicted of serious crimes, they should be punished less severely than the sane.[35]

For evidence that there is a distinct criminal class, "a degenerate or morbid variety of mankind," Maudsley refers to the work of J. Bruce Thomson, the prison physician who authored some of the earliest empirical studies of crime.[36] Well before they became familiar with the work of the Italian criminal anthropologist Cesare Lombroso, Maudsley and many Americans learned the fundamentals of criminal anthropology from Thomson's writings.[37] In fact, Lombroso himself acknowledged a debt to Thomson.[38]

Thomson begins an 1870 essay entitled "The Psychology of Criminals" with the proposition "that violent and habitual criminals are, as a class, moral imbeciles." He acknowledges that others have made this claim, but they did so with little or no "personal knowledge of criminals themselves." Thomson suffers no such deficiency: "In this respect I hold a vantage ground, being enabled to offer facts and figures drawn from acquaintance with criminals for the last 12 years in the General Prison of Scotland." [39]

Thomson's statistics, gathered from observation of almost 6,000 prisoners, show that habitual offenders are "born into crime." [40] These moral imbeciles can be identified by not only their long records but also their bodies: a "low type of physique" and such telltale signs as "extreme nervous debility and defective vital energy," deformities, epileptic fits, luxuriant hair (in females), imbecility, insanity, and early death. [41] Thomson compares moral imbeciles to members of primitive tribes that have not yet acquired the moral sense; even when well developed intellectually, they remain "savages." [42] Using the same sort of last-to-arrive, first-to-go argument that Maudsley employs, Thomson declares that the moral sense, the flower of civilization, is most vulnerable to degeneration. Unlike Maudsley, he is explicitly eugenical in his recommendations. For that 12 percent of the prison population that is congenitally irresponsible, the "cure" is "abolition of the parent stock" through incarceration. "If these *habituées* were confined for life, the residue outside would be small, and the propagation of the criminal class prevented." [43]

■ ■ ■

In sum, early and mid-nineteenth-century debates about the nature of moral disease evolved in several directions. Some writers simply rejected the concept. Early commentators who accepted the condition generally considered it to be rare; those writing after 1850 detected it more frequently. Whereas the first theorists considered it to be innate, later theorists considered it to be heritable as well. In other words, the thrust was toward biologization. The issue of criminal responsibility came to the fore. In addition, theorists increasingly associated moral disease with mental retardation. By the 1880s many psychiatrists, social scientists, and policymakers had concluded that moral disease is a fairly common and probably inherited mental weakness that diminishes criminal responsibility and is somehow related to feeblemindedness. Production of eugenic criminology—the theory that crime can be controlled through reproductive control—had begun.

Step Three: Producing Eugenic Criminology

In the United States one of the first groups to produce eugenic criminology was the superintendents' organization, the Association of Medical Officers of American Institutions for Idiotic and Feeble-Minded Persons (AMO). The superintendents were fast accumulating the trappings of professional success—large institutions, legislative acceptance, and systemwide growth

—but they lacked the specialized knowledge on which professional identity ultimately depends. As a substitute for specific information about the causes and cures of feeblemindedness, they began generating information about eugenics.

During the AMO's first phase of professionalization, 1876 through 1895, superintendents and their guests presented ten papers on moral imbecility at various annual meetings, accelerating production toward the period's end (see table 1). They used various names for the condition—not only *moral imbecility* but also *juvenile insanity, moral paranoia,* and *psychical epilepsy*—but all were writing about the compulsive unlawfulness that Prichard had called "moral insanity." Their papers constitute a series of collective "runs" at creating a criminalistic image for the feebleminded.[44] If the act of rereading deviants' histories in terms of their current misdeeds involves what sociologists call "retrospective interpretation," then these papers illustrate a phenomenon that might be called "prospective interpretation," an effort to project future misbehavior on current deviants.

In this as in many other aspects of the superintendents' professional development, Pennsylvania's Isaac N. Kerlin took the lead, presenting the first of the moral imbecility papers in 1879 and another in 1887. Most of the other papers were written by Kerlin associates. Dr. S. J. Fort, who knew Kerlin from childhood and later worked for him at Elwyn, authored two; John M. Broomall, a Media, Pennsylvania, lawyer, wrote another;[45] and Kerlin's chief assistant, Dr. Martin Barr, produced the final two. Kerlin's influence can also be gauged from the papers' references: whereas Kerlin himself cites Maudsley, Thomson, Rush, and Dugdale, and Barr cites Maudsley, Prichard, and Lombroso,[46] the other authors indicate no such familiarity with "outside" sources. Instead they refer to Kerlin's work, acknowledging that they are developing his theme.

In all ten papers the authors aim at establishing the underlying identity of feeblemindedness with criminality, and sometimes with other types of unfitness as well. As Kerlin puts it in the sequence's initial paper, the goal is to show that "there is a 'criminal diathesis' [congenital disposition] interwoven with tendencies to insanity and conditions of imbecility."[47] To support this contention, the papers present examples of moral imbecility, the Janus-faced condition that joins feeblemindedness with criminality. Those authors who deal with causation tend to attribute moral imbecility to hereditary degeneracy. Six of the eight papers that propose solutions to moral imbecility call for indefinite institutionalization, the method quickly emerging as American eugenicists' preferred response to degeneracy. In addition, two authors recommend sterilization, one to bring sexually perverted inmates under control and the other to "destroy the evil. . . . Heroic measures these, but it is the war of extermination."[48]

Table 1. Association Papers on Moral Imbecility, 1876–95

Author-Date	Label	Causes	Solutions
Kerlin 1879	Juvenile insanity	Spinal injury, degeneracy (curable)	Institutionalization; treatment
Carson 1886	Moral imbecility	[none given] (probably incurable)	Moral treatment in institution *might* help
Kerlin 1887	Moral imbecility	Degeneracy, reversion	[none given]
Broomall 1887	Moral imbecility, moral insanity	Heredity and environment	Institutionalization
Carson 1891	Juvenile insanity	Scarlet fever, head injury, degeneracy	[none given]
Rogers 1892	Mental and moral aberration	Sexual perversions	Moral training, asexualization
Fort 1892	Moral imbecility	[none given]	Mild punishment, moral treatment
Fort 1894	Psychical epilepsy	[none given]	Treatment or life restraint
Barr 1894	Inchoative paranoia (moral insanity)	Neurotic heredity	Institutionalization, punishment
Barr 1895	Moral paranoia (moral imbecility, moral insanity)	Degeneracy, environment, heredity	Institutionalization, temperance, prohibition on mothers' reading novels, sterilization

Although the authors do not agree on all of the moral imbecile's characteristics, they refer time and again to certain key traits. Moral imbeciles commit purposeless crimes, exhibiting "badness without reason, violence without motive, . . . thieving without acquisitiveness."[49] They are incorrigible, fearless, and defiant; some relish punishment. A few are mentally deficient, but most are intellectually normal and some are actually precocious. Egotistical, cunning, malicious, and unable to identify with others, moral imbeciles start causing trouble in childhood (Kerlin reports one case of a three year old).[50] It is this early display of uncooperativeness, the authors suggest, that probably most distinguishes the morally imbecilic from the morally insane, although they remain undecided on this point. What is clear is that "these moral imbeciles know too much"; thus they are able to manipulate an institution's staff and other inmates. Moral imbeciles, Dr. Fish wryly remarks, are the inmates who cause superintendents "gray heads and scanty hair."[51]

Several papers in the sequence mount a legal argument for eugenic isolation of moral imbeciles. Moral imbecility, they explain, is much like insanity: a condition that should excuse offenders from standing trial. Whereas the insane sometimes regain competency, however, moral imbeciles by definition never will. Thus when suspected of offending, moral imbeciles naturally must be committed for life. This argument is articulated most clearly in a paper titled "The Helpless Classes," by lawyer John Broomall. Incorrigible offenders, who Broomall estimates may constitute up to "one-fourth of the criminal classes," should be held "in restraint for life, and why not?" "The influence of heredity in keeping up the ranks of criminals would gradually diminish as incorrigible criminals came to be restrained of their liberty for life. It is humane and it is right for us to say that the incorrigible criminal, the lunatic, and the imbecile shall not be represented in the coming generations."[52] If criminality is recognized as a moral disease, it can be eugenically eradicated.[53]

As this series of papers progresses, the eugenic themes grow stronger. In the first paper (1879) Kerlin still straddles the fence, torn between the optimistic Lamarckian view that degeneracy can be reversed and the pessimistic hereditarianism of full-blown eugenics.[54] The final paper in the series, Martin Barr's address "Moral Paranoia" (1895), exhibits none of this ambivalence. To the contrary, in it Barr self-confidently incorporates hordes of people into the moral imbecile category and damns them all as incurable. Most idiots are moral imbeciles, Barr tells us, as are the intellectually normal and even bright people whom others call "morally insane." Also moral imbeciles are the "queer, nervous, misanthropical, moody; the weak dude; the silly coquette"; the lustful; gossips; "the dipsomaniac; the kleptomaniac; the pyromaniac"; murderers, harlots, *agents provocateurs;* epileptics; hypochondriacs; and egotists. "The religious hypocrite," Barr continues, "the confidence man; the bombast; the confirmed tramp—all belong to this class." Barr contends that moral imbeciles are "born not made," diseased instead of criminal.[55] Thus authority over them should be shifted from lawyers to physicians, who will place them in "institutions providing a happy and permanent home." "For the 'Crime of Law' wreaking vengeance upon the diseased and the impotent, substitute a beneficent

'Protection,' guarding the afflicted from society and from themselves, and the pure stock from contamination."[56] Between Kerlin's fumbling paper of 1879 and Barr's supremely assured address of 1895, the AMO discovered its eugenic mission.

Superintendents did not adopt a ready-made eugenics but discovered the doctrine on their own, generating it in fits and starts as they supervised their institutions and professionalized their occupation. Negatively eugenics gave them rationales for their failures to cure the feebleminded, for expanding their institutions, and for the financial burden their institutions imposed on states. Positively it provided them with a new medical problem (bad heredity), a larger and higher-status clientele (society in general, now including those members who were neither dependent, defective, nor delinquent), and room to elaborate their treatments (custodialism and, to a much lesser extent, sterilization). Eugenics also appeared to be scientific, thus conferring further professional legitimation.

But questions remain. How did the superintendents manage to attribute criminality to charges whom not long before they had perceived as sweetly innocent? How did their papers on moral imbecility relate to other eugenic discourses, and how did they affect peoples' lives? Finally, did the superintendents—who were, after all, practical men with institutions to run—actually believe that they could fold tramps, harlots, and murderers into their training school for feebleminded children? The answers lie in the ways the superintendents and other eugenicists used their rhetoric.

Born Criminals as Metaphors

Eugenicists saw no reason to draw clear lines between hereditary criminals and other degenerates. Indeed, their science initially rested on a perception of fundamental unity among dependents, defectives, and delinquents. "There is no sharp dividing-line between these three," John Broomall explained. "The ranks run into one another, and the individuals are readily interchangeable from one rank to the others."[57] Thus terms like *moral imbeciles* and *born criminals* could refer to a small subgroup of offenders or to all the feebleminded—or even to all "the unfit." In the pulsating language of eugenics, *born criminals* (and so on) could mean any or all at the same time.

Phrases like *born criminals* and *the unfit* were metaphors, multivalenced terms laden with symbolic meanings. To emanate multiple meanings, historian JoAnne Brown tells us, is a crucial function of metaphor: "The very vagueness and multiplicity of metaphorical meaning is what makes it so powerful a social adhesive."[58] The superintendents did not feel foolish when they equated tramps and criminals, or dipsomaniacs and paupers, with the "feebleminded" and "moral imbeciles," claiming jurisdiction over all, because they were using the terms *feebleminded* and *moral imbeciles* metaphorically, to denote a small and a large group simultaneously. According to Brown, "Each listener is likely to interpret a given metaphor differently, yet also perceive that interpretation to be widely shared, without ever realizing that the consensus is created by the vagueness of the metaphor itself." [59] In the case of the AMO superintendents and other eugenicists, metaphoric meanings varied not only from speaker to speaker but also for each speaker, with multiple meanings coexisting within a single utterance.

To understand completely the metaphoric content of eugenic criminology, one must identify those who produced it. In the United States eugenics doctrine was produced primarily by a loosely affiliated group of psychiatrists, psychologists, prison physicians, social workers, and institutional superintendents, many of them members of relatively new professions. [60] Their work was that of social welfare, and they were members of the emerging professional middle class. [61] These producers of eugenics theory constituted only a fraction of the new professional middle class, but they were indispensable to its postbellum project of reestablishing middle-class authority eroded by industrialization, immigration, urbanization, and the increasing hostility of the lower classes. [62] While other professionals tackled other issues, the social welfare specialists who articulated eugenics doctrine defined the middle class's essential and particular worthiness. They did so by structuring social values around two poles, assigning one element of each binarism to "born criminals" (and so on) and the other to "ourselves," as set forth in table 2.

The tracts of eugenic criminology (those already discussed and those reviewed in later chapters) devote their subtexts to establishing these polarities and setting up a charged field, with "us" at one end and born criminals at the other. Like magnets, each pole attracts filaments associated with class, gender, race, sexuality, and other key elements of identity. Moreover, the two poles are not merely different; they are opposites, relating to each other not as A to B but as A to not-A. Instead of being equals, one is the absolute contradiction and nullification of the other. [63] As eugenic discourses proliferated and these sets of associations became commonplaces, any term in the first column of table 2 summoned up the others. Thus any phrase in the "born-criminal" column—"feebleminded," "primitive," "pauperized," "unfit," and so on—became a metaphor for innate criminalism and hereditary unfitness.

Eugenicists who were less concerned with criminality than with other social problems focused on not born criminals but feeblemindedness, pauperism, or moral imbecility, and so on, heading their lists (so to speak) with the disability of choice. The lists themselves nevertheless remained remarkably similar from author to author, profession to profession, and de-

Table 2. Some Binarisms of Eugenic Criminology

Born Criminals	Ourselves
The unfit	The fit
Moral imbeciles	Altruists
Worthless	Worthy
Born (produced by "nature")	Bred (produced by "nurture")
Body	Mind
Pauperized	Self-supporting
Defective	Healthy
Feebleminded	Intelligent
Bestial	Civilized
Sexually indiscriminate	Heterosexual and monogamous
Fecund	Reproductively impoverished
Undeterrable	Disciplined
Require social control	Administer social control
Negro, dusky, "Gypsies"	White
Foreign-born	Native-born and Anglo-Saxon
Unstable (in abode, sexuality, gender, and manifestations of degeneracy)	Stable (in abode, sexuality, gender, and "heredity")
Lazy and unproductive	Diligent and socially useful
Unskilled	Professional
Primitive	Highly evolved
Other	Same
Lower class	Middle and upper class

cade to decade. It is thus impossible neatly to cordon eugenic criminology off from other aspects of eugenics discourse. Eugenic criminology can no more be separated from eugenic social work, eugenic psychiatry, eugenic psychology, and so on than dependents, defectives, and delinquents could be separated from one another.

With other eugenicists, eugenic criminologists structured the moral universe into dichotomies, dualistically defining themselves and other members of the middle class in terms of their opposites. As Charles Goring, an early twentieth-century eugenicist and criminologist, observed, "every judgment of abnormality presupposes a definition of what is normal."[64] Normality cannot exist without deviance, nor saints without sinners. Eugenic criminology was inextricably bound up in the social construction of both the new professional middle class and the underclass. More than a

class-based doctrine, eugenic criminology actively furthered class formation.

The producers of eugenics doctrine hardly spoke in unison, however,
and at times they competed for jurisdiction over born criminals. Such in-
fighting becomes predictable when one recalls that they belonged to various occupations, many of them new and in the process of professional
self-legitimation. To advance themselves, these individuals occasionally attempted a hostile takeover of an adjacent jurisdiction,[65] claiming (as later
chapters show) to be better at identifying born criminals than were the
current authorities. To make such claims required little expertise, for it
was seldom difficult to argue that the current theory needed improvement.
Professionalization of the social welfare occupations advanced not despite
these disputes but because of them. Each new version of born-criminal
theory made social welfare seem more scientific.

The Rhetoric of Eugenics and the Altruistic Impulse

The production of eugenic rhetoric was thus closely tied to processes
of professionalization and class formation. The interrelationships among
these phenomena can be glimpsed in the way all three converged in the
concept of altruism. In her sensitive study of Sir Francis Galton, Ruth
Schwartz Cowan traces Galton's eugenicism to his desire to be helpful:
through eugenics Galton hoped to be, as he put it, "advantageous to future
inhabitants of the earth."[66] Later eugenicists shared Galton's service ideal.[67]
They hoped to ensure the future health of society and at the same time to
signify, through altruistic behavior, the worthiness that other eugenicists
recognized as a sure sign of hereditary fitness. Altruism was also intrinsic
to professionalism: to distinguish their work from other occupations, professionals need to demonstrate that they labor for a worthwhile cause, not
money alone. Altruistic behavior moreover confirms character, distinction,
and middle-class standing.

But altruism requires an object for its attention; there can be no altruism (from the Latin for "other," *alter*) without an Other. During 1875–1925
eugenicists defined degenerates in general and born criminals in particular as all that they themselves were not. In constructing the born criminal,
they simultaneously constructed themselves as altruistic, fit, and worthy.
They elaborated these metaphors until the 1920s, when, with their professions firmly established and the threat of lower-class insurrection fading,
their demonstrations of altruism began to seem less necessary. Gradually
they lost interest in eugenics.

By recognizing the altruistic content of eugenic criminology, one can
avoid interpreting eugenic rhetoric in purely instrumentalist terms. It is

certainly true that eugenics dogma, with its facile attributions of unfitness and almost casual demands for life sentences, invites a self-interest interpretation. It is also true that those who produced this dogma were deeply concerned with class control and that, to a degree, they realized it. Eugenicists nonetheless achieved powers far more extensive and subtle than those of heavy-handed oppression. By taking into account the intersections among eugenics, professionalization, social-class formation, and altruism, one can move beyond the self-interest explanation of eugenics (itself facile and tinged with a Darwinian view of human struggles). It becomes clear that eugenicists achieved social control by defining middle-class professionals as experts able to diagnose and treat individuals and society itself. This rhetorical structuring of social power was all the more effective in that any one of its positively charged terms automatically conjured up the negative pole and the evil genie of the born criminal.

Notes

1. See. e.g., Carlson and Dain 1962; Werlinder 1978.
2. Pinel [1801] 1962:151.
3. Ibid.
4. Prichard [1837] 1973:89.
5. Ibid., 279-83.
6. Fink [1938] 1962:2; Savitz, Turner, and Dickman 1977.
7. Combe 1879: appendix 1; Spurzheim 1883:323-28; Bakan 1966.
8. See E. T. Carlson 1958; Cooter 1976, 1984; J. Davies 1955; Fink [1938] 1962; Noel and Carlson 1970; and Savitz, Turner, and Dickman 1977.
9. For example, Prichard ([1837] 1973:325-36) concludes his *Treatise* with an argument against phrenology.
10. Cooter 1976; Spurzheim 1883:295-99.
11. E.g., Farnham 1846; Sampson 1846.
12. Cooter 1984:110 (emphasis in original).
13. Spurzheim (1883) speaks of heredity as the strongest and most permanent influence on the organization of the mind (chap. 1) and recommends proto-eugenic solutions to crime and other problems (pp. 46-47, 274). A strong hereditarian and often eugenic current ran through most phrenological writing (Rosenberg 1976:42).
14. Rush originally ([1786] 1815:106) used *micronomia* and *anomia* to refer, respectively, to partial and total disease of the moral faculty; later (Rush 1812) he settled on *partial* and *total moral derangement*. To avoid terminological confusion, I use *moral derangement* throughout.
15. Rush [1786] 1815:95. On Rush's relation to phrenology, see Noel and Carlson 1973.
16. Rush 1812:360.

17. Rush [1786] 1815:97.

18. Ibid., 99; also see Rush 1812:358.

19. Rush [1786] 1815:101-2.

20. Rush 1812:360, 358.

21. Rush [1786] 1815:99.

22. Also see Werlinder 1978:30.

23. In fact, Rush may have originated the term *phrenology;* see Noel and Carlson 1970.

24. Howe 1848:19-20 (emphases in original).

25. Ibid., 80.

26. Ibid., 56-57.

27. Ibid., 80, 73, 55.

28. Ray defines *moral imbecility* as a condition in which the mental faculties remain intact while the moral faculties are undeveloped. His enthusiasm for phrenology enabled him to conceive of moral imbeciles as a "class of subjects in whom the mental defect consists in a great deficiency, if not utter destitution of the higher *moral* faculties, the intellectual, perhaps, not being sensibly affected" (Ray [1838] 1983:122; emphasis in original). Disagreeing with Rush, who had personally encountered only three morally deranged patients, Ray asserts that moral imbeciles are "more common in society than is generally suspected" (ibid., 125).

In his *Treatise* Ray also discusses "moral mania," his term for moral insanity. See, in addition, Ray 1861-62.

29. Ray [1838] 1983:75; cf. Rush [1786] 1815:100.

30. For reviews of born-criminal theory in the period 1840-80, see Dain 1964; Fink [1938] 1962; Kiernan 1884; Mohr 1993; Rosenberg 1968; and Werlinder 1978. As the next section indicates, Werlinder is not entirely correct in stating that the "discussion ebbed" in the 1880s (48); rather, moral insanity was displaced by the concept of moral imbecility, and heads of institutions for the feebleminded picked up the discussion where psychiatrists left off.

31. Maudsley 1876:34, 58.

32. Ibid., 67, 31.

33. Ibid., 62, 22.

34. Ibid., 29, 62.

35. Ibid., 29, 24-28.

36. Ibid., 29-31.

37. Thomson (1870:323) in turn cited Maudsley. The intellectual world in which born-criminal theory developed was thinly populated.

38. Lombroso-Ferrero [1911] 1972:xxiii.

39. Thomson 1870:321-22.

40. Ibid., 330.

41. Ibid., 327-28. Thomson does not consider that incarceration itself—especially under conditions of perpetual solitary confinement, as at Perth—could have produced many of these traits, including the long hair.

42. Ibid., 342.

43. Ibid., 331, 339.

44. Garfinkel (1956) calls this sort of series a sequence of denunciatory "tries."

45. I assume that Kerlin and Broomall were acquaintances: both lived in Media; Broomall here expresses Kerlinian ideas; and someone must have invited him to address this AMO meeting, apparently the only one he attended. The meeting was held at Lakeville, Connecticut.

46. Kerlin 1879, 1887; Barr 1895.

47. Kerlin 1879:94.

48. Rogers 1892:325; Barr 1895:531 (quotation).

49. Kerlin 1887:37.

50. Kerlin 1879:87.

51. Dr. W. B. Fish in Association of Medical Officers of American Institutions for Idiotic and Feeble-Minded Persons, *Proceedings, 1894*, pp. 475, 474.

52. Broomall 1887:40.

53. Fort (1894) mounts a similar legal argument.

54. This paper (Kerlin 1879) uses *juvenile insanity* instead of *moral imbecility*, the term Kerlin came to prefer.

55. Barr 1895:524–25.

56. Ibid., 529–30.

57. Broomall 1887:40.

58. J. Brown 1992:13.

59. Ibid., 14.

60. Haller 1963; Kevles 1985; Larson 1995.

61. On the emergence of the new professional middle class, see Wiebe 1967; also see Bledstein 1976.

62. Rafter 1994. For a similar argument, related more specifically to the social work profession, see Ehrenreich 1985.

63. Similarly, as Paula Bennett (1993:251) observes, women have been defined not as different from men but as "man's negative obverse: not-A to his A." On the born criminal as Other, see Sekula 1986 and Pick 1989.

64. Goring [1913] 1972:22.

65. See Abbott 1988 on jurisdictional invasions.

66. Cowan 1985:53, quoting from Galton's *Hereditary Genius*.

67. Others who stress the altruistic current in social welfare work or eugenics include Burnham (1960); Ehrenreich (1985); Haber (1964:116); Lubove (1965); and MacKenzie (1981).

Phrenological diagrams illustrating the location and nature of the various mental "faculties." From J. G. Spurzheim, *Education: Its Elementary Principles Founded on the Nature of Man* (New York: Fowler and Wells, 1883), 322.

Hervey Backus Wilbur, founder and first superintendent of the Syracuse Asylum for Idiots. From Association of Medical Officers of American Institutions for Idiotic and Feeble-minded Persons, *Proceedings, 1884–85,* facing p. 291.

Wilbur's first home in Barre, Mass., where he began educating idiots. From New York State Archives, ser. A4228, Hebberd Commission, photographs of custodial institutions for the mentally deficient, ca. 1910–14.

Original building of the Syracuse Asylum for Idiots, where Wilbur lived and taught idiots from 1855 until his death in 1883. From New York State Archives, ser. A4228, Hebberd Commission, photographs of custodial institutions for the mentally deficient, ca. 1910–14.

Josephine Shaw, founder of the first U.S. eugenic institution, and her fiancé, Col. Charles Russell Lowell, ca. 1863. From William R. Stewart, *The Philanthropic Work of Josephine Shaw Lowell* (New York: Macmillan, 1911), facing p. 38.

The institution Lowell founded, the Newark Custodial Asylum for Feeble-minded Women. Frontispiece to State Custodial Asylum for Feeble-minded Women, Newark, N.Y., *Annual Report, 1908.*

Embroidery work at the Newark Custodial Asylum for Feeble-minded Women. From New York State Archives, ser. A4228, Hebberd Commission, photographs of custodial institutions for the mentally deficient, ca. 1910–14.

Clearing rough land at the Templeton, Mass., Colony for the Feeble-Minded.
From New York State Archives, ser. A4228, Hebberd Commission, photographs
of custodial institutions for the mentally deficient, ca. 1910–14.

Statue of Sophocles illustrating the ideal
of the well-developed man. Frontispiece to
Henry M. Boies, *Prisoners and Paupers* (New
York: Putnam's, 1893).

"A Group of 'Incorrigibles' from a Reformatory" (probably Elmira),
used to illustrate degenerates' deviation from a somewhat hazily conceived norm. From Henry M. Boies, *Prisoners and Paupers* (New York:
Putnam's, 1893), facing p. 172.

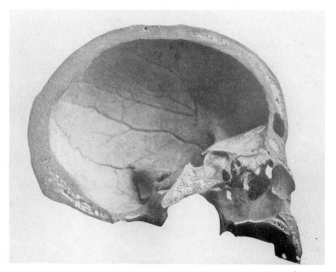

"Skull of a Negro Murderer," meant to illustrate degeneration. Frontispiece to G. Frank Lydston, *The Diseases of Society*
(Philadelphia: Lippincott, 1905).

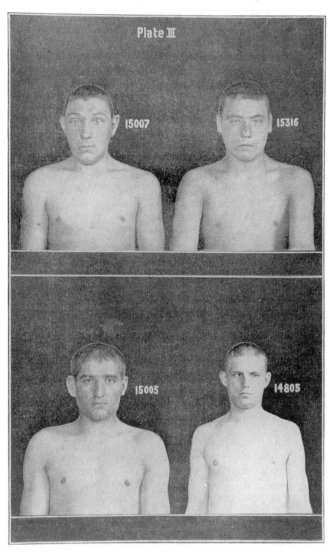

"Defectives" at the Elmira Reformatory during Zebulon Brockway's superintendency. From New York State Reformatory at Elmira, *Annual Report, 1892*, pl. 3 (following p. 11).

EARS.

LONG. LONG, OUTSTANDING.

SMALL. SMALL, OUTSTANDING.

MEDIUM. MEDIUM, OUTSTANDING.

"Ears," from Dr. Hamilton Wey's studies in criminal anthropology at Elmira, showing his interest in photography and the stigmata of criminality. From New York State Reformatory at Elmira, *Annual Report, 1895*, following p. 72.

"The Nose," another of Wey's contributions, showing how closely he associated the Bertillon method of criminal identification with criminal anthropology. From New York State Reformatory at Elmira, *Annual Report, 1895,* following p. 72.

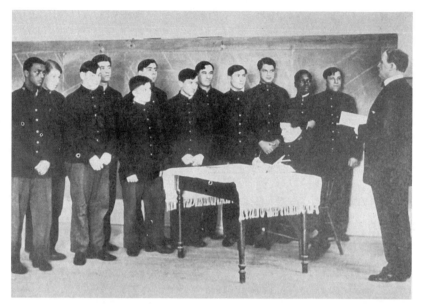

Elmira superintendent Frank Christian interviewing the special training class, to which Fenix Whipple probably belonged at this time (ca. 1916). From F. C. Allen, *A Hand Book of the New York State Reformatory at Elmira* (Elmira, N.Y.: Summary [Elmira Reformatory], 1916), facing p. 128.

5

Degenerates Appear in the Prison System

There is a physical basis for all mental action.

Elmira Reformatory physician Hamilton D. Wey in
New York State Reformatory at Elmira, *Annual Report, 1889*

While Isaac Kerlin and his colleagues were discovering moral imbeciles in the mental retardation system, prison officials began detecting another type of born criminal, the "degenerate" or "incorrigible" offender. Officials in both systems drew on a common fund of beliefs about degeneracy, the tendency to devolve to a more primitive state, to explain the behavior of these particularly difficult inmate types. Thus the mental retardation system's moral imbecile and the prison system's degenerate criminal bore a family resemblance. Like twins separated at birth, however, these two figures matured independently, nurtured by their separate institutional systems. They remained apart until, late in the nineteenth century, welfare workers began to associate and fuse them in the image of yet another biological offender, the anthropological born criminal.

Within the prison system the degenerate criminal was discovered first at a new type of penal institution, the adult reformatory, which states started founding in the late nineteenth century. Adopting the goal of juvenile reformatories, adult reformatories attempted to rehabilitate offenders. Inevitably it was these reformatories, and not old-fashioned penitentiaries, that took the lead in detecting degenerates: rehabilitative institutions are keenly aware of their failures, whereas merely punitive or custodial institutions have no reason to distinguish between reformable and incorrigible inmates. The degenerate criminal made his initial appearance at the nation's first reformatory for men, the New York State Reformatory at Elmira, which opened in 1876. In this chapter I investigate the processes through which the Elmira Reformatory's founding superintendent, Zebulon Reed Brockway, constructed biological criminals at his institution.[1]

Brockway profoundly influenced nineteenth-century thinking about crime and punishment. The first prison superintendent to claim that he could tell which offenders had been reformed and which were incurable, Brockway took a major step in the professionalization of prison management. In the 1820s, when he was an infant, prisons were run by political appointees, men who lacked experience and had little time to gain it before the next election. By midcentury, when the youthful Brockway entered prison work as a clerk, prison management was becoming more stable. Wardens were now able to accumulate experience and become penologists, or specialists in the treatment of offenders. When wardens spoke of the causes of crime, their analyses now commanded respect. By the century's end penologists had been displaced as authorities on the causes of crime, superseded by criminal anthropologists, who claimed more scientific knowledge about the criminal body. Brockway became prominent just before penologists lost their jurisdiction over crime causation to criminal anthropologists. He presented himself (and contemporaries recognized him) as a "scientific" penologist,[2] someone with criminological as well as penological expertise. Brockway's identification of the degenerate served to justify this claim.

Before the Elmira Reformatory opened, neither penologists nor the general public perceived physical differences between criminals and law-abiding citizens. Midcentury phrenologists had interpreted criminal behavior in terms of abnormal development of the brain's various "faculties," and psychiatrists such as Isaac Ray had begun to somaticize criminality and claim jurisdiction over offenders they deemed diseased, but at this point few other Americans viewed criminals' bodies as fundamentally different from their own. By the century's end, however, criminal anthropologists were writing about "the" criminal, a monstrously abnormal type of human being, perhaps a different species. Brockway's theory of crime fell midway between these two poles. He identified degeneracy, the heritable tendency to devolve, as an important cause of crime, but because he also believed in the inheritance of acquired characteristics, he thought that bad heredity could be ameliorated. Brockway, along with Richard Dugdale, Isaac Kerlin, and other writers of the 1870s, expected training to reverse the degenerative tendency in all but the most profoundly criminal. From this mildly hereditarian, Lamarckian position, Brockway ushered in the more extreme hereditarianism of eugenic criminology.[3]

In his ideas about prisoner treatment, Brockway again carried U.S. prisons through an important transition. Before the Civil War policymakers still pictured most offenders as mentally normal, responsible beings who freely willed their actions and therefore deserved punishment. Policymakers hoped that incarceration would deter further crime and perhaps induce repentance, but their main aim was simply punishment, and they did not design prison routines to rehabilitate the body or mind. Brockway rose to prominence just as the Lamarckian, or partially determinist, version of degenerationist thought took hold. It was he who famously taught that criminals need rehabilitation and who showed others how to reverse degenerative tendencies. At the century's end, however, degenerationists discarded Lamarckianism, along with the blend of environmentalism and hereditarianism that characterized early degenerationist thought. In their works heredity became more determinative and the criminal correspondingly less salvageable. Nevertheless, even fervent criminal anthropologists, who held no hope at all for the born criminal, continued to draw on Brockway's methods. The wisest course, they taught, is to sentence everyone to an indefinite or fully open-ended term. Penological experts will know when to release those who have been rehabilitated, and they will be able to retain incorrigibles for life.

Brockway fought long and hard for totally indefinite sentencing. He achieved only a weakened version of it: the indeterminate sentence that enabled penologists to hold incorrigibles until their maximums expired while granting early release on parole to those who had reformed. Indeterminate sentencing was itself a major revolution, however, and it boded well for the ideal of fully indefinite sentencing.[4]

Again anticipating criminal anthropology, Brockway translated degeneration theory into medical terms, describing criminality as a disease that must be diagnosed and cured. "No sound prison system can be devised," he declared, "until examination is had of antecedent social phenomena" — the environmental as well as physical causes of the disease of criminality: "What is the molecular condition or quality of those who gravitate to vicious and criminal society and practices? How is the mind affected by a degraded physical organism? How are the tastes formed, the purposes and desires moulded, and the moral sense obscured by such a mind? Do men make themselves what they are voluntarily, or is there a law of transmission . . . ? What cures and tones up?"[5] Elmira's became the first prison to claim to operate on the assumption that inmates are sick and in need of treatment (the "medical model" of criminality).[6] In portraying his reformatory as a "moral hospital" for "prisoner patients"[7] and in identifying the incurable degenerate, Brockway spread the perception of criminals as somatically diseased and therefore dangerous quite apart from whatever offenses they might commit.

Hundreds of Americans theorized about the degeneracy of criminals, but Brockway figured out how to marry degeneration theory to prison management and apply it to offenders. This chapter follows him as he accomplished these feats at the Elmira Reformatory. The first of the following sections outlines the origins and substance of the reformatory plan. It is followed by a section describing how the plan was implemented at Elmira and how it worked there to sift out a bottom layer of degenerates. The next section explores another sense in which Brockway produced degenerates: by so brutalizing inmates that they became too weak to reform.

The Reformatory Plan

The momentous occasion on which American prisons adopted rehabilitation as their primary mission occurred in 1870, when over 250 men and women from twenty-four states and several foreign countries gathered in Cincinnati for the National Congress on Penitentiary and Reformatory Discipline.[8] Many of the Cincinnati delegates headed prisons or reform schools; others were trustees of such institutions, educators, or members of charity boards and prison reform organizations. They were liberal reformers, forward-looking activists who were willing and indeed anxious to experiment with innovative methods of social improvement. Until recently they had devoted their energies to winning the Civil War and abolishing slavery. Now freed by the war's end to rechannel their social concerns, the Cincinnati reformers hoped to address serious problems that had developed in the prison system.

All too often party politics still dictated the appointment of prison administrators, toppling experienced officials from positions of authority. Postwar prison overcrowding and recent prohibitions against the brutal punishments of the past had left wardens in need of new disciplinary tools. Above all, however, the Cincinnati delegates were troubled by prisons' inability to accomplish anything in the way of inmate reformation. The "revolver," or habitual criminal, seemed to prove the inadequacy of traditional retributive and deterrent methods. Those methods, moreover, now appeared shamefully vindictive. A recent survey of North American penal institutions by the reformers Enoch C. Wines and Theodore W. Dwight had led to the disappointing conclusion that "there is not a prison system in the United States . . . which seeks the reformation of its subjects as a primary object."[9] Delegates such as Franklin B. Sanborn, the recent secretary of Massachusetts's Board of State Charities, hoped that American prisons would adopt methods of rewarding prisoners for good behavior that had recently been introduced in Australia and Ireland.[10] Disillusioned with current approaches to crime and punishment and critical of past experiments that had proved to be unworkable, the delegates endorsed a document entitled *Declaration of Principles,* which launched prison management on the correctional trajectory it would follow (in theory if not necessarily in practice) for the next hundred years.[11]

Zebulon Brockway, then superintendent of the Detroit House of Correction, played a central role at the Cincinnati convention. His speech, "The Ideal of a True Prison System for a State,"[12] most thoroughly articulated the new goal of rehabilitation. Brockway had drafted the *Principles* with Enoch C. Wines, Franklin B. Sanborn, and Ohio governor Rutherford B. Hayes,[13] and he had already introduced a form of indeterminate sentencing at his Detroit institution. Other delegates looked to Brockway, the most progressive penologist in the United States, to lead them into the future.

The *Declaration of Principles* rejected the retributive philosophy, which called for punishment equal to the offense. Retribution, although it had guided responses to crime since biblical times, had manifestly failed to curb crime. Moreover, to the Cincinnati delegates, retribution seemed unnecessarily harsh, little more than "the infliction of vindictive suffering."[14] Instead the delegates embraced the twin goals of rehabilitation and social defense.[15] They continued to hold offenders responsible for their behavior, but those who drafted the *Principles* had started to conceptualize crime as a "sort of moral disease, of which punishment is the remedy. The efficacy of the remedy is a question of social therapeutics, a question of the fitness and measure of the dose."[16] Brockway pushed the analogy of crime to disease even further in his own address, speaking of "the constitutional condition of criminals" and holding that reformation necessarily involves "change in the constitutional tendencies."[17] But all the delegates were aware that their interest in reformation directed attention "to the criminal rather than to the crime."[18] From now on they would focus more on the offender than on the offense.

The *Principles* recommend a number of specific methods for achieving prisoner rehabilitation: a "mark system" of rewarding good conduct, ethical and industrial training, educational programs, abolition of degrading disciplinary practices, and supervision of discharged prisoners. Nonetheless, principle 8, endorsing indefinite sentencing, and principle 19, recommending separate prisons for the incorrigible, recognize that some criminals may be beyond reformation. Although the delegates spoke of not "indefinite" but "indeterminate" sentences, to them *indeterminate* did not denote (as it does today) sentences with maximums beyond which unparoled prisoners must be released, as their eighth principle makes clear:

"Peremptory [flat or fixed] sentences ought to be replaced by those of indeterminate length. Sentences limited only by satisfactory proof of reformation should be substituted for those measured by mere lapse of time."[19] In thus advocating sentences with no fixed termination, the delegates repudiated a touchstone of Western jurisprudence, the belief that punishment should fit the crime. They realized that legislatures would be reluctant to abandon this principle of proportionality and were willing to accept, as an interim compromise, the indeterminate sentence with a maximum, which Brockway had recently introduced in Detroit. But totally open-ended sentencing lay near the heart of their reformatory plan.

Applying the Reformatory Plan at Elmira

The most closely watched penal experiment in Western history got underway in 1877, when the Elmira Reformatory, which had opened the previous year, adopted the principles of the Cincinnati prison congress.[20] All three aspects of the system that Brockway instituted at Elmira—indeterminate sentencing, rewards for good behavior, and training programs— flowed from the delegates' conviction that reformation must appeal to the convict's "self-interest," so that "the prisoner shall choose for himself what his officer chooses for him."[21] Brockway discovered, however, that success with some implied failure with others: "when earnest effort is put forth for the rescue of all, some will be saved, and the incorrigible will go to their inevitable decay."[22] In this sense Elmira's "incorrigibles" (or "degenerates" or "defectives"; Brockway used the three terms interchangeably) were products of the reformatory plan itself.

Indeterminate sentencing formed what Massachusetts prison reformer Franklin B. Sanborn called the "keystone of the arch" of the effort to induce inmates to accept authorities' values.[23] Elmira held inmates on indeterminate sentences capped by the maximum terms possible for their various offenses. Men who satisfied requirements could be paroled well before the maximum expired. Technically Elmira's board of managers was supposed to approve the superintendent's parole decisions, but in practice it rubber-stamped his recommendations.

Brockway's second means of encouraging compliance involved classifying prisoners into a series of levels or grades. As inmates advanced, they were rewarded with larger cells, better food, and increased privileges. Earlier prisons had classified convicts by rudimentary criteria such as sex. More ambitious, Elmira's officials aimed at classifying them according to what Sanborn called "degree of criminality."[24] To the question of how criminality could be gauged, the reformatory plan in effect answered, "Let convicts classify themselves." New inmates started in the middle grade, from which they could move up through earning marks for good conduct, industrious labor, and school progress. In theory only top-grade men could be paroled. Insubordination, laziness, or scholastic slowness resulted in demotion to the bottom grade.

Third, officials at Elmira attempted to instill the values of keeper in the kept through programs of ethical, industrial, and scholastic training. By law the reformatory could receive only promising cases—men between the ages of sixteen and thirty with no previous felony convictions. Initially confident that such novices in crime could be transformed by proper tutelage, Brockway made extravagant claims about his programs' success. His 1886 report, for example, assured readers that "any one passing along our corridors" might see prisoners "reading by gas-light . . . the *Prologue* of the Canterbury Tales, the tragedy of Hamlet, Emerson's *May-Day,* or the story of Evangeline."[25] Frank Sanborn, one of Brockway's strongest admirers, described in enthusiastic detail the work of convict scholars at "the Elmira prison university."[26] "In the pursuit of pleasure," an inmate revealed on an ethics exam, "I have found a great amount of my shortcomings," while another insightful student of ethics reported that "by the help of the lectures, discussions, etc., I see already the fallacy of the Epicurean theory I was unconsciously following."[27] The prisoners had no textbooks, however; they attended classes only twice a week (in the evening, after a day of labor that started at 5:15 A.M.); and their teachers were often other inmates.

Indeterminate sentencing, grading, and training produced three types of failures at Elmira, those deemed to be troublesome, indolent, or intellectually slow. The three sank together to the bottom grade, where their image began to fuse. Even though they were demoted for different reasons, the superintendent had only one index for the three sorts of failure—segregation in the lowest division, where they mixed with one another and with the invalids who were also assigned there. Brockway began using the terms *incorrigible, incompetent, stupid, diseased,* and *abnormal* as synonyms.

By 1885 Brockway had reached an impasse. Externally Elmira's reputation was soaring. Pursuing an aggressive "policy of publicity,"[28] the superintendent mailed the institution's annual reports and its in-house newspaper, *The Summary,* to hundreds of officials, libraries, and interested citizens. College presidents, professors and students, politicians, writers such as Samuel Clemens, and "many thousands"[29] of other visitors toured the reformatory to observe Brockway's techniques. Books lauding his achievements would soon appear on both sides of the Atlantic,[30] and Brockway himself boasted that "never before in my long years of experience has the problem of reclaiming to society a large majority of convicted criminals seemed so easy."[31]

Internally, however, the Elmira system was crumbling.[32] Crowding—

which Brockway encouraged by expanding and claiming "probable reformation" rates of over 80 percent[33]—made individualized treatment impossible. He responded creatively to legislative constraints on the types of goods inmates could manufacture, but idleness nevertheless became problematic. Furthermore, an increasing number of inmates either could not or would not work their way out of the bottom grade. Trapped between his claims of accomplishment and Elmira's actual performance, Brockway's chief concern became pushing inmates through the system. To meet the pressure for parole, the superintendent developed training programs designed to stimulate the "sodden" bodies and "dormant mental powers" of the growing numbers in his lowest division.[34]

Elmira's Physical Training Programs

Elmira's physical training programs grew out of Brockway's belief that weaknesses of the mind and will must reflect an underlying physical deterioration. Physical degeneracy, Brockway explained, "is a common subjective cause of criminal conduct; . . . mental powers enfeebled, untrained, uninformed, characterize the mass of criminals on admission, a condition evidencing physical degeneration as its source; . . . they are not always and altogether responsible."[35] This analysis led Brockway and the reformatory's physician to hope that physical treatments might "nullify" prisoners' "defective heredity."[36]

During the reformatory's tenth year, its physician, Hamilton D. Wey, started "an experiment of physical treatment for mental and moral improvement . . . with twelve selected inmates of [the] lowest type, apparently incorrigible."[37] This physical culture experiment continued the next year with thirty-one inmates who were "dullards or physically deficient, shop-worn, and those recently admitted who were poorly nourished and undersized."[38] Variations on this program thenceforth constituted Elmira's primary method of reformation. "Oftener than is imagined," Brockway explained, "unfavorable physical conditions obstruct . . . normal, healthful mental activity, which is one of the essentials of lawful, useful conduct."[39]

The superintendent built a marble-faced gymnasium with a pool, Turkish baths, massage rooms, and other "scientific apparatus" to improve the "physical tissue" of the "defectives and dullards."[40] According to a reformatory report, bathing increases "the activity of the skin, one of the chief eliminative organs of the body; while the massage stimulates the peripheral nerves . . . [and] nerve-cells within the brain."[41] Another physiological program used dietary restrictions to make convicts' bodies and brains more supple. In addition, Brockway instituted a manual training program for the "specially defective" class into which more and more inmates fell. Sanborn, the reformatory's closest outside observer, attributed the expansion of manual training to the presence of dullards: "Like most of the improvements made at Elmira, . . . this one had for its stimulus a pressing need of increasing the number qualified for parole, so that the reformatory should not become too crowded and the lower grades too full of slowly promoted prisoners."[42]

The manual training program distinguished among "mathematical defectives," "control defectives," and "general defectives." The control defectives—"those who, even in the Reformatory community, are anti-social"[43]—were Elmira's equivalents of the mental retardation system's "moral imbeciles." General defectives, the program's director found, resembled the genuine, hereditary imbecile:

> This class of inmates are [sic] those who are among the lowest intellectual and physical order in prison society, men in whom hereditary influences for generations back of their existence has [sic] left them a legacy of diseased bodies, and disordered weak brains.
>
> These are between the imbecile and the densely ignorant; many of them should have never been sent to the Reformatory, but to a permanent home for imbeciles.[44]

Dr. Wey realized that the reformatory's defectives resembled the born criminals being identified by the Italian criminologist Cesare Lombroso. Soon after introducing his physiological experiments, Wey began remarking on the criminal's peculiar "physiognomy," a head shape that reminded him of "idiocy."[45] Thereafter he peppered his reports with references to Lombroso's theory of the criminal as an atavism, or a throwback to a more primitive evolutionary stage; to Sir Francis Galton's work on heredity; and to Moriz Benedikt's research on the criminal's primitive brain.

Wey's interest in the gymnasium as "a favorable place for studies in criminal anthropology"[46] intensified with the increasing popularity of the Bertillon system, a method for detecting offenders through body measurements. As described by its creator, the French police official Alphonse Bertillon, this system was based on the belief that "nature never repeats herself. Choose any part of the human body, examine it, and compare it carefully with the same part of another person, and differences will appear."[47] The Bertillon system took various measurements of each apprehended offender (head length and width, length of right ear and left foot, forehead slope, etc.) and then filed these according to a complex method that enabled rapid retrieval; thus a recidivist, even one who gave a false name, could be identified as such.

As photography historian Allan Sekula points out, Bertillon's system was based on no theory of a criminal type.[48] Bertillon's anthropometrics and his general concern with knowing the criminal body nevertheless naturally reminded Hamilton Wey of the new science of criminal anthropology. Wey began measuring the bodies of Elmira inmates and using his annual medical reports to present numerical data, graphs of the criminal nose, and chilling photographs of deformed criminals. His aim was not to identify recidivists but to elucidate the causes of crime. Despite some reservations about Lombroso's work, the physician nonetheless recited information on tattooing and occipital protuberances in the Italian fashion.[49] Such discussions provided Brockway with a rationale for the reformatory's burgeoning number of apparently unreformable cases; he hoped that criminal anthropology would soon explicate "the true source of anti-social behavior." [50]

"No part of the system pursued at Elmira," Sanborn observed of its physiological training programs, "has attracted so much attention as this among sanitarians and alienists, and the course adopted has increased materially the scientific knowledge of the world respecting the much-debated class of 'degenerates.' " [51] Through his Elmira reports and talks before the National Prison Association,[52] Wey helped to introduce Americans to the concept of the anthropological criminal. In addition, his Elmira research was widely cited in criminal anthropological treatises such as Havelock Ellis's *The Criminal* and Henry Boies's *Science of Penology*. Many Americans understandably got the impression that Brockway had validated criminal anthropology.

Brockway and Wey reconfigured the profile of the biological criminal. Their degenerate, although not entirely distinct from the moral imbecile described by the superintendents of institutions for the feebleminded, is more insentient and physically decayed. The mental retardation superintendents (as chap. 3 shows) modeled their moral imbecile on the intellectually normal and physically able inmates who, although they were constant troublemakers, performed invaluable institutional chores. Brockway and Wey characterize their degenerates as more frail and less manipulative. These degenerates more closely resemble the habitual criminals identified by Dr. J. Bruce Thomson a few years earlier at Perth prison: deformed, mentally dense, low in energy, and liable to insanity.

Brockway and Wey describe prisoners in the physical training programs as "diseased," "effeminate," "feeble-minded," "incompetent," "incorrigible," "insubordinate," "lacking in moral sense," "morbid," "ox-like," and "vicious." According to the two officials, these prisoners are "cranks," "mattoids" (a Lombrosian term Brockway used to indicate mental feebleness), "moral imbeciles," "perverts," "psychopaths," and "stupids." These terms place particular emphasis on the degenerate's mental weakness. By implication, those who identify degenerates must be intelligent.

The one-third of Elmira's prisoners who by the century's end had accumulated in the lower grade contradicted Brockway's claims of success. They were "incorrigible" in the sense that they did not respond to the attempts to remake them. To Brockway this type of incorrigibility indicated that, if released, the men would probably relapse into crime. This interpretation followed logically from his degenerationist premises, according to which physical, mental, and moral defects do not exist independently of one another.

Like a sediment, hundreds of lower-grade "defectives" were precipitated by the reformatory system itself. There was also a second sense in which Elmira produced degenerates, however. The superintendent so debilitated prisoners as to physically create the diseased bodies that both encouraged and confirmed attributions of degeneracy.

Creating Degenerates

Two investigations of Brockway's management practices revealed that the high rates of physical and mental disease at Elmira were caused by abuse. The New York State Board of Charities (SBC) opened the first investigation in 1893 in response to newspaper allegations of cruelty at the reformatory. Although the SBC confirmed these charges, Brockway survived its investigation, partly because his do-nothing board, itself under fire, defended him and partly because then-governor Roswell Flower, loath to dismiss the prestigious reformer, sidestepped the SBC report. The second, less formal investigation occurred during the 1899–1900 fiscal year, when a new board of managers, forced on the reformatory by Governor Theodore Roosevelt, uncovered patterns of gross neglect and brutality. The new board concluded that "defectives" might be not born but made: "many . . . would not have become 'incorrigible' under wiser treatment." [53]

Letters from nearly 1,000 convicts and interviews with over 200 witnesses persuaded the first set of investigators that Brockway had inflicted "very severe and cruel punishment . . . for the slightest causes," using as a "paddle" a "heavy leather strap one foot ten inches long, three inches wide and nearly a quarter of an inch thick, affixed to a strong hickory handle." [54] His public opposition to harsh punishment notwithstanding, Brockway had regularly taken prisoners to an isolated bathroom (known among them as the "slaughter house"),[55] strung them up, and beaten them with the paddle strap or a rubber hose. Some prisoners were injured for life; others, as mournful parents testified, died. The stunned SBC declared, "The brutality practiced at the reformatory has no parallel in any modern penal institution in this country." Indulging in these orgies of viciousness an average of twice daily, the superintendent must have "absolutely brutalized" himself.[56]

Some prisoners resisted Brockway's onslaughts, only to incur further bodily harm. When those who were to be flogged refused to spread themselves against the wall, Brockway had two burly assistants throw them on the marble floor, where they were "kicked and pummelled into subjection, the blows being given on the face, in the head or in the stomach."[57] One inmate "barricaded his cell when threatened with punishment and was forced out with hot iron hooks"; another "was made so desperate through inability to perform the task set for him that he poured molten iron on his foot."[58] But the managers defended the superintendent's "spanking treatments" as a tool of "moral regeneration."[59]

Five years after the first investigation, Governor Roosevelt's replacement board found that Brockway had not only persisted in flogging prisoners but also invalided them through various forms of mismanagement. Incoming convicts had not been examined for communicable diseases, and those free of illness were often celled with infected inmates; moreover, the herd that supplied their milk was tubercular. Dr. Wey had pursued a private practice, giving no more than "perfunctory attention to his duties at the institution."[60] An "initially healthy" prisoner was dead within six months, and over 100 of the sick had to be granted special paroles. Another 74 inmates were transferred to the Matteawan hospital for insane criminals.[61] Whereas Dr. Wey had blamed inmates themselves for the reformatory's high rates of mental disorder, the new board concluded that in some cases, reformatory conditions had induced insanity.[62] It found Elmira's food supply to be adulterated and its water supply "a menace to health."[63] The new board fired nearly every officer, including Dr. Wey (son of the former board's president), and with enormous difficulty persuaded Brockway to resign.

Degenerates and the Evolution of the Criminal Body

The degenerate as characterized by Brockway and Wey appeared midway through the process that Michel Foucault, in his genealogy of the dangerous individual, calls the " 'pathologification' of crime."[64] Although the degenerate was more deeply penetrated by criminality than the mid-nineteenth century's normal offender, his body and mind were not scarred with the stigmata that deformed the next type of biological offender, Lombroso's born criminal. Brockway's degenerate, moreover, was less ferocious and less mature than Lombroso's savage adult; reflecting the relative youthfulness of Elmira's population,[65] Brockway's degenerate was punier, weaker mentally, and more passive. Brockway hoped to remediate the degenerate's body; Lombroso's born criminal is by definition beyond reformation.[66] And the degenerate's heredity, although defective, is not yet dysgenic.

Instead of diminishing his prestige, Brockway's ouster brought condolences from other superintendents and illustrious speaking engagements. In addresses at Brown, Yale, and Cornell Universities and at professional meetings, Brockway called for life imprisonment of incorrigibles and indefinite sentences for misdemeanants. He inspected jails for the Prison Association of New York, became mayor of the town of Elmira, and was designated honorary president by the 1910 international prison congress. Far and wide, social welfare specialists praised him as "the Nestor of modern penology" and "St. Paul" of the prisoner reformation movement.[67]

Even those who acknowledged Brockway's culpability continued to endorse the reformatory system's principles and its view of the criminal as diseased. In an 1894 letter to the *New York Evening Post,* Josephine Shaw Lowell argued that, although Brockway had allowed Elmira to expand to a size that made individual treatment impossible, its methods were nonetheless sound.[68] Elmira's new board reinforced the medical model by inviting Dr. Frank Robertson, the mental disease specialist initially hired to replace Dr. Wey, to become Brockway's successor. Elmira's first post-Brockway report requested additional "anthropological" equipment and included an uncritical section on "Defectives."[69]

■ ■ ■

Although the mental retardation system and the prison system developed their ideas about moral imbeciles and degenerate criminals in relative isolation, toward the end of the nineteenth century officials of the two institutional networks overcame their professional parochialism and began taking an interest in related welfare work. The result was a cross-fertilization and a pooling of ideas that led to the conceptualization of the criminal imbecile early in the next century.

Exchange of ideas was encouraged by the formation in 1874 of the National Conference of Charities and Correction (NCCC), an umbrella organization that brought various welfare workers together for annual meetings. At the NCCC's 1884 meeting Isaac Kerlin, superintendent of the Pennsylvania Training School, delivered his powerful eugenical speech on the "great host of crime-doers who are not so much criminals as mental and moral imbeciles."[70] This talk cited Elmira data,[71] and during Kerlin's 1885 speech to the NCCC, Brockway was present in the audience. Brockway opened the following discussion by agreeing that "something that may be called imbecility lies at the foundation of a vast amount of crime . . . . The prime cause of criminal conduct, if not arrested development, is undevelopment [sic]. I think any man who has undertaken to grade the prisoners of a prison establishment . . . will have found a residuum that may be called imbeciles." [72] Thus encountering one another at the NCCC convention, Kerlin and Brockway discovered common ground.

Toward the century's end other officials of institutions for the feebleminded also opened up to outside influences. In 1891, for instance, Dr. William B. Fish, the superintendent from Illinois, remarked to his colleagues: "There are doubtless members of this conference who have read the very interesting report of Dr. H. D. Wey, physician of the Elmira Reformatory in New York, published in 1887. In the photographs of his class in physical culture types of adult idiots are clearly discernible." [73] By 1895 Martin Barr of the Pennsylvania Training School had integrated Lombroso's work on criminal anthropology into his own thinking about moral imbecility, publishing the result in a paper entitled "Moral Paranoia." [74] Arthur MacDonald, who had recently authored the first American book on criminal anthropology, attended the meeting where Barr read this paper on moral imbecility. Finally, George Knight, director of Connecticut's institution for the feebleminded, reported corresponding with Elmira's Dr. Hamilton Wey. [75] These crossings of professional borders fortified the belief that the disorderly classes were interrelated through bad heredity. They made it particularly apparent that little divided imbeciles from criminals.

Notes

1. The Elmira Reformatory as run by Brockway is probably the most written-about penal institution in the world. Most of this literature is highly flattering to both Brockway and the institution; see, e.g., McKelvey [1936] 1972; Winter 1891. Few writers have recognized that Brockway constructed a new criminal type, the "degenerate" or "incorrigible" offender (but see Grupp 1959 and Zeman 1981) or that he habitually violated his own stated principles of prison management (but see Pisciotta 1983). The definitive work on Elmira, and an excellent source of information on Brockway, is Pisciotta 1994.

2. Brockway 1871:39–45; Brockway [1912] 1969:85, 308–9; Boies 1901: chaps. 8 and 9.

3. Brockway opened Elmira five years before the first criminal anthropological book (Benedikt 1881) appeared in the United States and probably a decade before he himself learned the details of Lombroso's doctrine. He was nonetheless already familiar with a concept that became central to Lombroso's biological determinism: the idea that the criminal is a throwback to a more primitive form of humanity, "a relic of a vanished race," as Lombroso put it (Lombroso-Ferrero [1911] 1972: 135). At times Brockway, too, conceived of the criminal as a distinct and savage

type of being (Brockway 1871:41; New York State Reformatory at Elmira (hereafter Elmira Reformatory), *Annual Report, 1878,* p. 11).

4. For Brockway, moreover, completely open-ended sentencing was ideal not for eugenic reasons but because it increased penologists' power over prisoners. Despite his own mildly eugenical beliefs (Brockway 1871:43), Brockway remained more interested in reforming the majority of his inmates than in controlling the reproduction of the degenerate minority.

5. Brockway 1871:40.

6. At midcentury phrenologist Eliza Farnham had run the women's division at Sing Sing prison on the medical model (Rafter 1990a:17–19), but the experiment was short-lived and attracted much less attention than did Brockway's application of the medical model at Elmira.

7. Ellis 1890:271; Elmira Reformatory, *Annual Report, 1893,* p. 14.

8. The delegates are listed in the first few pages of E. Wines 1871. I have taken the numbers from Pisciotta 1994:12.

9. Wines and Dwight 1867:62.

10. Sanborn 1871. For a useful review of earlier experiments in penal and convict reformation that influenced the 1870 delegates, see F. Wines 1919, esp. chap. 9.

11. The transactions of the Cincinnati congress, including the *Declaration of Principles* in draft and final form, appear in E. Wines 1871. This Cincinnati meeting turned out to be the founding meeting of the organization that became the National Prison Association and is today the American Correctional Association, the main professional society of prison administrators.

12. Brockway 1871.

13. Pisciotta 1994:13.

14. Principle 2 in E. Wines 1871:541.

15. Principles 1 and 2 in ibid.

16. Ibid., 548.

17. Brockway 1871:40, 45.

18. Principle 2 in E. Wines 1871:541.

19. Principle 8 in ibid., 541–42.

20. Pisciotta 1994:17 notes that a year passed before Elmira adopted the *Principles* as its guide and that three more years went by before Brockway, having completed the prison's construction, could start applying the principles therein.

21. E. Wines 1871:541–42.

22. Elmira Reformatory, *Annual Report, 1889,* pp. 22–23.

23. Sanborn 1900a:29.

24. Sanborn 1871:408.

25. Elmira Reformatory, *Annual Report, 1885,* p. 26.

26. Sanborn 1900b:43.

27. Elmira Reformatory, *Annual Report, 1888,* p. 52.

28. Brockway [1912] 1969:236.

29. Ibid., 237.

30. E.g., Boies 1901; Ellis 1890; Henderson 1893; Winter 1891.

31. Elmira Reformatory, *Annual Report, 1884,* p. 12.

32. If the Elmira system worked to reform prisoners at any point, it did so between 1880 and 1885. According to Brockway himself, until October 1880 "the reformatory differed only in name from a common, rough, state prison" (Brockway [1912] 1969:174). By the end of the 1884-85 reporting period, the population averaged 650 inmates—too large a number for individualized treatment, as New York's State Board of Charities frequently complained. Dr. Wey's physiological treatments for incorrigibles, the first obvious sign that the system was in trouble, began during the fiscal year 1885-86.

33. E.g., Elmira Reformatory, *Annual Report, 1892*, pp. 24, 27.

34. Elmira Reformatory, *Annual Report, 1886*, pp. 20, 60.

35. Elmira Reformatory, *Annual Report, 1892*, p. 9.

36. Elmira Reformatory, *Annual Report, 1895*, p. 74.

37. Elmira Reformatory, *Annual Report, 1886*, p. 20.

38. Elmira Reformatory, *Annual Report, 1887*, p. 72.

39. Elmira Reformatory, *Annual Report, 1886*, p. 21.

40. Elmira Reformatory, *Annual Report, 1889*, p. 19.

41. Elmira Reformatory, *Annual Report, 1887*, p. 73.

42. Sanborn 1900b:44.

43. Elmira Reformatory, *Annual Report, 1899*, p. 114.

44. Ibid., 120.

45. Elmira Reformatory, *Annual Report, 1886*, p. 61.

46. Elmira Reformatory, *Annual Report, 1892*, p. 146.

47. Bertillon 1891:331.

48. Sekula 1986:25.

49. Elmira Reformatory, *Annual Report, 1895*, p. 67 and accompanying illustrations. Wey denies the existence of a criminal type or separate criminal species in Elmira Reformatory, *Annual Report, 1895*, p. 73-74, there also declaring that a healthy environment can "nullify" defective heredity. He is similarly optimistic in his National Prison Association (NPA) presentation, "Plea for Physical Training" (Wey 1888). Yet a somewhat later NPA report entitled "Criminal Anthropology" (Wey 1890) is deeply Lombrosian.

50. Elmira Reformatory, *Annual Report, 1891*, p. 18.

51. Sanborn 1900b:42.

52. Wey 1888, 1890.

53. Elmira Reformatory, *Annual Report, 1900*, p. 29-30.

54. New York State Board of Charities 1894:xiii, xiv.

55. Pisciotta 1983:621.

56. New York State Board of Charities 1894:xxxiii, xxvi.

57. Ibid., xxi.

58. ibid., 6, 5.

59. Elmira Reformatory, *Annual Report, 1894*, p. 17.

60. Elmira Reformatory, *Annual Report, 1900*, p. 13.

61. Ibid., 12.

62. Elmira Reformatory, *Annual Report, 1899*, pp. 146-47; Elmira Reformatory, *Annual Report, 1900*, p. 15.

63. Elmira Reformatory, *Annual Report, 1900*, p. 28.

64. Foucault 1988:133.

65. Fifty-six percent of the prisoners committed to Elmira during Brockway's superintendency were between sixteen and twenty years old, and another 34 percent were between twenty and twenty-five (Elmira Reformatory, *Annual Report, 1898*, p. 48).

66. Lombroso-Ferrero [1911] 1972:101.

67. National Prison Association, *Proceedings, 1910*, pp. 162, 169. For an example of his calls for life incarceration of incorrigibles and indefinite sentencing of misdemeanants, see Brockway 1901:210–12; this paper is prefaced by one of the condolences. Also see S. Barrows 1900 for a volume in which article after article praises Brockway without reservation.

68. Josephine Shaw Lowell, letter to the editor, September 27, 1894, as cited and quoted in Stewart 1911:461

69. Elmira Reformatory, *Annual Report, 1900*, pp. 106–7, 92.

70. Kerlin 1884:255.

71. Ibid., 255–56.

72. National Conference of Charities and Corrections, *Proceedings, 1885*, pp. 444–45.

73. Fish 1891:205.

74. Barr 1895:526–27.

75. Association of Medical Officers of American Institutions for Idiotic and Feeble-Minded Persons, *Proceedings, 1895*, p. 597.

6

The Anthropological Born Criminal

Ladies and gentlemen, herein lies the source of failure
of the old methods of study and reform of the criminal
class—their bodies were forgotten.

G. Frank Lydston, "Some General Considerations
of Criminology"

Essentialism *is* cultural construction.

Marjorie Garber, *Vested Interests*

The first biological theory of crime to attract
widespread attention was that which Cesare
Lombroso, its best-known proponent, named
"criminal anthropology." According to Lombroso and his followers, incorrigible offenders
are "born criminals," apelike throwbacks to a
more primitive evolutionary stage. Born criminals differ so radically from lawful people that
scientists can identify them by their physical and
mental abnormalities, just as physical anthropologists can identify members of different races
by their physical characteristics. The Americans who elaborated Lombroso's doctrine did
so not as training school superintendents or
prison officials but as contributors to a new
field—criminology—dedicated to the production
of scientific information about crime and criminals.[1] This chapter analyzes the kind of information that American criminal anthropologists
produced during the two decades, 1890–1910,
that their doctrine was in vogue.[2]

A New Science

There was something novel in the relationship between American criminal anthropologists and their subject matter. This becomes clear if we compare the way they thought of their work with that of earlier commentators on crime. Most of their American predecessors had speculated on crime causation without aspiring to contribute to a body of scientific knowledge that would have value in and of itself. Some had been prison officials and thus primarily concerned with producing practical penological information. Others had been members of prison reform organizations and thus mainly concerned with gleaning information that could lead to prisoner rehabilitation. The point is not that these predecessors conceived of themselves as something other than "criminologists," for that term did not gain currency until criminal anthropologists popularized it.[3] Rather, it is that they did not think of themselves as specialists in the production of scientific information about crime. The two partial exceptions to this rule, Zebulon Brockway, the superintendent of New York's Elmira Reformatory, and Hamilton D. Wey, Elmira's physician, did attempt to collect data of primarily scientific value; but their professional identities remained those of prison administrator and physician, respectively, not scientists.

American criminal anthropologists, like Lombroso himself, insisted that their work was a "new science," one that carried the study of crime causation across the great divide between idle speculation and hard fact.[4] Mocking the amateurishness of his predecessors, the American criminal anthropologist G. Frank Lydston wrote in 1896 that "criminology, until recent years, was a very simple subject for study. The entire field of research was covered from the inquiring, searching eye of science, by a blanket of dogmatic and egotistic reasoning—or rather a lack of reasoning. How simple the doctrine that the delinquencies of criminal man are due to the fact that he is bad—that he is not so good as we are! And how simple the remedy— to punish him and preach to him, and make him as good as we are!"[5] Lydston advised his audience of prison officials to renounce the absurd view that criminals have free will in favor of "modern criminal anthropology": "With all due respect to moralistic methods in the prevention and correction of crime, I believe that no advance has been made, or can be made, that is not founded upon scientific materialism."[6] Similarly Hamilton Wey wrote that "of criminologists there are, generally speaking, two schools, the theological or spiritualistic and the material or anthropological."[7] August Drähms, another American criminal anthropologist, echoed Lydston and Wey by comparing "two distinct schools of criminological investigation . . . : the Positivist, or materialistic" school of criminal anthropology "and the Spiritualistic, or classical" school.[8]

With such remarks criminal anthropologists drew a firm line between themselves and earlier commentators on crime who had unscientifically included God and free will in the causational picture. Unlike their predecessors, they would examine only phenomena rooted in the natural world of matter. When they described their school as "materialist" or "positivist," they invoked a philosophical position according to which all phenomena can be explained in terms of physical laws. Like other scientists, they would investigate the laws of matter, ignoring such foolishness as free will.

Lombroso's American followers did not always refer to their new science as "criminology." Because the field was just beginning to take shape, they sometimes folded the study of criminals into other fields—"scientific sociology," "the science of penology," or the "scientific" study of degeneracy.[9] They all considered their work to be "scientific," however, a term they used to express their commitment to empirical methods and dispassionate analyses. "A large part of the most rigid science," we learn on the first page of the first American treatise on criminal anthropology, Arthur MacDonald's *Criminology*,[10] "consists in simple and exact description, which should be given, of course, without regard to any views that one may consciously or unconsciously hold."[11] They would measure criminals' bodies with scientific equipment such as calipers, the dynamometer, and the aesthesiometer, objectively recording facts. And they would use induction and quantitative methods to formulate causal laws. Like other true scientists, they would work up to whatever theory the facts indicated.

Their materialist premises led criminal anthropologists to their central assumption that the body must mirror moral capacity. Lombrosians took for granted a one-to-one correspondence between the criminal's physical being and unethical behavior. Criminals, wrote the American criminal anthropologist Henry Boies, are "the imperfect, knotty, knurly, worm-eaten, half-rotten fruit of the human race," their bodies illustrating "the truth of the reverse Latin adage, *'insana mens insano corpore.'* "[12] Nature had made the expert's task relatively simple: to detect born criminals, one needed only the appropriate apparatus. Degree of criminality could be determined by measuring the number and extent of the offender's "stigmata," or physical deformities.

The assumption that offenders literally embody their criminality led criminal anthropologists to present not just graphs and statistical tables but also drawings and photographs, pictures that claim a direct access to reality and purport to present the criminal's essence. The illustrations of criminal anthropology in effect deny that they are representations and hence constructions. As photography scholar David Green puts it, they assert "a seamless relation between the photographic image and appearances whereby . . . the image [can] function as reality itself."[13] Charts and photographs become a rhetorical gesture, a means of signifying science and objectivity. Reducing the social problem of crime to a biological problem, the visual and verbal languages of criminal anthropology also reduce themselves to thin air, claiming to be media through which perception flies, unobstructed, straight to the essence of the criminal body. "The naivete, but also the force, of this positivism," Daniel Pick remarks in a history of degeneration theory, "lay in its attempt to deny the presence of metaphor." [14] Criminal anthropology owed much of its appeal and plausibility to its visual rhetoric. [15]

Criminal Anthropology in the United States

While producing criminal anthropology, the first American criminologists were also produced by it. They appropriated a body of knowledge that gave them and their own writings scientific status. [16] Although they elaborated on the doctrine, they added little to its scientific core, the perception that the worst criminals constitute an atavistic, anthropologically unique type. To understand the relationship between the formation of their field and its content, we need to distinguish among three groups that generated criminal anthropological information: the Europeans who formulated the theory in the first place (whom I call "originators"), those who initially gave Americans access to the originators' work ("channelers"), and the Americans who then reiterated and expanded on the channelers' materials ("American criminal anthropologists"). By distinguishing the contributions of these three groups, we can also trace the process through which criminal anthropology migrated to and took root in the United States.

Originators

The first book on criminal anthropology published in the United States, Moriz Benedikt's *Anatomical Studies upon Brains of Criminals,* appeared in 1881, well in advance of any work by Lombroso. A Hungarian who taught in Vienna, Benedikt was inspired to study criminals' craniums and brains by the work of Franz Joseph Gall, the founder of phrenology. [17] Dissections led Benedikt to conclude that "the brains of criminals exhibit a deviation from the normal type, and criminals are to be viewed as an anthropological variety of their species, at least amongst the cultured races." [18] This finding excited debate in the United States, especially among physicians, on the existence of an anatomically distinct criminal type. [19] Furthermore, Benedikt's statistics, his complicated medical terminology, and his detailed diagrams of animal and human brains contributed to the growing sense that criminology would constitute a hard science. Benedikt's book was nevertheless too abstruse to have much impact on mainstream American thinking about the causes of crime, and its method—brain dissection—was not one that social scientists could easily adopt. In addition, this was Benedikt's only book to be translated into English. As a result *Anatomical Studies* became little more than a footnote in the work of American criminal anthropologists.

The other originator, Cesare Lombroso,[20] exercised far greater influence, but for years Americans knew his work mainly through secondary sources. Lombroso's own writings appeared slowly in English and at first in the form of introductions to books by American followers and articles. Arthur MacDonald's *Criminology* (1893) carried one of these introductions; August Drähms's *The Criminal* (1900), another. Subscribers to a journal called *The Forum* could read Lombroso's "Criminal Anthropology: Its Origin and Application," an 1895 survey of the field. Portions of one of his major studies also appeared in English in 1895 as *The Female Offender,* just two years after its initial Italian publication, and this work was reprinted six times before 1911. Nonetheless, Americans who knew only English had to wait another sixteen years before they could read even a digest of Lombroso's key work, *L'uomo delinquente,* the first Italian edition of which had appeared in 1876. This summary, compiled by Lombroso's daughter with his assistance and carrying yet another of his introductions, was published in 1911 as *Criminal Man.* His *Crime: Its Causes and Remedies* appeared in the same year.[21]

Americans who could not read Lombroso's oeuvre in Italian or French translation thus had little direct access to it until the heyday of criminal anthropology had passed.[22] This meant that those who built on his research worked at some distance from their source material. Their own writings were often doubly derivative, dependent not only on Lombroso's research but also on the channelers who gave them access to it.

Channelers

Among the channelers who provided access to the originators' work, translators played an important role by determining, through their initiatives, which European works would reach American audiences. Americans might never have heard of Benedikt, for example, had E. P. Fowler, a New York physician, not translated his *Anatomical Studies upon Brains of Criminals* from German—a task he undertook, Fowler tells us, to establish "a scientific basis for the prevention of crime."[23] Henry P. Horton, who translated Lombroso's *Crime: Its Causes and Remedies* from French and German sources, helped to introduce Americans to Italian criminal anthropology.

Horton's significance as a channeler is eclipsed, however, by that of the organization that arranged this translation, the American Institute of Criminal Law and Criminology. Although this professional association was not founded until enthusiasm for criminal anthropology had begun to fade, it immediately evinced a deep and relatively sophisticated interest in biological theories of crime. Criminological historian Leonard Savitz suggests that the organization's publication policies contributed to Lombroso's American "triumph": "The powerful American Institute of Criminal Law and Criminology, very fierce adherents to the Positivist School, translated Lombroso, Garofalo and Ferri, but, of the French environmentalists, only Tarde."[24] The institute opened a door through which Lombrosian works passed into the United States while closing that door to studies in alternative theoretical traditions.

European criminal anthropology further flowed to the United States through writers who, by summarizing the originators' work in English, first alerted Americans to it. Of these, far and away the most influential was Havelock Ellis, author of *The Criminal* (1890). The multilingual Ellis, an English eugenicist, wrote on an enormous range of subjects, from art to sexology. Although *The Criminal* was his only foray into criminal anthropology, it proved to be an extended one: by 1911 the book was in its fourth edition and had gone through nine printings. Ellis relied on numerous sources for the book, including reports produced by New York's Elmira Reformatory, but primarily on Lombroso's own writings. He illustrated *The Criminal* with graphs, drawings, and photographs, all purporting to convey important scientific information. *The Criminal's* main message is that Ellis is a learned scientist and the criminal is an anthropological freak. This book became the well into which many Americans dipped for data on born criminals.[25]

Early American reports on Lombroso's work, although much briefer than *The Criminal*, formed yet another artery through which the doctrine passed into the United States. Joseph Jastrow, a psychology professor, produced one of the first articles of this type, "A Theory of Criminality," for the journal *Science* in 1886. Noting that "a change in our view of crime and criminals seems about to take place," Jastrow uncritically outlines Lombroso's theory of criminality as "a morbid phenomenon, . . . a defect," deriving his information from a French review by Lombroso.[26] In 1888 William Noyes, a physician at New York's Bloomingdale Asylum, published a paper entitled "The Criminal Type" in the *American Journal of Social Science;* the article emphasizes the criminal's bad heredity and primitive nature. Based on a French edition of *L'uomo delinquente*, Noyes's paper is undilutedly Lombrosian.[27]

Criminal anthropology is better digested in the two presentations by Hamilton Wey that introduced members of the National Prison Association to criminal anthropology. Citing Benedikt, Francis Galton, and Have-lock Ellis as well as Lombroso, Wey supplements his outline of criminal anthropology with data gathered through his own Elmira Reformatory re-search.[28] His relatively critical attitude toward Lombroso's ideas and the fact that he did original research make Wey a transitional figure between the channelers and the first generation of U.S. criminal anthropologists. More than a translator or mere herald, Wey could be regarded as the first American criminologist if his output were more extensive. He stood on the threshold that others were about to cross.

American Criminal Anthropologists

As news of Lombroso's theory spread, many Americans began writing about it; thus the third group of producers, American elaborators of crimi-nal anthropology, greatly outnumbers the other two. We can identify its key members, however, by defining them as authors of book-length works that to some degree endorsed the concept of the criminal as a physically distinct, atavistic human being and that are frequently cited in both the primary and secondary literature on criminal anthropology.[29] Applying this definition, I found that there were eight leading American criminal anthropologists who together produced nine works of this sort (Henry Boies having au-thored two). Their names, their books' titles, and publication data appear in table 3.

The initial book in this series, Arthur MacDonald's *Criminology,* was apparently the first American treatise to identify its subject as "crimi-nology" and its author as a specialist in the area. MacDonald asserts ex-pertise by listing his credentials and claiming that his findings have sci-entific status. He also dedicates his book to Lombroso, "the founder of criminology," who has written its introduction. For these reasons we may take *Criminology*'s 1893 appearance as the field's starting point. As other titles in table 3 suggest, however, for some time to come the study of crime and criminals remained intertwined with investigations of other "degener-ate" types.

These major American books on criminal anthropology addressed three overlapping audiences. Charles R. Henderson's *Introduction to the Study of the Dependent, Defective and Delinquent Classes* was designed as a text-book for college students and social welfare workers; Philip A. Parsons' *Responsibility for Crime,* originally a Columbia University dissertation, also seems to have been written for classroom use. Two of the studies (Eugene S. Talbot's erudite *Degeneracy* and G. Frank Lydston's massive *Diseases of Society*) were at least partially directed toward other professionals. The rest were written to inform—in some cases to alarm—the general public.[30]

Table 3. Major American Books on Criminal Anthropology

Author	Title	Date of First Publication	Other Dates of U.S. Publication
MacDonald, A.	*Criminology*	1893[a]	1893
Boies, H.	*Prisoners and Paupers*	1893	—
Henderson, C. R.	*An Introduction to the Study of the Dependent, Defective and Delinquent Classes*	1893	1901, 1908, 1909
Talbot, E.	*Degeneracy*	1898	1904
Drähms, A.	*The Criminal: His Personnel and Environment*	1900	—
McKim, W. D.	*Heredity and Human Progress*	1900	1901
Boies, H.	*The Science of Penology*	1901	—
Lydston, G. F.	*The Diseases of Society*	1904	1905, 1906, 1908
Parsons, P.	*Responsibility for Crime*	1909	—

[a] The 1893 edition of McDonald's *Criminology* was copyrighted in 1892 and is labeled "Second Edition." However, the 1892 "first" edition was merely a thirteen-page reprint of an article published earlier that year. Moreover, although a fourth edition of 1892 is listed in the *National Union Catalog*, it evidently was merely a reprint of the 1893 edition. I have found no trace of a third edition.
Source: Library of Congress, *National Union Catalog,* for all except Drähms (1900).

The authors of these books were all well-educated, male professionals. Those common denominators aside, however, the group was characterized by occupational diversity: its members included social welfare workers (Boies, Drähms, and Henderson), educators (Henderson, Lydston, Mac-Donald, Parsons, and Talbot), physicians (Lydston, McKim, and Talbot), and ministers (Drähms and Henderson; MacDonald, too, had studied theology). As the overlaps in the preceding examples suggest, professional heterogeneity characterized most of the individuals as well. W. Duncan McKim had both Ph.D and M.D. degrees; Lydston was a physician, sexologist, university professor, and successful author; Henderson, a minister heavily involved in charity work, taught sociology at the University of Chicago; MacDonald, a self-described specialist in the education of "the abnormal and weakling classes,"[31] had studied (but not earned degrees in) law, medicine, and theology and had attended lectures on criminology by Lombroso;[32] and Talbot, a professor of dental and oral surgery with a special interest in degeneracies of the jaw and teeth, held both M.D. and D.D.S. degrees.

This multiplicity of professional interests indicates something quite important about American criminal anthropologists: like Lombroso, who was trained as a physician, they came to criminology from the outside, as amateur specialists. MacDonald's European studies included some formal training in criminology, and at least four of the other authors had had extensive contact with prisoners,[33] but otherwise American promulgators of the new science had few qualifications other than an ability to digest their sources and proclaim criminological opinions with confidence. This situation was inevitable. Like social science in general, criminology was still in what MacDonald called its "formative period."[34] Criminal anthropology constituted the first sustained scientific discourse on crime and criminals. Even after the turn of the century, sociologist Frances Kellor noted that "with but two or three exceptions, universities offer no courses in criminal sociology and abnormal psychology."[35] The writers under discussion helped to create the base on which the discipline developed, but that base was almost unavoidably derivative and amateurish.

The Substance of American Criminal Anthropology

A Criminal Class

American criminal anthropologists used their texts to demonstrate that there exists a criminal class, physically and psychologically different from normal citizens. They devoted their treatises to describing the abnormalities of that class, but by implication they were also establishing criteria for the normality of noncriminal classes. Boies's *Prisoners and Paupers,* for example, explicitly argues that to be criminal is to be different and abnormal; implicitly it argues that those who are physically normal cannot be truly criminal. "Every member of the actual criminal class diverges in some essential respects from the normal type of mankind. . . . Abnormality becomes in itself an indicative characteristic of the class. Conversely, there is never found in the criminal or pauper class, except by accident, a normal, well developed, healthy adult. At least not in America."[36] To make this point visually, Boies presents photographs of immigrants at Ellis Island (e.g., "Typical Russian Jews" and "A Group of Italians"), of deformed "incorrigibles" at Elmira, and of ragged, misshapen "Paupers in an Almshouse." The "well-developed" ideal type is represented by photographs of art objects: an imposing Roman statue of Sophocles, a cast of the Venus de Milo, and a painting of American statesmen. Through these illustrations we gather that to be good is also to be beautiful, healthy, middle- or upper-class, normal, and socially valuable; and we gather that to be bad is to be poor, sickly, ugly, criminal, lower-class, abnormal, and a social nuisance. As photographic historian Allan Sekula points out, "the invention of the modern criminal cannot be dissociated from the construction of a law-abiding body."[37]

In his *Introduction to the Study of the Dependent, Defective and Delinquent Classes,* Charles R. Henderson divides "all the members of society" into two groups. The "Progressive Class" consists of those who are "self-supporting, self-respecting, law-abiding, industrious, and under the educational influences of schools, churches, newspapers and the public sentiment of Christian civilization." The "Stationary or Retrogressive Class," on the other hand, is made up of dependents, defectives, and delinquents, degenerate types linked by "a very close and organic connection."[38] With such statements Henderson and other American criminal anthropologists established themselves and their sort as normal while relegating their inferiors to a common pool, the biologically dangerous, criminalistic underclass.

According to these criminal anthropologists, members of the criminal class are bestial, childish, drunken, and drawn to urban squalor. Including disproportionate numbers of foreigners, Catholics, and Negroes, the criminal class breeds more rapidly than upright citizens, producing ever more paupers, imbeciles, and criminals. The most self-conscious of the American criminal anthropologists, August Drähms, recognized the doctrine's class biases: "What experts claim as an indication of criminal degeneracy can hardly be construed as anything more than simple class characterization."[39] This realization did not stop Drähms from propounding the doctrine, however. His work, like that of the other authors listed in table 3, conflates the lower class with the criminal class, defining both as hereditarily unfit.

When criminal anthropologists referred to "the criminal class," they meant sometimes only criminals and sometimes all members of the lower classes. Similarly, as I have shown, when superintendents of mental retardation institutions used terms like *moral imbeciles* and *the feebleminded,* they meant sometimes only a subset of the unfit and sometimes all the unfit, their referents constantly expanding and contracting. In both cases the terminology was imprecise because it was a way of indicating a universe through a particular, of discussing all social problems by speaking of one. In the same way criminal anthropologists defined *the born criminal* as but one of several criminal types while often equating that term with all criminals. Again, imprecision was crucial to their meaning.

The *Criminal*

According to American criminal anthropologists, of all offender types, the born (or instinctive, or incorrigible) criminal departs most profoundly from normality. Covered by the stigmata of crime, he[40] is most obviously atavistic in origin. Lawbreakers of this sort, Talbot writes in a typical passage, "form a variety of the human family quite distinct from law-abiding men. A low type of physique indicating a deteriorated character gives a family likeness due to the fact that they form a community which retrogrades from generation to generation."[41] American criminal anthropologists gleefully repeat Lombroso's litany of the born criminal's physical anomalies — his heavy jaw, receding brow, scanty beard, long arms, and so on. They also closely follow Lombroso by enumerating the criminal's "psychical" anomalies — his laziness and frivolity, his use of argot, his tendency to inscribe his cell with hieroglyphs and his body with tattoos, and his moral insensibility and emotional instability.

The Americans augment Lombroso's picture of the born criminal, however, by placing greater emphasis on the criminal's weak intelligence. In the 1911 condensation of *Criminal Man,* Lombroso pays little attention to the criminal's mentality aside from stating that "*Intelligence* is feeble in some and exaggerated in others."[42] In contrast, four of the eight Americans carry Lombroso's implications to their logical conclusion by finding that criminals are mentally as well as morally weak. Talbot, for example, explains that "there is truly a brute brain within the man's, and when the latter stops short of its characteristic development, it is natural that it should manifest only its most primitive functions."[43] This American concern with the criminal's poor intelligence reflects the growing body of literature on moral imbecility.

The American authors, realizing that degeneracy could explain the criminal's bad heredity, thoroughly integrate criminal anthropology with degeneration theory. Lombroso himself was slow to adopt the degenerationist explanation, relying at first on the notion of atavism, according to which born criminals are throwbacks to earlier stages of evolution.[44] His American followers emphasize that the born criminal comes (in McKim's words) "of a degenerate line"; like Lombroso in his later work, they picture the born criminal as a product of not freakish heredity but continuous devolution.[45] Stressing the close connections among socially problematic groups, American criminal anthropologists argue that poverty, disease, and crime are interchangeable and almost indistinguishable. Henderson writes, "The Degenerate Stock has three main branches, organically united, — Dependents, Defectives and Delinquents. They are one blood."[46] Historian Mark Haller has pointed out that the term *criminal anthropology* was "in a sense . . . a misnomer," for the doctrine "was concerned with the nature and causes of all classes of human defects."[47] This was especially true of American criminal anthropology.

Other Criminal Types

Just as Lombroso eventually distinguished between the born criminal and higher offender types, so did most of his American followers create typologies that located incorrigibles at the bottom of the criminal class and ranked other offenders by the degree to which they approached normality. Ultimately these distinctions were statements about the biological causes of crime. The typologies show that whereas incorrigibles are irrevocably doomed to criminality by their bad heredity, offenders further up the evolutionary ladder are increasingly impelled by environmental forces. The American criminal anthropologists seem to have been most at ease when describing the more reformable varieties of offenders. Although they delight in reporting Lombroso's galvanizing findings about born criminals, five of the eight writers simultaneously question these findings. Uncomfortable with what we might call "hard" criminal anthropology, these authors turn with apparent relief to the "softer" form of Lombrosianism that permitted multifactorial explanations of criminal behavior and did not rule out rehabilitation for lesser offenders.

The Americans' typologies fall along a continuum that starts with the crude typification of one of the first, Boies's *Prisoners and Paupers* (1893), and ends with the highly developed typology of the series' last work, Parsons's *Responsibility for Crime* (1909). *Prisoners and Paupers* reviews the causes of degeneration at length but does not relate them to degrees of criminality. Boies's typology, moreover, is rudimentary, distinguishing merely two sorts of criminals. On the one hand are the "born" or "incorrigible" offenders who have "inherited criminality" and constitute 40 percent of the "criminal class"; the remaining 60 percent are "the victims of heteronomy [various other factors], the subjects of evil associations and environment." Only the latter can be reformed. Boies vaguely indicates that incorrigibles can be identified by number of convictions and offense seriousness, but in this first book he mostly avoids the issue of how to sort the hereditary from the heteronomic criminal.[48]

Chronologically and substantively, Drähms's book *The Criminal* (1900) marks a midpoint in the process by which criminal anthropologists articulated a hierarchy of criminal types differentiated by the causes of their offenses and their degrees of abnormality. Drähms recognizes three criminal types. The *instinctive criminal*'s "biological, moral, and intellectual equipments are the results of hereditary entailment from prenatal sources." The *habitual criminal* "draws his inspirational forces from subsequent environment rather than parental fountains." And the "essentially social misdemeanant," whom Drähms labels not a "criminal" but rather a *single offender*," is "possibly as free from the anti-social taint as the average man." The average or normal man is never a true, biological criminal; instead, "He is a criminal because the law declares it." [49]

Identifying even more criminal types, Parsons's *Responsibility for Crime*, the last work in the series, begins with the most abnormal type, the *insane criminal*, thereafter describing the *born criminal* ("His normal condition is abnormal . . . he is born to crime. It is his natural function"), the *habitual criminal* ("He is capable of something else, at least in one period of his life. The born criminal never is"), and the *professional criminal* ("frequently of a high order of intelligence,—often a college graduate. His profession becomes an art in which he sometimes becomes a master"). Of the next type on his list, the *occasional criminal*, Parsons informs us that "here, for the first time, environment plays an important part in the nature of the crime committed." The occasional criminal, moreover, "frequently possesses a keen sense of remorse" and is "frequently a useful citizen." Parsons's typology is topped by the *criminal by passion or accident*, characterized by a high "sense of duty" and "precise motive," unmarred by anomalies, and requiring neither cure nor punishment. [50]

Whereas Boies in 1893 had trouble explaining how to distinguish among criminal types, Parsons in 1909 uses explicit criteria: the frequency of physical and mental anomalies; degrees of reformability, intelligence, skill, and remorse; the extent to which environment plays a part; and the offender's ability to exercise free will ("precise motive"). Parsons has finally unraveled the implications latent in Boies's 1893 distinction between hereditary and heteronomic criminals, arriving at a hierarchy of criminal types that corresponds to social-class divisions. At the bottom of the scale is the born criminal, rough in appearance and manners, uneducated, and poor. At the summit stands the gentlemanly normal offender, anomaly-free, produced by not heredity but environment, intelligent and skilled, conscience-stricken and reformable, capable of self-determination, and requiring no state intervention.

Criminal anthropologists' "upper" groups, Thomas Zeman points out in a dissertation on the American criminological tradition, "made it possible to maintain a sharp separation, not just of degree, but of essence, between the motivation and character of the ordinary respectable citizen and that of the lower-class offender." [51] One might extend Zeman's insight by observing that this "essence" was what criminal anthropologists called "heredity." In the process of distinguishing among types of criminal bodies, criminal anthropologists established a biological hierarchy in which worthiness is gauged by class attributes. They not only constructed typologies but also structured the social and moral world around two poles, one associated with the lower-class born criminal and the other, with the middle-class professional.

Criminal Anthropology and Eugenics

Urging that punishments be tailored to fit the offender types they had identified, criminal anthropologists hoped to make justice, as well as criminology, a "science" based on the lawbreaker's biology.[52] Much as some Americans had gone beyond Lombroso in developing aspects of criminal anthropology, so too some outdid the master in deriving eugenic conclusions from his doctrine.

In *Criminal Man* and *Crime: Its Causes and Remedies*, Lombroso argues merely for individualization of consequences: "Punishments should vary according to the type of criminal." Criminals of passion and political offenders should "never" be imprisoned. For the upper-level criminaloids, probation and indeterminate sentencing are appropriate.[53] Even habitual and born criminals may be improved under the indeterminate sentence, but those who continue to demonstrate incorrigibility should be kept in "perpetual isolation in a penal colony" or, in extreme cases, executed. Lombroso makes these last recommendations not to prevent reproduction but "to realise the supreme end—social safety."[54] Only in a posthumously published article, evidently written shortly before his death in 1909, does Lombroso speak eugenically, and this in a casual remark about how life confinement of insane criminals will protect society, "making at the same time their propagation impossible."[55]

Like Lombroso, four of the eight American criminal anthropologists show little or no interest in eugenic solutions.[56] The other four champion them, however. Two—Boies and Parsons—support life sentences on the grounds that these would prevent criminals from breeding. In *Prisoners and Paupers* Boies considers himself to be a pioneer in making this argument. Most penologists, he observes, call for "permanent seclusion of the incorrigible, for the good of society; but none, so far as I am aware, have so far urged this most important of all reasons for it, the natural extirpation of this class." Boies is especially anxious to see the class "exterminated" because, he declares with his usual gusto, "the sexual sense is abnormally developed in them. They spawn their noxious progeny with as little care as the fish of the sea, and with almost equal prolificacy." Heteronomic offenders can be placed on probation; after a first or second conviction, criminals should receive completely indefinite sentences; but for those who are convicted a third time, thus revealing themselves to be born criminals, life incarceration is the solution. "The gangrened member must be cut off from the body politic."[57] Boies reiterates these eugenic recommendations in *The Science of Penology,* and Parsons essentially repeats them in *Responsibility for Crime.*

In addition to urging prophylactic life sentences, the Americans propose other eugenic measures. Several recommend marriage restrictions. "The marriages of all criminals should be prohibited," Boies explains, "but the utmost vigilance should be exercised to prevent the marriage of the instinctive."[58] Some American criminal anthropologists promote sterilization. In *The Diseases of Society* Lydston, who also authored one of the first papers on "asexualization" as "a remedy for crime," urges that rapists be castrated and all habitual criminals (male and female) be sterilized: "The confirmed criminal . . . is simply excrementitious matter that should not only be eliminated, but placed beyond the possibility of its contaminating the body social."[59]

The most extreme eugenic solution came from W. Duncan McKim. For "the *very* weak and the *very* vicious *who fall into the hands of the State,*" McKim proposes "a *gentle, painless death*" by "carbonic acid gas." This is the "surest, the simplest, the kindest, and most humane means for preventing reproduction among those whom we deem unworthy of this high privilege." Criminal types that should be thus extinguished include most murderers, the insane, the incorrigible, and "nocturnal house-breakers" (a type with which McKim evidently had suffered unhappy personal experience). Their execution would result in "a tremendous reduction in the amount of crime."[60]

As Lombroso's example indicates, there was no necessary connection between criminal anthropology and eugenics. What we see in the works of American criminal anthropologists is rather a convergence of the two doctrines, especially after the turn of the century.

The Broader Context

Few Americans were as impressed by Lombroso's theory as were these eight authors. When Hamilton Wey spoke on criminal anthropology before the National Prison Association in 1890, for example, a prison chaplain named Williams retorted, "We of the theological school are very clear in the conviction that the criminal tendencies are to be reversed by an infusion of the spiritual. . . . It seems to me that this matter of heredity is run into the ground. . . . I don't believe in Darwin."[61] Frederick H. Wines, a prominent penologist and statistician, advised that the scientific foundation for criminal anthropology was shaky indeed, and a sociologist from the University of Minnesota warned that "if the criminal anthropologist should be let loose in society to pick out criminals . . . , there is no telling who of us would escape."[62] Even advocates of criminal anthropology cautioned that "Lombroso's views are by no means universally accepted as final."[63]

Whereas few Americans abandoned themselves completely to criminal anthropology, however, many found the doctrine to be appealing and persuasive. Of the factors that nurtured American receptivity, three were particularly influential: the buildup of positivist research on criminal biology, developments in the natural sciences, and perceptions of social deterioration.

The Positivist Tradition

Although Lombrosians liked to contrast their empiricism and determinism with the free-will assumptions of earlier discussions of crime, the distinction between "new" and "old" was far less pronounced than they claimed. Their work merely made explicit a tendency to associate crime with biological defects that had been evolving throughout the nineteenth century. Benjamin Rush, Isaac Kerlin, and others who had studied innate incorrigibility had not always used quantitative or strictly inductive methods, but they had attempted to identify the physical ("material") grounds of compulsive lawbreaking. Moreover, they were determinists in that they portrayed moral imbeciles and incorrigibles as helpless, irresponsible victims of a mental ailment. Owing to the persistence of positivist methods and the theme of moral incorrigibility in U.S. work on crime causation, Americans easily digested Lombroso's scientism and his lesson that born criminals lack the "moral sense."[64]

Criminal anthropology also had much in common with phrenology, another contributor to the development of positivism. While Lombroso was still an infant, phrenologists were studying criminal skulls and adopting the medical model of crime as disease. As G. Frank Lydston observed, most criminal anthropologists "consciously or unconsciously" relied on phrenological concepts and language to explain the born criminal's moral and mental weaknesses.[65] They extended phrenology's equation of inner with outer—its belief that skull shape reflects the faculties within—from the head to the entire body, so that not only cranial protuberances but also the arm's length, the nipple's coloration, and the foot's prehensility became signs of criminality. For both groups, moreover, mind was inherited and morality based in biology.

The great degenerationists of the 1870s and 1880s, too, advanced the positivist approach to the study of crime while articulating ideas and techniques that Lombroso later adopted. Zebulon Brockway and Hamilton Wey, Richard Dugale, and J. Bruce Thomson all developed empirical methods to investigate the nature of criminality. Brockway, again with Wey, pioneered in the use of photographs to convey criminal anthropological data. Dugdale's genealogical *"Jukes"* study seemed to prove that criminality can be inherited; Lombroso himself cited *"The Jukes"* as evidence that "there are whole generations, almost all the members of which belong to the ranks of crime, insanity, and prostitution." [66] Henry Maudsley was writing about "born" criminals when Lombroso published his first book on the subject; six years earlier J. Bruce Thomson had itemized the congenital criminal's stigmata. Moreover, degenerationists came close to speaking as experts on criminality. They claimed no such specialization, of course, for they were equally concerned with pauperism and physical defects, but the line separating degenerationist studies from those of criminal anthropologists was thin indeed. Incorporating aspects of psychiatrists' and phrenologists' work, degenerationists carried forward the positivist tradition that finally freed criminal anthropologists to speak of themselves as specialists in the production of scientific knowledge.

Developments in the Natural Sciences

Criminal anthropology flourished at a time when science enjoyed an admiration verging on awe. The doctrine's particularly close fit with physical anthropology and evolutionary biology—sciences that promised to unlock the secrets of human history and human nature—made it inherently attractive and conferred on its advocates prima facie respectability. Criminal anthropology, like physical anthropology, focused on comparative anatomy and physiology. It, too, aimed at classifying humankind into types through the study of skulls. For a public familiar with research on American Indian tribes and the extensive anthropological collections at the Smithsonian and other museums, it was but a short step to the classification of the criminal, a type as exotic as any Inca or Hottentot.

Speculation about evolution and humans' relationship to less complex organisms ran strong from the early years of the nineteenth century, nourished by work in the natural sciences and by the English sociologist Herbert Spencer, who coined the phrase "survival of the fittest." [67] Such speculation intensified with the 1859 publication of *The Origin of Species,* in which Darwin argues that "the innumerable species, genera, and families of organic beings, with which this world is peopled, have all descended . . . from common parents." [68] Commonly misunderstood as a "monkey theory" of evolution, Darwin's ideas seemed to be congruent with the notion of the criminal as an animalistic holdover from the primitive past. [69] Passages in which Darwin remarks on "rudimentary, atrophied, or aborted organs," moreover, could easily be read as confirmations of Lombroso's reports of the criminal's snakelike teeth and other animalistic anomalies. [70]

Many natural science findings suggested that evolution is purposeful, its goal an ever-higher civilization. If this is true, then it follows that the criminal must be primitive, a holdover from an earlier evolutionary stage. Some of Darwin's own statements appear to equate adaptation with progress. In the final pages of *The Origin of Species* he rhapsodizes that "from the war of nature, . . . the most exalted object which we are capable of conceiving, namely, the production of the higher animals, directly follows." *The Descent of Man* (1871), in which Darwin applies his theory of evolution specifically to humans, argues that man's "intellectual and moral faculties" are "inherited" and "perfected or advanced through natural selection." [71] With nature itself apparently striving to advance civilization, surely progressive nations should help by getting rid of born criminals.

America's Deterioration

As the nineteenth century drew to a close, middle-class Americans increasingly perceived a deterioration in the nation's health. One source of weakness seemed to be the hordes of "new immigrants" from southern and eastern Europe. As the photographs in Boies's *Prisoners and Paupers* graphically demonstrated, Syrians, Sicilians, and Russian Jews came from decaying stock. In neither body, mind, nor morals did they measure up to earlier, Anglo-Saxon immigrants. Pouring into American cities, the new immigrants were creating a host of sanitary, educational, and political problems that further drained the nation's energies.

A close look, moreover, revealed that even native-born Americans were less sturdy than in former years and that the sickliest among them had begun to contaminate rural areas, those cradles of American tradition and values. For example, sociologist Frank Blackmar, dean of faculty at the University of Kansas, discovered that a "social residuum" of tramp families, Juke-like clans with "pauper and criminal tendencies," was fastening on country communities, causing "social degeneration." [72] "Considered in themselves, they seem scarcely worth saving," Blackmar observed. "But from social considerations it is necessary to save such people, that society may be perpetuated. The principle of social evolution is to make the strong stronger that the purpose of social life may be conserved, but to do this the weak must be cared for or they will eventually destroy or counteract the efforts of the strong. We need social sanitation." [73] Sapped by immigrants on the one hand and native-born paupers on the other, the nation's health was in alarming decline.

Henry Boies perceived "a general degeneracy" everywhere: the " 'lower tenth' " of the population was multiplying rapidly while all ranks were being depleted by " 'constitutional' defects" and by imbecility, suicide, and insanity. "Stature is decreasing," Boies warned, "the proportion of normal perfectly healthy people diminishing, the general average of physical endurance and vitality becoming lowered . . . ; hair, the common indication of vigor, is disappearing, and bald heads becoming numerous early in life; weak nerves, weak stomachs, weak hearts, weak heads are ordinary ailments. All these are indicative of a general deterioration, which must be due to faulty breeding."[74] W. Duncan McKim similarly warned of an "ever-strengthening torrent of defective and criminal humanity."[75]

Not only individuals but the body politic was deteriorating. Many Americans now perceived their nation as a vast organism, its parts interconnected by the hidden currents of blood and heredity. If one part grew ill, its poisons might secretly infect the whole. The crime problem, then, included not only criminals but also criminality, the biological taint that flowed from criminals into the body of society. It seemed obvious that the crucial need was to increase control over the bodies of those who, like the anthropological born criminal, propagated the diseases of society.

Notes

1. Conceptually this chapter is indebted to Haskell 1977 and Ross 1979, 1991.

2. By 1911 leading writers had rejected Lombroso's doctrine; see, e.g., Parmelee [1911] 1918.

3. Werlinder (1978:71) suggests that the term *criminology* was coined at a criminal anthropology conference in 1883.

4. On Lombroso's own attitudes, see Lombroso-Ferrero [1911] 1972:5.

5. Lydston 1896:347–48.

6. Ibid., 349.

7. Wey 1890:275.

8. Drähms [1900] 1971:22.

9. MacDonald 1893:173; Boies 1901; Talbot 1898:viii.

10. Henry Boies and Charles R. Henderson, both of whom also produced criminal anthropological books in 1893, have equal claim to publishing the first American book on criminal anthropology. I give priority to MacDonald partly because his book was copyrighted a year earlier and partly because it is labeled "Second Edition." The "second edition" claim is a false one, however, and in taking it into consideration I am in effect allowing MacDonald's misrepresentation to bully me. For more on MacDonald, including his tendencies to bully and to oversell himself, see Gilbert 1977.

11. MacDonald 1893:17.

12. Boies 1893:266, 265.

13. Green 1985:10.

14. Pick 1989:115.

15. For more on this rhetoric, see Sekula 1986. Interestingly, some of the best recent analyses of criminal anthropology have come from historians of photography.

16. Garland (1985:93) makes a similar point when he writes that "in claiming to have discovered criminality in the bodies or the brains or the milieux of criminals, criminology claimed a social and scientific space for itself."

17. Benedikt 1881:vii; he was also aware of Lombroso's investigations.

18. Ibid., 157 (original entirely capitalized for emphasis).

19. Fink [1938] 1962:107–9 reviews the impact of Benedikt's study on U.S. physicians.

20. I do not deal here with the work of Lombroso's colleagues, Enrico Ferri and Raffaele Garofalo, partly because they were so closely associated with him and partly because I could not confidently gauge their impact on U.S. criminal anthropology. Some American criminal anthropologists cite Ferri; as a group they were poor footnoters, however, and it is sometimes tempting to conclude from internal evidence that they were using secondary sources instead of the Italian and French originals that they cite.

21. Lombroso 1893, [1900] 1971, 1895; Lombroso and Ferrero [1895] 1915; Lombroso-Ferrero [1911] 1972; Lombroso [1911] 1918. Neither *The Female Offender* nor *L'uomo delinquente* has been completely translated into English. A French edition of *L'uomo delinquente, L'Homme criminel,* became available considerably earlier (1887, 1895) than the English translation; several American criminal anthropologists cite it as their source on Lombroso's work.

22. Indeed, access to Lombroso's work remains limited. Because much of it remains untranslated, I have no way of tracing his development over time.

23. Fowler in Benedikt 1881:xi.

24. Savitz 1972:xix. I was unable to identify the translators of *The Female Offender* (Lombroso and Ferrero [1895] 1915) and *Criminal Man* (Lombroso-Ferrero [1911] 1972).

25. In addition to writing *The Criminal,* Ellis wrote on criminal anthropology in his preface to Winter's *New York State Reformatory at Elmira* (Ellis 1891). On how he came to write *The Criminal,* see Grosskurth 1985:115–16.

26. Jastrow 1886:22, 20.

27. Noyes 1888.

28. Wey 1888, 1890.

29. After formulating this definition of "leading American criminal anthropologists," I listed all books mentioned in the relevant chapters of three secondary sources on U.S. criminal anthropology: Fink's *Causes of Crime: Biological Theories in the United States, 1800–1915* ([1938] 1962); Haller's *Eugenics: Hereditarian Attitudes in American Thought* (1963); and Zeman's dissertation on the American criminological tradition (1981). When I excluded books on juvenile crime and general sociology from these lists and reduced Arthur MacDonald's many criminal anthropological works to one, *Criminology* (his major study), I ended up with nine books by eight authors. I then read the nine books to discover whether they frequently cited other works that fit my definition. I found that, writings by the originators and channelers aside, they primarily referred to previously published books already on my list. This made me confident that my nine books were indeed influential and that their authors did constitute a core group that included the major American writers on criminal anthropology.

30. Henderson 1893:ix. Parsons subsequently wrote two works clearly designed as textbooks (1924, 1926), and he authored no other books. Talbot (1898:viii) states that *Degeneracy* "has been written with a special intention of reaching educators and parents"; however, its density of scientific detail would have made it more appealing to scholars. Lydston ([1904] 1905:9) states that *The Diseases of Society* is "intended primarily for professional readers," although he hopes that it will also do "a little missionary work" among "the reading public."

31. MacDonald 1893: cover page.

32. Gilbert 1977:176.

33. Boies and Henderson had direct contact with prisoners as social welfare workers; Drähms, as San Quentin's chaplain; and Lydston, as resident surgeon at New York's Blackwell Island Penitentiary.

34. MacDonald 1893:271, speaking of "social science" but referring to criminology.

35. Kellor 1901:5.

36. Boies 1893:265–66.

37. Sekula 1986:15; also see Zeman 1981:378–79.

38. Henderson 1893:13–14.

39. Drähms [1900] 1971:31.

40. Lombroso's *Female Offender* (1895) had little influence on the American criminal anthropologists discussed here; with the partial exception of Lydston ([1904] 1905), they pay almost no attention to female born criminals. Because my main interest here lies in the substance of writings by American criminal anthropologists, I follow their lead by focusing on male born criminals and using masculine pronouns in this chapter. On nineteenth-century female criminals, see Gibson 1982, 1990; and, more generally, Fee 1979.

41. Talbot 1898:18.

42. Lombroso-Ferrero [1911] 1972:41 (emphasis in original); also see Lombroso and Ferrero [1895] 1915:170–71.

43. Talbot 1898:18. Lydston (to give a second example) observes that "a defective moral sense is most likely to be associated with defective development of the brain in general," concluding that it is "not surprising that the typic or born criminal should lack intelligence" ([1904] 1905:496). The two other works that deal with the criminal's intelligence are MacDonald's *Criminology* (1893), which devotes an entire chapter to the subject, and Drähms's *The Criminal* ([1900] 1971), which goes so far as to reverse the typical Lombrosian presentation by discussing the criminal's mental and moral abnormalities before his physical stigmata.

44. On the lateness of Lombroso's embrace of degeneration theory, see Parmelee [1911] 1918:xxix; Pick 1989:120; and Wolfgang 1972:247, 249.

45. McKim 1900:23.

46. Henderson 1893:114.

47. Haller 1963:16.

48. Boies 1893:184, 178, 185.

49. Drähms [1900] 1971:55–57.

50. Parsons 1909:35–44.

51. Zeman 1981:390.

52. E.g., Parsons 1909:194.

53. Lombroso-Ferrero [1911] 1972:185, 186–87. By "indeterminate sentence" Lombroso seems to have meant a sentence that has no maximum but nonetheless anticipates the offender's eventual release.

54. Lombroso-Ferrero [1911] 1972:198, 208; also see Lombroso [1911] 1918: part 3, chaps. 2 and 3, p. 216.

55. Lombroso 1912:60. This is the only eugenical remark by Lombroso that I have found, but one might get a very different impression from works not yet translated into English.

56. Talbot (1898:347–48) explicitly rejects eugenics, while MacDonald (1893) and Drähms ([1900] 1971) recommend life imprisonment to incapacitate born criminals physically but not reproductively. Henderson (1893:229) proposes "a life sentence for recidivists" for mildly eugenical reasons ("to reduce the supply of morally deformed offspring"), but merely in passing.

57. Boies 1893:181, 175–76, 178–90, 267.

58. Boies 1901:239.

59. Lydston [1904] 1905:8, 424, 564, 566. Marriage restriction is also recommended by Boies (1893:280), Lydston ([1904] 1905:557–62), and Parsons (1909: 198–99). Sterilization is advocated by Boies (1893:270–73; 1901:123), as well as by Lydston.

60. McKim 1900:188 (emphases in original), 193 , 188, 192, 255. Boies and Parsons praised McKim's proposal while reluctantly rejecting it, Boies (1901:53) because he feared that "public sentiment does not yet support the purely scientific plan of Dr. McKim" and Parsons (1909:90) because it was too violent.

61. National Prison Association, *Proceedings, 1890,* pp. 290–91.

62. F. Wines 1895: chap. 11; S. Smith 1896:255.

63. Henderson 1893:113; also see Lydston [1904] 1905:25–26; MacDonald 1893:60–61; and Parsons 1909, *inter alia.*

64. Lombroso-Ferrero [1911] 1972:28.

65. Lydston [1904] 1905:156. For an example of how another criminal anthropologist relied on phrenological concepts, see Talbot 1898:8, explaining that "a predisposition to certain diseases, *seated in parts contiguous to the seat of insanity,* often descends from parents to their children" and that insanity sometimes perverts the "moral faculties" while at others bypassing "all the faculties of the mind" (emphases added).

66. Lombroso-Ferrero [1911] 1972:139.

67. On pre-Darwinism evolutionary theory and Spencer, see Burrow 1985 and Hofstadter 1955.

68. Darwin [1859] 1985:434.

69. P. Becker (1994) argues that Lombroso derived his theory of the criminal as atavism not from Darwin but from other evolutionists who stressed recapitulation, the idea that every human starts at step one in the evolutionary process. Criminals differ from the lawful in that they do not evolve as far.

70. Darwin [1859] 1985:428; Lombroso-Ferrero [1911] 1972:7.

71. Darwin [1859] 1985:459; Darwin [1871] 1986:496.
72. Blackmar [1897] 1988:57, 64, 56.
73. Ibid., 65.
74. Boies 1893:278–79.
75. McKim 1900:iii.

7

The Criminal Imbecile

Psychology needs the defective.

Henry Herbert Goddard, "Psychological Work
among the Feeble-Minded"

Early in the twentieth century a Parisian physician proposed an ingenious new method for identifying repeat offenders. If detectives were to inject a bit of paraffin under the skin of each person they arrested, the physician pointed out, the permanent small bumps would enable police to recognize recidivists.[1] This proposal to brand the criminal's body says as much about the decline of criminal anthropology as about alarm over habitual offenders: if the criminal body must be marked, then faith has been lost in Lombroso's doctrine of the stigmata of crime.

In the United States the decline of criminal anthropology merely whetted appetites for a better biological theory of crime. The first two decades of the twentieth century are often called the "Progressive Era" for their energetic liberal reforms, their optimism, and their environmentalist attacks on social problems; they were also decades during which the eugenics movement enjoyed its greatest popularity. But there is no real contradiction here. Although hereditarian themes hardened in the early twentieth century, confidence in the efficacy of reform persisted as well.

Reformers continued to conceive of society as an organism, a living body whose health depends on the strength of its members' germ plasm.

Earlier, drawing on Lamarck's theory of the inheritance of acquired characteristics, they had been able to hope that individuals might be able to upgrade the quality of their own germ plasm, improvements that in time might spread to the whole. Recent advances in genetics forced them to abandon that hope, but there was still ground for optimism: a vigorous eugenics program could reduce the number of mental defectives in the next generation. Progressive men and women remained buoyant about the future by substituting for the old, "individual" Lamarckism a "social" Lamarckism in which the social body would acquire new characteristics through eugenics. Far from undermining the confidence with which Progressive reformers faced the future, eugenics reinforced it. Reformers thus experienced no tension between their desire to improve society and their calls for stern measures against the unimprovable. They proudly asserted their ability to be liberal and conservative at the same time.

The intellectual and emotional currents that had encouraged American receptivity to Lombroso's work built in intensity. Fear of social deterioration persisted, with its sense of contamination by swarthy-skinned immigrants and native-born dependents, defectives, and delinquents, but this fear merely strengthened the Progressive determination to improve social control. The American reverence for science blossomed in enthusiasm for eugenics and the related sciences of psychology, psychiatry, and statistics. And although criminal anthropology had failed to deliver on its promise, positivists discovered an even more promising tool for identifying and classifying offenders in newly devised tests of intelligence.

The Advent of IQ Testing

The Vineland, New Jersey, Training School for Feeble-minded Boys and Girls led in constructing a new born-criminal type, the criminal imbecile.[2] Picking up where the Elmira Reformatory had left off, in the early twentieth century Vineland became the nation's most fertile site for the production of eugenic criminology. Vineland received state cases, but because it remained under private control, it was able to attract private funding and to conduct eugenics research that could not have been undertaken in a public setting.[3] Its superintendent, Edward R. Johnstone, became a leader of the American eugenics movement. Whereas most superintendents of institutions for the retarded were physicians, Johnstone was an educator. This background meant that "the professor" (as colleagues called him) was less defensive than other superintendents when nonmedical personnel from the new profession of psychology began diagnosing feeblemindedness.[4] It also meant that if scientific research were to be done at Vineland, he would need to call in an outsider.

The outsider whom Johnstone hired was Henry Herbert Goddard, a psychologist teaching at the nearby State Normal School in West Chester, Pennsylvania. Goddard had recently received a Ph.D from Clark University, where he had studied psychology under G. Stanley Hall, a specialist in child development. The field of psychology was in the process of emancipating itself from philosophy, where it had long found its disciplinary home, and becoming an empirical science. Psychologists were still trying to define their knowledge base, to identify the areas of life to which their field would be relevant, and to validate their claims to scientific expertise. During the Progressive period they exhibited what one historian describes as an "extremely self-conscious and relentless concern for full-scale development, and for stature" as scientists and professionals.[5] Goddard's Vineland work showed how the "new" psychology could use mental testing to bring the problems of feeblemindedness and crime under social control. In the process of helping to create the criminal imbecile, Goddard also helped to establish psychology as a science.[6]

The Johnstone-Goddard collaboration began in 1901, when the training school's new director and the young psychology teacher, already slight acquaintances, met at a child study conference in New Jersey. On the train back to Philadelphia, Johnstone proposed formation of what became jocularly known as the "Feeble-Minded Club," a group that included Goddard and met biannually to discuss issues related to feeblemindedness. The club soon began projecting plans for a psychological research division, modeled after the in-house laboratories of academic psychologists, where "problems of human growth and development" could be "scientifically studied under controlled conditions."[7] Johnstone obtained funding from local philanthropists—Samuel Fels, a soap manufacturer, contributed especially generously to the laboratory's work—and wrote to G. Stanley Hall to ask whom he should invite to become the division's director. Probably no one was surprised when Hall recommended his former student, Henry Goddard. Thus in 1906 Goddard became director of research at the Vineland Laboratory.

Goddard soon realized that psychologists had woefully few resources for helping superintendents to train and manage the feebleminded. The superintendents were unable to define their clientele precisely and lacked a foolproof method for screening out the insane, who were still sometimes confused with the feebleminded. The superintendents were also vulnerable to accusations of accepting improper commitments (a charge to which, in their perplexity, some freely pleaded guilty), and they worried about accidentally institutionalizing someone brilliant, such as the blind and deaf Helen Keller. At Vineland Goddard had to rely on old-fashioned methods of classifying the feebleminded according to their motor reactions and ability to perform simple peg-in-hole tasks. An early paper entitled

"Psychological Work among the Feeble-Minded" shows him groping for something that he, as a psychologist, can contribute to the understanding of feeblemindedness. Nonetheless, he is already certain that "the problem of the feeble-minded is a psychological and educational problem," not primarily a medical one. Psychology, he states, has much to learn from the study of defective minds, but "if psychology needs the defective, vastly more does the defective need the psychologist." [8]

Searching for better methods, in 1908 Goddard traveled to Europe to study the work of Continental institutions for the feebleminded. In Belgium he learned of a new method of measuring intelligence through questions keyed to levels of mental development. Alfred Binet, a French psychologist, and his collaborator, Dr. Théodore Simon, were asking children to perform groups of tasks that were graded in an order of increasing difficulty and that corresponded to stages in normal development. Thus the Binet method permitted the tester to scale results by "mental age." This system produced easily understood standards, and unlike earlier methods of testing, it measured complex mental processes. [9]

Goddard found Binet's method to be promising but initially doubted its efficacy as a tool for classifying the feebleminded. On returning to the United States, he described the Binet-Simon tests to the superintendents of institutions for the feebleminded while expressing his own preference for traditional classification criteria: "I have a feeling that a [sic] motor control—how the child handles its muscles—may be ultimately a stronger basis of classification than the mental process,—the more purely psychological. Mind is a very evanescent thing; . . . it is the sum of processes and experiences and consequently very difficult to measure." [10] Nevertheless, the superintendents in the Association of American Institutions for the Feeble-Minded (AAIF) (as the AMO had been renamed) realized that a classification scheme based on the Binet-Simon tests would be more rapid, accurate, and precise than were current methods. It would enable them to shelve the medical classifications that had proved to be unsatisfactory, such as "microcephaly" and "Mongolism," and it could give them uniform standards for admitting and classifying inmates. Goddard came around to their point of view. After some verification of Binet's system at the Vineland Training School, Goddard excitedly deemed it a method of "marvelous accuracy" and "remarkable perfection." He revised, translated, and published Binet's questions. Between 1910 and 1914 the Vineland Laboratory distributed 20,000 test booklets and 80,000 record blanks, supplying the materials to anyone who requested them. [11]

Educators, prison physicians, and psychologists greeted the Binet tests with open arms. Never before had Americans had an efficient, quantitative means of gauging intelligence. Goddard's reworking of Binet's 1908 questions served as the principal method of testing intelligence in the United States until Lewis M. Terman's Stanford Revision appeared in 1916.[12]

As other psychologists soon realized, however, Goddard's version of the Binet-Simon tests produced inaccurate results. As early as March 1912 Lewis M. Terman, a Stanford University psychologist, identified a major failing: "The scale originally offered by Binet is, in general, far too easy at the lower end, while in the upper range it is too difficult." Moreover, Terman continued, some of Binet's specific tests were "objectionable or unsatisfactory for other reasons."[13] Frederick Kuhlmann, a psychologist at the Faribault, Minnesota, school for the feebleminded, observed that Goddard's standardization of the Binet scale on 2,000 normal children was marred. Some children had coached one another in the answers, the tests had been administered too quickly, Goddard's data did not always support his conclusions, and he had failed to follow his own "previous conclusions as to which tests are misplaced in the scale entirely."[14] Goddard's colleagues were also troubled by the way he encouraged amateurs to use the tests. The Vineland psychologist had announced that "even novices may use the Binet Scale, provided that they use it with ordinary good sense," and he accepted "evidence" that research assistants obtained by bypassing the tests entirely in favor of "subjective" assessments of feeblemindedness, some on persons long dead.[15]

Goddard was not the only Progressive psychologist to use intelligence testing carelessly and for eugenical ends,[16] but many of his colleagues insisted on higher scientific standards. Goddard's biographer suggests that the tests' usefulness in institutions for the feebleminded may have blinded him to their faults.[17] Their usefulness to eugenicists, who quickly perceived the tests' potential for identifying the unfit, may have blinded him as well.

Discovering the Criminal Imbecile

Goddard began contributing to born-criminal theory in 1910, when he collapsed two earlier categories of mental defect, upper-grade "feeblemindedness" and "moral imbecility," into the single concept of the criminalistic "moron." The AAIF superintendents had recently arrived at something close to this revision on their own, but Goddard completed it and confirmed its validity. His definition of the moron delivered the coup de grace to criminal anthropology, replacing its version of the born criminal with a more psychological one.

On hearing Goddard outline the diagnostic potential of the Binet scale in 1909, the AAIF superintendents appointed a committee, including Goddard, to recommend a new method of classifying the feebleminded based on intelligence testing. The next year Goddard reported that Vineland research with the Binet tests now enabled him to define the levels of mental retardation by mental age: *idiots* were those who tested under one or two years, *imbeciles* tested at ages three to seven, and *the feebleminded* tested between years eight and twelve. Because no Vineland inmate had tested above twelve in mental age, and because he assumed that the institution held no erroneous commitments, Goddard further proposed mental age twelve as the cutoff point for feeblemindedness.[18]

Goddard went on to point out that members of the upper-level category lacked a clear identifier, since *feebleminded* might also refer to everyone who was intellectually subnormal. To denote high-grade defectives more precisely, Goddard suggested a new term—*moron*, "from the Greek word meaning foolish." [19] He hoped to sensitize laypeople to the moron's unfitness:

> The public is entirely ignorant of this particular group. Our public school systems are full of them, and yet superintendents and boards of education are struggling to make normal people out of them. One of the most helpful things that we can do would be to distinctly mark out the limits of this class and help the general public to understand that they are a special group and require special treatment,—in institutions when possible, in special classes in public schools, when institutions are out of reach.[20]

Thus Goddard consciously sought to expand perceptions of mental subnormality and to bring more of the feebleminded under institutional control. The AAIF adopted his "moron" terminology and his mental-age definitions for the grades. Their decision to use intelligence tests diagnostically, historian Leila Zenderland observes, "marked a stunning victory, not only for Goddard but for applied psychology, for it defined and institutionalized a new diagnostic function for the emerging profession." [21]

Not yet done, at the momentous 1910 meeting Goddard went on to equate the moron with the moral imbecile. He had administered Binet tests to the Vineland school's moral imbeciles, "those children that give trouble because of their inability to either understand the simplest moral law or to conform to it at all," including cases of "marked sexual disturbance." All twenty-three cases had tested between the mental ages of nine and twelve.[22] Drawing on the evolutionary explanation of moral backwardness that criminal anthropologists had used before him, Goddard hypothesized that the "primitive" instincts "that lead the child to become what we loosely call a moral imbecile, ripen about the age of nine years; now if a child is arrested in his development at just about that time then he is a liar, a thief, a sex pervert, or whatever else he may be, because those instincts are strong in him. . . . Had he been arrested in his development a year or two sooner, he would not have been a moral imbecile because the instincts that lead to it had not developed." Or, if development stopped later, "he would have developed sufficient reasoning power to enable him to overcome and control those instincts." Morons, because their moral evolution stopped "at just that critical period of nine," would inevitably be liars, thieves, and other criminal types.[23]

Goddard's contemporaries were preaching much the same message about the evils inherent in the upper-grade feebleminded, but with less precision and force. For example, in the twentieth century's first major work on mental retardation, *Mental Defectives*,[24] Martin Barr spoke of the feebleminded as "low and . . . bestial, . . . ignorant and . . . weak, . . . silly and irresponsible, . . . festering sores in the life of society."[25] Barr continued to treat moral imbecility as a separate category, but superintendent Walter E. Fernald of Massachusetts threw it out about two years before Goddard defined the moron. In a landmark paper entitled "The Imbecile with Criminal Instincts," Fernald concluded that "*every imbecile, especially the high-grade imbecile, is a potential criminal.*" These imbeciles, Fernald maintained, are equivalent to the instinctive criminal of criminal anthropology, and they are equally marked by "physical and psychical stigmata."[26] Anticipating Goddard's "moron" category, Fernald threw out the traditional distinction between moral imbeciles and high-grade imbeciles: the former used to be considered cases "without intellectual defect," he explained, but "long observation and close analysis" had now "demonstrated that they were cases of true imbecility."[27]

Goddard applauded Fernald's critique of the older distinction between mental and moral imbeciles: "The notion that a child may be born with his natural faculties all right and his moral faculties all wrong is a notion that belongs to the middle ages of sociology and ethics as well."[28] When he later coined the term *moron*, Goddard was merely suggesting a more concise label for Fernald's "imbecile with criminal instincts."

Goddard far outstripped contemporaries, however, by using science to define and verify the concept of the criminal imbecile, or moron (he used both terms), and by popularizing it. Once he had formulated the concept, it became strategically important for Goddard to measure the intelligence of offenders. If he could show that criminals are inherently moronic, he could bolster his claim that morons are inherently criminalistic. Goddard started with juvenile delinquents, and like others who administered early versions of Binet's tests to institutionalized offenders, he found that the majority were intellectually inferior.[29]

In *Feeble-Mindedness: Its Causes and Consequences* (1914) Goddard reviews sixteen studies of institutionalized delinquents that yielded figures on defectiveness ranging from 28 to 89 percent. He professes to find it "most discouraging to discover that the more expert is the examiner of these groups, the higher is the percentage of feeble-minded found."[30] He nevertheless feels compelled to accept the test scores' evidence. From these data on youthful offenders, Goddard generalizes to "criminals," speculating that 25 to 50 percent of adult prisoners are mentally defective. "*The so-called criminal type is merely a type of feeble-mindedness*," he concludes. Then, openly bidding to replace the criminal anthropologist, Goddard claims that "*it is hereditary feeble-mindedness not hereditary criminality that accounts for the conditions.*"[31] His criminal imbecile theory provides the true explanation of innate criminality.

Criminals without Crimes

Goddard reduced the born criminal to a youthful potential offender. Lombroso's born criminal had been a full-grown, hairy monstrosity; Goddard's was an incorrigible child, chronologically as well as mentally. Moreover, although Goddard did write about a few underage killers, the majority of his cases were at worst guilty of antisocial behavior. Menaces rather than monsters, they were merely incapable of managing their affairs "with ordinary prudence."[32] Fernald describes them as "criminals who have actually committed no crime."[33] One could now be a born criminal without breaking the law.

This infantilization of the born criminal was crucial to the argument of Progressive criminologists: to establish the oneness of criminals and the feebleminded, they had to define both conditions quite loosely. In a revealing passage Goddard notes that mental testers are able to identify larger proportions of defectives in juvenile reformatories than in adult prisons "partly because it is difficult to believe that an adult man or woman who makes a fair appearance but who lacks in certain lines, is not simply ignorant. We are more willing to admit the defect of children."[34] In the literature on crime "the criminal" had been looming in importance and the criminal act receding into the background since the 1870s. Now the act disappeared entirely as Goddard and others defined the criminal in terms of fundamental incapacity.

Goddard brought to fruition ideas about criminal responsibility and treatment that had been ripening for decades. Delegates to the 1870 prison congress had questioned the responsibility of even ordinary offenders, and criminal anthropologists had held that the born criminal is no more responsible than the insane. Goddard streamlined the criminal anthropologists' typologies, with their series of discrete categories, by representing responsibility as a continuum corresponding to the continuous distribution of intelligence itself: "there are all grades of responsibility, from zero to the highest," and "all grades of intelligence from practically none up to that of the genius or most gifted. *Responsibility varies according to the intelligence.*"[35] Feebleminded offenders are predestined to behave irresponsibly. The fault lies not with them but with their biology.

The Inheritance of Feeblemindedness

To show that the moron is a eugenic threat, Goddard had to prove that feeblemindedness is inherited. Criminal anthropologists and other degenerationists had been able to show no more than an *association* between mental defect and bad heredity. Goddard used recent advances in genetics to demonstrate that the relationship is causal. According to Goddard, a single unit character (what we would call a "gene") inevitably produces mental defect. Feeblemindedness is inherited as a recessive trait. Coupled with Goddard's finding that "every feeble-minded person is a potential criminal," this account indicated that criminality too is transmitted by heredity.[36]

Fifty years earlier Gregor Mendel, an Austrian monk, had formulated laws of inheritance from experiments with garden peas. According to Mendel's laws, parental traits do not blend in offspring; rather, some are dominant and others recessive, with different combinations producing predictable ratios of dominants to recessives in subsequent generations. European biologists unearthed this forgotten law in 1900, just as the work of another nineteenth-century geneticist, August Weismann, gained acceptance. Weismann had rejected Lamarck's theory of the inheritance of acquired characteristics and advocated the theory of the continuity of germ plasm—the idea that chromosomal germ cells determine heredity. The work of Mendel and Weismann stimulated the growth of both modern genetics and eugenics, fields that overlapped in the early twentieth century.[37]

American eugenicists, assuming that many human traits are transmitted as unit characters, as is height in Mendel's peas, produced scores of studies showing that bad temper, epilepsy, feeblemindedness, and other negative attributes obey Mendel's laws. Their research was orchestrated by Charles B. Davenport, a prominent figure in the American eugenics movement and director of both the Station for Experimental Evolution and the Eugenics Record Office at Cold Spring Harbor, Long Island. In 1909 Davenport organized groups to study various aspects of inheritance, appointing a committee on feeblemindedness that included Fernald and Goddard.[38] It was probably through this contact with Davenport that Goddard absorbed Mendel's formula.

The difficulties inherent in performing genetic research on living humans forced Goddard, as well as other eugenicists, to fall back on pedigree studies, a type of investigation for which Galton's *Hereditary Genius* and Dugdale's *"Jukes"* provided prototypes. With more financial assistance from Samuel Fels, Goddard trained eugenic field-workers to investigate the genealogies of Vineland's inmates.[39]

In his preliminary report on these investigations, an article titled "Heredity of Feeble-Mindedness" that appeared in a 1911 issue of *The Eugenics Review*, Goddard uses the vivid iconography that became characteristic of Progressive Era pedigree studies. This set of symbols, which Goddard evidently invented,[40] distills the argument of eugenics to a simple visual code. Whereas Galton, Dugdale, and other previous genealogists had written in names on their family trees, Goddard uses squares to indicate males and circles to indicate females, presenting all members of a single generation in one row. Within each square or circle, he indicates normality with an N and feeblemindedness with an *F*, thus visually conveying his assumption that N and F are dichotomous.[41] Those squares or circles marked *F* are blackened, betokening the evil of the feebleminded. In this preliminary article Goddard presents the heredity charts with few comments — but few are needed, for the charts clearly demonstrate that the mating of two feebleminded persons produces feebleminded offspring.[42] The charts seem to track not individuals but heredity itself.

In his more definitive report on the genealogies of Vineland's inmates, *Feeble-Mindedness: Its Causes and Consequences*, Goddard "confesses to being one of those psychologists who find it hard to accept the idea that the intelligence even *acts like a unit character*. But there seems to be no way to escape the conclusion from these figures." The book presents pedigree charts, photographs, and graphs that force readers to the same conclusion. "Normal-mindedness is, or at least behaves like, a unit character; is dominant and is transmitted in accordance with the Mendelian law of inheritance." When this determiner is absent, the result is feeblemindedness. Goddard also recognizes "nonhereditary" causes of feeblemindedness such as spinal meningitis, but these constitute fewer than one-third of his cases. The primary cause of feeblemindedness, he shows, is inheritance; unions of the feebleminded "practically always give defective children." More complicated matings between people with one normal and one feebleminded parent yield "three normals to one defective" — just as Mendel's formula predicts.[43]

Incorporating Mendel's and Weismann's theories, Goddard carefully specifies that bad heredity causes feeblemindedness, with feeblemindedness in turn causing crime, alcoholism, prostitution, truancy, and other social ills. Such statements seem to reject the degenerationist idea that feeblemindedness, criminality, and other social problems are interchangeable. Nonetheless, degenerationist premises lurk just below the surface of *Feeble-Mindedness: Its Causes and Consequences*, encouraging Goddard to begin with the idea that dependency, defectiveness, and delinquency must be related. He was not the only Progressive Era eugenicist to have one foot in nineteenth-century degenerationism and the other in twentieth-century genetics. Many of his contemporaries, including Davenport, Fernald, and Terman, also continued drawing on degeneration theory, even while recasting it in twentieth-century terms.[44]

Marketing the Criminal Imbecile

Henry Goddard was the first American born-criminal theorist to reach a mass audience. Although the majority of his publications were semischolarly, as were those of his predecessors, Goddard produced two books for a wide readership. The first, *The Kallikak Family* (1912), proved the criminality of the feebleminded. The second, *The Criminal Imbecile* (1915), proved the feeblemindedness of criminals.

Goddard viewed *The Kallikak Family* (a pedigree study reprinted eight times during his lifetime) and *The Criminal Imbecile* (an account of "three remarkable murder cases" reprinted in 1922) as tools for educating "the lay reader" about psychometrics and eugenics.[45] In this respect they were part of a eugenics propaganda literature that included other studies of cacogenic, or bad-gened, families. In these books, however, Goddard delivers his message in narrative form. Moreover, whereas other authors get lost in a wilderness of data, Goddard focuses clearly on his theme of the born criminal.[46]

The Kallikak Family describes two branches of one family, one good (*kali* in Greek) and the other bad (*kako*), but both sired by one Martin Kallikak Sr. The first branch began with Martin's liaison, in a tavern during the Revolutionary War, with "a feeble-minded girl." From this coupling flowed over 480 illegitimate, alcoholic, epileptic, and above all feebleminded and criminalistic descendants, down to Deborah Kallikak, one of Goddard's main characters. Deborah ends this half of the story biologically as well as narratively: because she is an inmate of the Vineland school, there will be no more bad Kallikaks. The other branch stemmed from Martin's marriage to "a respectable girl of good family"; their 496 descendants were all normal or superior in intelligence, "men and women prominent in every phase of social life."[47] Goddard believed that in the Kallikaks, nature had provided a kind of controlled experiment, one that held the sire constant while varying the consort. The two-branched family seemed to demonstrate, as Dugdale's monolithic Jukes family could not, that "no amount of education or good environment can change a feeble-minded individual into a normal one."[48]

Having argued in *The Kallikak Family* that the feebleminded are hopelessly delinquent, Goddard argues in *The Criminal Imbecile* that delinquents are hopelessly feebleminded. Concentrating on the issue of criminal responsibility, he contends that imbeciles should be exempted from criminal punishment, just as the insane are. He himself recently secured an acquittal "on the ground of criminal imbecility" for Jean Gianini, a boy who had committed a seemingly "cold-blooded murder of the most atrocious character . . . with a fiendishness seldom seen among human beings." Owing to Goddard's work for the defense, "For the first time in history psychological tests of intelligence have been admitted into court and the mentality of the accused established on the basis of these facts." [49] Physicians who testified at Gianini's trial failed to recognize his imbecility. Thus (Goddard broadly hints) psychologists should replace them as courtroom experts on mental disability. If psychologists are permitted to identify and institutionalize such individuals while they are still young, the world's Jean Gianinis can be prevented "from becoming criminals." "Feeble-mindedness as related to crime may be exterminated in a few generations if we will but use our intelligence to attack this problem at its root." [50]

Both books are framed by stories in which science confronts a problem and discovers a solution. Science is one hero here; by implication Goddard, the scientist in question, is another. He encourages us to identify with his sleuthing, thus positioning us to adopt his ideological perspective as well. Goddard presents his narratives of the cacogenic within the framing stories, tracing the Kallikak genealogy in the first instance and events of the three murders in the second. These narratives are sustained versions of the "horror stories" that Josephine Shaw Lowell and others had used earlier to mobilize sentiment against the retarded. Goddard develops the horror story into an extended tale of sex and violence, degradation and depravity.

The Kallikak Family owes its fame — a reputation so great that the name entered the English language as a term of opprobrium — to the skill with which Goddard confers on its narrative the religious and poetic dimensions of myth. Like many myths, *The Kallikak Family* explains the origins of sin and sorrow and points the way to redemption. Its roots stretch back to the story of Adam's loss of innocence and fall from the Garden of Eden; like Adam, Martin Sr. succumbs to a temptress (the feebleminded tavern girl), thus damning future generations. Its roots also lie in the biblical story of Esau and Jacob, of whom it was prophesied that "two peoples, born of you, shall be divided; the one shall be stronger than the other, the elder shall serve the younger." Esau, like the bad Kallikaks, was primitive, a hairy hunter; Jacob set the pattern for the good Kallikaks with his quiet domesticity. [51]

Portraying a universal struggle between darkness and light, *The Kallikak Family* echoes morality literature and fairy tales. The book's central contrast of good and evil is literally embodied in the family's two branches; it recurs in the framing story, where the good scientist learns how to slay the dragon of bad heredity; and it is brilliantly summarized in the name *Kallikak*. This triple realization of its theme gives *The Kallikak Family* a powerful unity. At the end Goddard invites the reader to participate in the eugenicist's battle against evil. Observing that "the real sin" lies in "peopling the world with a race of defective degenerates," he recommends measures we can take to prevent more of "their horrible progeny." [52]

Secrecy forms a major theme in both books. Goddard repeatedly exposes the illusions of his characters and even his readers, stressing the difficulty of penetrating appearance to the underlying reality. Many of his characters present deceptive faces; others are unaware of fundamental facts about their lives. Martin Sr., for example, "could not have begun to realize the evil that had been done" by his union with the feebleminded girl. Photographs that show Deborah Kallikak as an apparently normal young woman, sewing and setting a table, illustrate the impossibility of reading feeblemindedness from a countenance. (The gruesome photographs of criminal anthropology make the opposite point.) One Kallikak anecdote tells how "a defective man on the bad side of the family was found in the employ of a family on the normal side and . . . neither suspects any relationship." [53] Goddard, tantalizing the reader, keeps the good family's actual name a secret.

Carrying the secrecy theme forward, *The Criminal Imbecile* mystifies what had seemed to be clear by insisting that "we *cannot believe all that he* [Jean Gianini] *says in his confession.*" Goddard tells us that the "facts" showing that Gianini premeditated his teacher's murder "indicate nothing of the kind," that apparently correct responses to intelligence-test questions are faulty, and that a strong memory and good school performance are not reliable signs of intelligence.[54] This insistence on secrecy and mystery keeps the reader turning the pages in search of truth. It underscores the inscrutability of feeblemindedness. And it sets the scene for science to ride to the rescue by revealing the world as it actually is.

Feeding the nation's hunger for scientific information, Goddard provides easily digested stories in which the heroic scientist searches for clues and triumphantly solves the conundrums of human heredity. Drawing on the pervasive fear of social deterioration, in the same works Goddard provides cheering tales in which virtue enlists eugenics to win the struggle against defective germ plasm. Appealing to both conservative and liberal impulses, *The Kallikak Family* and *The Criminal Imbecile* show readers how they can contribute to eugenic reforms. These books, often ridiculed as bad science, are rarely recognized for also being extraordinarily clever propaganda and early examples of "pop" psychology.

■ ■ ■

Until late in the nineteenth century, physicians—particularly those who superintended institutions for the feebleminded and the insane—had a monopoly on born-criminal theory. With the advent of criminal anthropology, professionals from other fields joined the physicians, thus loosening the ties between born-criminal theory and medicine. The connection further atrophied with the arrival of Goddard and other psychologists who used the new technology of intelligence testing to construct the criminal imbecile.

At a time when psychology was searching for scientific legitimacy, for ways to be socially useful, and for professional standing, Goddard's production of eugenic criminology opened up new professional territory. Through identifying criminal imbeciles in particular and the feebleminded in general, he and like-minded psychologists performed seemingly crucial eugenics work. For a few years after 1910 Goddard was the most powerful criminologist in the country, the national expert on the causes of crime. Critiques by other psychologists eventually brought him down, but before he fell, his criminal imbecile acquired another label, *defective delinquent*, and launched a movement for eugenic sentencing.

Notes

1. *Journal of Criminal Law and Criminology* 2 (1911–12): 272.

2. Vineland actually included two institutions, both established in 1888, one the State School for Feeble-minded Women, modeled after New York's Custodial Asylum at Newark, and the other the training school for children.

3. Leiby 1967:74. At the celebration for the twenty-fifth anniversary of the training school's laboratory, New Jersey's commissioner of institutions and agencies, William J. Ellis, remarked: "One of the real reasons why it has been possible here to develop this Laboratory is that the institution has been under private control. I do not believe that Dr. Goddard would have been given the opportunity or that Professor Johnstone could have done with public funds what they did with private support" (in Doll 1932:20.)

4. On the Progressive Era struggle between physicians and psychologists for authority to diagnose feeblemindedness, see Trent 1994 and Zenderland 1987.

5. Camfield 1973:70.

6. Zenderland 1987. Henry Herbert Goddard was born in Maine in 1886 into a Quaker family; his was father a farmer, and his mother was a minister (Cravens 1986). After earning a B.A. and an M.A. at Haverford College, Goddard went on to Clark University, where G. Stanley Hall's hereditarianism and interest in child development helped to set Goddard in the same directions (Ross 1972:350–54).

7. Edgar A. Doll in Doll 1932:xix. Johnstone describes the origins and work of the Feeble-Minded Club in *Journal of Psycho-Asthenics* 14 (1909–10): 122 and in Doll 1932:6–8, where he gives 1902 as the date of his first meeting with Goddard.

For Goddard's version and dating of the meeting to 1901, see his "Anniversary Address" in Doll 1932:55–57.

8. Goddard 1907–8:23, 19.

9. Terman 1913:93–95; Kuhlmann 1911.

10. Goddard 1909–10:49.

11. *Journal of Psycho-Asthenics* 14 (1–4) (1909–10): 52–54; Goddard 1914a:91 (quotations); Kite n.d.:24 n.

12. Sarason and Doris 1969:281.

13. Terman 1912:103.

14. Kuhlmann 1912:144–45.

15. Goddard 1914a:88; Kite 1912:84, 86–87. For an objection to amateur administration of the tests and Goddard's response, see *Journal of Psycho-Asthenics* 16 (4) (June 1912): 192–93.

16. See, e.g., Terman 1914:120.

17. Zenderland 1987:67.

18. Goddard 1910:26, 18.

19. Ibid., 27.

20. Ibid.

21. Zenderland 1987:46.

22. Goddard 1910:28.

23. Ibid., 29–30.

24. Barr's *Mental Defectives: Their History, Treatment and Training* (1904) helped to popularize the term *mental defect,* which was supplemented during the Progressive period by yet another new term for feeblemindedness, *mental deficiency.*

25. Barr [1904] 1973:190.

26. W. Fernald 1909–10:33 (emphases added), 35, 30. Fernald's paper was originally presented at the May 1908 annual meeting of the American Medico-Psychological Association (ibid., 16).

27. Ibid., 32.

28. Goddard in *Journal of Psycho-Asthenics* 14 (1–4) (1909–10): 37. The English continued to classify the moral imbecile apart from other "aments" (as the feebleminded were sometimes called in England), distinguishing among four grades: idiots, imbeciles, feebleminded persons (equivalent to the Americans' "morons"), and moral imbeciles. See *Journal of Psycho-Asthenics* 19 (2) (Dec. 1914): 112 and Tredgold 1916: chap. 5.

29. This finding resulted from the difficulty of his upper-level tests, but because there were no alternative tests as yet, Goddard's results were not easily challenged.

30. Goddard 1914b:8.

31. Ibid. (emphases added).

32. Ibid., 5.

33. W. Fernald 1909–10:19.

34. Goddard 1914b:8.

35. Ibid., 2 (emphases added).

36. Ibid., 514.

37. Goddard explains Mendel's laws in *The Kallikak Family* ([1912] 1923:109–

13) and in *Feeble-Mindedness: Its Causes and Consequences* (1914b: chap. 6). Ludmerer (1972:42) estimates that about half of all early twentieth-century American geneticists subscribed to eugenics; also see Barker 1989.

38. Haller 1963: chap. 5; Rosenberg 1976: chap. 4.

39. D. Smith 1985:44–45 quotes a 1910 letter from Goddard to Samuel Fels that discusses a $1,000 gift used in part to "start a field worker." Goddard dedicated *The Kallikak Family* (1912) to Fels, "who made possible this study," and again acknowledged Fels's help in *Feeble-Mindedness: Its Causes and Consequences* ("the very existence of the research work on its present extended plan is largely dependent upon one man. . . [,] Mr. Samuel S. Fels, of Philadelphia, friend, adviser, inspirer and promoter of this work" [1914b:x]).

40. A January 1910 bulletin of the American Institute of Criminal Law and Criminology outlines a system of recording data concerning criminals and explains how to devise a heredity chart. It presents the method described here, saying that it is "modified from the one devised and used by Dr. H. H. Goddard" (American Institute of Criminal Law and Criminology 1910:88). A May 1911 bulletin of the Eugenics Record Office entitled "Methods of Collecting, Charting and Analyzing Data," authored by Davenport, Goddard, and others, attributes the "plan of charting" heredity to "the decisions of a committee of the American Association for the Study of the Feeble-Minded held at Lincoln, Illinois, in 1910," a committee that consisted of Johnstone, Goddard, and four physicians (Davenport et al. 1911:2–3).

41. This assumption must have given Goddard pause, as Sarason and Doris (1969:260) point out, for his research with the Binet tests was yielding a continuous distribution of intelligence scores; also see Barker 1989:355.

42. Goddard 1911 (this article originally appeared in 1910 in the *American Breeders Magazine*). Whether Goddard or Davenport invented this iconography, it was certainly Goddard who popularized it.

43. Goddard 1914b:441, 556. For a critical analysis of how Goddard reached these conclusions, see Barker 1989.

44. Goddard outlines the causal sequence in 1914b: chap. 1. For more on degenerationism in his thinking, see Trent 1982:129–31; for a more general discussion of "the mating of Mendelian theory with the degeneration theories," see Sarason and Doris 1969:253–55.

45. In his preface to *The Kallikak Family,* Goddard explains that he is addressing not other scientists but "the lay reader" ([1912] 1923:x), and he begins *The Criminal Imbecile* by offering the book "to the public" ([1915] 1922:v).

46. For examples of other bad-family studies, see Rafter 1988.

47. Goddard [1912] 1923:18, 29–30.

48. Ibid., 53.

49. Goddard [1915] 1922:1–2.

50. Ibid., 85–87, 104, 108.

51. Genesis 25.

52. Goddard [1912] 1923:102–3, 113.

53. Ibid., 102, 51.

54. Goddard [1915] 1922:17 (emphases in original), 19, 34, 36–38.

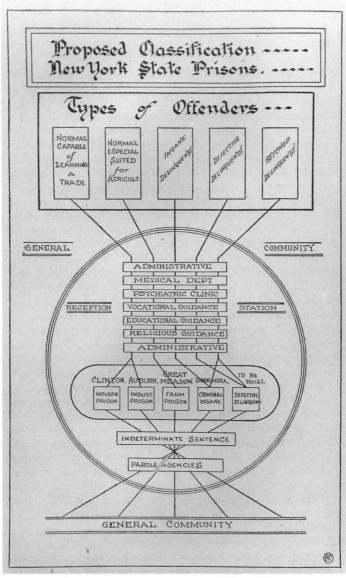

Diagram of Bernard Glueck's plan to centralize New York's men's prisons, classify them by offender type, and isolate defective delinquents. From B. Glueck, "Types of Delinquent Careers," *Mental Hygiene* I (1917): 172.

Orlando Faulkland Lewis, leader of New York's campaign to establish an institution for male defective delinquents. From Prison Association of New York, *Annual Report, 1922,* facing p. 13.

The Napanoch Institution for Defective Delinquents, 1920, a year before Fenix Whipple was transferred there. From New York State Archives, ser. A3045, instructional lantern slides and negatives and positive transparencies, 1911–39.

Fenix Whipple about 1921, when he was diagnosed as a defective delinquent. From New York State Archives, ser. 14610-88B, inmate case files, 1920–56, case 298.

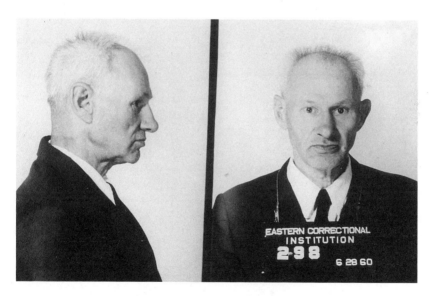

Fenix Whipple in 1960, after nearly forty years at Napanoch. From New York State Archives, ser. 14610-88B, inmate case files, 1920–56, case 298.

One of Fenix's "writes of habeaus copos," a petition to
Judge Mamackin, July 22, 1929, requesting release. From
New York State Archives, ser. 14610-88B, inmate case files,
1920–56, case 298.

A cellblock at Napanoch in 1920, just before Fenix's commitment. From New York State Archives, ser. A3045, instructional lantern slides and negatives and positive transparencies,
1911–39.

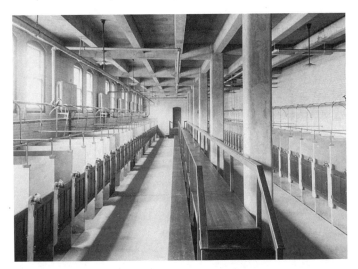

Shower stalls at Napanoch, 1920, as they would have looked to Fenix when he arrived the next year. From New York State Archives, ser. A3045, instructional lantern slides and negatives and positive transparencies, 1911–39.

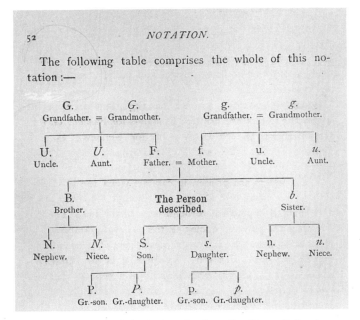

The following table comprises the whole of this notation :—

G. = *G.*		**g.** = *g.*
Grandfather. = Grandmother.		Grandfather. = Grandmother.
U.   *U.*   **F.** = *f.*   u.   *u.*
Uncle.   Aunt.   Father. = Mother.   Uncle.   Aunt.
B.   **The Person**   *b.*
Brother.   **described.**   Sister.
N.   *N.*   **S.**   *s.*   n.   *n.*
Nephew.   Niece.   Son.   Daughter.   Nephew.   Niece.
P.   *P.*   p.   *p.*
Gr.-son. Gr.-daughter.   Gr.-son. Gr.-daughter.

Sir Francis Galton's method of tracing heredity. From Galton's *Hereditary Genius* (1869; repr., New York: Horizon, 1952), 52.

J. E.'S FAMILY[1]

M. Died of cancer of stomach. Æt. 66. — F. [Wife] Died in a fit. Æt. 54.

- M. A suicide. Æt. 56. Married. No issue.
- M. Died of convulsions. Æt. 13 weeks. Died of cancer of stomach. Æt. 58. Left five children.
- F. Died of consumption. Married several years. No issue.
- F. Died of consumption. Æt. 16.
- M. Healthy. Has seven children.
- M. Epileptic. Twice insane. Married. No issue.

[1] Dr. S. A. K. Strahan, *loc. cit.*, p. 49.

Method of showing the impact of degeneration on heredity, derived from the work of S. A. K. Strahan. From W. Duncan McKim, *Heredity and Human Progress* (New York: Putnam's, 1900), 89.

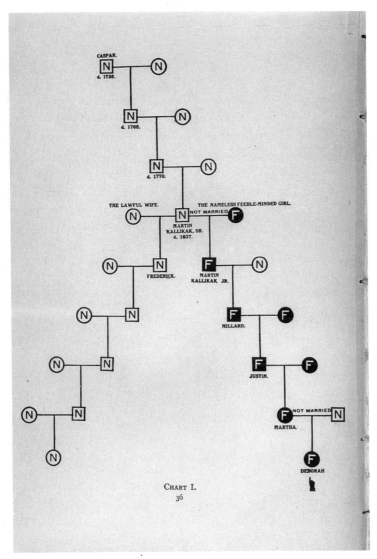

CASPAR.
N — N
d. 1735.

N — N
d. 1765.

N — N
d. 1770.

THE LAWFUL WIFE.   THE NAMELESS FEEBLE-MINDED GIRL.
N — N NOT MARRIED F
MARTIN
KALLIKAK, SR.
d. 1837.

N — N   F — N
FREDERICK.   MARTIN
KALLIKAK JR.

N — N   F — F
     MILLARD.

N — N   F — F
     JUSTIN.

N — N   F NOT MARRIED N
     MARTHA.

N   F
     DEBORAH

CHART I.
36

Henry H. Goddard's method of showing the inheritance of feeble-mindedness (F) and normal intelligence (N). From Goddard's *Kallikak Family* (New York: Macmillan, 1912), chart 1, p. 36.

Creating eugenic heredity charts at the Faribault, Minnesota, School for Feeble-Minded, ca. 1915. From New York State Archives, ser. 4221, Hebberd Commission, box 2, folder labeled "Minnesota."

8

Defective Delinquents

Both appear to be degenerates of the worst type, small
of head, with close set wicked eyes, and cruel mouths.
They have been compared in appearance with the
Apaches of Paris. Both are said to be afflicted with
contagious and loathsome diseases.

New Orleans Daily Picayune, on two men
arrested in 1911 for a murder

Defective delinquents: this new term for the
feebleminded criminal, adopted widely and en-
thusiastically just after 1910, became a rallying
cry for Progressive reformers as they renewed the
campaign for indefinite sentences. Up-to-life sentences for all offenders became a key goal of men
and women intent on eradicating crime. "The
criminal should never be set free until he shall
have given satisfactory evidence of . . . rehabilitation," wrote Robert Gault, editor of the *Journal
of Criminal Law and Criminology,* in a typical passage. "If this involves life imprisonment let the
prisoner be confined for life regardless of the specific nature of his criminal activity."[1] Reformers
failed to achieve this goal fully, but they did realize it partially in the case of eugenics-based up-
to-life sentences for defective delinquents. This
chapter describes the events that led to the first
implemented defective delinquent law, enacted
for the eugenic control of "feebleminded" inmates at New York's prison for women. It also
explores the meanings and social significance of
the term "defective delinquent."

Identifying Defective Delinquents at the Bedford Hills Reformatory

No Progressive penologist had greater impact on eugenic criminology than Katharine Bement Davis, superintendent of New York's Bedford Hills Reformatory for Women from 1901 through 1913. Davis attributed female criminality to social factors, but she also pioneered in imposing eugenic controls on the minority whose offending seemed to be caused by bad heredity. At the height of the Progressive and eugenics movements, just as Goddard completed the criminalization of the feebleminded, Davis's systematic intelligence testing of prisoners completed the "imbecilization" of the criminal.[2]

Davis came to corrections relatively late in life and indirectly. A Vassar graduate, she taught high-school science and supervised a settlement house until 1897, when, in her late thirties, she began doctoral studies at the University of Chicago. There she specialized in political economy, not criminology. Nonetheless, as biographer Ellen Fitzpatrick has shown, the culture of the new university's social sciences departments deeply affected Davis's subsequent prison work:

> Political science, sociology, and political economy took shape at Chicago at a time when American social science itself was being defined. Professors who joined the university represented divergent strands that wove the tapestry of late-nineteenth-century social science. Together they designed a program that drew on both the amateur tradition of social inquiry in America and the rapidly professionalizing fields of academic social science. In so doing, they created an intellectual hybrid that prepared their students to use the science of society to address social policy.[3]

Davis emerged from the university primed to apply her expertise to social problems.

Shortly before Davis's *cum laude* graduation, the university's dean of women received a letter of inquiry from Josephine Shaw Lowell, who, after founding the Newark Custodial Asylum for Feeble-minded Women, had continued to play an active role in establishing institutions for criminalistic women. Lowell asked the dean to suggest a candidate for the superintendency of a women's reformatory that New York was about to open at Bedford Hills. The dean recommended Katharine Davis.[4]

Not long after assuming the superintendency, Davis began making eugenic recommendations for the prevention of crime, although like many contemporaries she avoided using the specific term *eugenic*. In a 1906 paper entitled "Moral Imbeciles," she identifies a class of people whom "we can not cure . . . of their moral disease." Although "all" Bedford Hills Reformatory inmates are "victims of bad heredity or environment, or both,"

the moral imbeciles "come largely with bad heredity. . . . They are not necessarily ignorant girls. Some of them have good minds; but it seems to be
impossible for them to distinguish between right and wrong when it concerns themselves." [5]

Davis argues that society needs protection against moral imbeciles and
moral imbeciles against it. Female moral imbeciles, who are by definition
sexually promiscuous, "become a fearful menace . . . more dangerous than
if they stole money"; for the same reason, however, "They will not have any
happiness" if released.[6] Davis then invokes Newark as an example of the
solution she has in mind: "We have . . . a custodial asylum for women of
child-bearing age who have proved that they are not capable of being educated to be self-supporting women. It is not safe to leave them outside. . . .
I believe that the day will come and the public will feel that it is the duty of
the State to also segregate and colonize these women who are dangerous
to the community, who are moral imbeciles, just as we have colonized the
mental imbeciles."[7] Davis proposes isolating her reformatory's moral imbeciles on a farm colony where "they could be made quite self-supporting."
Supremely confident in her own judgment and the science of eugenics, the
superintendent assures her audience of prison administrators that "I would
not commit anyone to a farm colony for life until I had thoroughly experi-
mented. But let us take that further step and prevent there being brought
into the world children who, if there is anything in heredity, have only to
look forward to a life of hopeless misery, such as their mothers have suffered before them."[8]

Davis had accepted the superintendency on condition that she be allowed to run Bedford Hills as a rehabilitative institution, so why did she
conclude that some prisoners required custodial care? The answer lies in
a combination of institutional dilemmas and the availability of eugenic
solutions. Like other reformers, Davis found that the recent innovation of
probation was siphoning off the reformatory's most remediable cases; as
a result the institution was receiving "a perceptibly more difficult class of
women."[9] Then too, she was reluctant to release women who had not been
reformed, but the majority of her inmates had led immoral lives (many had
been prostitutes), and it was hard to interest them in chastity.[10] In addition Bedford Hills' promises of rehabilitation, which encouraged judges
to flood it with commitments, led to overcrowding and disciplinary problems. To explain her failures Superintendent Davis turned, as Superintendent Brockway had before her, to biological explanations, concluding that
her most troublesome inmates were too "abnormal" to be released at the
end of their up-to-three-year sentences.[11] Eugenics theory was now abun-
dantly available to support this reasoning, and indefinite sentencing enjoyed
widespread support.[12] Davis argued that eugenic control of the unreform-

able minority would enable her to concentrate on rehabilitating the rest. By the end of 1912 she was calling those unreformable cases "defective delinquents."[13]

The Clearinghouse Plan

To screen out unreformable defectives, Davis proposed to establish a "clearinghouse" where prisoners could be diagnosed and classified.[14] The clearinghouse concept was just then taking the field of criminal justice by storm. Court and prison administrators borrowed the idea from psychiatrists who a decade earlier had begun to establish psychopathic hospitals or central laboratories to screen incoming patients, sift the treatable cases from the untreatable, and conduct scientific research. To centralize, improve efficiency, and individualize treatment were the goals both of psychiatrists and of criminal justice administrators who backed the clearinghouse plan. In criminal justice the plan eventually led to prison "laboratories," or reception centers for the classification of new inmates, and to court clinics for the diagnosis of prisoners before sentencing.[15] In Davis's mind the clearinghouse plan was inseparable from the idea of eugenically segregating defectives.

Davis outlined her clearinghouse plan during a 1910 visit of New York City magistrates and court reformers to Bedford Hills. One visitor asked her to put the plan in writing; the upshot was "A Rational Treatment of Women Convicted in the Courts of New York City," an article originally distributed in pamphlet form by the Charity Organization Society.[16] In it Davis proposes coordinating the work of all New York State courts and agencies that deal with criminal women so that the feebleminded can be identified and isolated on indefinite sentences.[17] When Davis learned of Goddard's work with mental testing at Vineland, she incorporated Binet's tests, "given with a minimum of difficulty and almost no apparatus," into the clearinghouse plan.[18] Bedford Hills eventually instituted its own reception center, but Davis regarded this postcommitment clearinghouse as less than ideal. Ultimately she hoped to see established a series of clearinghouses at which physicians, psychologists, and eugenic field-workers would classify convicted offenders "before sentence was passed."[19]

Eugenicists had decided that life segregation on farm colonies or in other institutional settings was the best way to prevent criminals from reproducing. Some endorsed sterilization as a supplement to segregation, and in fact in 1912 New York passed a law authorizing sterilization of criminals as well as the feebleminded, insane, and epileptic. This law had little public support, however, and only one prisoner (a male) was sterilized under its aegis.[20] Sterilization was widely practiced in some institutions for the feebleminded, and the U.S. Supreme Court upheld Virginia's sterilization statute in the 1927 case of Carrie Buck, a feebleminded woman.[21] Sterilization was also practiced in some criminal justice settings, albeit not programmatically, most notoriously at the Indiana State Reformatory, where, starting in 1899, the aptly named Dr. H. C. Sharp performed vasectomies on 236 young men.[22] But most eugenicists were horrified by the thought that, if sterilized and released, the unfit might fornicate with impunity, and of course the operation could not prevent crime in this generation. Thus for feebleminded criminals, life segregation seemed to be the best eugenic solution.

The clearinghouse, then, would be a place where experts would determine which offenders should go to regular state prisons and which to eugenic institutions. The plan's efficiency and "rationality" commended it, as did its stress on administrative discretion. Clearinghouses would complete the process, begun by indeterminate sentencing, of taking responsibility for setting prisoner release dates away from judges and placing it in the hands of scientific experts. Davis touted yet other virtues of the plan. Clearinghouses, by leading to the segregation of prostitutes (a group feebleminded almost by definition), would greatly reduce vice; they would enable penologists "to diagnose before instead of after treatment"; and they would fit treatment to the criminal—all goals high on the Progressive agenda.[23] In short the plan would bring science to bear on prison management.

Davis took the first step toward establishing a clearinghouse in the summer of 1909 when she invited Jane Day, a staff member of the eugenical New York Public Education Association, to study Bedford Hills' "most difficult" inmates.[24] Day examined prisoner records, interviewed officials, and concluded that 15 percent of Davis's 300 cases were mentally defective. This finding encouraged Davis's hope of developing a device to predict recidivism. The next summer she invited Mount Holyoke College psychologist Dr. Eleanor Rowland to study the mentality of three dozen selected inmates. Binet's tests were not yet available, but Rowland did measure these prisoners' reaction times, memory, attention spans, and suggestibility. She found that thirteen were mentally subnormal, thus confirming Davis's hunch that the key to classification lay in mental testing.[25]

With $3,000 in grants from the New York Foundation,[26] Davis next established a temporary clearinghouse administered by Dr. Jean Weidensall, a psychologist who had worked at the Juvenile Psychopathic Institute in Chicago. Davis sent Weidensall to Vineland to study the new Binet method of intelligence testing with Henry Goddard. A genealogical researcher from the New York School of Philanthropy and a field-worker from the Eugenics Record Office completed Weidensall's team. Within two years of her first scientific probe, then, the superintendent had attracted private funding for research on the intelligence and heredity of state prisoners, with an eye to segregating some for life.

Next Davis enlisted John D. Rockefeller Jr. in her cause. Rockefeller, one of America's wealthiest men, had recently chaired a grand jury to investigate prostitution, which he viewed as a vice associated with feeblemindedness and disease. To help bring prostitution under scientific control with "a certain freedom from publicity,"[27] he had formed the Bureau of Social Hygiene, a philanthropy that he funded mainly out of his own pocket and personally supervised. Rockefeller invited Davis, whom he considered to be the cleverest woman he had ever met,[28] to become part of the four-member bureau. Her clearinghouse pamphlet had impressed him, and as a eugenicist in charge of an institution filled with prostitutes, she was ideally situated to further the struggle against the unfit.

The First Defective Delinquent Law

The Bureau of Social Hygiene purchased land adjacent to the reformatory on which it built a clearinghouse, the Laboratory of Social Hygiene, where experts would scientifically examine the heredity, history, psychology, and pathology of every incoming inmate; the bureau committed itself to funding the project for up to five years. From New York's attorney general Rockefeller obtained an opinion declaring the laboratory permissible so long as "the State would bear the mere cost of maintenance of the inmates just as if they remained within the present boundaries of the institution grounds." This opinion clearly indicates the Davis-Rockefeller intention: "Such defective individuals [as would be identified by the laboratory] can then be sent to custodial asylums, such as that at Newark, instead of being set free at the end of a short period of detention and thus allowed to add to the population of defective and criminally inclined persons."[29] In other words, private funds were to be used to identify candidates for up-to-life incarceration, and a private citizen would actually own part of a state prison. The laboratory commenced operations in September 1912.

Davis left Bedford Hills in 1914 to become New York City's commissioner of correction, and her successors lost control of the reformatory. Inmate protests and riots plagued Bedford Hills into the 1920s. As far as the records show, these disturbances stemmed from managerial incompetence and extraordinarily harsh punishments for minor violations. But the prisoners' rebelliousness may also have stemmed from fears of intelligence testing. Poor test scores could lead to transfers to civil institutions for the feebleminded, and (as inmates may also have realized) they might eventually lead to commitment to the reformatory's projected division for defective delinquents. In any case the laboratory continued to identify the feebleminded, whose defects officials then used to explain the reformatory's problems. Inmate unrest and the laboratory's testing program increased pressure for custodial segregation of defective delinquents.[30]

When the reformatory's dollar-a-year lease on the Rockefeller property approached its expiration, Davis, now general secretary of the Bureau of Social Hygiene, drafted legislation under which New York would purchase the laboratory for use as a classification center. This legislation failed, however, and after a year's renewal of the lease, the laboratory closed in June 1918. Persistent inmate rioting brought requests that Rockefeller reopen the laboratory, but Rockefeller refused to cooperate until the state promised to purchase the complex for use "as a clearing house in connection with a state-wide system for the care of mentally defective women."[31]

The legislature finally complied, passing New York's first defective delinquent law in 1920. According to this law, any woman over sixteen years old in a state-supported institution for delinquents or criminals who was found "to be mentally defective to an extent to require supervision, control and care" was to be committed to a section of the Bedford Hills Reformatory called the Division for Mentally Defective Delinquent Women. The law did not specify how such women were to be identified, but it did state that their sentences were to be indefinite, with decisions about parole and discharge to be made by reformatory officials. Thus the plan for removing the feebleminded from the reformatory to a custodial unit was finally realized. For the first time in the United States, prisoners deemed feebleminded received open-ended sentences. After considerable foot-dragging, in 1923 the state purchased the Rockefeller property for $175,000.[32]

As Rockefeller's public sponsorship of this defective delinquent legislation indicates, eugenic criminology constituted an inoffensive and indeed respectable type of reform. There was evidently no public objection to the fact that such projects created alliances between capitalists and the state against marginal groups. In fact, to judge from the *New York Times* coverage, Rockefeller's promotion of eugenic criminology improved his reputation at a time of national outrage over his family's violent suppression of a miner's strike in Colorado. Financing eugenic programs enabled him to meet Charles R. Henderson's definition of a philanthropist as one who aims at improving the welfare not "of dependent *persons*" but "of the *community* and of the future *race*." In improving social control of fallen women, Rockefeller found a means to make what he termed "warfare against the forces of evil."[33] Many contemporaries also assumed a link between biology and criminality and admired those who, like Rockefeller, acted on that assumption.[34]

"Neither Fish, Flesh, nor Fowl": Male Defective Delinquents

Since at least the 1880s, when Frederick Howard Wines published a census report on "the defective, dependent and delinquent classes," the terms *defective, dependent,* and *delinquent* had been closely associated.[35] Thus it was likely that someone, somewhere, would eventually invent the term *defective delinquent.* The phrase was probably coined by eugenicist Orlando F. Lewis, executive director of the Prison Association of New York.[36] In 1910 the association established a "special committee on . . . the physical and mental characteristics of defective delinquents"—evidently the first use of the term.[37]

But Walter E. Fernald, superintendent of the Massachusetts School for the Feeble-minded, may also have coined the phrase. In April 1910 Massachusetts established a commission headed by Fernald to "investigate the question of the increase of criminals, mental defectives, epileptics and degenerates." The commission's report, submitted in January 1911, identifies a "special class of defective criminals" that "has been variously described as moral imbecile, high-grade imbecile, psychopath, criminal imbecile, imbecile with criminal instincts, etc. The combination of slight mental defect and irresponsibility with the criminal propensities of the entire group is well expressed by the term 'defective delinquent.' "[38] Fernald may have created the term independently or borrowed it from the title of Lewis's previously formed committee on defective delinquents.

Defective delinquent quickly entered the criminological vocabulary. By the end of 1912 all the significant audiences, including charity workers, institutional superintendents, judges, physicians, and teachers, had been exposed to it.[39] Officials at many prisons had been administering intelligence tests and discovering that large proportions of their populations were feebleminded. The new term gave them a convenient label for these feebleminded offenders.

Prison officials and reformers immediately produced articles urging eugenic measures against defective delinquents. These authors agreed that defective delinquents form a subgroup of the feebleminded, characterized by criminal tendencies. They were reluctant to exempt intellectually normal inmates from the category, however. When some Elmira prisoners passed the mental tests, for example, Frank Christian, the reformatory's physician and assistant superintendent, concluded that the "experienced psychologist or physician" must take "a number of other equally important [but unspecified] factors into consideration" before arriving at a final diagnosis of defective delinquency. Guy Fernald, physician at the Concord, Massachusetts, men's reformatory, wrote that defective delinquents are "border-land cases between the feeble-minded and the competent, between the sane and insane and the 'moral imbeciles.' " William Hickson, formerly a member of the Vineland research team and now director of a Chicago court laboratory, dismissed the problem of intellectual normality with a verbal sleight of hand: he explained that some defective delinquents who passed intelligence tests "show a mental defect instead of mental defectiveness." [40]

Those who wrote on defective delinquency were likewise reluctant to use rigid criteria for delinquency. They unanimously equated the defective delinquent with the recidivist, but they included "potential" recidivists and even "potential" criminals in the classification. Casting a wide net, Guy Fernald described the defective delinquent as one who "is smart enough to get into trouble but is not smart enough to keep out of it." Others included insane, alcoholic, crippled, and homosexual prisoners in the defective delinquent category. In the term's vagueness lay much of it appeal. [41]

The authors of these articles stress the defective delinquent's moral turpitude. The defective delinquent, according to Guy Fernald, "lacks high ideals and real morality." He "is seldom influenced by an appeal to the higher mental qualities: ambition, gratitude, reverence, remorse, etc., [and] in fact it often seems that self-interest is almost the only motive. . . . Some exhibit arrogance and conceit with small basis therefor. . . . As a class their patriotic and altruistic feelings are weak, and . . . they are apt to be cowardly and cruel. They often falsify, lacking a love of truth for its own sake." [42] According to Frank Christian, defective delinquents "are selfish, vain, and cruel." They act "principally upon impulses" and are "vindictive and revengeful." [43]

Earlier writers had attributed similar traits to moral imbeciles and anthropological criminals. Thus to some extent those who described the defective delinquent were merely updating an older concept. But definitions of the defective delinquent also echoed concerns specific to the Progressive period. At a time of strikes and unemployment, extreme polarizations of capital and labor, growth of a mass socialist movement, and obsessive worries about worker efficiency, writers described the male defective delinquent as a laborer who *could* not cooperate with modern management. From Chicago William Hickson reported that defective delinquents failed to live up to the "new efficiency ideals maintained by most business houses." Even when they did manage to gain employment, they were "the first to be laid off in periods of retrenchment." In Massachusetts Guy Fernald announced that defective delinquents "cannot support themselves"; they are "incapable of long endurance and sustained effort and concentration of attention, and so can neither acquire skill and knowledge nor accumulate wealth." In New York Frank Christian found that if the defective delinquent "has worked at all, it has probably been at 'odd jobs' that afforded plenty of intermittent diversions, for this type can not be depended upon to do any task without supervision."[44] Defective delinquency explained management's problems in terms of workers' defects.

These writings advanced the reconceptualization of dangerousness as not violent behavior but a condition, an invisible hereditary defect carried by even minor offenders. Expanding the territory of deviance, they peopled it with defectives whose abnormalities, although almost imperceptible, nonetheless pose a dire social threat. As Hastings H. Hart, a Russell Sage Foundation official, observed in 1912, "Five years ago . . . the average prison warden or reformatory superintendent would have estimated the number of feeble-minded persons in such institutions at not more than ten per cent. of the population," but according to current estimates "25 per cent. is moderate and conservative. At that rate we should have . . . a total of 26,000 defective delinquents in actual custody, not to mention those . . . at large."[45]

Authors warned against permitting defective delinquents to reproduce. The defective delinquent class, Guy Fernald wrote, "is very prolific and each generation encounters it in augmented numbers."[46] "While we can hardly assert that criminality is inherited," Frank Christian stated in a typical passage, "yet we are certain that insanity, degeneracy and feeble-mindedness when combined with criminality will reproduce only more material to populate the asylums and prisons." Thus the "public has every right to be protected not only from him [the defective delinquent], but also from his offspring."[47]

Authors gave different (and sometimes contradictory) accounts of the causal connection between defectiveness and delinquency. Some explained that the feebleminded cannot understand the law; others, that they cannot control their lower instincts; and yet others, that they become the easy prey of more intelligent criminals. Goddard sometimes emphasized mental defectives' inability to associate cause with effect, as a result of which they cannot learn from punishment. He and others also held that the feebleminded are more emotional than normal people. "The feebleminded are subject to attacks of depression and exaltation," wrote an Indiana prison physician, "and their mental equilibrium being very unstable, the baser elements of their natures assert themselves . . . in deeds of violence."[48]

Superintendents of the feebleminded now argued that delinquent and disruptive defectives should be removed to more secure, prisonlike quarters.[49] Following suit, prison officials used *defective delinquent* to designate *their* institutional problems, arguing that intractable prisoners should be segregated in specialized, hospital-like institutions.[50] Nonetheless, a spokesperson for the Massachusetts Board of Insanity pointed out, defective delinquents should definitely not be sent to hospitals for the mentally ill, for they tend to escape and commit sex offenses and arson.[51] A consensus formed that defective delinquents, because they were "neither fish, flesh nor fowl," should be segregated in a new type of institution that would combine elements of the training school for the feebleminded, the prison, and the mental hospital while providing permanent custodial care.[52]

"Scum of the Earth": Female Defective Delinquents

Defective delinquency was a highly gendered explanation of crime. Whereas authors partly defined male defective delinquents as inefficient workers, they almost totally defined female defective delinquents as sex offenders, the lascivious, hyperfecund mothers of criminals and other degenerates. "Whether the delinquency has been immorality or something else," wrote Ohio field-worker Mary Storer, every defective delinquent girl "is potentially immoral." Eugenicists did not always label the unchaste feebleminded woman a "defective delinquent," perhaps because the women who concerned them most were promiscuous rather than legally delinquent. Nevertheless, all would have agreed with juvenile court judge Harry Olson that "the fallen woman defective is the female equivalent of the boy delinquent-defective."[53]

Writers pictured the female defective delinquent's body as profoundly and pervasively deviant. Her unfitness emanated from her reproductive organs as well as her feeble brain. Such women were "primitive," a "barbarian type," beyond hope of reformation, and "by far the most dangerous individuals we have at large." "Defective delinquent women," a New Jersey official declared, "are the scum of the earth." A more sexualized concept than that of the male defective delinquent, the idea of the feebleminded woman was also more static. When Walter Fernald's 1911 commission reported that female defective delinquents were "certain to become sexual offenders, and to spread venereal disease, or to give birth to children as degenerate as themselves," it essentially reiterated Josephine Shaw Lowell's 1870s conceptualization of the degenerate woman.[54]

Descriptions of the female defective delinquent negatively defined the "true woman" in a period when that nineteenth-century construct was fast losing its relevance. Joining the paid work force, engaging in sex outside of marriage, using birth controls, clamoring for the vote—women throughout the nation were rejecting the ideal of the cloistered lady.[55] Faced with such signs of moral decay, defective delinquency theorists charged the feebleminded woman with a plethora of sexual sins. One was sexuality itself: she fornicated for pleasure, with no thought of the consequences. Another was lack of discrimination: the feebleminded woman mated with multiple and often highly unsuitable partners—very old, very young, or feebleminded men and sometimes other women.[56] Then too, she was "the most fertile source for the spread of all forms of venereal disease."[57] Worst of all, she showed no remorse. "They do not exhibit shame," observed Walter Fernald, giving this as a reason for concluding that several delinquent girls were feebleminded. "She tells about her [sexual] practices like a child," a scandalized Ohio superintendent complained, explaining that this was why he had labeled a feebleminded girl delinquent.[58] Writers attributed sexual deviance to male defective delinquents as well, but they were far more affronted by female promiscuity.

The vigorous antiprostitution campaigns of the Progressive period escalated anxieties about defective delinquency. "Most prostitutes are feebleminded," announced a Michigan physician; "This is one cause of prostitution."[59] Countless studies confirmed his conclusion. These studies were conducted by officials of women's prisons, vice commissions, the U.S. army's mental testers (who during World War I measured the intelligence of not only soldiers but camp followers), and a meticulous researcher who administered intelligence tests in brothels on Sunday afternoons, when work had not made the women weary.[60] Many of those who participated in antiprostitution crusades and confirmed the low mentality of prostitutes were eugenicists. Sex-purity and crime-control campaigns coincided in eugenicists' efforts to immobilize reproductively women who undermined traditional morality.

Eugenicists emphasized fertility in the case of both male and female defective delinquents, but fertility was easier to prove with females. Because children tend to be attached to their mothers, "the evidence of unchastity is with the mother rather than the father," as a Philadelphia report on degenerate women observed. Moreover, the author of this report reasoned, "more children are born to feeble-minded women than are born to feeble-minded men" because the "feeble-minded man is a repulsive person to a normal woman, but the unfortunate feeble-minded woman does not escape from wicked men."[61] Goddard found that feebleminded women were three times more likely to find a mate than were feebleminded men, and Walter Fernald determined that they were "twice as prolific as the normal woman."[62] From the female defective's womb issued the degenerates who threatened to overwhelm civilization.

Eugenicists marshaled examples of defective delinquent women to whip up support for their programs.[63] "Obviously," wrote Mary Storer, "the feeble-minded girl must be protected all her life."[64] Some eugenicists pitched this argument in terms of chivalry. If "left without protection," warned Hastings Hart, the defective delinquent girl would be "hunted by evil-minded or thoughtless men as ruthlessly as a rabbit." (By implication, she would also produce as many offspring.) Thus institutions for the feebleminded should give "preference . . . in admissions to girls of child-bearing age."[65] So compelling was this rhetoric that an Ohio judge tried to commit a college woman to an institution for the feebleminded.[66] After the age of nineteen, psychologist Fred Kuhlmann found, females were institutionalized as feebleminded more readily than males and released more slowly: "From a third to half of the female admissions is during the child bearing period."[67]

Opposition to Defective Delinquency Theory

For almost a decade the equation of criminality with feeblemindedness enjoyed immense popularity, more than any other biological theory of crime before or since. Particularly during 1912–15, when intelligence tests seemed to confirm defective delinquency theory and prison officials as well as mental retardation specialists endorsed it, eugenic criminology was relatively impervious to challenges. By 1915, however, critics had started to emerge.

Some of the doubters had legal backgrounds. On the basis of long experience, William N. Gemmill, a Chicago municipal court judge, derided equations of the criminal with the unfit: "Through our criminal courts is moving a long line of perfectly natural, healthy, able-bodied people. . . . Thousands . . . of those who are arrested . . . are women charged with being inmates of disorderly houses. . . . Are they all so ignorant, feeble-minded or defective? No, most of them are as intelligent and as sane as the average in the community."[68] Charles A. Boston, a New York City attorney and legal ethicist, vehemently opposed sterilization.[69] And most jurists rejected feeblemindedness as a defense against criminal charges.[70]

Opposition also came from those psychologists who objected to free-and-easy mental testing procedures. If psychologists hoped to obtain accurate estimates of offenders' intelligence, Frederick Kuhlmann maintained, they must improve their methods.[71] Bedford Hills researcher Mabel R. Fernald measured the intelligence of 100 prisoners by nine different scales, finding that the proportion of feebleminded varied from 34 to 100 percent.[72] During a trip to Iowa J. E. W. Wallin, a St. Louis psychologist, administered Goddard's 1911 version of the Binet-Simon tests to successful farmers, a businessman, and a housewife; all failed.[73] By insisting on careful intelligence testing, Kuhlmann, M. R. Fernald, Wallin, and others cast doubt on the offender test scores that had seemed to prove defective delinquency theory.

Also effective as critics were psychiatrists who insisted that mental defectiveness is but one of many mental abnormalities that can lead to criminal behavior. Members of a medical group that was just beginning to flex its professional muscles, these psychiatrists (as the next chapter shows) had no intention of giving psychologists the final say in the matter of crime causation. To counter defective delinquency theory, they proposed the broader and more flexible theory of psychopathy. And as the psychiatric theory of psychopathy gained acceptance, physicians' voices again came to dominate in discussions of born criminals.

Notes

1. Gault 1911–12b:790–91. For good general analyses of social control in the Progressive Era, see Rothman 1978 and Schlossman and Wallach 1978.

2. I here emphasize the eugenic side of Davis's work; readers who want to know more about her rehabilitative methods should consult Fitzpatrick 1990: chap. 5; Freedman 1981; and Rafter 1990a. Davis was only one of many prison officials who demonstrated the biological defectiveness of criminals, and Bedford Hills was only one of many prisons that conducted eugenics research, but reformers throughout the Western world regarded them as leaders in penological science (Fitzpatrick 1990:92; McKelvey [1936] 1972:214; Ruggles-Brise 1911-12).

3. Fitzpatrick 1990:40.

4. Ibid., 76–77. In addition to founding the Newark Custodial Asylum for Feeble-minded Women, Lowell helped to establish New York State reformatories for females at Hudson, Albion, and Bedford Hills.

5. Davis 1906a:345, 346–47.

6. Ibid., 347, 349.

7. Ibid., 349.

8. Ibid., 349–50.

9. Ibid., 345–356; also see Davis 1906b:789–90; Davis 1912:1849; and Gault 1914–15e:1.

10. For an example of an inmate insisting on sexual autonomy, see Davis 1906a: 348.

11. Davis 1916:ix.

12. See, e.g., Allison 1904 and Lamb 1906.

13. Davis 1913–14:407, 406. Davis originally presented this paper in December 1912.

14. Ibid.; also see Davis 1920.

15. On the psychiatric movement to establish psychopathic hospitals, see Grob 1983:126–42. The literature on the clearinghouse, or laboratory, movement is large; see, for example, Gault 1914–15a, 1914–15c; B. Glueck 1917a; Henderson 1900; Kellor 1901 (esp. chap. 2); B. Lewis 1921: chap. 6; McCord 1917; Olson 1915–16; and Town 1913. For secondary sources, see Cravens 1987; Haller 1963 (esp. 42–43); and Rothman 1980:123–26.

16. Davis 1916.

17. Davis 1913–14. Fitzpatrick (1990:103, 105) indicates that the original pamphlet was nearly identical to the article Davis later published in the *Journal of Criminal Law and Criminology* (Davis 1913–14). For a later version of the plan, see Davis 1921.

18. Davis 1912:1850.

19. Davis 1916:xi; Davis 1913–14:405.

20. S. Davies 1930:99–101. The law was declared unconstitutional in 1915 and repealed in 1920.

21. *Buck v. Bell, Superintendent,* 274 U.S. 200 (1927); also see Haller 1963; Larson 1995; and Reilly 1991.

22. Hart 1912:221; Pisciotta 1994.

23. Davis 1913–14 (titled "A Plan of *Rational* Treatment"):405, 408; Davis 1912:1850; Davis 1913–14:403.

24. Davis 1916:x. The Public Education Association's interests are reflected in Moore 1911, a report prepared for the organization and one of the most stridently eugenical documents of the period. Also see Public Education Association 1913. On the significance of Moore's report and of the PEA as a eugenic pressure group, see S. Davies 1923:65–66.

25. Davis 1912:1850. Moore (1911:71–80) summarizes Day's findings. Weidensall (1916:1) describes slightly later experimentation at Bedford Hills as aimed at securing data "that would prove prophetic of her [the inmate's] reformability."

26. New York Foundation n.d.:62. The New York Foundation's board included some of New York's wealthiest Jews: Jacob Schiff, his son Mortimer Schiff, and his son-in-law Felix Warburg. During the Progressive years the foundation also contributed to New York City's police department and department of correction, Bedford Hills' Laboratory of Social Hygiene, and the eugenical New York Committee on Feeble-mindedness (New York Foundation n.d.:56–63).

27. Rockefeller 1913:viii.

28. Fitzpatrick 1990:114.

29. Rockefeller Archive Center, ser. 3, box 25, f. 360 (New York State Office of the Attorney General, n.d., "Reformatory for Women at Bedford. Power of Board of Managers").

30. Kennedy 1920; New York State Reformatory for Women at Bedford Hills, *Annual Report, 1918,* pp. 54–55.

31. Rockefeller Archive Center, ser. 3, box 25, f. 360 (Davis n.d., "Tentative draft of an act to establish a state clearing house for delinquent women"); Fitzpatrick 1990:127; Kennedy 1920:79–80; John D. Rockefeller Jr., letter of December 6, 1919, as quoted in Kennedy 1920:79.

32. New York State, *Laws of New York, 1920,* chap. 774, enacted May 14, 1920; New York State, *Laws of New York 1923,* chap. 450.

33. Henderson 1899:2 (emphasis added); Rockefeller 1913:viii.

34. The full story of the financing of the eugenics movement remains to be told, although Allen (1975, 1986) has made an admirable start (also see Hahn 1980). I have already mentioned industrialist Samuel Fels's support of eugenic research at Vineland and the New York Foundation's contributions to eugenic causes. Other clues are scattered throughout the primary literature on eugenic criminology. The annual reports of the Prison Association of New York (PANY) show that scores of wealthy men and women contributed to the organization after director O. F. Lewis turned it into a lobby for eugenic programs. Through the National Committee on Mental Hygiene, the Rockefeller Foundation for Medical Research funded establishment of a eugenically oriented psychiatric clinic at Sing Sing prison (B. Glueck

1917a:104; this clinic's work is discussed in chap. 9). Josephine Shaw Lowell contributed funds to the Bedford Hills Reformatory in its early days (Stewart 1911:316, 318; New York State Reformatory for Women at Bedford Hills, *Annual Report, 1904*, pp. 28–38), thus starting a tradition that later members of the reformatory board perpetuated by funding studies of inmate genealogies and heredity (New York State Reformatory for Women at Bedford Hills, *Annual Report, 1911*, p. 18). On the financing of the Eugenics Records Office by the Carnegie Institution of Washington, Mary Williamson Harriman, J. D. Rockefeller Jr., and others, see Allen 1986. Goddard (1912–13:367–68) mentions "a philanthropic woman in the city of Newark" who donated funds so that children who came before the juvenile court could be tested. S. Davies (1923:53 n. 3) indicates that the Russell Sage Foundation financed O. F. Lewis's research on feebleminded delinquents. On the financing of the eugenic family studies, see the introduction to Rafter 1988. For nineteenth-century background on "philanthropy as social control," see Gettleman 1963, 1975.

   We need a way to theorize the involvement of Jewish philanthropists in financing New York's defective delinquent campaigns; in this regard, see Lewis 1984 and Proctor 1991:189.

   35. F. Wines 1888.

   36. The Prison Association was one of the oldest and most fashionable of U.S. private prison reform associations. During the Progressive period its patrons included many of the state's wealthiest and most socially prominent citizens.

   37. Prison Association of New York, *Annual Report, 1910*, p. 22. This committee set to work by helping Katharine Davis to secure funds to identify defective delinquents at Bedford Hills.

   38. Massachusetts 1911:32. Fernald's commission recommended legislation that would have made it possible to commit defective delinquents permanently to special institutions (Massachusetts 1911:43–44, 50). Massachusetts immediately enacted the nation's first defective delinquent bill (Massachusetts, *Acts and Resolves, 1911*, chap. 595), but this legislation remained ineffective until, a decade later, the state established a defective delinquent unit, analogous to the one Davis and Rockefeller had founded at Bedford Hills. These acts and their results are described in more detail in chapters 10 and 11.

   39. Readers of the *Journal of Criminal Law and Criminology* encountered the term *defective delinquent* in reviews of the Fernald commission's report (see Healy 1911–12; "F.G." 1911–12). In 1911 O. F. Lewis introduced the topic of defective delinquency before the National Conference on Charities and Correction, the New York Conference of Charities and Correction, the American Prison Association, and the state board of magistrates (Prison Association of New York, *Annual Report, 1911*, p. 49). In addition Lewis arranged for Hastings H. Hart, an official of the Russell Sage Foundation, to speak on "the extinction of the defective delinquent" at a meeting of the American Prison Association (Hart 1912). Guy G. Fernald read a paper describing tests for defective delinquency before the Boston Society of Psychiatry and Neurology in October 1911; this was published the next April in the *American Journal of Insanity* (G. Fernald 1912a). In November 1912 Guy Fernald again used *defective delinquent*, this time in a paper read at the annual meeting of the

American Prison Association (G. Fernald 1912b). Walter E. Fernald used the term in an address to the Massachusetts Medical Society and again at the 1912 annual meeting of the American Association for the Study of the Feeble-Minded (as the Association of Medical Officers of American Institutions for Idiotic and Feeble-Minded Persons had been renamed), whence it passed into the pages of the *Journal of Psycho-Asthenics* (W. Fernald 1912:91, 95). And in March 1912 PANY distributed a stridently eugenical pamphlet (probably written by O. F. Lewis) demanding a state custodial asylum for "defective delinquents" (Prison Association of New York 1912).

40. Christian 1913:277 (also see Prison Association of New York 1912:v, quoting Goddard to the same effect); G. Fernald 1912b:867; Hickson 1914:400. Also see Anderson 1914:343, speaking of "mental defectives who have the gift of language, appearing bright"; and Rossy 1915, explaining why subjects who did relatively well on intelligence tests were classified as feebleminded.

41. G. Fernald 1912b:870; W. Fernald 1909-10:19; G. Fernald 1912a:529 (quotation). Other defective types are folded into the defective delinquent category by G. Fernald 1912a:526; Hart 1912:203; Hickson 1914:403; and New York State Commission of Prisons 1918:16.

42. G. Fernald 1912a:525 (also see G. Fernald 1912b:868-69).

43. Christian 1913:279-80.

44. Hickson 1914:402; G. Fernald 1912a:523, 525; Christian 1913:279.

45. Hart 1912:206-7.

46. G. Fernald 1912a:526. In one sense it was true that the feebleminded were multiplying rapidly, for definitions were expanding. S. Davies (1923:46) makes this point by noting that whereas Dugdale had identified only one feebleminded Juke, an idiot, Arthur H. Estabrook, in his follow-up study *The Jukes in 1915* (1916), found that 50 percent of the Jukes were feebleminded. Davies (1923: chap. 4) provides a good overview of the rising percentages of feebleminded persons detected in Progressive Era studies.

47. Christian 1913:284 (also see Hart 1912).

48. Goddard 1912-13:366; Bowers 1914-15:410. Also see Hoag and Williams 1923:70.

49. Massachusetts 1911:31-32; S. Davies 1930: chap. 9.

50. Christian 1913:282; G. Fernald 1912a:551-53; G. Fernald 1912b:873; New York State Commission of Prisons 1918:17; and Gault 1911-12c (quoting O. F. Lewis).

51. Stearns 1916:433.

52. Prison Association of New York 1912:vi. On the best type of institution for the defective delinquent, see, for example, Hart 1912; Prison Association of New York 1912; and Stearns 1916.

53. Storer 1914:28; Olson 1915-16:62.

54. Peyton 1913-14 ("primitive" and "barbarian"); Emerick 1914:21 ("the most dangerous individuals"); American Association for the Study of the Feeble-Minded 1917a:109 ("scum of the earth"); Massachusetts 1911:32.

55. Connelly 1980 (esp. intro. and chap. 2); Peiss 1986; Rosen 1982.

56. Bruce 1909-10:45; W. Fernald 1909-10:20.

57. Bullard 1909–10:15.

58. W. Fernald in Massachusetts 1911:31; American Association for the Study of the Feeble-Minded 1917a:103. Also see Emerick 1914:21.

59. Vaughan 1914:134. Also see W. Fernald 1912:92.

60. McCord 1915–16. For reviews of this literature, see Connelly 1980:41–43; Lubove 1962; Miner 1918:128–41; and Rosen 1982:21–23.

61. Neff, Laughlin, and Cornell 1910:4; also see Butler 1901 and Miner 1918:246.

62. Goddard as cited in Hart 1912:214; W. Fernald 1912:91.

63. E.g., W. Fernald 1909–10.

64. Storer 1914:29.

65. Hart 1912:215, 214. For an example from the period shortly before the term *defective delinquent* was coined, see Kentucky Institution for the Education and Training of Feeble-Minded Children 1897:16.

66. American Association for the Study of the Feeble-Minded 1917b:29–30. Fortunately the institution's superintendent resisted.

67. Kuhlmann 1916:22.

68. Gemmill 1914–15:173.

69. Boston as quoted in Editors 1914–15:747; also see Boston 1913–14.

70. Woodbridge 1939.

71. Kuhlmann 1914–15:667. Drawing on his research at Minnesota's institution for the feebleminded, Kuhlmann also pointed out that "many cases of even low grade feeble-mindedness are entirely negative as to causes, either hereditary or acquired, and many persons of normal intelligence have a very bad heredity" (ibid.).

72. M. Fernald 1916–17:727. Also see Fernald, Hayes, and Dawley 1920:527–29 and Weidensall 1916:3–5, 15.

73. Wallin 1915–16.

9

Psychopaths and the Decline of Eugenic Criminology

> Some individuals because of their psychological makeup, either qualitative or quantitative, are absolutely and permanently incorrigible and present a problem which can be dealt with in only one effective way — namely, permanent segregation and isolation from society. It is on this very important account that the psychopathologist's place in criminology is fully justified.
>
> Bernard Glueck, *Studies in Forensic Psychiatry*

Biological theories of crime turned yet another corner about 1915, when psychiatrists began introducing the concept of psychopathy. This was in fact the third phase in born-criminal theory since the turn of the century. During the first, when criminal anthropology still reigned supreme, biological explanations were dominated by the riveting specter of a born criminal whose entire body displayed the stigmata of evil. During the second phase, when criminal anthropology gave way to feeblemindedness theory and the Lombrosian born criminal was displaced by the "criminal imbecile" and "defective delinquent," the idea of born criminality retreated, so to speak, from the body to the brain. In the third stage, when psychopathy eclipsed feeblemindedness theory, the idea of inborn criminality again retreated, this time from the brain to the less palpable mind and its emotions. Thus the sequence — from criminal anthropology through feeblemindedness theory to psychopathy — was one in which the somatic territory of the born-criminal idea steadily shrank. By the mid-1920s it had almost vanished.

The psychiatrists who produced the new theory taught that most psychopaths are intellectually normal. Unlike defective delinquents, they have sound brains. But psychopaths are unstable and undeterrable. Psychiatrists defined *psychopathy* as a biologically based (but not necessarily inherited) condition, a mental disease that causes criminal behavior and other social problems. In their view most offenders suffer from psychopathologies — diseases of the psyche, or mind. Psychopaths are more dangerous than other offenders, however, because their mental disease is inherent, inborn. By definition, few psychopaths can be cured of their condition.

Much as criminal anthropology had been bound up with the professionalization of criminology and feeblemindedness theory with the professionalization of psychology, psychopathy was closely tied to the professionalization of psychiatry. Like their predecessors, some of the psychiatrists who isolated the condition of psychopathy sympathized with the eugenics program. The psychopath emerged as a criminal type as the eugenics movement began losing momentum, however. Professionally psychiatrists were less invested in eugenics than in mental hygiene, a distinct although overlapping social movement aimed at detecting and treating mental disabilities in the general population. Although some eugenicists remained loyal to feeblemindedness theory, crusading for institutions for defective delinquents, less fervent advocates of the doctrine enlisted in the mental hygiene campaign against psychopathy and other forms of mental illness. Owing to its proponents' weaker professional involvement in eugenics, psychopathy was a less eugenical concept than defective delinquency. Associated only loosely with bad heredity, it had little somatic content. Furthermore, because psychopathy was less tightly coupled to bad heredity, it generated less alarm than defective delinquency theory had.

This chapter deals with the evolution of the concept of psychopathy and the psychiatrization of criminology until about 1925. To establish the context in which psychopathy theory developed, the chapter begins by outlining the rise of a "new" psychiatry aimed less at treating the insane than at helping communities cope with daily problems such as crime. The next section shows how the "new" psychiatrists managed to reclaim the born-criminal concept from psychologists who backed feeblemindedness theory. After summarizing the general picture of the psychopath that emerges from the literature, the chapter illustrates the literature's diversity by examining the work of three particular psychiatric criminologists: Bernard Glueck, William Healy, and Edith Spaulding.

The "New" Psychiatry

As the profession responsible for care of the insane, psychiatry was almost as old as the nation itself; Dr. Benjamin Rush, the first prominent specialist in diseases of the mind, had been a member of the Continental Congress. In the nineteenth century Rush's professional descendants superintended insane asylums. After completing medical school, they trained for their specialty through apprenticeship, becoming assistants to asylum superintendents. Psychiatry was thus confined within institutions and limited to treating patients so severely ill as to be diagnosed insane. Psychiatrists had little professional mobility, and isolated behind asylum walls, they tended to become parochial in outlook. As William A. White, superintendent of St. Elizabeth's Hospital in Washington, D.C., later remarked, "The very fact that [in the nineteenth century] mental disease was largely coextensive with insanity in the public estimation and that insanity involved segregation in a public institution necessarily separated the practice of psychiatry in a very material and effective way from the other medical specialties."[1]

By the late nineteenth century psychiatry had become what historian Gerald Grob describes as "a specialty adrift" from mainstream medicine, a backwater.[2] Earlier treatment techniques had devolved into custodialism; the "cult of curability"[3] had given way to a pessimistic hereditarianism that anticipated few cures of the insane. Psychiatrists were unable to explain the causes of insanity. They also lacked a coherent diagnostic system. Absorbed by the tasks of managing asylums, they did little research. In his final crusade on behalf of the mentally disordered, Hervey Backus Wilbur took psychiatrists to task for their overreliance on chemical restraints.[4] With other critics Wilbur established a reform organization, the National Association for the Protection of the Insane and the Prevention of Insanity (NAPIPI). This association collapsed soon after Wilbur's death in 1883, but physicians, charity board commissioners, and even former insane asylum patients remained publicly critical of psychiatrists, whose practice had become an administrative rather than a medical specialty.

Psychiatry rescued itself from this cul-de-sac not by reforming insane asylum practices but by overleaping asylum walls to identify an entirely new clientele. Toward the century's close a new generation of physicians began interesting itself in mentally disordered members of the general population, whom it proposed to diagnose in community-based clinics. Leaving the chronic insane behind in state hospital wards, these psychiatrists turned their attention to less profound (and more prevalent) mental disorders, including barely discernible "borderline" syndromes. Unlike their predecessors, they would keep up with scientific developments in medicine and do clinical research themselves.[5]

In short, advocates of the new psychiatry developed career opportunities independent of the mental hospital system. Rejecting the old-fashioned title *alienist* in favor of the more modern term *psychiatrist*,[6] they disassociated themselves from mental hospital superintendents and returned to NAPIPI's theme of prevention: through mental hygiene work they would detect emotional disorders in their early stages or even forestall them entirely. In many ways psychiatrists of this new generation fit the mold of the early twentieth-century Progressive reformer. Optimistic and activist, they introduced scientific reforms, stressed the wisdom of prevention, and aimed at creating a more manageable, efficient society.[7]

These shifts within the profession unsettled definitions of who could qualify as a psychiatrist. By tradition the psychiatrist had studied general medicine; some newer practitioners had specialized in neurology, the study of nervous diseases. Medical schools offered scant training in the diagnosis or treatment of mental diseases, however, and as psychiatrists severed ties with insane asylums, they lost the opportunity for learning through apprenticeship. Any physician who specialized in mental disorders might now claim to be a psychiatrist. Guy Fernald and other physicians who ran prison laboratories did so,[8] and William Healy, earlier a neurologist, became known as a psychiatrist by virtue of his court clinic work.[9] Dr. Walter E. Fernald, superintendent of the Massachusetts school for the retarded, became a leading Progressive psychiatrist by developing a method to diagnose mental retardation and promoting the mental hygiene movement.[10] So loosely was the title defined that Charles B. Davenport tried to appropriate it for the eugenic field-workers he trained at the Eugenic Record Office, many of whom held no more than a B.A. degree.[11] Davenport's bid failed, and medical training remained a prerequisite for psychiatry. Otherwise, however, qualifications for the psychiatric profession remained unclear.

Psychiatry versus Psychology

Early twentieth-century psychology was another field in flux. Although the academic route to becoming a psychologist was better established than was the route to becoming a psychiatrist, untrained physicians and laypeople administered intelligence tests, and there was no agreement as to how the emerging specialty of clinical psychology would interface with psychiatry. Armed with mental tests, some psychologists tried to take over the psychiatric function of diagnosing mental disorders; armed with even more esoteric diagnostic procedures, psychiatrists fought back.[12] The outcome of this professional struggle determined which group ultimately had jurisdiction over criminality. Although the ostensible battle was for authority to diagnose mental disabilities (feeblemindedness, mental illness, or both), a hidden stake was for authority to diagnose criminals. The struggle, which began as a diagnostic dispute between psychiatrist Walter E. Fernald and psychologist Henry H. Goddard,[13] raged through the 1910s.

Leading psychologists gleefully anticipated taking over psychiatric functions. Robert M. Yerkes, for example, hoped that psychologists would soon have tests to identify the maladies of mentally disturbed lawbreakers, those "affectively peculiar delinquents or criminals" who are even more "dangerous to society" than the feebleminded are. Yerkes conceded that the psychologist's "mental examination alone is wholly inadequate for the solution of such complicated human problems as court cases almost invariably present." He also admitted that feeblemindedness (an affliction psychological tests *could* identify) accounted for only one-quarter of all crime. Yet Yerkes went on to argue that "it is the great task of progressive psychological examiners to devise and perfect" methods for studying the "remaining seventy-five per cent or more" of criminals, among whom are "numerous cases of peculiar mental constitution, and especially of overdeveloped, underdeveloped, or exceptionally related affective, emotional, or instinctive traits."[14]

Psychologist Lewis M. Terman, too, called for "quantitative evaluation of emotional and volitional traits" by members of his field. Like Yerkes, moreover, Terman condemned intelligence testing by the untrained: "That positions in clinical psychology . . . should so often be entrusted to physicians who have no psychological training to speak of is most unfortunate."[15] Terman aimed this barb at all physicians who presumed to use mental tests for diagnostic purposes.

Terminological imprecision encouraged this professional sparring. In the mid-1910s psychologists and psychiatrists alike blurred the lines between mental retardation and mental disease. This dissolution of boundaries did not reflect an inability to differentiate between the two afflictions, as it had in the mid-nineteenth century. Rather, it flowed from the realization that mental retardation and mental illness were not mutually exclusive[16] and from a desire to reconceptualize both problems as subdivisions of the larger phenomenon of mental disorder, or psychopathology.[17] Nonetheless, the new usages temporarily muddied distinctions between the jurisdictions of psychology and psychiatry, encouraging members of these fields to raid one another's professional territory.

Psychiatrists, indignant over psychologists' presumption of diagnostic equality, struck back. In 1916 the New York Psychiatrical Society appointed a committee to rein in clinical psychologists. Including two giants of the mental hygiene movement, Adolf Meyer[18] and Thomas W. Salmon, this committee observed with much distrust . . . the growing tendency of some psychologists . . . to deal with the problem of diagnosis, social management and institutional disposal of persons suffering from abnormal mental conditions. We recognize the great value of mental tests . . . but . . . most of such work . . . is carried on in schools, courts, correctional institutions and so called "psychological clinics," quite independently of medically trained workers. . . .

We recommend that the Society express its disapproval . . . of the application of psychology to responsible clinical work except when made by or under the direct supervision of physicians qualified to deal with abnormal mental conditions.[19]

Psychiatrists should have the final diagnostic say, even over the interpretation of intelligence test results.[20]

An Indiana psychiatrist, incensed by psychologists' presumption, argued that "if we wish to know the mental status of any individual we must place the results of our mental examination in proper relation with the individual's life history. *We must make longitudinal sections of the individual, so to speak, and not mere cross sections.*"[21] The psychiatrists' "longitudinal," or life-history, approach won the day. In the ensuing truce psychologists stopped claiming final diagnostic authority and psychiatrists stopped administering intelligence tests.[22] Intelligence test scores became but one part, a "mere cross-section," of the full diagnostic picture now assembled by members of the psychiatric profession. Within psychopathic clinics and laboratories, psychologists became assistants to psychiatrists.

Psychiatrists triumphed in this professional struggle partly because physicians—including Frank Christian in New York, Guy Fernald in Massachusetts, and William Healy in Chicago—had already become directors of court clinics and prison clearinghouses or laboratories. Initially these physicians had few qualifications for psychiatric status other than their medical training and conviction that crime indicates some sort of mental disease. By administering intelligence tests, however, some had gained expertise in diagnosing mental disorders. Their medical background inclined them to identify with the new psychiatrists, not psychologists, and in any case psychiatry was in ascendancy. It was the diagnostic wave of the future, a more arcane and prestigious business than "mere" intelligence testing.

The physician-directors of court and prison laboratories thus adopted the title "psychiatrist." In turn they helped to ensure the dominance of psychiatry by making their laboratories beachheads for the mental hygiene movement. Psychologists could take comfort insofar as they participated in the psychiatrists' victory. They, too, became "psychopathologists," specialists in disorders of the mind, albeit specialists subordinate to psychiatrists. The ultimate victory went to the medical interpretation of criminality as a disease, now understood as a disease of the psyche.

Psychiatry owed some of its new appeal to the erosion of eugenics doctrine, a loss of explanatory power that created openings for more mentalistic accounts of the etiology of crime and other social problems. By the mid-1910 the Mendelian formula of inheritance, which had seemed so plausible just a few years earlier, was becoming the eugenics movement's Achilles' heel. Moreover, superintendents of institutions for the retarded were starting to retract their blanket indictment of the feebleminded. By 1915 enough doubt had been raised to tip the scale toward the view that mental disease rather than mental defect produces most crime. Eugenicists did not abandon their beliefs overnight; for instance, Walter E. Fernald, who had relaxed his hard line against the feebleminded, continued to maintain that most criminals "are really congenital defectives."[23] Nonetheless, they began to concede that hereditary feeblemindedness might be only one cause of crime, and perhaps a less significant cause than mental illness.

The psychopath thus displaced the defective delinquent as part of a more general phenomenon, the reinterpretation of criminal behavior as a function of mental disturbance.[24]

Defining the Psychopath

The term *psychopathy*, from the Greek for "soul" or "mind" (*psyche*) and "suffering" or "illness" (*pathos*), was evidently coined about 1845, when it made its first documented appearance in an Austrian psychiatric textbook. This text, by Ernst von Feuchtersleben, was translated into English two years later as *The Principles of Medical Psychology*.[25] Thus it is entirely possible that Americans began encountering the term *psychopathy* in the mid-nineteenth century. The criminological psychiatrists who popularized the term in the early twentieth century, however, cite not von Feuchtersleben but two more recent authorities on psychopathy, the Germans Richard von Krafft-Ebing and Emil Kraepelin, both of whom wrote influential textbooks that were translated into English.[26]

The American psychiatrists who championed psychopathy in the early twentieth century admitted that the concept was "most difficult to define."[27] Psychopaths, they tell us, are usually not mentally deficient: although some test as subnormal, others are bright. Nor are they insane, although the condition appears to overlap with the psychoneuroses and psychoses.[28] One report describes psychopaths as "semi-insane"; another, as "misfits among the misfits."[29] Early discussions also depict psychopaths as impulsive, inhibitionless, emotional, unbalanced, unadjusted, unemployable, poor in judgment, disruptive, rancorous, cruel, and deceitful.[30] "These psychopathic personalities," a Missouri report explains, "range from eccentric but harmless cranks through the group termed 'pathologic liars and swindlers' to the dangerous anti-social persons who are emotionally unresponsive to the feelings of others and are extremely selfish. Many of our repeated [*sic*] offenders belong to this group."[31]

Psychiatrists agreed that the mental and physical peculiarities of psychopaths appear early in life and are therefore probably "constitutional," or inherent. When they found similar abnormalities in the subject's family history, they took these as evidence that the constitutional defects had been inherited. Some commentators still used *degeneracy,* the nineteenth-century term for heritable mental and physical deterioration, as a synonym for *psychopathy.* After all, they reasoned, the condition must signify a decline in the vitality of the germinal matter.

This thumbnail sketch, although not inaccurate, is misleading insofar as it masks the remarkable diversity of the early twentieth-century literature on psychopaths. To recapture some of that definitional diversity and give an idea of how the psychopath concept developed between 1915 and 1925, it is instructive to explore the work of three influential psychiatric criminologists: Bernard Glueck, William Healy, and Edith R. Spaulding. Glueck studied male psychopaths, whereas Spaulding concentrated on their female counterparts and Healy on juveniles (male and female); thus the work of these three enables us to see how the "psychopath" label was applied to a range of subjects. Moreover, because Glueck and Spaulding studied New York State populations, their research enables us to continue tracing the evolution of born-criminal theory in that state. In addition, because their research on psychopathy, like the Bedford Hills research on defective delinquents, was sponsored by John D. Rockefeller Jr., it enables us to continue tracking outside funding for the development of born-criminal theory.

Glueck, Healy, and Spaulding drew different conclusions about the nature of the psychopath, but collectively their writings repudiate eugenic interpretations of criminal behavior. Their work helped to inaugurate a new interpretation in which psychopathy is a mental condition quite independent of the body.

Bernard Glueck

Bernard Glueck (1884–1972), a psychiatrist who was born in Poland but educated mainly in the United States, did more than any other single American to turn the tide against feeblemindedness theory and toward psychiatric understandings of criminality.[32] After earning his medical degree at Georgetown University Medical School in 1909, Glueck began work at St. Elizabeth's Hospital for the Insane in Washington, D.C., where he studied the criminally insane. That led to his 1915 appointment as head of the first psychiatric clinic in a men's penal unit, at New York's Sing Sing prison.[33]

This clinic had been established as part of the broader effort to centralize New York State's prison system; it was the first step in a plan to turn Sing Sing into a clearinghouse for the state's male prisoners, who after classification would be sent to prisons that specialized in types of mental disability, including defective delinquency. Supported by funds from John D. Rockefeller Jr. through the National Committee on Mental Hygiene,[34] Glueck's Sing Sing research was closely watched and frequently cited by other psychiatrists and lay reformers.

Glueck believed that criminal behavior reflects an underlying mental disorder. "Criminology is an integral part of psychopathology," he wrote, and "crime is a type of abnormal conduct which expresses a failure of proper adjustment at the psychological level."[35] Thus psychiatrists rather than judges should have ultimate authority in criminological matters. Glueck was familiar with the great German treatises on psychopathy, and he perpetuated their interpretation of mental disorders in degenerationist terms, attributing psychopathy to a deteriorating "constitution." In this respect he approached psychopathy as a clinician. At the same time, however, as a Progressive activist, Glueck was keenly interested in making the psychopath category administratively useful.

Glueck described the psychopath in a series of articles written in the mid-1910s, when he was on the cutting edge of the new psychiatric criminology.[36] These essays, most of them reporting the results of his Sing Sing research, identify the psychopath, or "constitutional inferior," as one of three major criminal types, along with defectives and the insane. Constituting about 20 percent of Glueck's Sing Sing sample, psychopaths differ from defectives in that they are often normal in intelligence and from the insane or mentally diseased in that their disorders are constitutional, not acquired.[37] Their psychopathic constitution, Glueck tells us, is usually inherited, induced by such factors as a father's alcoholism or a mother's sexual promiscuity.[38] Psychopaths with antisocial tendencies are the most dangerous of all criminals.[39]

To define the psychopath as a distinct clinical type, Glueck marshals a host of opprobrious adjectives: *impulsive, irritable, emotional, promiscuous, vicious, unadaptable, recidivistic,* and *incapable.* Psychopaths, he continues, are drinkers, drug addicts, gamblers, and sex perverts.[40] Often their constitutional inferiorities—nomadism, dizzy spells, sexual precocity—show up in early childhood.[41] Glueck's efforts to define the psychopath clinically founder, however, partly because many of the same traits characterize his other criminal types and partly because his psychopath seems to be more unpleasant than abnormal. "It is very difficult," Glueck admits, "to convince the uninitiated that we are dealing here with a pathological personality."[42] The psychopathic group "constitutes beyond a doubt, the most baffling group in our classification. . . . It is often difficult to convince the layman, or even the physician, that one is dealing here with a distinctly abnormal personality."[43]

Glueck is far more persuasive in defining the psychopath as an administrative category. Echoing Krafft-Ebing, he explains that psychopathic delinquents "are the most troublesome element in a penal institution. They are subject to outbreaks of pathological emotionalism and excitement, and cannot be given proper care in the average prison."[44] Thus they should be sent to specialized psychiatric facilities.

Glueck's writings on the psychopathic criminal illustrate a new cautiousness about eugenics. The enthusiasm with which eugenicists had endorsed defective delinquency theory just a few years earlier had faded. After 1915 those who remained loyal to eugenics tended to cloak their arguments in ambiguous language, advocating life sentences, for example, on the grounds that these would prevent crime while muffling their sentiments about reproduction. Glueck may have been using such a code of circumspection when he recommended life sentencing for psychopaths and other mentally abnormal offenders: "That permanent segregation in a proper institution is the only solution in a considerable percentage of these cases, we do not doubt for one moment, and it is hoped that the work done by the [Sing Sing] Clinic will succeed in furnishing sufficiently reliable data to justify Society in taking care in a more permanent, and hence a more rational manner, of those individuals who are obviously and palpably incapable of adjusting themselves to the demands of modern Society."[45] These sound like eugenic recommendations, and eugenicists would have understood them as such. Nevertheless, it is impossible to tell whether Glueck's rationale for permanent segregation is limited to defense against crime or includes defense against bad germ plasm as well. His motives may well have been eugenic: he presents psychopathy as a constitutional condition; his brother and sister-in-law, Sheldon and Eleanor Glueck, endorsed eugenic solutions into the 1930s;[46] and Glueck's studies were supported by a eugenicist, John D. Rockefeller Jr., through the National Committee for Mental Hygiene, an organization that in this period was dominated by eugenicists.[47] But the eugenic themes that sounded so loudly in the work of defective delinquency theorists have grown faint here. The somaticism that had dominated biological theories since Lombroso's vision of the born criminal was waning.

William Healy

Many Americans converted to psychiatric criminology on reading *The Individual Delinquent: A Textbook of Diagnosis for All Concerned in Understand-*

ing Offenders (1915). This study by the physician William Healy (1869–1963) became the period's most respected criminological treatise, one of the switches that rerouted criminology from the explanatory track of feeblemindedness theory onto that of mental deviation.[48] A monumental work of 830 pages, *The Individual Delinquent* analyzes data Healy collected as director of the Chicago Juvenile Psychopathic Institute, the nation's first and most influential court clinic, opened in 1909. It includes an entire chapter on "psychic constitutional inferiority," Healy's preferred synonym for *psychopathy.*[49]

The Individual Delinquent associates criminality with five major types of mental abnormality. One of these is mental defectiveness, but this disability, so prominent in the reports of defective delinquency theorists, afflicted only about 10 percent of Healy's total sample of 1,000 repeat juvenile offenders.[50] Healy does not specify the number of cases of psychic constitutional inferiority in his sample but suggests that this category was even smaller. To judge from numbers, then, constitutional inferiority plays a relatively minor role in offending. In nonstatistical passages, however, Healy dissolves distinctions between constitutional inferiority and criminality. Conceptually one category flows into the other, so that it is impossible to keep them separate. In these passages constitutional inferiority takes on a significance far greater than its numerical representation suggests, seeming at times to be the cause of all criminal behavior.

Healy treats psychopathy as a clinical category, but like Bernard Glueck, he has difficulty arriving at a precise and plausible definition. Psychic constitutional inferiority, he writes, is a "borderline" condition between feeblemindedness and insanity that in some unexplained way "unfits" those afflicted from leading "a law-abiding life."[51] Constitutional inferiors are "egocentric, selfish, irritable, very suggestible, easily fatigued mentally." Most exhibit "distinct bodily abnormalities," such as dwarfish growth, delayed puberty, facial tremors or tics, and weak eyesight. But even more characteristic than the "so-called stigmata of degeneracy" is their weakness of will. Constitutional inferiors are simply unable to exercise self-restraint.[52]

Healy describes female constitutional inferiors in terms close to those that earlier born-criminal theorists applied to criminalistic women. He begins by remarking that criminalistic female constitutional inferiors are relatively rare. Like Lombroso, with whose work he was familiar, Healy then draws on egg-sperm imagery to explain the low female rates: "The notable comparatively small number of female constitutional inferiors found in court work may be best explained, I think, by the greater freedom and restlessness of the male sex. The females of this class become more of the drudge type than offenders."[53] Over the course of these two sentences, the "comparatively small" category of female constitutional inferiors balloons to include all women who are stolid and poor. Such women, moreover, are negatively defined from the viewpoint of a disdainful middle-class male ("drudge type"). Healy, who throughout *The Individual Delinquent* describes girl delinquents in terms of their attractiveness, concludes this passage by associating impoverished women with the familiar archetype of the female degenerate. Some female constitutional inferiors, he writes, "yield to temptation and later become, in spite, perhaps, of unattractiveness, members of the low prostitute class. Almost worse for society is the fact that they live in various relationships with a low class of men in camps or shanties, and frequently produce offspring, who, in turn, become problems to society." [54] In just a few sentences the constitutionally inferior or psychopathic woman has gone from rarely offending to becoming another Ada Juke, the whorish mother of paupers, criminals, and mental defectives. She moreover has been set up as the opposite of the middle-class male, who becomes the standard against which deviation is to be defined.

Healy describes male constitutional inferiors as effeminate homosexuals. Here he may be following the lead of Emil Kraepelin, the German psychiatrist who had previously made effeminacy a defining characteristic of the male psychopath. [55] Alternatively, Healy may simply have been reflecting the growing awareness and fear of homosexuality. [56] In any case, the first of his several long examples of male constitutional inferiority describes a youth of sixteen whose delinquencies include truancy, running away, and petty theft: "Voice high and weak for his age. Stammers a little. Backward in signs of puberty . . . very few manly traits. . . . Got into bad sex habits when he was 10 or 12 years old. His stepmother has warned him of the danger of going insane through these things [masturbation]. Says when he has been in the country in the summer, tramps have approached him for these purposes. Whenever we talk with him he cannot get along without crying." [57]

Healy does not explicitly attribute homosexuality to his second example, although he does report this fourteen-year-old boy to be poorly developed, high voiced, emotional, and unmanly ("an arrant coward"), [58] but the third example presents a full-scale portrait of sexual "degeneracy." [59] This seventeen-year-old boy, arrested for truancy and "sex perversions," is physically weak, with "unusually long, delicate hands" and prominent hips. "Complains of occasional marked swelling in one breast. Has supernumerary nipples. Uses his eyes in most peculiar way; drops the eyelids and snaps them in girlish fashion." Always regarded as a "sissy," as a child he played with dolls, loved to sew and iron, and avoided athletics. In adolescence he adopted the name of "Hattie" and began cross-dressing. Soon he was engaging in "the most effeminate type of sex perversions" and earning his living by female impersonations. [60] It is just *because* this boy is so womanly that Healy concludes that he is constitutionally inferior: "The incongruous combination of poor general physical conditions, stigmata of degeneracy, delicate bodily organization, effeminacy of mind, dishonesty, show of natural affection, engaging in female occupations by choice, . . . and absolute weakness of purpose, show him to be a marked type of constitutional inferior."[61] In males effeminacy, criminality, and psychopathy have become interchangeable afflictions.

Healy's descriptions of female and male constitutional inferiors serve to demonstrate that heterosexual, middle-class masculinity is the standard by which other sexualities and genders will be judged and found wanting. His comments on psychic constitutional inferiors are devoid of eugenic content, but like earlier versions of born-criminal theory, they too distribute authority in the moral world.

Edith R. Spaulding

Progressive Era studies that deal exclusively with the female psychopath often portray her as an institutional troublemaker who impedes rehabilitative work with other inmates. Unlike the inert, barely sentient defective delinquent woman, but also unlike Healy's psychopathic "drudge," the psychopathic woman was constructed as defiant, someone who organizes prisoner resistance.[62] Even more so than Bernard Glueck's male psychopath, the female of this type was defined from an administrative perspective.

The gender differences ascribed to institutionalized psychopaths are by and large artifacts of the methods researchers used to select their subjects. Studies of male psychopaths usually began with a general population, such as Sing Sing's, that was then classified into subgroups, one labeled psychopathic. The leading studies of female psychopaths instead began with groups preselected as institutional headaches or psychopaths. Such women were then studied to determine the female psychopath's characteristics.

Edith R. Spaulding's *Experimental Study of Psychopathic Delinquent Women* (1923), the period's most detailed portrait of the female psychopath, reports research at the psychopathic hospital at Bedford Hills. This hospital was a separate unit built and operated on the reformatory's grounds from September 1916 through June 1918 with funds from John D. Rockefeller Jr.'s Bureau of Social Hygiene.[63] Spaulding, the hospital's director, had previously been resident physician at the Massachusetts Reformatory for Women, where, having become dissatisfied with mental testing methods and feeblemindedness theory, she had begun diagnosing some inmates as "psychopathic" in their tendencies. Spaulding had then started an experiment in which, as she described it, "a group of the most unstable were segregated in a part of the institution where they had a different regime intended to give more outlet and an atmosphere of therapy."[64] The experiment had failed, however, because the Massachusetts psychopaths, living up to reputation, discovered ways to continue disrupting the general population.

Bedford's psychopathic hospital was established "for the special study and treatment of the unstable cases that were constantly interfering with the progress of the more stable types."[65] They were the troublemakers who remained in the reformatory's population after the defective delinquents had been weeded out. These psychopathic women were characterized by neither mental backwardness nor mental disease but rather "conduct deviation."[66] All were "psychopathic" in the general sense of having been segregated in a psychopathic hospital for treatment of some sort of psychopathology or mental abnormality. In addition, of the total of thirty-three "patients" treated at the hospital, nineteen, or 58 percent, were "psychopathic" in the more specific sense that their formal psychiatric diagnosis included this word: eight were diagnosed as "psychopathic personality," two as "psychopathic personality with episodes of excitement," another two as "psychopathic personality with manic-depressive constitution," and so on.[67]

Spaulding painstakingly examined her patients for "stigmata of degeneracy,"[68] but she was unable to discover much evidence that the psychopathic condition is "constitutional." She did find that biological factors such as menstruation played a causal role in the disciplinary outbreaks that periodically rocked the hospital, that "in 39.4 per cent of the cases inheritance appeared to have been an unfavorable element," and that "in many instances, there was an emotional make-up that suggested the force and abandon of primitive races."[69] Spaulding's use of such biological and anthropological details is less explanatory than invocational, however, a genuflection to anthropological German writings on psychopathy that by then had lost their relevance. Instead of reaching conclusions about degenerate constitutions, she remarks that the psychopaths had "surprisingly few organic conditions." In an explicit rejection of eugenics, moreover, Spaulding recommends *against* "a truly indeterminate sentence . . . that would impose the equivalent of a life sentence," for it would remove the "incentive of freedom" desperately needed in work with the female psychopath.[70]

Presenting the psychopathic woman almost exclusively as a disciplinary problem, Spaulding lists the traits that make her administratively difficult: her "intense antisocial manner, the defiance of authority, the suspicion and attitude of defense, and the susceptibility to group hatred."[71] There is little clinical material here, even in the detailed case histories, as shown by the case history of Pearl W., a sixteen-year-old "mulatto girl" committed to Bedford Hills for petit larceny. When Pearl demonstrated "emotional instability" in the reception cottage, Laboratory of Social Hygiene officials transferred her to the psychopathic hospital for study and treatment.[72] There Spaulding's team discovered that Pearl had become a prostitute at the age of eleven and that she drank, used drugs, stole, and showed no remorse about her way of life. In the hospital "she associated with the most unstable girls and was easily influenced," becoming "excited and assaultive, especially if any of the other patients made remarks about the colored people and if she thought the colored girls were being discriminated against. She was often disobedient, defiant, and boisterous, . . . always scolding and dissatisfied."[73] Hospital officials further described Pearl as sullen, aggressive, irritable, combative, and sly—all signs of her uncooperativeness. Eventually they diagnosed her as a psychopathic personality.[74] For Spaulding and her associates, "psychopathic" was primarily a managerial category, a label for inmates who gave them trouble. "Altogether," she concludes of Pearl, "there was little of a constructive nature in her make-up."[75]

Although nearly all Bedford Hills' inmates were incarcerated for sex-related offenses or diseases, Spaulding refrains from speculating on a possible causal connection between psychopathy and promiscuity. Nor does she relate the condition to lesbianism, notwithstanding her awareness of extensive pairings among inmates. Spaulding does remark on the infatuations of the "white girls" for the "colored girls," a racial crossing she attributes to the whites' substitution of color "for the masculine companionship they were temporarily denied." Although she thus racializes lesbianism from a white, heterosexual perspective, however, Spaulding makes no attempt to pathologize it. Her sole concern is that the "undercurrent of the emotions aroused in such infatuations is felt at times throughout a large group of girls and the emotional explosions are difficult to control."[76]

Spaulding's disinterest in attributing abnormality to her subjects' bodies or sexual behaviors reflects her study's timing. She did not publish *An Experimental Study of Psychopathic Delinquent Women* until the 1920s, nearly a decade after Glueck and Healy published their studies; in the interim degenerationism and the German psychiatric tradition, both of which had treated departures from the role of the good woman as forms of mental and biological deviance, had become even more attenuated—so much so that their influence barely grazes Spaulding's book.

Two of the era's most respected prison superintendents, Jessie D. Hodder and Katharine Bement Davis, reinforced Spaulding's description of the female psychopath as a rebellious—and hence pathological—inmate. In works of their own, Hodder and Davis actually go far beyond Spaulding, portraying psychopathic women as monsters of defiance who refuse to be intimidated by lumbar punctures, stomach pumpings, or transfers to institutions for the insane or feebleminded.[77] The period's literature describes male psychopaths as disorderly as well, but not mutinous on such a grand scale. Women superintendents may have worried more than their male counterparts about maintaining discipline, or they may actually have had more disciplinary problems, since they aimed at greater prisoner control.[78] Whatever their reasons, Hodder and Davis frankly use the concept of psychopathy for control purposes, agreeing that a consistently uncooperative woman must be "psychopathic" and hence not treatable in *their* institution. As Hodder puts it, "An unmanageable woman prisoner is so because of nervous or mental defect, or both, and no prison discipline will overcome that defect."[79] Such "psychopaths" should be transferred to mental institutions.

"A Large Unclassified Group"

There was, then, considerable variation among these first American portrayals of the psychopath, variation influenced by the authors' research goals, their sample selection processes, and such personal characteristics as their sex, attitudes toward gender and sexuality, and familiarity with classics of German psychiatry.

For Bernard Glueck, classifying male prisoners in an experiment possibly guided by eugenic principles, *psychopath* was a label for difficult prisoners who, although they could not be diagnosed as feebleminded or insane, nonetheless seemed mentally abnormal and in need of permanent segregation. In Glueck's work psychopathy remains a form of degeneration, a constitutional and inherited disability. For Healy, too, psychopathy, or psychic constitutional inferiority, is a type of mental abnormality that leads to crime and reveals itself in physical and mental anomalies. In Healy's case, however, the physical and mental anomalies are heavily freighted with sex/gender content, and they are unambiguously free of eugenic content.

Spaulding and others who report on incarcerated female psychopaths show little interest in either constitutional degeneracy or sex/gender pathologies, instead stressing the psychopathic woman's willful disruptiveness of prison routines. Two of these authors, Davis and Hodder, were not physicians but prison superintendents; Spaulding, although she practiced medicine and conducted her Bedford Hills experiment during the 1910s, did not complete her study before biological theories of crime had begun to wane in popularity. Thus these authors characterize psychopathy less as a physical disease than as a behavioral deviation. In their work psychopathy has already become a purely mental disease.

As a concept psychopathy roused relatively little resistance. When a group of psychiatrists met in 1923 for a symposium on "the psychopathic individual," few had substantive criticisms. One argued that the "term constitutional psychopath is objectionable because it implies that an individual of this type is born so, and that, therefore, there is nothing to do about it." The same psychiatrist observed that his profession had not developed a sufficiently clear terminology for the "large unclassified group" of mentally ill people "who are lumped together under the heading psychopathic."[80] But the only true critique came from William A. White, who declared, "Psychopathic as a prefix has come to be a wastebasket into which all sorts of things have been thrown. It is a sort of middle ground for the dumping of odds and ends, as the praecox group used to be."[81]

That psychiatrists embraced the concept of psychopathy is not surprising: it was the condition that proved that mental disorder causes crime. It formed the conceptual bridge over which born-criminal theory passed out of psychology and into psychiatry. Psychologists were unable to prevent this loss. Having been subordinated, they lacked authority to criticize psychiatrists' diagnostic categories or to object to the psychiatric takeover of jurisdiction for crime.

These early works on psychopathy had much in common with earlier biological theories of crime. In them psychopathy is a highly flexible concept, one that can be derived from various samples and applied in widely different situations. In them, too, the born-criminal concept expands and contracts, referring sometimes to a small subcategory of offenders and sometimes to all criminals. The authors of these studies, like their predecessors, purport to describe the worst type of offender, and again, *worst* is defined in terms not of dangerous behavior but of an internal condition. They, too, use their born-criminal concept to reassert the authority of middle-class professionals, in this case the authority of psychiatrists to examine the criminal's body and mind and pass judgment on their quality.

Notes

1. White 1917:7.
2. Grob 1983:30.
3. Deutsch 1949: chap. 8.
4. Wilbur 1881b.
5. For helpful accounts of the rise of the "new" psychiatry, see Grob 1983 and Lunbeck 1994.
6. Southard 1917:567–68.
7. See esp. Burnham 1960.
8. G. Fernald 1916–17, esp. p. 396, where Fernald says he has "abandoned" intelligence testing in favor of "the clinical psychiatrist's methods"; also see p. 397, where Fernald calls himself an "alienist."

9. See, e.g., Jones 1986.

10. W. E. Fernald was nominated president of the Massachusetts School of Psychiatry and New England School of Psychiatry (Brenzel 1986:285), and he was a member of the executive committee of the National Committee for Mental Hygiene.

11. Davenport [1916] 1988:212.

12. See, for example, Healy 1922; MacCurdy 1921b:182; and MacCurdy 1921a.

13. Zenderland 1987.

14. Yerkes 1916–17:366–69.

15. Terman 1916–17:533–35; also see Yerkes 1916–17:369–70.

16. See, for example, Taft 1918, esp. p. 438, where the author asks, "may not the standard of feeblemindedness indicating segregation be as much a matter of type of emotional and impulsive make-up as a matter of degree of intellectual defect?"

17. For instance, Murray and Kuh, psychiatrists at the Chicago House of Correction, used *mental defectives* to denote both the mentally deficient and the mentally ill (1917–18:840); similarly, see White 1917:12.

18. Meyer helped to lead the mental hygiene movement even though he broke with the National Committee for Mental Hygiene; see Grob 1983:149–56.

19. Notes and Abstracts 1917–18:266–67.

20. Similarly, see W. Fernald 1917b:232–33.

21. Bowers 1917–18:309 (emphases added).

22. But see Southard 1917:569, proposing a new psychiatric specialty in "metric psychiatry," or mental testing. Except for Healy, few on either side in this dispute had much tact.

23. W. Fernald 1917a:42.

24. For another, less criminological view of psychopathy's role in the development of psychiatry, see Lunbeck 1994.

25. Werlinder 1978:86 n. 2.

26. Krafft-Ebing 1904; Kraepelin [1912] 1917.

27. B. Glueck 1917a:98; also see G. Fernald 1918:454 and Scott 1922:360.

28. Anderson 1916:693; also see Anderson 1914:344 and Karpas 1913.

29. Missouri Association for Criminal Justice 1926:405; Spaulding 1916:5.

30. This chapter is based on discussions of psychopathy in Adler 1917–18, 1920; Anderson 1914, 1916, 1917–18; Bowers 1914–15, 1915; S. Brown 1924; Bryant 1917–18; Clark 1916; Davis 1919–20, [1923] 1969; Deiser 1919–20; Diefendorf 1907; Dooley 1924; Farnell 1920–21; G. Fernald 1916–17, 1917, 1918; B. Glueck 1917a, 1917b, 1918a, 1918b, 1919; S. Glueck 1925; Goddard 1920–21, 1921; Healy 1915; Hoag and Williams 1923; Hodder 1918, 1920; Karpas 1913, 1916; Karpman 1924; Keniston 1910; Love and Davenport 1919, 1920; McCord 1924; Meyer [1905] 1951, [1907] 1952, [1916] 1952; Missouri Association for Criminal Justice 1926; Montague 1919; New York State Commission of Prisons 1925; New York State Prison Survey Committee 1920; Pollack 1921; Prison Association of New York, *Annual Report, 1916;* Prison Association of New York, *Annual Report, 1917;* Rosanoff 1927; Salmon 1917, 1919–20; Scott 1922; Southard 1916; Spaulding 1914–15, 1916, [1923] 1969, 1925; Stearns 1918–19; Strecker 1921; U.S. War Department 1918; Visher 1922; Williams and Anderson 1924; and Yerkes, 1916–17.

31. Missouri Association for Criminal Justice 1926:405. It was Kraepelin who identified the "morbid liars and swindlers" group (Kraepelin [1912] 1917:295-309).

32. Werlinder (1978:143) emphasizes the role played by another psychiatrist, Adolf Meyer, in introducing Americans to German psychiatric thought. Also a European immigrant, Meyer developed his own psychiatric theory ("psychobiology" [Meyer 1957]), taught at Johns Hopkins, and contributed greatly to the transformation of psychiatry from an institutional to a community-based specialty. Yet his writings on psychopathy ("constitutional inferiority"; see Meyer [1905] 1951 and [1907] 1952) were neither as specific nor as widely cited in criminological circles as were Glueck's. It is possible that Werlinder, working in Sweden, was simply unfamiliar with most of Glueck's work, which is obscure relative to Meyer's and has not been collected. On the other hand, Werlinder's main interest lies in psychiatry, not criminology, and in the former field Meyer certainly outshone Glueck.

33. For a brief biography, see Lebensohn 1973, which is my source for the 1915 date.

34. B. Glueck 1917a:104.

35. B. Glueck 1916:vii.

36. See B. Glueck 1917a, 1917b, 1918a, 1918b, and 1919.

37. B. Glueck 1917a.

38. B. Glueck 1918b:121. This analysis suggests that to some extent, Glueck still relied on Lamarckian theory, according to which acquired characteristics can become hereditary.

39. Ibid., 123. Glueck repeats this claim in 1918a:206 while at the same time describing psychopaths as "perhaps the most promising group from a therapeutic point of view."

40. Without defining *sex perverts,* Glueck indicates that he applies the term to heterosexuals as well as those who are "biologically sexually inverted" (B. Glueck 1917a:103). The day of the "sexual psychopath" lay ahead (see Freedman 1987); in the early American literature psychopathy is just beginning to be associated with sexual deviation.

41. B. Glueck 1917a:102-3.

42. B. Glueck 1917b:188.

43. B. Glueck 1918b:91.

44. B. Glueck 1917b:173; Krafft-Ebing 1904:623.

45. B. Glueck 1917a:104. Glueck (1916:vi) also makes the following claim, however: "some individuals because of their psychological makeup, *either qualitative or quantitative,* are absolutely and permanently incorrigible and present a problem which can be dealt with in only one effective way—namely, permanent segregation and isolation from society" (emphasis added). In particular, "qualitative" here hints at poor germ plasm, but again it is impossible to be sure. For other eugenically tinged statements, see B. Glueck 1917b:182 and B. Glueck 1918a:184, 188.

46. Glueck and Glueck 1934.

47. In addition, Bernard Glueck advocated institutions for defective delinquents, which in the 1910s were invariably conceived as eugenic institutions, and eugenicists such as O. F. Lewis were enthusiastic about his work (O. Lewis 1916).

48. Mental hygienists, court personnel, criminologists, and prison reformers revered *The Individual Delinquent* as one of the pivotal books of their day. " 'The Individual Delinquent' is undoubtedly the greatest American contribution in the field of criminology," wrote one reviewer. "Indeed, it is one of the greatest contributions of any country" (Klein 1915:8). A textbook explained that "for the real beginning of the new science of criminal diagnosis . . . we must look to the Juvenile Psychopathic Institute in Chicago," where Healy had uncovered "the dominating part played by mental factors in the etiology of crime" (F. Wines 1919:270, 291). The *Journal of Criminal Law and Criminology* devoted eleven pages to reviewing Healy's book, and although its reviewer had some reservations, he reported that "Doctor Healy has completely succeeded" as "a scientist of the characterology of juvenile criminals" (Stevens 1915–16:858). "For those who have doubted the wisdom and the value of expert psychopathic work as an adjunct to judicial procedure," this reviewer concluded, "no more adequate answer could be given than reference to the volume before us" (ibid.).

49. Healy uses *psychic constitutional inferiority,* a term he borrowed from German psychiatry, instead of *psychopathy* to avoid any implication of insanity (Healy 1915:576).

50. Healy 1915:139 (of the 1,000 offenders, 97 are either morons or imbeciles).

51. Ibid., 444, 576.

52. Ibid., 576–77.

53. Ibid., 588–89.

54. Ibid., 589.

55. Kraepelin [1912] 1917:281–85.

56. Hansen 1992.

57. Healy 1915:578–80.

58. Ibid., 580–83.

59. Ibid., 588.

60. Ibid., 584–85.

61. Ibid., 586.

62. But see Scott 1922, describing female court cases.

63. Davis [1923] 1969:xiv.

64. Spaulding 1914–15:711; Spaulding [1923] 1969:4.

65. Davis [1923] 1969:xiii.

66. Spaulding [1923] 1969:3.

67. Ibid., 68. In addition to treating the thirty-three "patients," the hospital also treated eleven inmate "workers" deemed mentally defective (feebleminded). Although Spaulding sometimes calls these workers "patients," she makes it clear that they were brought into the hospital to hold down the cost of treating the *real* problems, who are now perceived as not feebleminded but psychopathic.

68. Ibid., 158.

69. Ibid., 97, 102, 119.

70. Ibid., 112, 133.

71. Ibid., 69.

72. Ibid., 177.

73. Ibid., 179.

74. Ibid., 68.

75. Ibid., 179.

76. Ibid., 273.

77. Hodder 1918, 1920; Davis 1919–20.

78. Rafter 1990a.

79. Hodder 1918:444. For a comparable statement by Davis, see Davis 1919–20:389.

80. Dr. Loren B. T. Johnson in Karpman 1924:177.

81. White in Karpman 1924:175.

10

Defective Delinquent Legislation

Flies are nuisances. They carry and breed disease. . . .
Necessary as it is to give a lusty whack at each individual fly whenever we can reach him, we shall not do
any radical work in the job of ridding the community of
flies unless we get at the breeding grounds. It is so with
criminals.

Arthur Woods, *Crime Prevention*

With a stroke of the governor's pen, in 1921
New York's reformatory for men at Napanoch
became an institution for defective delinquents,
the nation's first freestanding eugenic prison.[1]
The Napanoch law carried biological theories of
crime to the goal toward which they had been
tending since the late eighteenth century: formal,
mandated isolation of those predestined to commit crime. It realized the 1870 Cincinnati prison
congress's vision of institutions where incorrigible criminals could be segregated for life, and
it put into practice Zebulon Brockway's ideal of
the prison as a hospital for moral invalids. In
the areas of criminology and criminal justice, it
constituted the eugenics movement's most significant victory.

That victory arrived at a most peculiar moment, however, well after the enthusiasm for
defective delinquency theory had passed. The
most propitious time for such legislation would
seem to have been in 1911, when both the eugenics and Progressive movements were at full
crest, intelligence testing was starting to yield its
astounding results, and the galvanizing term *defective delinquent* had just been coined. As O. F.
Lewis, general secretary of the Prison Associ-

ation of New York, observed in 1912, "The problem [of feebleminded de-
linquents] is just now in the foreground. Sympathy is notably frequent in
the discussion of the question; legislators are inclined to see a great light."[2]
Why were institutions for defective delinquents not established then instead of a decade later, when the "great light" had gone out?[3]

In fact, Massachusetts did enact a defective delinquent law in 1911, creating—on paper—departments to which courts might commit mentally
defective defendants in criminal cases and troublesome mental defectives
from state training schools. This legislation authorized prison units to
which such criminalistic defectives could be committed on indefinite terms,
but the law remained a dead letter until the early 1920s. A similar New
York State bill, also introduced in 1911, got nowhere until 1920, when the
division for female defective delinquents was established at Bedford Hills,
and it did not finally succeed until 1921, when Napanoch was designated
the state's prison for male defective delinquents. Thus we confront a paradox: early efforts to establish institutions for defective delinquents (IDDs)
failed despite many factors in their favor, whereas later efforts succeeded
in a far chillier climate.

With a closer look the paradox vanishes. The first IDD proposals were
so fiscally naïve and politically simpleminded as almost to invite rejection.
Much more than enthusiasm was needed for eugenic solutions to become
law. The "good" feebleminded had to be distinguished from the "bad."
Criminal justice agencies, through mental testing, had to build up pressure
for institutions to isolate the defective delinquents they identified. Before
prisons could be classified by inmate type, New York's prison system had to
be centralized. And even when all these conditions had been met, if World
War I had not depopulated New York's prisons, the legislature probably
would have balked at setting aside an institution for defective delinquents.

Sorting Good from Bad

Attitudes toward the mentally retarded shifted yet again during 1911–21,
with well-set currents reversing themselves and innovative ideas carving
new channels. The decade was one in which Goddard and his followers
paired feeblemindedness with criminality, seemingly fusing the two devian-
cies for all time. At the same moment, however, others started uncoupling
the two concepts. While one current flowed toward the criminalization of
low intelligence, another ebbed toward normalization.

Eugenicists began differentiating among the objects of their fears, distinguishing the "good" feebleminded from the "bad." Some, acknowledging the impossibility of institutionalizing every feebleminded person, realized they would have to make distinctions among those who did and did

not require segregation. Others, when they learned that mental defectiveness was not heritable as a unit characteristic, wondered whether some of
the feebleminded might not be kept in the community after all. Still others
reversed their attitudes for professional reasons. For example, Walter Fernald, a decade after producing his inflammatory "Imbecile with Criminal
Instincts" paper, announced: "I am getting back to my old proposition that
there are both bad feeble-minded and good feeble-minded, that not all the
feeble-minded are criminalists and socialists and immoral and anti-social;
we know they are not. . . . We have really slandered the feeble-minded."[4]
As historian James W. Trent Jr. argues, Fernald and other psychiatrists had
become uncomfortable with the success of psychologists such as Goddard
"in spreading the message of the menace of the feebleminded throughout
the nation. . . . By distancing themselves from what they had so recently
helped create [fear of the feebleminded], they were separating themselves
from a challenge to their own authority and influence."[5] For one reason or
another, then, eugenicists relaxed their hard line against the feebleminded
as a class—but simultaneously they took an even stronger stand against the
subgroup of defective delinquents.

Mirroring these developments, the language of mental disability underwent yet another transmutation, with *mental defectives* and *mentally deficient* replacing *the feebleminded* and *feeblemindedness*. *Mental defectives* was
a more precise and arguably less denigrating term than *feebleminded*, and
mental deficiency, lacking the historical associations of *feeblemindedness*
with children's training schools, was less infantilizing. In addition the new
terms were relatively free of eugenic content. Whereas the feebleminded
had long been accused of social and genetic sins, "mental defectives" had
fewer negative associations. Taking steps to "lessen the odium," in 1919
New York officially replaced *feebleminded* with *mental defectives* and *feeblemindedness* with *mental deficiency*.[6] Other states made similar changes.

At the same time, however, *defective delinquent* superseded older terms
such as *moron* and *criminal imbecile* for the "bad" feebleminded. The
newer phrase was catchier, and it enabled eugenicists to engage in minor
self-deceptions that terms such as *feebleminded felon* or *mentally defective
murderer* would have made difficult. *Delinquent,* although a synonym for
criminal, sounded less threatening. Delinquents might be children, adult
misdemeanants, or even adult felons—but the term did not conjure up
visions of safecrackers or violent mobsters. Thus it gave those who advocated IDDs room to feel benevolent. Indefinite sentencing of adults became
palatable when the offenders were conceived as irresponsible "defective delinquents."

In sum, there developed a terminological double track for those formerly undifferentiated as "feebleminded." *Mental defectives* and *mentally*

deficient decontaminated the "good" feebleminded, while *defective delinquents* villainized the "bad."

More favorable attitudes toward mental defectives were encouraged (and in turn reinforced) by modifications in the colony plan. This plan dated back to 1882, when Hervey Backus Wilbur had devised what might be called a *Ferris-wheel model* of satellite colonies encircling a central institution. Wilbur conceived of colonies as adjuncts to the Syracuse Asylum, sheltered communities where older inmates who lacked families might live and work in relative normalcy. Pennsylvania superintendent Isaac Kerlin introduced an *umbrella model* for colonizing the feebleminded—holding retarded persons of all levels and ages for life under one institutional roof. Imperialistic in design and eugenic in aim, this second type of colony welcomed borderline "moral imbeciles" who, although they got into mischief, worked efficiently, thus holding down institutional costs. Early in the twentieth century the colony plan was again reconceptualized, this time according to what might be called a *funnel model,* designed to siphon the retarded out of closed institutions and back to life in the community. New York State led the way in this development, and New York in turn was led by Dr. Charles Bernstein, superintendent of New York's Rome Custodial Asylum.[7]

In one sense Bernstein merely revised Wilbur's Ferris-wheel plan. New York had never adopted Pennsylvania's umbrella model; instead, it classified by institution, with children going to Syracuse, adult females to Newark, and other custodial cases to Rome. Looking for ways to expand institutional capacity and reduce costs, early in the twentieth century Bernstein established the first Rome colony by settling twenty men on a nearby farm. This experiment cleared over $300 in the first six months, encouraging him to establish five more men's colonies over the next decade. These differed from Wilbur's colonies in that they became stepping stones to parole and complete discharge. Later Bernstein tackled the more sensitive task of establishing colonies for retarded women. These colonies demonstrated that mentally defective females could live in relative freedom without corrupting the community. The colony plan was evolving into a track for the "good" feebleminded.[8]

Simultaneously, however, Bernstein was working for more restrictive institutions for the "bad" feebleminded. His interest in these defective delinquents, like the attraction of nineteenth-century superintendents to moral imbeciles, lay in the hope of drawing able-bodied inmates into his institution to do the difficult work and reduce costs. In 1911 Bernstein begged the state to send defective delinquents to Rome: "We are very, very sure that the defective criminal, if he is anything, he [*sic*] is a good gardener, and if he can dig in the dirt and work a farm or garden, then he can help to support his less fortunate brethren, and this is our principal reasons for wishing to establish a department for this class at Rome. We feel they can be very helpful."[9] At first, then, Bernstein conceived of defective delinquents as controllable feebleminded males who could raise his institution's vegetables.

A decade later Bernstein changed his tune. In the interim the state's criminal courts had started committing retarded defendants to Rome rather than to reform schools or jails. Among those awaiting admission to Rome in 1921, one had been "arrested four different times for felonious assault," another was of "8 year mentality . . . implicated in at least two fires where buildings were burned," and a third had "shot the head off another man."[10] Clearly such cases would not make good gardeners. Bernstein now threw his weight behind the bill to turn Napanoch into an IDD.

The softening of old prejudices against mental defectives and simultaneous hardening of attitudes toward defective delinquents was also apparent in the work of New York's Commission to Investigate Provision for the Mentally Deficient, a body chaired by Robert W. Hebberd, secretary of the State Board of Charities. Established in 1914, the Hebberd commission caught defective delinquency in its fullest bloom. The commission's purpose, like that of investigative bodies established about the same time in other states, was to coordinate action for the care and control of the feebleminded. Parts of the commission's massive report are as rabidly eugenical as anything written by Henry H. Goddard. The first words, for example, warn that "feeble-mindedness is a grave social menace. To it can be attributed a very definite proportion of the vice, crime and degeneracy that tend to destroy the peace and prosperity of our communal life. Not only is it a fundamental cause of misery, but it possesses the quality of hereditary transmission, thus ensuring the continuance of misery through generations to come."[11] But the body of the Hebberd commission's report tells a different story. From it we learn that mental deficiency "can be induced by the factors of environment," that intelligence testing has been misused to exaggerate eugenic fears, and that normal children can be misdiagnosed as mentally deficient.[12] The commissioners go so far as to caution that vocational education for the weak-minded could create "definite labor groups or economic classes in the community—a tendency which is distinctly antagonistic to all ideas of democracy." With adequate training, they assert, some "high grade" defectives might "be given entire freedom."[13] In the course of educating themselves about mental deficiency, the commissioners shed their fear of the "good" feebleminded.

The Hebberd commission nevertheless remained adamantly hostile toward defective delinquents. Of twenty-six witnesses consulted about the need for IDDs—including Elmira Reformatory assistant superintendent Dr. Frank Christian, Charles B. Davenport from the Eugenics Record Office, Katharine Bement Davis, Walter E. Fernald, Hastings Hart of the

Russell Sage Foundation, and O. F. Lewis, all strong eugenicists—only one clearly objected. The exception was Charles Bernstein, who still believed that delinquent defectives could "be very helpful" at Rome.[14] Thus the Hebberd commission concluded "that separate institutions of a custodial nature should be established, one for the care of each sex, for the safe keeping of the mentally defective delinquent class."[15] A residue of eugenic fears remained to fuel campaigns against defective delinquents.

Pressure from Criminal Justice Agencies

Pressure for IDDs also flowed from criminal justice agencies, which now had the capacity to identify mentally subnormal offenders but no place to segregate them. Intelligence testing had provided a technology for identifying the mentally defective, and court clinics and prison clearinghouses were busy applying it. Such work was pointless, however, if there were no institutions to which weak-minded criminals might be sent.

The story of the Psychopathic Laboratory, operated by New York City's police department between 1915 and 1917, illustrates how such pressure built up. This laboratory's goal was twofold: to show how "science—psychology, medicine, and sociology"—could contribute to crime control[16] and to bypass trial in some cases by sending mental defectives straight from the streets to permanent custodial care.[17] The laboratory was instituted by reform-minded police commissioner Arthur Woods, a graduate of Groton and Harvard who had married into the wealthy Morgan family. A pilot program begun late in 1915 demonstrated the need: of twenty-nine (no doubt astonished) men pulled from morning lineups for mental testing, twenty-one proved to be mentally abnormal.[18]

Temporarily discontinued for lack of funds, the program was reintroduced the next year through $18,000 in private donations.[19] (According to the *New York Times,* donors included the millionaires Andrew Carnegie, F. W. Vanderbilt, Daniel Guggenheim, Mortimer L. Schiff, William Rockefeller, and Mrs. George B. Alexander.)[20] The advisory board, which had originally included Raymond B. Fosdick (an associate of John D. Rockefeller Jr.) and psychologist Edward L. Thorndike, was now joined by Thomas H. Salmon, chair of the National Committee for Mental Hygiene.[21] The staff fluctuated in number but at its height included three psychiatrists, one psychologist, a social worker "loaned by Dr. Davenport of Cold Spring Harbor," and two secretaries.[22] Examiners administered Binet and other tests to prisoners selected from the daily lineups or referred by magistrates. According to the police department's report for 1916,

> As soon as a definite conclusion is reached as to the particular form of abnormality of any of these persons they have been taken to court with a . . . recom-

mendation . . . that the prisoner be confined in an institution for treatment or for permanent care, rather than be put on trial. This procedure, the authorities believe, is far more economical and humane than to try to secure a conviction and send the prisoner to a penal institution . . . where they may be started on their way through the old in and out system of hopeless punishment, and through this become a menace to society by reason of their irresponsible mental condition.[23]

The laboratory, in short, would reduce "the old in and out" to an "in." It constituted a police-level counterpart to the laboratories at Bedford Hills and Sing Sing.

By May 1, 1917, the Psychopathic Laboratory had processed 502 cases, of which only 84 fell into the "not obviously abnormal" category. Eighty-two were diagnosed as mentally defective and another 43 as "psychopathic characters."[24] The Psychopathic Laboratory recommended seven imbeciles for commitment, but its significance to the defective delinquency movement lay largely in the number of defectives it identified who were *not* institutionalized. Those were the cases that created pressure for an IDD. A report on the program describing over a dozen horrific cases concluded: "What is most urgently needed at the present time is an institution for feeble-minded criminals."[25]

For three years the police department's annual reports used similar scare tactics and reached openly eugenic conclusions. When Woods resigned as commissioner, he published *Crime Prevention*, a book that relates additional horror stories from the laboratory's records and concludes that "there are on the average twenty-five persons a day arrested in New York who are mentally defective. . . . Plainly the proper course of action is to segregate him [the defective criminal] in some sort of institution . . . of the hospital type . . . until cured."[26] Citing laboratory data, a highly eugenical special report by the state's Commission of Prisons concluded that New York needed to turn the Bedford Hills and Sing Sing prisons into clearinghouses and establish no fewer than *four* institutions for defective delinquents.[27]

Under the headline "Sleuths to Be Taught How to Differentiate Mental Defectives from Crooks," the *New York Times* publicized the Psychopathic Laboratory's work: "The Commissioner figures that it is going to save his men a great deal of work if they can stand on a corner and by psychological tests tell what passer-by is the thief of yesterday for whom they are seeking, or spot the one whose guilty conscience betrays the presence of decks of cocaine in his pocket. If the policeman is uncertain he may march his suspect up an alley and apply the Binet test."[28] Professional journals and books also ran laudatory reports on the police laboratory's work.[29]

In this instance as in that of intelligence testing at Bedford Hills and Sing Sing, philanthropists financed a eugenics experiment within a criminal justice agency. Some who endowed the police laboratory supported the prison experiments as well; others knew the sponsors of the prison experiments through organizational, social, or family networks. Like the prison programs, the police department experiment confirmed eugenics dogma, intensified fears of mentally defective offenders, and identified "actual" offenders of this type, thus increasing the need for IDDs. At the same time many (perhaps most) of the donors were contributing to the Prison Association of New York, the New York Committee on Feeblemindedness, and other eugenics lobbying groups.

  Given the class interests inherent in the eugenics movement, it is tempting to speculate that those who financed the police laboratory hoped to transform criminal justice agencies into a tool for class control. Had that been their goal, however, they probably would have donated much more generously to the cause. The $18,000 that financed the police laboratory was a trifling sum for these particular donors. More likely, they endowed the Psychopathic Laboratory as a way of participating in the reform movements of their day. To bring criminal justice practices into line with the new sciences of human behavior was a goal dear to many Progressive reformers. What better way to achieve it than to integrate intelligence testing with policing and (as one observer phrased it, with the Eugenics Record Office's field-workers in mind) make "every patrolman a field worker"?[30]

Centralizing the Prison System

Delegates to the 1870 prison congress had recommended that "prisons, as well as prisoners, should be classified or graded so that there shall be prisons for the untried, for the incorrigible and for other degrees of depraved character."[31] Fifty years later New York implemented this recommendation. The institution at Napanoch, previously a men's reformatory, became a prison for "incorrigibles" as part of a broader effort to centralize the prison system and classify both prisons and prisoners.

A Masterplan for Change

The driving force behind New York's effort to centralize its prisons and create specialized institutions was the Prison Association of New York. A watchdog organization founded in 1844, the association had a long and distinguished record as the oldest private prison reform organization in the country.[32] Under Enoch C. Wines, the strongest of its nineteenth-century directors, it had attracted large donations from the wealthy, for whom it served as a fashionable philanthropy. The association was a logical candidate to lead Progressive penological reforms—if it could attract another powerful executive. That it did in 1910, when O. F. Lewis became its general secretary.

  Orlando Faulkland Lewis was born in 1873 and graduated from Tufts

College in 1895. After studying in Munich and Paris, he received a Ph.D
in 1900 from the University of Pennsylvania. Lewis taught modern languages at the University of Maine for the next five years but then moved
to New York City, where he found his métier in social welfare work, joining first the Charity Organization Society and later the Prison Association.
His major publication was a book on prison history,[33] but he also wrote
prize-winning short stories and edited *The Delinquent*, a eugenical criminal justice journal. Lewis served the American Prison Association as both
general secretary and a member of its executive committee before dying
suddenly of pneumonia in 1922, at the age of forty-nine. According to one
observer, he was "an able and orderly executive,"[34] an impression that sur-
viving records bear out.[35]

At the Prison Association O. F. Lewis (as he signed himself) rivaled
Enoch Wines's record in attracting generous gifts. The organization's en-
dowment climbed from $9,000 in 1910, the year he became general secre-
tary, to nearly $200,000 in 1921;[36] in the latter year contributors included
the New York Foundation, the senior and junior J. D. Rockefellers, the
Laura Spelman Rockefeller Memorial, and Mortimer Schiff, as well as a
galaxy of Morgans, Tiffanys, and Guggenheims. On joining the Prison
Association, Lewis made establishing an institution for male defective delinquents a top priority. The best way to achieve this goal, he recognized
from the start, was as part of a general overhaul of the state's prison system.[37]

Beginning the push toward centralization in 1913, O. F. Lewis created a
subdivision within the Prison Association, the three-member Bureau of Inspection and Research, the tasks of which included writing a masterplan
for the state's prison system. Affluent Prison Association members, some
of whom had already contributed to efforts to eugenicize criminal justice,
covered the salaries of the bureau's staff.[38]

In 1916 this bureau produced a blueprint with the tripartite goal of
centralizing New York's prison system, classifying its prisons by inmate
type, and establishing eugenic institutions for incorrigibles. Specifically the
plan called for the state to create a department of correction; abolish the
state's traditional division into separate judicial districts, "each sentencing
its State prisoners to a different prison"; and redesignate Sing Sing as a
"receiving and distributing station for all the State prisons."[39] Sing Sing
seemed to be a logical candidate to become a clearinghouse because it was
close to New York City, from which the majority of prisoners came. (This
was probably also why Sing Sing was chosen for Bernard Glueck's classification experiments, which began the same year. Glueck's work demonstrated the effectiveness of a reception and diagnostic center at Sing Sing.)[40]
The state's men's prisons should be reorganized to specialize by inmate
type, with Napanoch reserved for defective delinquents.[41]

Justifying the Master Plan

The United States entered World War I in 1917; its participation brought prison reform to a halt. When O. F. Lewis returned to the Prison Association after the war, he faced the problem of finding an adequate rationale for his centralization plan. Although prison classification could be used to justify segregation of defective delinquents, could the desire to segregate defective delinquents be made to justify a classification program that would involve expensive clearinghouses, extensive prisoner transfers, and new legislation? The Prison Association's argument—that cardiac, feebleminded, perverted, psychotic, and tubercular cases should be held at separate institutions—was not particularly compelling; after all, New York had managed without this classification plan in the past. A more positive rationale for reorganizing the prison system was necessary.

This justification was provided by a prison survey committee appointed in 1919 to streamline inmate labor.[42] The committee conducted a year-long study, developing a comprehensive plan to make New York's prisons more profitable and more effective at training skilled workers. In the committee's view these goals required linking the state's prisons into a centralized, coordinated system.[43] That system would have to classify prisoners to give them the vocational training they needed to reform. Merging the medical model with the principles of scientific management, the committee's 1920 report recommended not only clearinghouses and institutions for defective delinquents but also the specialization of prisons by the type of goods (cloth, school desks, etc.) they would produce. This vision of treating inmates through industrial as well as medical methods broadened the appeal of prison reorganization.

Adolph Lewisohn, a well-to-do industrialist who for many years had presided over the National Committee on Prisons and Prison Labor, chaired the Prison Survey Committee. A member of the Prison Association, Lewisohn would also have known O. F. Lewis through their mutual work on the eugenical New York Committee on Feeblemindedness.[44] To further his study, Lewisohn sought advice from a wide range of experts, including penologists and psychiatrists who endorsed defective delinquency theory. Katharine Bement Davis, Bernard Glueck, O. F. Lewis, Thomas W. Salmon, and psychiatrists who had headed the Bedford Hills psychopathic hospital all contributed suggestions.[45] Thus the committee's report became a conduit through which IDD proposals formulated in philanthropic and mental hygiene circles flowed into the prison system.

The Prison Survey Committee's report urged New York to pay prisoners generously as an incentive for hard work. It anticipated, however, that the state would be unable both to offer good wages and to make ends meet without reducing its prison labor force by 50 percent. Thus, the report concluded, inefficient workers should be assigned to custodial institutions to perform unpaid, menial labor.[46] All incoming male prisoners should be sent to Sing Sing for physical, mental, and psychiatric examinations. The "normal" should then be transferred to prisons with industries appropriate to their abilities.[47] Others, including the approximately 20 percent of the total prison population whom the committee estimated to be mental defectives, should be sent to hospital-like institutions for special care and permanent custody.[48] Under headings such as "A Human Scrap Heap," "Always Segregable," and "Hardly Reform Cases," the report explains that mental defectives "are or will be repeaters."[49]

> These defectives are . . . incapable of handling their own affairs. They are often prolific and bear inheritable types of mental defect. . . . These mental defectives retard the progress of the normal or nearly normal population and make it impossible to effect on the latter any permanent or lasting reform. . . .
> Custodial care should be permanent, not as punishment but as a precaution required because he [the mentally defective criminal] has cellular defects in his brains for which he is in no way responsible.[50]

A life sentence for the offender with "cellular defects in his brains": the language is new, but the logic of eugenic prevention is at least as old as the Newark Custodial Asylum.

Defective Delinquent Legislation

Two states, Massachusetts and New York, took fairly elaborate steps to incorporate the defective delinquency concept into their prison systems. The processes through which they founded their defective delinquent units are described in the following two sections. The next chapter examines the consequences of these and other defective delinquent laws.

Massachusetts's Defective Delinquent Laws

Walter E. Fernald, superintendent of the Massachusetts School for the Feeble-minded, pushed the nation's first defective delinquent law through the Massachusetts legislature in 1911. He was anxious, he later explained, to rid his institution of defective delinquents. They were "only slightly defective"; they required "precaution against escape quite equal to that of a prison, which is costly"; and they were "very disturbing and very demoralizing" to other inmates.[51] At Fernald's instigation, in 1910 the Massachusetts legislature established its Commission to Investigate the Question of the Increase of Criminals, Mental Defectives, Epileptics and Degenerates. Led by Fernald, it included the directors of the Bridgewater State Farm, Massachusetts Hospital for Epileptics, Worcester State Hospital, and Charlestown State Prison. When this commission reported in January 1911, it recommended that Massachusetts establish separate facilities for "defective delinquents" [52] — one of the earliest usages of the term.

Six months later the legislature obliged most generously. The new law created a department for defective delinquents to which courts might commit any mental defective who might otherwise be sent to "the state prison, the reformatory for women, or any jail or house of correction, or to the Massachusetts reformatory, the state farm, or to the industrial school for boys, the industrial school for girls, the Lyman school, any truant school, or the custody of the state board of charity, for an offence not punishable by death or imprisonment for life." [53] The law required only that "it shall appear that the offender has committed the offence with which he is charged" and that he or she be "mentally defective" and neither insane nor "a proper subject for the schools for the feeble-minded." [54] *Offense* was defined to include persistent violation of institutional rules and indecent behavior. Units were to be set aside at the men's reformatory, women's reformatory, and Bridgewater State Farm to which defective delinquents could be committed for indefinite terms, with parole a discretionary function of the units' officials. [55]

This act pleased no one. It shot wide of the targeted populations of troublemakers at all institutions but Fernald's. When Massachusetts enacted the law, Edith Spaulding later explained, "it was generally supposed that all those who had been misfits in the various institutions . . . would be found to be defective intellectually as well emotionally and therefore would be fit subjects for permanent segregation. . . . When it was found on closer study that many, although defective in emotional control, ranked high when psychometric tests were applied, considerable doubt arose as to the legality of the commitment of such persons." [56] Then too, the 1911 law did not fund the new units. All it did, a critic later quipped, was to plan for "an extremely comprehensive round-up for the permanent custodial branding iron of defective delinquency." [57]

The Massachusetts law remained inoperative until the early 1920s, [58] when it was revived, apparently by two insurrections. Inmates at one institution for the retarded burned a barn, and a group at Fernald's school attacked five employees. At that point Massachusetts established a division for defective delinquents at Bridgewater. The hellions were transferred to it, and discipline at the regular training schools underwent "miraculous" improvement. "In fact," wrote Fernald, "overnight, the boys remaining . . . became courteous, obedient and willingly and cheerfully went to work." [59]

New York's Defective Delinquent Bills

New Yorkers took longer to enact defective delinquent legislation, but in the long run they achieved more. At first proponents fired off bills that hit wide of the mark. There followed a maturation period during which they garnered support, meshed the IDD proposal with other aspects of prison reorganization, and generally strengthened social control of mental defectives. During the final stage IDD supporters orchestrated enactment of defective delinquent legislation. They did so in a mood of weary disillusionment, however. Victory, when it finally arrived, came as something of a surprise and through unplanable events.

Stage One: The Initial Bills Misfire   New York's initial defective delinquent bills were bumbling efforts, more hopeful than realistic.[60] The first, drafted in April 1911 by Dr. Charles Bernstein in consultation with O. F. Lewis, called for "the transfer of idiots and imbeciles from penal and reformatory institutions to the Rome State Custodial Asylum" and an appropriation of $50,000 for a new building in which to hold them.[61] This draft was circulated for comments, but before it could be revised, Bernstein's board of managers submitted it to the legislature, which turned it down. The bill's plan for segregating defective delinquents at Rome was at best half-baked, and its wording antagonized a key player, Katherine Bement Davis, who feared that it would create an institution for both sexes. From experience she knew that the women would be treated as inferiors in such circumstances.[62] A second bill, this one providing for a commission to select a site for a male IDD, failed in 1912.[63]

O. F. Lewis concentrated on rallying support. In October 1911 he and Bernstein presented arguments for a defective delinquent bill to New York State's Conference of Charities.[64] To strengthen the Prison Association's Committee on Defective Delinquents, Lewis arranged for its members to meet Henry Goddard of the Vineland Training School and Frank Christian of the Elmira Reformatory.[65] When his wife chanced to find the records on which Richard Dugdale had based his 1877 *"Jukes"* study, Lewis forwarded them to the Eugenics Record Office, which did a follow-up study. In contrast to Dugdale, who had discovered only one mentally backward Juke, Arthur Estabrook, who wrote *The Jukes in 1915,* determined that "all of the Juke criminals were feeble-minded"[66]—more fuel for the fire. And Lewis enlisted a psychiatric examiner to test jail inmates for mental defectiveness.

In December 1911 O. F. Lewis arranged for this examiner, Dr. George M. Parker, to make a presentation on defective delinquency to the State Conference of Magistrates, a group whose courts Lewis considered to be "the gateway to the correctional institutions of this State."[67] Parker used a stereopticon to illustrate his remarks:

(Comments on the first picture.) Here is a fellow from Elmira. All these cases from Elmira . . . are feeble-minded. . . . In these cases that don't look bad, that are not degenerate in their face at all, you get . . . a weak mouth, a curious set of ears; the eyes in particular are flat.

(Next picture.) He isn't normal . . . you should immediately raise in your mind the question, whether that man is all right or not. You notice a bilateral difference in the face that is very marked.

(Next picture.) There is a rabbit type. That man has no resistance. He is inferior; he always has been inferior. You will see when you go through this series of pictures that it [defective delinquency] is more a set of general impressions, than any specific diagnostic thing you can put your finger on.[68]

Having sensitized the magistrates to recognize defective delinquents, Parker announced: "We are moving for an act for the creation of an institution for defective delinquents. . . . If you can send the defective there, . . . he will be treated. Correction doesn't do him one particle of good."[69] State Board of Charities secretary Robert W. Hebberd seconded Parker's remarks, and the magistrates formally endorsed defective delinquent legislation.[70]

Over the next few years various groups toyed with the possibility of writing another defective delinquent bill.[71] O. F. Lewis, however, seems to have shelved the idea, realizing that it would have to be embedded in a more general plan for prison reorganization.

Stage Two: Maturation   While the Prison Association's planning bureau developed its proposals, Lewis continued his public relations campaigns on behalf of IDDs. One natural ally in this effort was the Russell Sage Foundation, which with Lewis's help had earlier sponsored mental testing at Elmira. The foundation also pioneered in the development of traveling exhibits to publicize community problems. With the Prison Association and a women's prison reform group, the foundation put together a prison exhibit that opened in New York City in January 1916. Illustrated with electrical devices, posters, and motion pictures of prison life, this exhibit advocated various correctional reforms, including institutions for defective delinquents. From New York it traveled to the state's other major cities, returning to New York for a successful rerun that according to the Prison Association attracted 125,000 visitors.[72]

When Lewis took a leave of absence to join the war effort, leadership of the IDD campaign passed to New York's newly established Commission for Mental Defectives.[73] Established to systematize and centralize state provisions for mental defectives, this commission became New York's official mouthpiece on aspects of mental deficiency. Thus, when it lobbied for IDDs, its opinions carried considerable weight.

Those opinions were often eugenical. The commission had been created in part through the work of two eugenics lobbies, the New York Committee on Feeblemindedness and the State Charities Aid Association of New York. The commission's first chairman, Dr. Walter B. James, was a member of the New York Committee on Feeblemindedness. When James resigned early in 1919, he was replaced by another eugenics sympathizer, Dr. Pearce Bailey, also a member of the Committee on Feeblemindedness and during World War I a supervisor of the U.S. army's mental testing program. When Napanoch became an institution for defective delinquents, the Commission for Mental Defectives became its board of managers.

The commission addressed the problem of defective delinquents in its Mental Deficiency Law of 1919, an act that reorganized and systematized state care of the retarded. This law provided that judges could commit mental defectives who were over sixteen years of age and charged with a misdemeanor "to the Rome state school . . . where a separate building is to be set aside or constructed." Similarly judges could commit mentally defective defendants in felony cases to the unit at Rome "before or after trial or conviction."[74] A finding of mental defectiveness had to be made by two qualified and experienced physicians, or one physician and one experienced psychologist.[75] The law did not require intelligence tests, however, nor did it distinguish among levels of mental defect.

The commission's attempt to establish a unit for defective delinquents on the cheap was no more successful than the Massachusetts attempt of 1911 had been. When New York judges started committing accused or convicted offenders found to be mentally defective to the Rome State School, superintendent Bernstein threw up his hands, dropped his happy-gardeners line, and declared that the only sensible place for defective delinquents is a prison.

Stage Three: Success   Twin defective delinquent bills, one each for Napanoch and Bedford Hills, were passed unanimously by the New York State Senate on April 11, 1921, and by the assembly three days later. The Bedford Hills bill amended that institution's defective delinquent law of 1920,[76] which had established an entity named the Division for Mentally Defective Delinquent Women to which inmates could be committed from penal institutions. The new bill made possible two additional types of commitment: (1) from the state schools for mental defectives, in cases where the individual was charged with a criminal offense, and (2) directly from criminal courts, before or after trial.[77] The Napanoch bill converted the Eastern New York Reformatory at Napanoch into an institution for defective delinquents supervised and controlled by the Commission for Mental Defectives.[78] Like the Bedford Hills division, the facility at Napanoch could receive commitments from the courts, institutions for mental defectives, and prisons. In all cases, female and male, the defective delinquent had to be over sixteen years of age and certified mentally defective by two qualified examiners.

For women defective delinquents, commitment was automatically for "an indeterminate period" (i.e., up to life), with parole and discharge to be granted, if at all, by the superintendent.[79] For men, if the sentence expired (or, in unsentenced cases, if the *potential* sentence expired) and the prisoner remained mentally defective, the superintendent had to go through a court procedure to retain the inmate. Napanoch's superintendent could parole and discharge cases "reasonably safe to be at large." [80] Male (but not female) defective delinquents could challenge their confinement through habeas corpus proceedings.[81]

The bills' timing was fortuitous in that the prisons had been emptied by World War I, which enlisted the most crime-prone population—young men—and sent them overseas. In the second annual report of the Commission for Mental Defectives, Pearce Bailey wrote that "it is entirely possible for the State to take control immediately of defective delinquents, chronic recidivists, who play so large a part in the criminal annals of the community. . . . There are about 2000 vacancies in penal and correctional institutions in the State, and with no greater expense than that of maintenance the Legislature could provide that these different institutions fill their vacancies with such irresponsible criminals." [82] Similarly, in a letter to the governor's counsel, the secretary of the state's Board of Charities advised that "there is considerable room [for defective delinquents] at the State Reformatory for Women." [83] Had prisons been overcrowded, legislators might well have voted against the IDD bills.

The campaign for IDDs ended on a note of cranky exhaustion. The enthusiasm that had characterized earlier Progressive reforms had drained away during the war; the country's mood had turned conservative, even rancorous. In this context IDD supporters felt they were fighting a rearguard action. The Prison Association staff had "little hope" for "enactment of progressive legislation." In Albany they spent their time combating "reactionary and severe legislation, . . . introduced to cope with the so-called 'crime wave.' " [84] They saw IDD legislation as a liberal cause and a reminder of less repressive times.

Caught up in the legislative battles of the moment, IDD supporters wasted little time reiterating eugenic rationales. If New York's defective delinquent legislation ever had been a "moral crusade" in the sense of a self-righteous campaign,[85] it was no longer. Those who pressed for the Napanoch bill were mainly institutional managers, interested in the disciplinary bonanza they would reap from the existence of IDDs. Their arguments were more practical than idealistic.

That the Bedford Hills bill might fail must have seemed unlikely, for the governor received only two (perfunctory) letters in its favor.[86] The risk there was slight because the Division for Mentally Defective Delinquent Women had already been established. Moreover, as the bill's lack of a habeas corpus clause indicates, no one was particularly concerned about the liberty interests of mentally defective delinquent women.

The Napanoch bill's fate was far less certain, however. Leaving little to chance, its backers rounded up support from all quarters. Pearce Bailey led the lobbyists, using his annual report to inform the legislature that the "recurring trials" of defective delinquents "cost the state $1,000 a piece. . . . As things are now, on reaching the age limit, boys are discharged from the reformatories and on termination of sentence are discharged from the prisons. Thus every year are set loose proven criminals, gunmen, thieves, firebugs, vagabonds of all kinds who can never be anything else."[87] It was these remarks, Bailey later claimed, that persuaded legislators to vote for the Napanoch bill.[88]

At one time or another the establishment of a men's IDD had been endorsed by every relevant state group: the New York State Commission to Investigate Provision for the Mentally Deficient; the Hospital Development Commission; the Prison Association of New York; Lewisohn's Prison Survey Committee; the New York Committee on Feeblemindedness; the Board of Charities; the Charities Aid Association; and the Commission of Prisons and its Special Committee on Mental Disease and Delinquency. In addition, in what seems to have been a carefully orchestrated campaign, Governor Nathan L. Miller received nine personal letters urging him to sign the bill.[89]

Unlike earlier defective delinquent bills, those of 1921 appealed to multiple constituencies. Superintendents of state institutions for mental defectives would be able to transfer troublesome inmates to the IDDs, as would the heads of penal institutions. Judges who considered mental defectives to be incompetent to stand trial or genetically dangerous would now have a place to send such cases. The bills offered something to all the major groups they would affect.

Governor Miller signed the Bedford Hills bill on April 30, 1921, and the Napanoch legislation two days later. The Prison Association, having anticipated defeat, was pleasantly surprised.[90]

Notes

1. New York State, *Laws of New York, 1921*, chap. 483.

2. O. Lewis 1912:11.

3. A definitive sign that the light had burned out was the appearance in 1926 of Carl Murchison's *Criminal Intelligence,* which ridicules the feeblemindedness theory of crime and prisoner rehabilitation as "imbecilic" (p. 38).

4. W. Fernald 1918–19:98. For an even earlier recantation, see Fernald's comments in New York State Commission to Investigate Provision for the Mentally Deficient (hereafter New York State Commission for the Mentally Deficient) 1915:127.

5. Trent 1994:181.

6. New York State Commission for Mental Defectives, *Annual Report, 1919,* p. 6; New York State, *Laws of New York, 1919,* chap. 633.

7. New York's Mental Deficiency Act of 1919 renamed this the Rome State School for Mental Defectives. Massachusetts, too, contributed to the movement toward extra-institutional treatment; its leader was W. E. Fernald. See S. Davies 1923: chap. 7.

8. Bernstein 1914, 1916, 1918, 1920; S. Davies 1923: chaps. 8 and 9; S. Davies 1930: chaps. 13 and 14; Trent 1994: chap. 6. For biographies of Bernstein, see Ferguson 1994 and Trent 1986.

9. Bernstein in New York State Conference of Charities, *Proceedings, 1911,* p. 202, in New York State Board of Charities, *Annual Report, 1911,* vol. 1, appendix 1.

10. Memorandum on "Illustrative Cases" enclosed in Dr. Pearce Bailey to Governor Nathan L. Miller, March 18, 1921, in bill jacket to New York State, *Laws of New York, 1921,* chap. 483 (New York State Education Library, Albany, Bill Jacket Collection).

11. New York State Commission for the Mentally Deficient 1915:12.

12. Ibid., 20, 26–27, 69.

13. Ibid., 74, 112.

14. Ibid., 169.

15. Ibid., 254.

16. Keller 1918:84.

17. New York City Police Department 1915:xviii; New York City Police Department 1917:82.

18. Bisch 1916–17:82.

19. New York City Police Department 1917:83.

20. *New York Times,* October 12, 1916, p. 11. Funds for the laboratory may also have come from the New York Foundation, which in 1916 donated about $800 to the New York Police Department (New York Foundation n.d.:57). Mrs. Alexander (Wittpen) was a stalwart of the eugenics movement in both New Jersey and New York.

21. New York City Police Department 1915:xviii; New York City Police Department 1916:xxvii.

22. Keller 1918:84.

23. New York City Police Department 1916:xxvii–xxviii.

24. Keller 1918:86–87.

25. Bisch 1916–17:88.

26. Woods 1918:62–64.

27. New York State Commission of Prisons 1918:19, 23. This report was prepared with the help of the National Committee for Mental Hygiene.

28. *New York Times,* October 30, 1915, p. 5.

29. See, e.g., Gault 1914–15d, 1923; Salmon 1919–20.

30. Bisch 1916–17:83.

31. E. Wines 1871:543.

32. Heale 1975; Klein 1920:353-63.

33. *The Development of American Prisons and Prison Customs, 1776-1845* (O. Lewis 1922).

34. Lyon 1914-15:313.

35. Biographical details, some of them conflicting, appear in O. F. Lewis's *New York Times* obituary (Feb. 25, 1922, p. 13); Wickersham 1922;, and the Prison Association's memorial (Prison Association of New York, *Annual Report, 1922*, pp. 13-14).

36. Prison Association of New York (hereafter PANY), *Annual Report, 1921*, p. 17.

37. As early as June 1910 Lewis was circulating a paper entitled "The Possible Coordination of the Correctional Institutions of the State of New York" in which he advocated centralization, state control of local institutions, and "segregation of imbeciles and feeble-minded persons who are frequently committed to prisons for crime" (Ellwood 1910:98-99). Also see PANY 1912.

38. PANY, *Annual Report, 1916*, p. 189 lists these donors as E. S. Harkness, Cleveland H. Dodge, Jacob H. Schiff, Dean Sage, Samuel Untermyer, Frank A. Vanderlip, Felix M. Warburg, and Richard M. Hurd. Most were already either PANY "Life Patrons" ($500) or "Honorary Life Members" ($100). The bureau consisted of two staff members in addition to O. F. Lewis, and centralization was only one of its tasks (for the full list, see PANY, *Annual Report, 1916*, pp. 189-91).

39. PANY, *Annual Report, 1916*, p. 202.

40. George W. Kirchwey, Sing Sing warden and leader of criminal justice reforms, claimed that he was the one who selected Bernard Glueck to head the Sing Sing psychiatric clinic; see Kirchwey 1918-19:333. Kirchwey also personally urged the governor to sign the Napanoch bill.

41. PANY, *Annual Report, 1916*, pp. 118-35. The Prison Association had a comprehensive scheme in mind for female inmates, too, but because it had not yet worked out the details, it limited itself to recommending possible transformation of the prison farm at Valatie into an institution for female defective delinquents and utilization of the Bedford Hills Laboratory of Social Hygiene as a central clearinghouse.

42. O. F. Lewis, like many other reformers, shared the Prison Survey Committee's concern to improve prison industry efficiency; see O. Lewis 1911b:45-47. In fact, the Prison Survey Committee may have been Lewis's idea; see PANY, *Annual Report, 1912*, p. 33.

43. New York State Prison Survey Committee 1920:260-61.

44. New York Committee on Feeblemindedness, *First Annual Report* (n.d. [1917?]), pp. 3-4.

45. New York State Prison Survey Committee 1920:25-26.

46. Ibid., 89-90, 122.

47. Ibid., 122.

48. Ibid., 211, 118 (special institutions).

49. Ibid., 211-13.

50. Ibid., 109-10.

51. Fernald as quoted in New York State Commission for the Mentally Deficient 1915:166.

52. Massachusetts 1911:50.

53. Massachusetts, *Acts and Resolves,* chap. 595, sec. 1.

54. Ibid.

55. Ibid., secs. 2, 5–7.

56. Spaulding [1923] 1969:2n.

57. Ricker 1934:95.

58. According to Robinson (1933:363), "a brief and unsuccessful attempt" was made soon after 1911 "to establish a department for [defective] delinquent boys at the Massachusetts reformatory."

59. The Massachusetts events are described and Fernald is quoted in S. Davies 1930:136–37.

60. The bills described below were probably preceded by an earlier effort by Elmira's eugenical physician, Frank Christian. O. F. Lewis (1911a:190) reported that "Dr. Christian has written me that the general superintendent of the reformatory recommended to his board of managers the introduction into the legislature of 1911 of a bill permitting the reformatory to transfer the imbeciles now at Elmira Reformatory to a custodial asylum." However, Elmira's board apparently did not pursue this possibility.

61. O. Lewis 1911a:192. According to this account, Lewis had been alarmed in particular by an intelligence-testing study conducted at Elmira under a grant from the Russell Sage Foundation. This study showed 70 percent of the reformatory's inmates to be intellectually subnormal and 39 percent of them definitely feebleminded. Lewis himself had arranged for the study to be conducted under Prison Association auspices.

62. O. Lewis 1911a:194–95. Bernstein hotly retorted that Davis had "entirely overlooked the fact that" the bill concerned "male defective delinquents only," adding that the bill's authors "did nothing regarding females" in the hope that all females would soon be transferred from Rome to Newark "or some other institution for feeble-minded women" (New York State, Twelfth Conference of Charities, *Proceedings, 1911*, pp. 201–2, in New York State Board of Charities, *Annual Report, 1911*, vol. 1, appendix 1).

63. PANY, *Annual Report, 1912*, p. 60.

64. O. Lewis 1911a; also see Gault 1911–12a.

65. PANY, *Annual Report, 1912*, p. 66.

66. Estabrook 1916:85.

67. Lewis as quoted in New York State Probation Commission, *Annual Report, 1911*, p. 361.

68. Parker 1911:343–44.

69. Ibid., 347.

70. Towne 1911–12b:922. At another December 1911 meeting, representatives of correctional agencies similarly fell in line, adopting resolutions urging the governor to support defective delinquent legislation; see Towne 1911–12a.

71. For example, an unsigned news item in the *Journal of Criminal Law and Criminology* 5 (1914–15): 934 mentions two anticipated IDD bills, and PANY, *An-*

nual Report, 1916, p. 204 refers to a bill suggested by Dr. Thomas W. Salmon "for the permanent commitment of the feebleminded." Also see PANY, *Annual Report, 1916*, p. 165, mentioning a proposal of the New York Committee on Feeblemindedness to build an IDD for women at Newark.

72. "The Prison Exhibit," PANY, *Annual Report, 1916*, pp. 161–63.

73. Originally called the State Commission on the Feeble-minded, the body was soon renamed the Commission for Mental Defectives.

74. New York State, *Laws of New York, 1919*, chap. 633, sec. 24.

75. Ibid., sec. 25. By June of 1919, 245 New York State physicians and eleven psychologists had filed for certification, including eugenicists such as Clinton P. McCord of Albany and Frank L. Christian of Elmira. Eugenicists who had for years been warning about the genetic dangers of defective delinquents added little to the adversarial process.

76. New York State, *Laws of New York, 1920*, chap. 774.

77. New York State, *Laws of New York, 1921*, chap. 364.

78. Ibid., chap. 483.

79. Ibid., chap. 364, sec. 243.

80. Ibid., chap. 483, sec. 24-d, c.

81. Ibid., sec. 35.

82. New York State Commission for Mental Defectives, *Annual Report, 1919–20*, p. 16.

83. Memorandum from Charles H. Johnson to Honorable C. Tracey Stagg, counsel to the governor, April 28, 1921, in bill jacket to New York State, *Laws of New York, 1921*, chap. 364 (New York State Library, Bill Jacket Collection).

84. PANY, *Annual Report, 1921*, p. 89.

85. H. Becker 1973.

86. The first endorsement of the Bedford Hills bill was a response from Board of Charities secretary Charles H. Johnson to a query by the governor's counsel about the "propriety and effect of this bill." Charles H. Johnson to Hon. C. Tracey Stagg, counsel to the governor, April 28, 1921, in bill jacket to New York State, *Laws of New York, 1921*, chap. 364 (New York State Library, Bill Jacket Collection). The second endorsement, from E. R. Cass, assistant general secretary of PANY, to Hon. Nathan L. Miller, governor, April 19, 1921, endorsed the Bedford Hills IDD bill but without the formal action by PANY's board that the Napanoch bill received. At the time I examined this letter, it was misfiled in the bill jacket to New York State, *Laws of New York, 1921*, chap. 483, New York State Library, Bill Jacket Collection.

87. New York State Commission for Mental Defectives, *Annual Report, 1919–20*, p. 16.

88. New York State Commission for Mental Defectives, *Annual Report, 1920–21*, p. 5.

89. These letters, comprising the bill jacket to New York State, *Laws of New York, 1921*, chap. 483, are part of the New York State Library's Bill Jacket Collection (Albany). They came from Bird Coler, commissioner of New York City's Department of Public Welfare; Pearce Bailey; George A. Hastings, acting secretary of the state's Charities Aid Association, who wrote twice; Dr. Bradford C. Loveland, head

of the Bureau of Psychiatry, Syracuse Department of Health; Benjamin J. Shove, a justice of the Syracuse Court of Special Sessions; E. R. Cass, assistant general secretary of the Prison Association; George W. Kirchwey, former warden of Sing Sing and president of the American Institute of Criminal Law and Criminology; and Charles H. Johnson, Board of Charities secretary.

90. PANY, *Annual Report, 1921*, p. 89.

11

The Aftermath of Eugenic Criminology

> Now it is a fact, abundantly exemplified in human
> history, that a practice often lasts for a long time after
> the theory which inspired it has lost its hold on the
> belief of mankind.
>
> Henry Maudsley, *Responsibility in Mental Disease*

Eugenic criminology lost impetus in the 1920s
as the fears, hopes, and assumptions that had
sustained eugenics since the 1870s disintegrated.
Walter E. Fernald and others who had criminalized the mentally retarded recanted. Refinements
in intelligence testing made it increasingly difficult to label offenders "feebleminded," and genetics research discredited eugenicists' understandings of heredity. The Progressive movement, to
which the fortunes of eugenics had been tightly
bound, died out. Moreover, eugenicists simply
had less reason to pursue their cause. They had
achieved many of their specific goals. Middle-
class authority was once again secure, this time
on the basis of expertise. With their professions
now well established, social welfare workers had
less need for the legitimation that eugenics conferred. No longer pressed to define themselves
as altruistic worthies, they could discard the di-
chotomizing metaphors of eugenic criminology
and its crude division of people into bad and
good, ugly and fair, others and ourselves. Eugenics had always been "a movement of the experts,"
historian Mark Haller observes, and starting in
the 1920s, "experts abandoned it."[1]

Nevertheless, although weakened, eugenic
criminology did not expire. In the 1930s Har-

vard Law School professor Sheldon Glueck and his wife, Eleanor T. Glueck, published *Five Hundred Delinquent Women,* a study that confirms much of what Josephine Shaw Lowell had said about criminalistic women fifty years earlier. Examining social, psychological, and biological factors, the Gluecks conclude that their women offenders are a *"swarm of defective, diseased, antisocial misfits,"* burdened by "feeble-mindedness, psychopathic personality, and marked emotional instability." Ninety-eight percent of them had led sexually improper lives. Without using the term *eugenics,* the Gluecks recommend "a wholly indefinite sentence" with release (if any) to be determined by experts like themselves.[2]

In the late 1930s Ernest A. Hooton, a Harvard anthropologist who had helped the Gluecks with their study, published a more explicitly eugenic work, *The American Criminal.* It concludes that "the elimination of crime can be effected only by the extirpation of the physically, mentally, and morally unfit, or by their complete segregation in a socially aseptic environment."[3] In a companion volume, *Crime and the Man,* Hooton examines the anthropological characteristics of criminals by race and ethnicity, closing with a cartoon of a policeman hauling a criminal off to a prison labeled "Birth Control Clinic."[4] Inspired by Hooton, in the 1940s Harvard psychologist William H. Sheldon launched the field of "constitutional psychology," an attempt to correlate criminal tendencies with body type. Sheldon's self-described aim was to make "a direct attack on our most deadly enemy—careless reproduction."[5]

Nazi attempts to eliminate criminals, the mentally retarded, and other "degenerates" gave such overt eugenic talk a bad name. Research continues on biological factors in crime,[6] however, and when it purports to identify factors that are genetic, it has distinctly eugenic implications. In *The Bell Curve,* for instance, Richard Herrnstein and Charles Murray argue that "IQ is substantially heritable" and that low IQ scores are strongly associated with criminality. "In trying to understand how to deal with the crime problem," they write, "much of the attention . . . should be shifted to . . . cognitive disadvantage." Using logic similar to that of nineteenth-century degenerationists, they explain that this shift can be accomplished by terminating America's current subsidy of "births among poor women, who are also disproportionately at the low end of the intelligence distribution."[7] Futurists Alvin and Heidi Toffler predict the coming of a "crisis in eugenics. Give a totalitarian government the advanced tools made possible by the biological revolution, and we can see a world of competing eugenic strategies as arrogant regimes play God with future generations."[8] Like the horror film monster who only seems to die, the born criminal may be reviving for a sequel to earlier versions of eugenic criminology.

Of the many legacies left by turn-of-the-century eugenic criminology, the most influential (if most difficult to document) lies in the structuring of social values and assumptions about what (and who) is good or bad. Intelligence remains one of the most highly prized attributes in our society; advertisements, playing on our fear of appearing stupid, tell us that if we are *smart,* we will purchase such and such a product. We define beauty in terms of whiteness and refinement, and we associate "welfare mothers" with stupidity, hyperfecundity, illegitimacy, and criminalistic offspring. The eugenics movement contributed powerfully to our perceptual and valuative categories.

Moreover, eugenic criminology left behind institutions for defective delinquents (IDDs) that continued to operate for another fifty years. Carrying the medical model to its logical conclusion, the IDDs gave officials almost total and unchecked discretionary power. At first no conviction was required for an IDD commitment: courts and even state schools for the retarded could commit suspected offenders, before a finding of guilt, for indefinite terms. Prisons, too, could commit to the IDDs, and although in this case those committed had been convicted, their sentences were extended to up-to-life terms. For men and women committed indefinitely to hospitals for the criminally insane, there was always a possibility of recovery, however slim, whereas for defective delinquents, with their presumably irreversible mental defect, recovery was impossible.

In this chapter I investigate the institutional consequences of eugenic criminology. Examining the IDDs of New York and other states, I ask the following questions: What sorts of people were labeled defective delinquents? What triggered their commitment, and did they actually serve life sentences? How many states passed defective delinquent laws? Until the records of Napanoch and other institutions for allegedly feebleminded offenders are studied more systematically, answers to such questions must remain tentative, yet it is possible to reach some preliminary conclusions. The chapter concludes by returning to Fenix Whipple, the prisoner who, as I mention in the introduction, was committed to the Napanoch Institution for Defective Delinquents not long after it opened in 1921.[9]

New York's Institutions for Defective Delinquents

Napanoch

When the Napanoch prison became an IDD, it fulfilled a long-planned destiny. The facility at Napanoch had been built by Zebulon Brockway as a prison to which he could ship Elmira Reformatory incorrigibles on (he hoped) totally indefinite sentences. Napanoch opened in 1900 as the Eastern New York Reformatory, but underfunded and poorly constructed, it was a reformatory in name only.[10] Almost immediately eugenicists began eyeing it as a suitable institution for mentally defective criminals.[11]

An architectural throwback, with massive round towers at the corners of its central administration building, Napanoch resembled a medieval fortress more than a modern prison. From the administrative center extended two wings of cell blocks, both in a state of "protracted neglect" when the first defective delinquents arrived.[12] Underneath were six lightless, airless dungeons, "rest rooms" for the difficult.[13] Fittingly, Napanoch was located in rural Ulster county, homeland of Dugdale's dysgenic Jukes family.

In theory the Napanoch IDD was to be a hybrid institution, a combination of prison and state hospital for the retarded, and at first the state recognized this dual mission by requiring Napanoch officials to report to the Commission for Mental Defectives. Nevertheless, the first superintendent, Dr. Walter N. Thayer Jr., had headed Napanoch when it was the Eastern New York Reformatory and he was a career prison official. Moreover, when New York reorganized its government in 1927, it put Napanoch under the new Department of Correction, another sign that the IDD would function primarily as a branch of the prison system. From the start Napanoch's prison identity predominated.

Getting into Napanoch: Commitments to the Institution for Defective Delinquents   During its first year the Napanoch IDD received 409 prisoners (table 4). Other state prisons formed the leading source of commitments (almost 60 percent), followed by the Rome State School for Mental Defectives (28.6 percent) and the courts (12.5 percent). These sources fell to squabbling over IDD beds to which all felt entitled. Ultimately they were struggling for authority to define defective delinquents.

Dr. Charles Bernstein, superintendent of the Rome State School, had a proprietary interest in the new IDD: he had supported defective delinquent legislation for a decade. As soon as the IDD opened, Bernstein sent it 58 inmates. Of the 117 inmates Bernstein transferred to Napanoch in the first year, however, the IDD unceremoniously returned 40, and the next year it sent back another 24. Worse yet, the Commission of Prisons publicly reprimanded Bernstein for trying to use Napanoch as "a disciplinary institution for [his] disorderly inmates."[14] After attempting fifteen more transfers in the third year, Bernstein gave up,[15] defeated by Napanoch officials who defined the IDD as an arm of not the state training schools but the prison system.

Case records of three inmates in the initial shipment from Rome provide details on this definitional struggle. Bernstein transferred Henry Hanks,[16] a white youth from an impoverished farm family, to Napanoch for mis-

Table 4. Sources of Commitments to Napanoch Institution for Defective
Delinquents, June 1, 1921–June 30, 1922

Commitment Source	Number	Percentage
Penal institution transfers		
Auburn Prison	61	14.9
Clinton Prison	50	12.2
Great Meadow Prison	8	2.0
Sing Sing Prison	14	3.4
Dannemora State Hospital	9	2.2
Matteawan State Hospital	40	9.8
Elmira Reformatory	20	4.9
N.Y. County Penitentiary	17	4.1
N.Y. City Reformatory	9	2.2
House of Refuge	13	3.2
Subtotal	241	58.9
Direct court commitments	51	12.5
Rome State School transfers	117	28.6
Total	409	100.0

Source: New York State Commission for Mental Defectives, *Annual Report, 1922,* p. 10.

behavior—pederasty and running away. Tests showed Henry to have an IQ
of 42. After a lengthy delay, Napanoch returned him to Rome as "unsuitable for treatment here," evidently because he had not clearly committed a
criminal offense. Thereafter the youth went in and out of Rome until state
troopers picked him up for chasing cows with an ax and dumping a lighted
pipe in a barn. Before trial a court recommitted Henry to the IDD, which
no longer disputed his suitability.

In the second case Napanoch officials accepted the transfer from Rome
but hurried him through the system. Bernstein committed Skip LaRue,[17] a
small white boy, as a "thief and frequent runaway." Napanoch's officials
held Skip for three years, only to grant parole when his parents begged for
his release. ("He has been gone away from home ever since June 1913," his
mother wrote, "& it maby about time for him to come home on prole.")
However, Skip was returned to Napanoch seven years later for "pyro-
maniacy."

Napanoch's very first case shows that the institution's officials insisted
on clear signs of criminal conduct in transfers from Rome. Bernstein trans-

ferred Thomas Green,[18] a white sixteen year old, because he ran away frequently. Thomas was reputed to have stolen a sack of coal at the age of twelve but had no criminal record. The conduct that resulted in his indefinite commitment occurred at the IDD itself, where Thomas was insolent, assaultive, and "the passive party in at least four sodomy acts." Napanoch's psychiatrist, V. C. Branham, classified Thomas as "feeble-minded, stable, habitual." "His yielding suggestible nature makes him an easy dupe for anyone," Branham concluded. "He is obviously an institutional case and should be recommitted to Napanoch."

Going through a commitment process that soon became routine, Superintendent Thayer filled out a form alleging that Thomas Green had performed an act of criminal behavior. An Ulster County judge certified that the youth was confined at the IDD "on a criminal charge." Then two qualified examiners attested that Thomas was a mental defective, and the judge issued the commitment order.[19]

While skirmishing with Dr. Bernstein, Napanoch officials fought a more protracted battle with court officers over the type of cases that constituted proper IDD commitments. The first round of this fight occurred shortly after the IDD opened. Fewer than 15 percent of Napanoch's first-year commitments were "judicials" (see table 4), and over the next few years the proportion actually fell. Napanoch officials discovered that the examiners on whom courts relied to certify mental defect were demanding up to $250 per case,[20] thus discouraging judges from ordering examinations. To break this logjam, the IDD recommended that the state provide free mental examinations.

Judicial commitments then escalated dramatically, to constitute 60 percent of all new prisoners in 1930.[21] The high figure was as troublesome as the low one had been, however, for it left few beds for prison transfers. Moreover, judges were abusing their power to commit persons merely charged with or arraigned for a criminal offense. In some cases, Dr. Thayer reported to the governor's office, courts had committed to Napanoch men "who exhibited no degree of mental deficiency." Moreover, when Napanoch officials tried to return such cases, "the committing courts . . . declined to answer communications addressed to them in the premises."[22] Thayer, now commissioner of correction,[23] joined forces with the governor's office to trim judicial discretion. A 1931 amendment to the Napanoch law took the dramatic step of limiting judicial commitments to persons "convicted of a criminal offense."[24] In addition, Thayer's department drafted legislation, also enacted in 1931, enabling it to discharge unsuitable commitments and, if necessary, to deposit them with the local sheriff.[25]

Not all judges were irresponsible, of course, and before conviction became an admission requirement, Napanoch officials did approve some pretrial commitments, as in the case of William Dell,[26] charged with stabbing a policeman. A twenty-three-year-old black man with a history of head injury and assaultiveness, Dell had previously been committed to a juvenile reformatory and the Rome State School. His mother now filled out commitment papers attesting that William was "very backward" and unable to care for himself. At Napanoch his condition deteriorated. He flew into rages, became "careless and untidy about his personal appearance," and smiled "foolishly much of the time." When he became psychotic, Napanoch recommitted him to the Middletown State Homeopathic Hospital, where he died twenty years later. William Dell's history indicated that pretrial commitment might be appropriate in some cases, but Thayer was willing to forgo its benefits to force judges into line.

Napanoch fought the final round in its battle against judicial irresponsibility in 1934. A New York City judge was reopening the cases of defective delinquents who had been committed without trial prior to the 1931 amendment and then later paroled. Amazingly the judge was now trying these parolees on the original charges and sentencing them to regular state prisons. "Thus, the inmate is under two sentences for the same crime," an outraged Thayer complained to the governor, "one at Napanoch and the new sentence to state prison." Fourteen Napanoch inmates stood ready for parole, but Thayer refused to release them to such legal peril.[27] Legislation of 1934 resolved the situation by stating that a Napanoch commitment was final.[28]

Fending off unsuitable civil and judicial commitments, Napanoch officials preserved the IDD as a fief of the prison system. But they still had to force other penal institutions to accept their definition of the defective delinquent. Napanoch might be a dumping ground, but there were limits to the institutional refuse it would accept.

The IDD's officials complained that other prisons sent their most unpleasant inmates to Napanoch. "Psychopaths with a mental age of over 12 years should not be transferred to this institution," the Commission of Prisons admonished in 1923. "They include the most desperate criminals and are difficult to govern."[29] When Thayer surveyed Napanoch's population in the mid-1920s, he discovered that some inmates had mental ages above 11.2 years. (In them, as he tactfully put it, "the intelligence defect had ceased to be prominent.")[30] Fifteen years later this problem of overly bright commitments remained unsolved: a 1938 study based on intelligence testing of all New York State prisoners found that of 712 Napanoch inmates, 24 (3.4 percent) had IQs between 87 and 106.[31] According to officials who worked at Napanoch for decades, the majority of inmates did appear to be mentally retarded, but there were always some of normal intelligence who had been transferred to the IDD for disciplinary reasons.[32]

Case files from New York's Auburn prison provide glimpses of events that precipitated transfers to Napanoch. A penciled note in one file, signed "Prison Phys," reads, "Complynn [sic] with your request for a statement concerning [inmate's name] I would advise that we leave no record of any injury to knee and no × ray."[33] In this instance, apparently, physical brutality formed a prelude to punitive transfer. Other records are more explicit about the triggering event. Lynch, a black man classified as "Normal (Borderline)" and "Prolonged Tractable," had a series of run-ins with C. S. Trites, Auburn's psychiatrist. Seven years into his sentence Lynch complained about Dr. Trites, who was reprimanded. The next year Trites examined Lynch, afterward informing the principal keeper:

> This man is the most insulting, dastardly, impudent, shiftless, foul-mouthed, laziest Negro it has even been my experience to meet.
>
> He is of borderline intelligence (I.Q. 70%), assaultive, and a menace to all. . . .
>
> I would suggest he be located in a place where it would be impossible for him any longer to pursue his foul, unprincipled tactics.[34]

Lynch was transferred to Napanoch.

Some Auburn prisoners were sent to Napanoch not for punishment but simply because they were exasperating or unparolable. For example, officials were evidently irritated by Vincent Parisi, a middle-aged Italian who had been sentenced to life imprisonment under a fourth-felony law. (Parisi's fourth offense involved stealing shoes, for which he had been convicted of third-degree burglary.) Lack of English-language skills made it almost inevitable that Parisi would test feebleminded. He nevertheless had the wit to mock three physicians, as a transcript of his meeting with the prison's classification board shows:

Dr. Martin:
Q. What you want you can't get? [sic]
A. Beer and whiskey; can't get that.
Q. You don't eat that?
A. You drink it. . . .
Q. Guilty this time?
A. No, half guilty.
Q. How?
A. You get the stuff, but you don't steal it. [This may be a reference to receiving stolen property.]
Q. What did they say you stole?
A. Shoes.
Q. Where did you find them?
A. On a church step.
Q. You weren't going to church?
A. It was Monday. . . .

Dr. Trites:
Q. What language do you speak?
A. Broken English.

Dr. Martin:
Q. Why not good English? . . .

Dr. Argento:
Q. What is your name?
A. I don't know my name.

The board concluded that "since he is doing Natural Life and is feeble-minded, he is recommended for Napanoch." [35]

Napanoch officials tried to bar vindictive and opportunistic transfers. They returned inappropriate cases to the transferring prison and as early as 1924 started traveling to other prisons to screen potential transfers themselves.[36] But the most effective weapon in their fight against improper commitments proved to be more careful intelligence testing. In the 1930s Elmira's classification director began supplementing group examinations with individual Stanford-Binet tests, which gave more precise results. In the 1940s New York's prison system began testing all new commitments, not just troublemakers. By that time, moreover, professional educators trained at Columbia University's Teachers College had wrested control over mental testing from older psychologists and physicians. As mental testers became more cautious, the proportion of inmates classified as mentally defective steadily shrank. Regular prisons continued to use IDD transfers for disciplinary purposes, but they found it more difficult to do so.

Nappies   Who was the typical "Nappie" (as officials nicknamed the IDD's inmates) [37] in terms of age, ethnicity, and race? Defective delinquents tended to be younger at commitment than other state prisoners. In 1937, for example, almost half the prisoners committed to Napanoch were under twenty-one years old, whereas fewer than 10 percent of other state prison commitments were that young (table 5). With regard to ethnicity, Napanoch usually held a *smaller* proportion of foreign-born inmates than did other New York State prisons. Moreover, this proportion fell considerably below the proportion of foreign born in the state's general population. Nappies tended to be native born.[38] They also tended to be black, a disproportion that increased over time.[39]

It is not surprising that "defective delinquents" were so labeled while young; troublesome youths who seemed to be uneducable were naturally sent to the state institution that specialized in their training. Nor is it surprising that Napanoch's population was disproportionately black. Blacks were less likely than native-born whites to do well on intelligence tests

Table 5. Ages of Commitments to New York State Prisons,
July 1, 1936–June 30, 1937

| | Age in Years | | | |
	16–20	21–30	31 and over	Total
IDDs				
Napanoch (men)	91	65	41	197
	(46.2%)	(33.0%)	(20.8%)	(100%)
Albion (women)	23	14	8	45
	(51.1%)	(31.1%)	(17.8%)	(100%)
	114	79	49	242
	(47.1%)	(32.6%)	(20.3%)	(100%)
State prisons[a]	187	997	1027	2211
	(8.5%)	(45.1%)	(46.4%)	(100%)

[a] Attica, Clinton, Sing Sing, and Westfield State Farm (Bedford Hills).

Source: New York State Commissioner of Correction, Annual Report, 1937, pp. 12, 18.

normed on the latter population, and blacks, too, often felt the weight of officials' prejudices. Of one Auburn case, for example, the psychiatrist wrote, "This Negro is the commonly met with, good-natured irresponsible type. The examiner believes that he is of the suggestible kind, and could be easily led. He is definitely feeble-minded, and would be a suitable case for transfer to Napanoch."[40]

But it *is* surprising to find that Napanoch did not net a disproportionate number of foreign-born prisoners. Eugenicists often claimed that southern and eastern Europeans were lowering the average American intelligence quotient.[41] In addition, foreigners with little command of English, like Vincent Parisi, tended to score poorly on English-language intelligence tests. Moreover, officials who made the transfer decisions, such as Auburn psychologist Dr. William Argento, expected inferiority in immigrants.[42] Nevertheless, the published statistics on ethnicity are reinforced by data in Auburn and Napanoch case files showing that IDD officials—whatever their personal beliefs—tried to disentangle ethnicity from intelligence when reviewing records of foreign-born inmates.

For instance, Superintendent Thayer blocked commitment of a man who evidently was transferred to Napanoch simply because he was a Russian Jew. Samuel Cohen[43] had lived with his wife and five children in New York City before his arrest for running a "confidence game." He had a long record of clever swindles, claimed to be able to read and write in Hebrew and Russian, and at Auburn had an excellent disciplinary record. Nonetheless, Auburn's physician, Frank Heacox, described Cohen as "indolent, unstable, sexually promiscuous, inadequate." As "cause of present mental condition," Heacox indicated "heredity." (He also wrote, "Parents probably mentally defective," even though both had died years earlier in Russia.) Cohen's mental age, according to Heacox, was seven years. Thayer disagreed, writing that "because of language difficulty and foreign parentage, . . . binet-simon is unfair." Thayer further reasoned that "as [Cohen] has no education, and as he possesses an industrial record of holding one job at tailoring for 13 years, and having earned $75 per week as a tailor, and also as he has shown sufficient intelligence to organize and supervise the operation of our tailoring shop . . . he cannot be classed as feeble-minded." Thayer retransferred Cohen to Sing Sing.

In the case of Jake Kaplansky,[44] Napanoch officials again refused an Auburn commitment evidently based on ethnicity. Born in Poland, Kaplansky had been a crane operator and machinist until his conviction for grand larceny and receiving stolen property. At Napanoch his IQ tested at 57, but according to the examiner, he "answered all questions relevantly and promptly, with apparently no disturbance in the stream of mental activity. . . . Shows a fairly well balanced personality. . . . Suspicious or paranoid ideas could not be elicited. Nothing could be demonstrated at this time to indicate an essential psychopathic personality . . . ethical perception and judgment are relatively adult." Napanoch paroled Kaplansky to work in a steel mill.

The relatively low proportion of foreigners in Napanoch's population, then, probably reflected IDD officials' efforts to screen for ethnic prejudices. In the case of blacks, however, there was no such screening. In fact, assumptions of inferiority may have made troublesome black prisoners with low test scores seem natural candidates for IDD commitment.

Held for Life?   Did Napanoch officials try to achieve its founders' eugenic mission? Did they retain defective delinquents for life to prevent them from reproducing? The answer to both questions seems to be no. To judge from published records and my sample of cases, the IDD's eugenic goals were almost immediately shunted aside by the practicalities of prison management. As the years passed, the institution's eugenic rationale faded, replaced by a desire to parole prisoners and minimize costs. And then, in the 1960s and 1970s, U.S. Supreme Court decisions dismantled the tattered remnants of Napanoch's eugenic sentencing structure. Nonetheless, a few inmates, such as Fenix Whipple, were immured till cured.[45] They never managed to escape the snares of the IDD's original commitment law; in their cases the institution did in fact work to prevent reproduction, even though mid-twentieth-century officials may have had no eugenic intention.

Release was not nearly so rare as Napanoch's founders had hoped it would be. By the mid-1920s the IDD was paroling about 100 prisoners a year, a figure that rose to nearly 200 by the decade's end. Paroles drastically increased in the early 1940s (no doubt an effect of World War II) but dropped again in the late 1940s, remaining between 200 and 300 a year over the next decade.[46]

Most defective delinquents were granted at least one chance on parole. According to a former correctional officer, however, it was difficult for older Nappies in particular to achieve parole or do well on it. They could not easily line up an employment prospect (prerequisite to parole), and many had been institutionalized for so long that they were unable to function well on their own. Thus despite the parole possibility, some spent their last days at Napanoch.[47]

The Department of Correction harnessed indefinite sentencing to its own ends. Far less interested in hanging on to a lot of helpless elders than in maintaining the threat of an up-to-life sentence, the department held the possibility of an IDD transfer over the heads of inmates in other prisons. Indefinite sentencing remained, but it shed its eugenic rationale.

Under the vast discretion that the 1921 law granted to Napanoch officials lay a conviction that the needs of the state are more important than those of any individual. As the years passed, concern for individual freedoms whittled away at this view of the relationship between state and individual. Napanoch's founding legislation had provided a weak check against illegitimate commitments by requiring certification of mental deficiency by two qualified examiners. In the early 1930s, after courts freed over three dozen Nappies on habeas corpus petitions,[48] New York's attorney general recommended hearings at the time of commitment. Cases decided in the 1940s mandated hearings at the time of indefinite recommitment as well. These decisions made it increasingly difficult to commit as defective delinquents people who did not meet the sub-70 IQ standard for defective delinquency. Then, in 1966, the U.S. Supreme Court decided a case, *Baxstrom v. Herold,* that spelled death for the IDD.

The Closing of Napanoch   The *Baxstrom* decision pertained to mentally ill prisoners, not mentally retarded ones, but it implied that New York's defective delinquent laws were irreparably deficient in due process.[49] Johnnie K. Baxstrom, who had been convicted of second-degree assault in 1959 and sentenced to two-and-a-half to three years in a New York prison, was certified insane before his sentence expired and transferred to Dannemora State Hospital, where he was recommitted until he recovered. The Supreme

Court held that Baxstrom's constitutional right to equal protection had been denied because, unlike nonprisoners, he had not at the time of civil commitment had a jury review of his case, nor had a judge determined that he was *dangerously* mentally ill. Baxstrom's circumstances were similar to those of Napanoch's defective delinquents. Napanoch closed as an institution for defective delinquents in 1966, apparently a casualty of the *Baxstrom* decision. With a 1974 act eliminating transfer of "dangerously mentally defective" inmates in state schools to the Department of Correction, New York's defective delinquency system breathed its last.[50] Napanoch's residue of defective delinquents, mainly elderly men who had been there for decades, was moved to a unit adjacent to Matteawan State Hospital.

A subsequent U.S. Supreme Court decision, in the 1972 case *Jackson v. Indiana*,[51] completed the reversal in thinking about the rights of mentally disabled individuals. Theon Jackson, a severely retarded man who was both deaf and mute, had been accused of two minor robberies. Instead of being tried, Jackson had been committed to a civil institution until recovery. According to the *Jackson* Court, due process is violated by such an indefinite commitment of a criminal defendant solely on account of incompetency to stand trial. The nature and duration of commitment must bear a reasonable relation to the purpose of commitment—which Jackson's probable natural-life commitment for alleged petty thefts did not. Moreover (the Court continued), criminal responsibility at the time of the alleged offense and competency to stand trial are distinct issues; guilt should not be inferred from the fact of mental retardation. Finally, the Court feistily concluded, by in effect condemning Jackson to permanent institutionalization, Indiana subjected him to cruel and unusual punishment.

New York's Other Institutions for Defective Delinquents

New York established two other institutions for defective delinquents, one for women and the other for Napanoch's overflow. Although full histories of these institutions would be inappropriate here, brief overviews help to indicate the impact of the defective delinquency movement.[52]

Albion State Training School   The Division for Mentally Defective Delinquent Women established at the Bedford Hills Reformatory in 1920 soon proved to be a "mistake."[53] Prisoners isolated there grew restive when they realized that, unlike other prisoners, they could not be paroled.[54] Moreover, it was expensive to separate the defective delinquents from the reformatory population and provide them with separate programs. In the 1920s problems also developed at New York's other women's reformatory, the Albion State Training School, in the western part of the state. There psychological

testing identified women with low IQs who, it seemed, should be reclassi-
fied as defective delinquents. New York's governmental reorganization of
1927 solved both sets of problems by bringing Bedford Hills and Albion
under the new Department of Correction. Now the department could classify by prison. The department transferred Bedford Hills' defective delinquents to Albion and Albion's "normal" prisoners to Bedford Hills. Bedford Hills closed its special division, and Albion became an independent
institution for female defective delinquents.[55]

Developments at Albion tended to mirror those at Napanoch; for example, due process restrictions imposed on the men's institution eventually affected the women's as well. In 1957 the Western Reformatory for
Women was established on Albion's grounds to receive women with normal intelligence and reformatory sentences. Thereafter the defective delinquent population shrank while that of the reformatory grew. The legislature finally abolished the women's IDD in 1970, four years after phasing
out the IDD at Napanoch.[56] The slower closing, like the earlier opening,
reflected a lower level of concern for the constitutional rights of women.

Woodbourne Institution for Defective Delinquents   With Napanoch full but
commitments unabating, in 1932 New York appropriated $1,500,000 to
build a second male IDD about fifteen miles away.[57] The Woodbourne Institution for Defective Delinquents opened in 1935 under V. C. Branham,
formerly Napanoch's psychiatrist. All its defective delinquents were transfers from Napanoch, but Woodbourne also specialized in cases of borderline and dull-normal intelligence. It was the first of New York's three IDDs
to return to normal status. After 1954 Woodbourne no longer received prisoners defined as mentally retarded.

■ ■ ■

How many people did New York classify as defective delinquents over
time? Neither published reports nor case files definitively answer this question because both sometimes count parole violators—and transfers among
IDDs as well—as new cases. But it seems probable that the number of men
and women committed to New York State prisons as defective delinquents
totaled about 11,000.[58]

To gauge the IDDs' impact on New York's prison system is somewhat
easier because in this case, one can use total population statistics. Between
1922 and 1956 (after which "normals" and "borderlines" were mixed into
IDD commitment statistics), at least 5 percent of New York's total prison
population was diagnosed as defective delinquent, a figure that rose steadily
to peak at almost 13 percent in 1944 (table 6). Thereafter there was a slow

Table 6. Proportion of New York State Prisoners in Institutions for
Defective Delinquents, 1922–56

	Napanoch	Bedford Hills/ Albion	Woodbourne	Total Prison Population[a]	Percentage in IDDs
1922	320	41	—	6,890	5.2
1924	420	60	—	6,797	7.1
1926	596	75	—	7,351	9.1
1928	679	71	—	10,284	7.3
1930	772	69	—	11,367	7.4
1932	961	137	—	12,843	8.5
1934	966	190	—	13,487	8.6
1936	921	253	408	14,805	10.7
1938	1,087	373	653	17,402	12.1
1940	953	373	661	18,324	10.8
1942	973	301	608	17,198	10.9
1944	946	293	700	14,993	12.9
1946	891	262	645	14,458	12.4
1948	1,027	254	388	16,227	10.3
1950	1,006	213	290	17,161	8.8
1952	1,102	228	—[b]	17,555	7.6
1954	1,016	252	—	18,496	6.9
1956	953	243	—	19,292	6.2

[a] This column gives combined statistics on state prisons, reformatories, and institutions for defective delinquents.

[b] No data are given for Woodbourne for 1952 because "normals" are not clearly excluded from its 1952 population statistics. For earlier years, when two sources conflict on Woodbourne's population, the lower figure is used on the assumption that it excludes "normals."

Sources: New York State's annual Legislative Manual and the annual reports of New York's Institution for Defective Delinquents at Napanoch, Reformatory for Women, Commission for Mental Defectives, Commission of Prisons, Commissioner of Correction, and Department of Correction.

decline in the proportion of state prisoners held at IDDs, down to about 6 percent in 1956. Even at the lows of 5 and 6 percent, however, significant numbers of prisoners were subjected to the threat of negative labeling and indefinite sentencing.

Defective Delinquents in Massachusetts

Massachusetts, too, developed a fairly elaborate defective delinquent system.[59] This one took root at the Bridgewater State Farm, where Massachusetts had long held the criminally insane and other atypical prisoners. The state opened a men's unit for "DDs" (as Massachusetts officials called defective delinquents) in 1922, in Bridgewater quarters previously reserved for vagrants and drunks. In 1926, shortly after Harvard University criminologist Sheldon Glueck issued a strong plea for a "special institution for female defective delinquents,"[60] the state established a corresponding women's unit in Bridgewater's former almshouse hospital. Overcrowding led to creation of a second unit for female DDs at the Framingham women's reformatory in 1941 and a parallel men's unit at the Concord reformatory in 1942. Thereafter Massachusetts operated four DD units.[61] None was fully independent, but at one point they held over 15 percent of the state's total prison population.[62]

The secondary literature on institutions for defective delinquents, although scant and usually uncritical, includes a remarkable 1950 study of Massachusetts defective delinquents by Efrem A. Gordon and Lewis Harris, Harvard University law students. Gordon and Harris interviewed DDs themselves, collecting rare prisoner views on what it meant to receive this designation. According to Gordon and Harris, "The significant feature of the DD attitude . . . is despair. This hopelessness is not the product of incarceration alone, but springs from the rigorous discipline of the department and the fact that sentence to the DD department may be a life sentence. To the inmate who has no friends or relatives willing to assist him, and no funds to expedite the machinery of release by securing counsel, the outlook is discouraging indeed."[63] The Massachusetts DD law, Gordon and Harris found, ensnared some people who had been cleared of the original charges, who were normal in intelligence, or who had no criminal record whatsoever.[64]

Until the 1950s DD adjudications in Massachusetts could be made without a hearing, and mental "examinations" sometimes "took place without any meeting between examining physician and defendant. Even under the present [1950] practice, there is some evidence that examination consisted of questions like 'can you name the seven oceans' and 'can you count backward from one hundred by sevens.' "[65] Gordon and Harris unearthed one case in which a young man ("quite alert and responsive in conversation") was committed as a defective delinquent after *he himself* called police for help in retrieving belongings from the house where his mother was living with a new husband. The mother charged her son with being a stubborn child, and after "a six to seven minute examination by a state psychiatrist," he was declared a DD. In a second case a bad hangover was mistaken for mental defect, and in a third an "extremely unattractive" defendant with an IQ of 112 was framed by a wife who preferred other men.[66]

Gordon and Harris also tell of a DD who, after twenty years on parole "with a reputedly good adjustment," decided to take steps toward discharge: "He *requested* discharge, i.e., termination of his status as a DD and was sent to —— Hospital. There it was found that he was 'happy, cooperative and prevaricating like a moron,' that he used obscene language, and was difficult to arouse in the morning. His parole was terminated, but not by discharge. The subject was recommended for return to Bridgewater . . . and has been reconfined."[67] Officials in Massachusetts showed much less concern than did their counterparts in New York about careless and overtly senseless defective delinquent commitments, allowing the state's DD department to be "used as a 'dumping ground' by the courts and schools for the feeble-minded."[68]

Although Massachusetts officials discharged DDs with great reluctance, they were forced to grant two mass releases. The first occurred in 1947, when the legislature required mental examination of all DDs in custody; many proved to be intellectually normal and were freed.[69] And in 1950, as a result of a parent's petition, the state supreme court ruled that people facing a defective delinquent commitment had the right to notice and to defend themselves. Those who considered themselves to have been improperly committed, the court continued, should submit a writ of habeas corpus.

At first few DDs took advantage of this offer: most could not afford legal assistance, and the Department of Correction made no move to help. In 1953, however, a superior court judge agreed to accept a DD's letter as a writ of habeas corpus. The lid was off the pot. Within a year nearly half of Massachusetts's DDs had gained their freedom. Pressured by the *Baxstrom* and *Jackson v. Indiana* decisions, Massachusetts finally repealed its defective delinquent law in 1970.[70] When I visited the Bridgewater Treatment Center in 1995, however, the superintendent pointed out a few elderly men, one in a wheelchair, who had originally been committed as DDs.

Defective Delinquency in Other States

Specialists in mental disability and the criminal law have paid remarkably little attention to the defective delinquent classification. Their writings, although voluminous on the subject of mental illness, avoid discussing defective delinquent laws, sometimes assuming (incorrectly) that these were a form of (or were incorporated into) sex psychopath legislation.[71] What little literature there is on the treatment of defective delinquents outside New York and Massachusetts demonstrates nothing more clearly than it does the need for more and better research.

Pennsylvania appears to have been the only state other than New York to establish an independent institution exclusively for defective delinquents. After twenty years of effort, Pennsylvania enacted a defective delinquent law in 1937.[72] At first it sent defective delinquent males to a converted industrial school at Huntington, but in 1960 it opened a new $12 million facility, the Institution for Defective Delinquents at Dallas, Pennsylvania.[73] Female defective delinquents were sent to the Laurelton State Village, an institution modeled after New York's eugenic institution at Newark.[74] Pennsylvania permitted transfers from state training schools and prisons as well as direct court commitments, holding them all for up-to-life terms. "The Pennsylvania Defective Delinquent Act contains almost no procedural safeguards and is open to the greatest abuse," a 1967 law review article complained.[75]

Virginia established a state farm for defective misdemeanants. Opened in 1926, this institution received a wide range of offenders, including drug addicts, the feebleminded, psychopaths, the tubercular, and the venereally diseased.[76] According to Stanley P. Davies, a long-term student of programs for the retarded, the Virgina State Farm received felons as well as misdemeanants; it also accepted transfers from mental hospitals, mental retardation colonies, and juvenile training schools. Women defective delinquents were quartered separately.[77]

Californians began lobbying for a separate institution for defective delinquents in 1919, but when funds did not materialize, Fred O. Butler, the entrepreneurial head of the Sonoma State Home for the retarded, went ahead and built quarters for this group at his institution.[78] Between 1931 and 1941 Butler identified 1,438, or 39 percent, of his admissions as defective delinquents. All were under twenty years of age, the boys with IQs of 50–70 and the girls with IQs of 50–89. Again seizing the initiative, Butler sterilized over 74 percent of the boys and 86 percent of the girls.[79]

Taking the path of least resistance, a number of states sent low-IQ offenders, pre- or postconviction, to training schools for the retarded. This shunting of prisoners into the mental retardation system became a significant means by which states meted out up-to-life sentences without enacting formal defective delinquent laws. According to a special census of 1933, 9 percent of first admissions to state hospitals for mental defectives and epileptics were of people accused or convicted of crimes. In four states (Rhode Island, Minnesota, North Dakota, and West Virginia) the proportion exceeded 15 percent. Even in New York, with its formal defective delinquency system, the proportion was over 7 percent.[80]

Recently discovered documents from New Jersey's Reformatory for Women at Clinton Farms illustrate how eugenic criminology could affect prisoners in ways that are today almost undetectable. In the 1920s Clinton's board and superintendent transferred some prisoners who were "still of child-bearing age and . . . likely to propagate more feeble-minded if released" to the Vineland, New Jersey, institution for the mentally retarded.[81] They arranged for the sterilization of other inmates who seemed to be low in intelligence or had illegitimate or biracial children.[82] In 1937 Dr. Ralph J.

Belford of Princeton, N.J., delivered the baby of prisoner C. R., a single white woman, through Cesarean section, afterward reporting that "the tubes were ligated on both sides because of a history of . . . insanity in the family, and also due to the fact that this patient while she is twenty-six years of age is not mentally developed much above the stage of a moron." [83] After another Cesarean section, this one on E. E., a twenty-one-year-old "colored" woman, Dr. Belford dropped the uterus "back into the abdomen after double ligation and cutting of tubes between the ligatures." [84] Other prisons may similarly have taken low-visibility steps to prevent "defectives" from reproducing. [85]

Maryland resuscitated the defective delinquent concept in 1951 by establishing its Patuxent Institution for Defective Delinquents. The brainchild of a group of psychiatrists and psychologists, the Patuxent IDD's legislation defined a defective delinquent as "an individual who, by the demonstration of persistent aggravated anti-social or criminal behavior, evidences a propensity toward criminal activity, and who is found to have either such intellectual deficiency or emotional unbalance, or both, as to clearly demonstrate an actual danger to society." [86] This definition is but a short remove from the degenerationist thinking on which earlier definitions of defective delinquency were based: it associates criminal behavior with mental deficiency and psychopathy, and it conceptualizes criminality and dangerousness as states or conditions within the offender, something distinct from behavior. To be committed to Patuxent, a person had to be convicted and sentenced, but—as at Napanoch—once designated a "defective delinquent," he could be held on a completely open-ended sentence. [87] And although Patuxent held a broader range of offenders than Napanoch did, by the mid-1960s mentally retarded offenders (defined as those with IQs under 80) constituted over one-quarter of its population. [88] Patuxent closed in 1977, done in by disillusionment with the medical model and the same civil liberties concerns that closed Napanoch. [89]

Rudy Vallee Is a Racehorse

And what of Fenix Whipple, with whose story this book began? Brain damaged and already a recidivist when he arrived at Elmira, in 1921 Fenix was transferred to Napanoch by none other than Dr. Frank Christian, the eugenicist who helped to formulate the theory of defective delinquency. Dr. Christian himself diagnosed Fenix as "very low [in] intelligence . . . licentious . . . ignorant . . . an obvious misfit and unfit to be at large." After reexamining Fenix, Napanoch officials decided he was a "typical hereditary type" and, without a hearing, recommitted him on an indefinite sentence. [90]

For the next forty years Napanoch personnel went through the motions of preparing Fenix for an undefined future event, in the process piling up records that reaffirmed his defective delinquent diagnosis. They frequently retested his mental ability, for example. What follows are Fenix's responses to tests administered in 1934:[91]

Who is the President of the United States? Roosevelt
What is the longest river in the United States? East River
Who is the Dictator of Italy? [no answer]
Who discovered America? Lincoln

The tuna is a kind of fish. TRUE *FALSE*
The pancreas is found in a person's brain. TRUE *FALSE*
Goethe was a famous German Poet. TRUE *FALSE*
Women are not allowed to vote in Tennessee. TRUE *FALSE*

The Guernsey is a kind of HORSE, CHICKEN, *COW*, GOAT.
The Piccolo is used in HAIRDRESSING, SKATING, *PAINTING*, MUSIC.
Rudy Vallee is a DISEASE, CROONER, POLITICIAN, *RACEHORSE*.

Fenix, too, went through futile motions, repeatedly petitioning for release and repeatedly being blocked by Napanoch officials. Between 1927 and 1950 Fenix produced at least ten habeas corpus petitions, explaining in his erratic script and fractured legalese that he was not a mental defective and that his discharge would not endanger public safety. He began one "write of habeaus copus" by scribbling:

Supreme Court State of New York
Against the people of the State of New York to
Water N. Thauyer Md Supt of Institution for Men Defictive Delinquents Against me Command you that you have said body and prison.
by you imprisoned and detained.

All of Fenix's petitions were dismissed.

In 1930 Fenix withdrew a habeas corpus application because Napanoch officials told him it would harm his chances for parole. The judge, Daniel V. McNamee, acknowledged the application's withdrawal, writing:

I am very glad to have you take this course, because I am very confident that Doctor Battey [then superintendent of Napanoch] will be very considerate of the application for parol [*sic*] of any worthy man.

I think you also are very wise in placing your confidence in him, and regarding him as your friend.

On at least one occasion Napanoch and court officials conspired to remedy legal defects in Fenix's recommitment papers so that a judge could not grant his request for release.[92]

Fenix's file illustrates the phenomenon that sociologist Erving Goffman, in his study of social control within prisons and other "total" institutions, calls "looping."[93] Looping occurs when keepers encourage inmate behaviors (such as passivity or independence) for which they then blame the inmate ("You are too passive" or "You don't know how to obey"). Looping locks the prisoner into an endless cycle of criticism and frustration. Relieving the frustration with anger confirms one's inadequacies, but internalizing it is equally crippling. Fenix reexperienced looping every time he took an IQ test: institutionalized nearly all his life, he had no way to learn how to answer the tests' questions about piccolos and racehorses and the election laws of Tennessee, yet low test scores had led to his institutionalization at Napanoch in the first place. Looping occurred again when he was encouraged to file petitions that would never be granted and yet again when Judge McNamee advised him that Napanoch officials were his "friends."

Equally "loopy" were Fenix's efforts to achieve parole. After his initial failure on parole (see the introduction), Fenix frequently applied for rerelease. Relatives helped him to line up jobs and places to live, but Napanoch staff took months to check out these arrangements, during which time Fenix, who never became socially competent, would get a new disciplinary report. He would then have to wait an entire year to reapply for parole, at which time the process would start again from the beginning. Occasionally it was slowed even further by officials who announced that they would "have to study and treat him for a longer period of time." When Fenix had been in prison for thirty years, a psychologist, without a trace of irony, recommended "that he be given a long period of institutionalization."

Finally reparoled in 1958, Fenix had a cancer operation and then went to live with a farm couple who treated him kindly. They became frightened, however, when he stormed off, warning the wife that he would "clean her clock" and threatening her husband as well. His parole revoked, Fenix returned to Napanoch for the final time.

Napanoch officials extracted Fenix's remaining teeth so that he could be fitted for dentures. Because the first denture mold broke and the second one was misplaced, however, months passed before his false teeth arrived. These bureaucratic mishaps dehumanized Fenix. He could no longer eat ordinary food. Late photographs show him as truculent as in earlier pictures but now toothless, frail, and even more bewildered. Officials decided to dispose of a bicycle that had accompanied him to Napanoch in 1921. At Fenix's suggestion, they sent it to his young relatives.

Fenix had a heart attack in 1960. The next year his cancer returned. He died of cancer of the large intestine in January 1962 and was buried in the prison's graveyard. His life and death were the logical outcome of eugenic criminology as it had been formulated by Josephine Shaw Lowell in the 1870s and reiterated thereafter by Isaac Kerlin, Zebulon Brockway, criminal anthropologists, prison physicians, psychiatrist Walter E. Fernald, psychologist Henry H. Goddard, superintendents Katharine B. Davis and Charles Bernstein, and prison reformer O. F. Lewis. Just as Fenix had predicted, and as all those who had worked to have him incarcerated as a biological criminal had hoped, he left prison only in "a ruff Box."

Notes

1. Haller 1963:177-78.

2. Glueck and Glueck 1934:303 (emphasis in original), 299, 322.

3. Hooton 1939a:309.

4. Hooton 1939b:397.

5. Sheldon, Hartl, and McDermott 1949: dedication page; also see Sheldon and Stevens 1942 and Sheldon, Stevens, and Tucker 1940.

6. See, for example, Amir and Berman 1970; Mednick, Moffitt, and Stack 1987; Rowe and Osgood 1984; and Wilson and Herrnstein 1985.

7. Herrnstein and Murray 1994:105, 251, 548.

8. Dreifus 1995:48.

9. This chapter draws on both published and archival materials. The latter include the following items:

> correspondence about amendments to New York's Defective Delinquent laws (New York State Education Library, Bill Jacket Collection);

> a sample of the Napanoch IDD records (New York State Archives, ser. 14610-88B) [I went through the first nine boxes, recording information on the first and middle case in each box. In the text I refer to cases by their actual numbers but use disguised names.];

> a sample of records from New York's Auburn prison, drawn to investigate events that led to Napanoch transfers (New York State Archives, ser. 14610-77A) [When I used them, these records had not yet been sorted. The key to my case identification code—"NFH case 1" and so on—is on file at the State Archives. Again, I have disguised inmates' names.]; and

> records of eugenic treatments at the New Jersey Reformatory for Women provided by Dr. Mary Ann Hawkes and now at the New Jersey State Archives, Trenton.

In addition, this chapter draws on interviews with Captain Kai Rober, who had been a guard at Napanoch since 1946, and Dr. Glenn M. Kendall, a New York State prison education official from the 1930s into the 1970s.

10. Pisciotta 1994:111-12; New York State Department of Correction 1949b.

11. See, for example, Lamb 1906:829 and New York State Department of Correction 1949b:5-6.

12. New York State Commission of Prisons, *Annual Report, 1922*, p. 118.

13. New York State Commission of Prisons, *Annual Report, 1923*, p. 126. According to Captain Rober (1977 interview), troublemakers were held in these cells

until they became insane and could be shipped off to Dannemora State Hospital. Then "Dannemora would fatten them up and ship them back."

14. New York State Commission of Prisons, *Annual Report, 1923,* p. 132.

15. New York State Commission of Prisons, *Annual Report, 1924,* p. 170.

16. Napanoch case 52.

17. Napanoch case 26.

18. Napanoch case 1.

19. After going through this rigmarole, Napanoch paroled Thomas just six months later, and there his record ends. Apparently he was too clearly criminal to return to Rome but not troublesome enough to hang on to.

20. New York State Commission of Prisons, *Annual Report, 1923,* p. 132.

21. New York State Commissioner of Correction, *Annual Report, 1930,* appendix ("Inset of Annual Statistics of Institution for Male Defective Delinquents"), 11.

22. Thayer to Rosenman, counsel to the governor, April 2, 1931, in bill jacket to New York State, *Laws of New York, 1931,* chap. 280.

23. In addition to Thayer, other Napanoch superintendents also moved on to higher positions in prison administration. Rober (1977 interview) emphasized that the IDD created an excellent training ground, producing at least thirteen superintendents and several commissioners as underlings worked up through the ranks. The IDD was large enough, Rober explained, to provide a range of administrative experience but small enough to enable officers to become closely familiar with all aspects of prison operations.

24. New York State, *Laws of New York, 1931,* chap. 459.

25. Ibid., chap. 280.

26. Napanoch case 213.

27. Thayer to Hon. Herbert H. Lehman, April 12, 1934, in bill jacket to New York State, *Laws of New York, 1934,* chap. 267.

28. New York State, *Laws of New York 1934,* chap. 267.

29. New York State Commission of Prisons, *Annual Report, 1923,* p. 133.

30. New York State Institution for Defective Delinquents at Napanoch, *Annual Report, 1926,* p. 12.

31. Wallack, Kendall, and Briggs 1939:105.

32. Rober (1977 interview); Kendall (1977 interview).

33. New York State Archives, ser. 14610-77A, NFH case 3.

34. Ibid., NFH case 27.

35. Ibid., NFH case 43.

36. New York State Commission of Prisons, *Annual Report, 1924,* p. 170.

37. This nickname, so far as I can tell from the records, was merely a diminutive, not a racial epithet.

38. These statements about ethnicity and the following statements about race and paroles are based on annual reports of New York State's Commissioner of Correction, Institution for Male Defective Delinquents at Napanoch, Commission of Prisons, and Department of Correction.

39. Fewer than 5 percent of New York State residents were black in 1920; this fell to 3.3 percent in 1930 and rose 6.2 percent in 1950 (Dodd 1993:66). Commitments to both regular New York State prisons and the IDDs were about 15 percent

black during the 1920s and 20 percent black during the 1930s. Then, about 1940, Napanoch began admitting black prisoners in numbers disproportionate to those in regular prisons. In the 1950s about half of Napanoch's commitments were black; the proportion was roughly 35 percent at the Attica, Clinton, and Sing Sing prisons.

40. New York State Archives, ser. 14610-77A, NFH case 57.

41. See, e.g., Cannon 1922.

42. Auburn records include intelligence tests and Argento's comments on them. Of NFH case 55, a middle-aged Italian who tested at mental age 8.5, Argento wrote, "This man is an illiterate, ignorant ex-shepherd from the mountains of Calabria and, though he has lived in America 17 years, he has assimilated nothing." Not long before arriving at Auburn, however, this man had purchased a new home. Auburn's classification board declared him "an unsuitable case for transfer" to the Napanoch facility, but he was transferred anyway.

43. Napanoch case 256.

44. Napanoch case 241.

45. This phrase comes from Woods 1918:67.

46. Long after other prisons had handed release decisions over to a parole board, Napanoch's superintendent retained parole-granting authority. New York's IDDs were among the last U.S. prisons to abandon the nineteenth-century model of the nearly autonomous prison whose head had almost unchecked discretionary powers.

47. Rober (1977 interview). According to Kendall (1977 interview), for some defective delinquents parole was never a possibility at all. They got what eugenicists had intended: permanent custodial care. Until the Napanoch records are coded and computerized, we cannot estimate the number or proportion of defective delinquents who were held for life.

48. New York State Commissioner of Correction, *Annual Report, 1930*, appendix ("Insert of Annual Statistics of Institution for Male Defective Delinquents"), 11, 18–20.

49. *Baxstrom v. Herold*, 383 U.S. 107 (1966).

50. New York State, *Laws of New York, 1974*, chap. 629.

51. *Jackson v. Indiana*, 406 U.S. 715 (1972).

52. For more information on the Albion and Woodbourne IDDs, as well as the IDD at Napanoch, see Branham 1926; Branham and Thayer 1931; Davies with Ecob 1959; Robinson 1933; Thayer 1925; and Hahn 1978.

53. New York State Department of Correction, n.d.:9.

54. New York State Department of Correction, 1949a:6.

55. For a brief period in the early 1930s, the Albion facility was named the Institution for Mentally Defective Delinquent Women, but in 1932, concerned about possible stigmatization, the legislature reinstated the former name, Albion State School. The prison remained an institution for defective delinquents, however.

56. New York State, *Laws of New York, 1970*, chap. 476, sec. 67. According to a personal communication of November 1990 from archivist Richard Andress, the New York State Archives' Albion holdings now include several hundred files on the women transferred to Albion from Bedford Hills. Some of this data is reported in Alexander 1995.

57. New York State Department of Correction 1949c:4.

58. The New York State Archives holds between 7,000 and 8,000 Napanoch case files, some of which may be repeats if recommitments were logged in as new cases, and another 4,000 Albion files. Woodbourne prisoners need not be counted because its defective delinquents were originally committed to Napanoch.

59. In addition to appearing in the sources cited in notes 60–70, information on Massachusetts's defective delinquent units can be found in Bates 1928; Davies with Ecob 1959; and Robinson 1933; also see Overholser 1935.

60. S. Glueck 1925:64–65.

61. Farrell and Ogonik 1955:439. According to Tenney (1962:30), by the early 1960s two of these units had been shut.

62. Tenney 1962:28.

63. Gordon and Harris 1950:478. The comment about "rigorous discipline" refers to the fact that at Bridgewater, as at Napanoch, a military system was used to train male DDs, or at least to keep them busy. However, Bridgewater officials carried this system to the extreme of court-martialing rule breakers. Gordon and Harris (1950:472) describe it as "the most rigorous program of discipline in the entire [Massachusetts] penal system."

64. Gordon and Harris 1950; also see Ricker 1934 and Lekkerkerker 1931:79.

65. Gordon and Harris 1950:465.

66. Ibid., 466–68.

67. Ibid., 483–84 (emphasis in original).

68. Ibid., 473.

69. Ibid., 466.

70. Massachusetts, *Acts and Resolves 1970*, chap. 888, sec. 11.

71. See, e.g., Brakel and Rock 1971:342–43. Also see Brakel, Parry, and Weiner 1985, where defective delinquency slips between the cracks of insanity on the one hand and sexual psychopathy on the other.

72. H. I. Pollock 1951: 600 n. 40 and accompanying text; Barnes [1927] 1968: 345.

73. Gafni and Welsh 1967:590.

74. Barnes [1927] 1968:345.

75. Gafni and Welsh 1967:581.

76. Ballard 1941:313–14; Davies with Ecob 1959:79.

77. Davies with Ecob 1959:79.

78. According to F. Butler (1948:76), other buildings for DDs were build at the Pacific Colony for the retarded.

79. F. Butler 1942:7, 9.

80. U. S. Bureau of the Census 1936:22.

81. William J. Ellis, psychologist, "Report of Psychological Examining at State Reformatory for Women at Clinton Farms, N.J., July 1, 1922–June 30, 1923," p. 5 (typescript in New Jersey State Archives).

82. E.g., Minutes of Board Meeting, May 14, 1935, p. 4 (New Jersey State Archives).

83. R. J. Belford, report on the case of C. R., June 24, 1937 (New Jersey State Archives).

84. R. J. Belford, report on E. E., July 12, 1937 (New Jersey State Archives).

85. Another low-visibility procedure is recorded by Westwell (1951:287), according to whom a Dr. Charles Hawke of Kansas was castrating defective delinquents and experimenting to discover whether hormones caused their condition: " 'By giving our castrates rather heavy doses of testosterone . . . we were able to get a return of the delinquency in several cases that had been entirely free of delinquent tendencies since they had been operated upon. . . . Those tendencies were all cleared up on stopping testosterone.' "

86. Lejins 1977:122.

87. Patuxent held only men.

88. Boslow and Kandel 1965:647.

89. See the entire "Symposium Issue: Patuxent Institution," *Bulletin of the American Academy of Psychiatry and the Law* 5 (2) (1977), and *McNeil v. Director, Patuxent Institution,* 407 U.S. 245 (1972).

90. All information on "Fenix Whipple" comes from Napanoch case file 298.

91. The psychologist recorded Fenix's answers to the first set of questions and underlined his answers to the second and third set.

92. Letter of May 26, 1944, from Superintendent of Woodbourne IDD to Mr. John A. Lyons, commissioner, Department of Correction, in Napanoch Case file 298.

93. Goffman 1961:35-36.

Afterword

Today biological explanations are once again leading in efforts to account for human behavior, and biological theories of crime have once again begun to attract serious attention. Moreover, genetic screening, new reproductive technologies, and the promise of gene therapies have restored eugenics to respectability.[1] Some people hope that we are posed on the brink of a brave new world, free of chronic and inherited diseases and in control of a multitude of social problems. Others fear a return to "scientific" racism, the evils of Nazism, and dangerous fantasies of escaping the human condition. How are we to respond to the resurgence in biological solutions to human problems, and how can history guide us through this maze of hopes and fears?

One way in which the history of ideas can guide us is by revealing that the criminal body as defined by science is as much a metaphor as a tangible reality. No one will deny that people exist who in their physical being are considered to be abnormal, defective, inferior, and dangerous. However, what is considered to be abnormal, defective, inferior, and dangerous changes over time. One generation defines born criminals one way; the next, another. The definition reveals as much about the definers as the defined. What history suggests, then, is that the concept of the criminal body is a construct.

In this study I have argued that born criminals—people who are said to have some biological defect that drives them to break the law—are created by scientists and social-control specialists. That bodies are created and known through representations, Jennifer Terry and Jacqueline Urla observe, has become an "almost commonplace axiom."[2] Because bodies are part of the production of knowledge and distribution of social power, ultimately born criminals must be understood as epistemological phenomena, as metaphors. This is the conclusion toward which the history of biological theories of crime points. If this conclusion is right, then we should also approach contemporary biological theories as discourses.

It is difficult to think critically about the latest scientific pronouncement. Although we can spot the flaws in discarded scientific theories, current concepts are often irresistibly persuasive. Nonetheless, if the subjects of today's biological criminologies are, like their predecessors, creations of criminological science, then we must analyze them, too, as constructions, dissecting their imagery, exposing their implied value systems, and probing their political implications.

When we define criminal bodies, we also define ourselves. Normality and deviance are necessarily interdependent; one category cannot exist without the other. Since the late eighteenth century, scientists and social-control specialists have used the born-criminal concept to establish boundaries between the normal and abnormal. Anthropologists, degenerationists, geneticists, phrenologists, physicians, psychiatrists, psychologists, social scientists and social workers, superintendents of the feebleminded, and prison personnel—all at one time or another attempted to define where normality leaves off and inherent deviance begins. This historical eagerness to enter the fray indicates that the stakes have enormous social value, as does the fact that groups have fought one another for jurisdiction to define innate criminality. Given these historical patterns, one of the first things we should ask about a new biological theory is how it explains difference and characterizes abnormality. We should also ask what group formulated the new definition and what is at stake professionally.

Criminal bodies are inevitably politicized bodies, surfaces on which theorists project fears and hopes, ideologies and ideals. Eugenic criminology drew a bright line between those who did and did not belong in the body politic. Similarly today's biological theories of crime can become vehicles for distinguishing between the politically worthy and unworthy. *The Bell Curve,* for example, pits a highly educated white elite against a black, low-IQ underclass. For the sake of social health, the authors maintain, we should encourage births by smart people and discourage births by the mentally subnormal. What is at stake, Herrnstein and Murray recognize, is the very definition of democracy.[3]

In *Human Biodiversity: Genes, Race, and History* Jonathan Marks writes that "eugenics represented a major failure on the part of mainstream American science to divorce human history from biology."[4] Marks's point —and it is an important one—is that turn-of-the-century eugenicists failed to realize that differences in peoples' social positions and achievements are a result of history, not biology. At the same time, we cannot separate history from biology, nor should we try, for biology itself has a history. Knowledge is always produced in cultural contexts. These contexts, in turn, are changed by the forms of knowledge produced in them. Biological theories today are produced in a context in which, as at the turn of the century, a white elite nervously faces a much larger underclass, frets (with diminishing guilt) about its inability to solve social problems, and worries about its own future. Works such as *The Bell Curve* are produced in and in turn reinforce this environment and so become part of it.

History can help us to grasp the implications and possible consequences of current biological theories of crime. Biological explanations, as we have seen, are not necessarily hereditarian. (Early phrenologists said little about heredity, and a recent study concludes that one cause of aggressive behaviors is lead poisoning, an environmental factor.)[5] Some biological theories of crime are hereditarian, however, and these are usually eugenic in implication.[6] James Q. Wilson and Richard Herrnstein, in *Crime and Human Nature,* and Richard Herrnstein and Charles Murray, in *The Bell Curve,* stop short of making explicitly eugenic recommendations, but their contentions that inherited factors play a role in crime point toward eugenic conclusions. Those familiar with the history of eugenics can hear its echoes in these books.

Eugenics, as Marouf A. Hassian Jr. points out in *The Rhetoric of Eugenics,* is today almost "ubiquitous."[7] During the Bosnian civil war, Serbs slaughtered Muslims in the name of "ethnic cleansing." In 1995, although conservatives attacked President Clinton's nominee for surgeon general because he had performed abortions, no one complained that Dr. Foster had also performed hysterectomies to sterilize retarded women. The Chinese have adopted explicitly eugenic population policies. We sterilize our pets to prevent them from multiplying. Six years ago sociologist Troy Duster warned of eugenics returning through the "backdoor," but today it has entered through the front door as well and presented us with a wide range of biological solutions to social problems.[8]

As we try to sort out our reactions to the new eugenics, a clear view of the past becomes crucial. If we demonize turn-of-the-century eugenicists, or dismiss them as crackpots, we cannot learn from them. We need to look closely at America's previous involvement with eugenic experimentation, including crime-control efforts, to prepare ourselves for developments ahead. Soon we may be able to forecast which fetuses will grow into crime-prone adults. How would we deal with that information? Soon we may be able to predict the probability that certain offenders will have criminalistic offspring. Do we want to prohibit reproduction in such cases?

"If our society is going to engage in a profitable public debate on the issue of eugenics," Hassian writes, "we need rhetorical histories that look at the ways in which eugenical arguments have been deployed and reconfigured."[9] We need to map the networks along which eugenic reasoning traveled as it entered American consciousness. We need to recognize that altruism as well as fear inspired eugenic programs, including eugenic criminology. But even more is required than simply understanding how we got here. It is also necessary to recognize the dangers posed by the dominance of a theory that interprets social problems in biological terms and difference as biological inferiority.

Notes

1. On the resurgence see Degler 1991; Duster 1990; Fausto-Sterling 1992; Herrnstein and Murray 1994; Kevles 1985; Wilson and Herrnstein 1985; Wattenberg 1987; and the current issue of almost any newspaper.

2. Terry and Urla 1995.

3. Herrnstein and Murray 1994. Again, I have borrowed the term "politicized bodies" from Fausto-Sterling 1992:vii.

4. Marks 1995:92.

5. "Aggressiveness, Delinquency among Boys Are Linked to Lead Levels." *Boston Globe*, February 8, 1996, p. 10.

6. The only exception I can think of is the theory that some women are driven to crime by premenstrual tension syndrome (PMS); see Dalton 1977.

7. Hassian 1996:3

8. Duster 1990. On the Clinton nomination see "White House Widens Effort on Behalf of Its Nominee," *Boston Globe*, February 12, 1995, p. 25, and "White House Won't Back Out of Foster Fight," *Boston Globe*, February 13, 1995, p. 3.

9. Hassian 1996:23

References Cited

Sources are listed in three categories: (1) interviews; (2) unpublished material; and (3) published material (articles, books, chapters, dissertations, serials, and theses). Unless noted otherwise, serial documents are cited by the last year in the reporting period, not by the date of publication. Thus an annual report covering the fiscal year July 1, 1910, through June 30, 1911, would be cited as *Annual Report, 1911,* even if it were not published until 1912. Similarly conference proceedings are cited by the year of the conference, not the date of publication: AMO, *Proceedings, 1884,* p. 14.

Abbreviations

AMO	Association of Medical Officers of American Institutions for Idiotic and Feeble-Minded Persons
JCLC	*Journal of Criminal Law and Criminology*
JP-A	*Journal of Psycho-Asthenics*
NCCC	National Conference of Charities and Correction
NYSBC	New York State Board of Charities
PANY	Prison Association of New York

Interviews

Brown, Mary Hicks, and Durant Brown. 1976 (Nov. 4). Interview with
    N. Hahn [Rafter], Barre, Mass.
Kendall, Glenn M. 1977 (Mar. 4). Interview with N. Hahn [Rafter], Delmar,
    N.Y.
Rober, Kai. 1977 (Mar. 26). Interview with N. Hahn [Rafter], Eastern
    Correctional Facility, Napanoch, N.Y.

Unpublished Material

Amherst College Archives, s.v. "Hervey Backus Wilbur."
Harvard University, Houghton Library, Dix papers.
New Jersey State Archives, Trenton, Records of the New Jersey Reformatory
    for Women at Clinton Farms.
New York State Archives, Albany.
        New York State Commission to Investigate Provision for the Mentally
            Deficient (Hebberd Commission). 1914-15. Series A4221,
            institutional reference files; ser. A4223, public hearing testi-
            mony; and ser. A4228, photographs of custodial institutions
            for the mentally deficient, ca. 1910-14.
        New York State Education Department, Division of Visual Instruc-
            tion. 1911-39. Instructional lantern slides and negatives and
            positive transparencies of instructional photographic images.
        New York State Institution for Male Defective Delinquents at
            Napanoch. 1920-56. Series 14610-88B, inmate case files.
        New York State, Auburn Prison. 1914-50. Series 14610-77A, inmate
            case files (Classification Clinic).
        New York State Board of Charities. 1867-1902. Series A1977,
            correspondence.
New York State Education Library, Albany—Legislative Reference Library,
    Bill Jacket Collection.
New York State Office of General Services, Bureau of Land Management,
    Albany, Deeds to Newark Custodial Asylum.
Onondaga County (New York) Clerk's Office. 1854. Indenture, Elias W.
    Leavenworth and the State of New York, July 1, 1854, book 130, pp.
    385-86.
———. Surrogate Court, book Y (wills).
Rockefeller Archive Center, North Tarrytown, N.Y. Bureau of Social Hygiene
    Collection.

Published Materials

Abbott, Andrew. 1988. The System of Professions: An Essay on the Division of
    Expert Labor. Chicago: University of Chicago Press.

Adler, Herman M. 1917–18. "A Psychiatric Contribution to the Study of Delinquency." *JCLC* 8:45–68.

———. 1920. "The Criminologist and the Courts." *JCLC* 11:419–25.

Alexander, Ruth. 1995. *The "Girl Problem": Female Sexual Delinquency in New York, 1900–1930.* Ithaca, N.Y.: Cornell University Press.

Allen, Garland E. 1975. "Genetics, Eugenics and Class Struggle." *Genetics* 79 (June, supplement): 29–45.

———. 1986. "The Eugenics Record Office at Cold Spring Harbor, 1910–1940: An Essay on Institutional History." *Osiris,* 2d ser., 2:225–64.

Allison, H[enry] E. 1904. "Defective Inmates of Penal Institutions." In National Prison Association, *Proceedings, 1904,* pp. 292–302.

American Association for the Study of the Feeble-Minded. 1917a. "Minutes of the Association, 1916." *JP-A* 21 (3 and 4) (Mar. and June): 100–127.

———. 1917b. "Minutes of the Association, 1917." *JP-A* 22 (1) (Sept.): 20–60.

American Institute of Criminal Law and Criminology. 1910. "Bulletin no. 2, January 1910. Report of Committee A: System of Recording Data Concerning Criminals." *JCLC* 1 (2): 84–97.

American Prison Association. 1910. *Proceedings.*

Amir, Menachem, and Yitzchak Berman. 1970. "Chromosomal Deviation and Crime." *Federal Probation Quarterly* 34:55–62.

Anderson, Victor V. 1914. "An Analysis of One Hundred Cases Studied in Connection with the Municipal Criminal Courts of Boston." *Boston Medical and Surgical Journal* 171 (9): 341–46.

———. 1916. "A Classification of Border-line Mental Cases amongst Offenders." *JCLC* 7:689–95.

———. 1917–18. "A Comparative Study of Feeble-mindedness among Offenders in Court." *JCLC* 8:428–34.

Association of Medical Officers of American Institutions for Idiotic and Feeble-Minded Persons. 1876–95. *Proceedings.*

———. 1964. *Proceedings 1876–1886.* Repr. New York: Johnson Reprint.

Backus, Frederick F. 1846. *Report of the Committee on Medical Societies and Medical Colleges, on That Portion of the Census Relating to Idiots.* New York Sen. doc. no. 23.

———. 1847. *Report of the Committee on Medical Societies and Medical Colleges, Relative to the Bill Proposing the Establishment of an Asylum or School for Idiots, &c.* New York Sen. doc. no. 44.

Bakan, David. 1966. "The Influence of Phrenology on American Psychology." *Journal of the History of the Behavioral Sciences* 2:200–220.

Ballard, Frances Anne, comp. 1941. *Mental Hygiene Laws in Brief: Summaries for Each of the States and the District of Columbia.* New York: National Committee for Mental Hygiene.

Bannister, Robert C. 1979. *Social Darwinism: Science and Myth in Anglo-American Social Thought.* Philadelphia: Temple University Press.

Barker, David. 1983. "How to Curb the Fertility of the Unfit." *Oxford Review of Education* 9:197–211.

———. 1989. "The Biology of Stupidity: Genetics, Eugenics and Mental Deficiency in the Inter-War Years." *British Journal for the History of Science* 22:347–75.

Barnes, Harry Elmer. [1927] 1968. *The Evolution of Penology in Pennsylvania: A Study in American Social History*. Repr. Montclair, N.J.: Patterson Smith.

Barr, Martin W. 1894. "An Incohative Paranoiac." In AMO, *Proceedings, 1894,* pp. 406–15.

———. 1895. "Moral Paranoia." In AMO, *Proceedings, 1895,* pp. 522–31.

———. [1904] 1973. *Mental Defectives: Their History, Treatment and Training.* Repr. New York: Arno.

———. 1934. "A Brief Review of the Life of Isaac Newton Kerlin, M.D." *JP-A* 58:144–50.

Barrows, Isabel. 1894. "Manual Training for the Feeble-Minded." In AMO, *Proceedings, 1894,* pp. 441–49.

Barrows, Samuel J., ed. 1900. *The Reformatory System in the United States.* Washington: Government Printing Office.

Bates, Sanford. 1928. "Practical Problems of the Defective Delinquent." In American Association for the Study of the Feeble-Minded, *Proceedings, 1928,* pp. 110–14.

Beatty, Barbara R. 1986. "Lowell, Josephine Shaw." In *Biographical Dictionary of Social Welfare in America,* ed. Walter L. Trattner, 511–15. New York: Greenwood.

Becker, Howard S. 1973. *Outsiders: Studies in the Sociology of Deviance.* New York: Free Press.

Becker, Peter. 1994. "Controversy over Meanings: The Debate between Cesare Lombroso and His Critics about the Signs and the Habit of Criminals." Paper delivered at the 1994 annual meeting of the American Society of Criminology, Miami.

Benedikt, Moriz. 1881. *Anatomical Studies upon Brains of Criminals.* New York: William Wood.

Bennett, Paula. 1993. "Critical Clitoredectomy: Female Sexual Imagery and Feminist Psychoanalytic Theory." *Signs* 18:235–59.

Bernstein, Charles. 1914. "A State's Policy toward the Care of the Feeble-Minded." *JP-A* 19:51–54.

———. 1916. "Colonizing the Feebleminded." *The Delinquent* 6:1–4.

———. 1918. "Self-Sustaining Feeble-Minded." *JP-A* 22:150–61.

———. 1920. "Colony and Extra-Institutional Care for the Feebleminded." *Mental Hygiene* 4:1–28.

Bertillon, Alphonse. 1891. "The Bertillon System of Identification." *The Forum* 11:330–41.

Best, Joel. 1987. "Rhetoric in Claims-Making: Constructing the Missing Children Problem." *Social Problems* 34:101–21.

———, ed. 1989. *Images of Issues: Typifying Contemporary Social Problems.* New York: Aldine.

Bisch, Louis E. 1916–17. "A Police Psychopathic Laboratory." *JCLC* 7:79–88.

Blackmar, Frank W. [1897] 1988. "The Smoky Pilgrims." In *White Trash: The Eugenics Family Studies, 1877–1919,* ed. Nicole Hahn Rafter, 56–65. Boston: Northeastern University Press.

Blake, L. J. 1892. "Some Practical and Speculative Views Derived from Six Months' Experience at Elwyn." In AMO, *Proceedings, 1892,* pp. 313–17.

Bledstein, Burton J. 1976. *The Culture of Professionalism.* New York: Norton.

Boies, Henry M. 1893. *Prisoners and Paupers.* New York: Putnam's.

———. 1901. *The Science of Penology.* New York: Putnam's.

Boslow, Harold M., and Arthur Kandel. 1965. "Psychiatric Aspects of Dangerous Behavior: The Retarded Offender." *American Journal of Psychiatry* 122:646–52.

Boston, Charles A. 1913–14. "A Protest against Laws Authorizing Sterilization of Criminals and Imbeciles." *JCLC* 4:326–58.

Bowers, Paul E. 1914–15. "The Recidivist." *JCLC* 5:404–15.

———. 1915. *Clinical Studies in the Relation of Insanity to Crime.* Michigan City, Ind.: The Dispatch Print.

———. 1917–18. Review of "The Binet Scale and the Diagnosis of Feeble-Mindedness," by Lewis M. Terman. *JCLC* 8:307–10.

Bragar, Madeline C. 1977. "The Feebleminded Female: An Historical Analysis of Mental Retardation as a Social Definition, 1890–1920." Ph.D. diss., Syracuse University.

Brakel, Samuel J., John Parry, and Barbara A. Weiner. 1985. *The Mentally Disabled and the Law.* 3d ed. Chicago: American Bar Foundation.

Brakel, Samuel J., and Ronald S. Rock, eds. 1971. *The Mentally Disabled and the Law.* Rev. ed. Chicago: University of Chicago Press.

Branham, V[ernon] C. 1926. "The Classification and Treatment of the Defective Delinquent." *JCLC* 17:183–217.

Branham, V[ernon] C., and Walter N. Thayer Jr. 1931. *The Classification of the Prison Inmates of New York State.* Supplemental report, addendum 2, to New York State Commission on Prison Administration and Construction, *Report by Commission to Investigate Prison Administration and Construction.* N.p.: New York State Department of Correction.

Brenzel, Barbara M. 1983. *Daughters of the State: A Social Portrait of the First Reform School for Girls in North America, 1856–1905.* Cambridge, Mass.: MIT Press.

———. 1986. "Fernald, Walter Elmore." In *Biographical Dictionary of Social Welfare in America,* ed. Walter I. Trattner, 284–86. New York: Greenwood.

Brockway, Zebulon R. 1871. "The Ideal of a True Prison System for a State." In *Transactions of the National Congress on Penitentiary and Reforma-*

tory Discipline, 1870, ed. E. C. Wines, 38–65. Albany, N.Y.: Weed, Parsons.

———. 1901. "Prevention of Crime." In National Prison Association, *Proceedings, 1901,* pp. 202–19.

———. [1912] 1969. *Fifty Years of Prison Service: An Autobiography.* Repr. Montclair, N.J.: Patterson Smith.

Broomall, John M. 1887. "The Helpless Classes." In AMO, *Proceedings, 1887,* pp. 38–41.

Brown, Catherine W. 1897. "Reminiscences." *JP-A* 1:134–40.

Brown, George. 1884. "In Memoriam—Hervey B. Wilbur, M.D." In AMO, *Proceedings, 1884,* pp. 291–95.

Brown, JoAnne. 1992. *The Definition of a Profession.* Princeton, N.J.: Princeton University Press.

Brown, Sanger. 1924. "The Psychopathic Child." *JP-A* 29:226–30.

Bruce, Hortense V. 1909–10. "Moral Degeneracy." *JP-A* 14:39–47.

Bryant, Louise Stevens. 1917–18. "The Women at the House of Correction in Holmesburg, Pennsylvania." *JCLC* 8:844–89.

Bullard, William N. 1909–10. "The High-Grade Mental Defectives." *JP-A* 14:14–15.

Burnham, John C. 1960. "Psychiatry, Psychology and the Progressive Movement." *American Quarterly* 12:457–65.

Burrow, John W. 1985. Editor's Introduction. In Charles Darwin, *The Origin of Species by Means of Natural Selection,* 11–48. London: Penguin Classics.

Burton, Robert. [1621] 1989. *The Anatomy of Melancholy.* Repr. Oxford: Clarendon.

Butler, Amos W. 1901. "A Notable Factor of Social Degeneration." *Science,* n.s., 14 (351): 444–53.

Butler, Fred O. 1942. "The Defective Delinquent." *American Journal of Mental Deficiency* 47:7–13.

———. 1948. "California's Legal Approach and Progress in the Rehabilitation of the Defective and Psychopathic Delinquent." *American Journal of Mental Deficiency* 53:76–79.

Camfield, Thomas M. 1973. "The Professionalization of American Psychology, 1870–1917." *Journal of the History of the Behavioral Sciences* 9:66–75.

Cannon, Cornelia James. 1922. "American Misgivings." *The Atlantic Monthly* 129:145–57.

Carlson, Elof A. 1980. "R. L. Dugdale and the Jukes Family: A Historical Injustice Corrected." *Bioscience* 30:535–39.

Carlson, Eric T. 1958. "The Influence of Phrenology on Early American Psychiatric Thought." *American Journal of Psychiatry* 115:535–38.

Carlson, Eric T., and Norman Dain. 1962. "The Meaning of Moral Insanity." *Bulletin of the History of Medicine* 36:130–40.

Carson, J[ames] C. 1886. "A Case of Moral Imbecility." In AMO, *Proceedings, 1886,* pp. 407–12.

————. 1891. "Juvenile Insanity—Report of Three Cases." In AMO, *Proceedings, 1891*, pp. 186–90.

————. 1915. "News and Notes." *JP-A* 19:171–72.

Chamberlin, J. Edward, and Sander L. Gilman, eds. 1985. *Degeneration: The Dark Side of Progress.* New York: Columbia University Press.

Christian, Frank L. 1913. "The Defective Delinquent." *Albany Medical Annals* 34:276–84.

Clark, Taliaferro. 1916. "The School as a Factor in the Mental Hygiene of Rural Communities." In NCCC, *Proceedings, 1916*, pp. 215–23.

Clayton, W. W. N.d. *History of Onondaga County, N.Y., 1615–1878.* Syracuse, N.Y.: D. Mason.

Collinson, George. 1812. *Treatise on Law concerning Idiots, Lunatics, and Other Persons Non Compotes Mentis.* London: W. Reed.

Combe, George. 1879. *Education: Its Principles and Practice.* London: Macmillan.

Connecticut Commissioners on Idiocy. 1856. *Report to the General Assembly.* New Haven, Conn.: Carrington and Hotchkiss.

Connelly, Mark Thomas. 1980. *The Response to Prostitution in the Progressive Era.* Chapel Hill: University of North Carolina Press.

Conrad, Peter, and Joseph W. Schneider. 1980. *Deviance and Medicalization: From Badness to Sickness.* St. Louis: Mosby.

Cooter, Roger. 1976. "Phrenology and British Alienists, c. 1825–1845." *Medical History* 20:135–51.

————. 1984. *The Cultural Meaning of Popular Science: Phrenology and the Organization of Consent in Nineteenth-Century Britain.* Cambridge: Cambridge University Press.

Cowan, Ruth Schwartz. 1985. *Sir Francis Galton and the Study of Heredity in the Nineteenth Century.* New York: Garland.

Cravens, Hamilton. 1978. *The Triumph of Evolution: American Scientists and the Heredity-Environment Controversy, 1900–1911.* Philadelphia: University of Pennsylvania Press.

————. 1986. "Goddard, Henry Herbert." In *Biographical Dictionary of Social Welfare in America*, ed. Walter I. Trattner, 325–28. New York: Greenwood.

————. 1987. "Applied Science and Public Policy: The Ohio Bureau of Juvenile Research and the Problem of Juvenile Delinquency, 1913–1930." In *Psychological Testing and American Society, 1890–1930*, ed. Michael M. Sokal, 158–94. New Brunswick, N.J.: Rutgers University Press.

Dain, Norman. 1964. *Concepts of Insanity in the United States, 1789–1865.* New Brunswick, N.J.: Rutgers University Press.

Dalton, Katharine. 1977. *The Premenstrual Syndrome and Progesterone Therapy.* London: Heinemann.

Darwin, Charles. [1859] 1985. *The Origin of Species by Means of Natural Selection.* London: Penguin Classics.

———. [1871] 1986. *The Descent of Man and Selection in Relation to Sex.* Repr. N.p.: Telegraph.

Davenport, Charles B. [1916] 1988. Preface to Anna Wendt Finlayson, *The Dack Family: A Study in Hereditary Lack of Emotional Control.* Repr. in *White Trash: The Eugenic Family Studies, 1877-1919,* ed. Nicole Hahn Rafter, 212-14. Boston: Northeastern University Press.

Davenport, Charles B., H. H. Laughlin, David F. Weeks, E. R. Johnstone, and Henry H. Goddard. 1911. *The Study of Human Heredity: Methods of Collecting, Charting and Analyzing Data.* Eugenic Records Office Bulletin no. 2. Cold Spring Harbor, N.Y.: Eugenic Records Office.

Davies, John. 1955. *Phrenology: Fad and Science—A 19th Century American Crusade.* New Haven, Conn.: Yale University Press.

Davies, Stanley P. 1923. *Social Control of the Feebleminded: A Study of Social Programs and Attitudes in Relation to the Problems of Mental Deficiency.* New York: National Committee for Mental Hygiene.

———. 1930. *Social Control of the Mentally Deficient.* New York: Thomas Y. Crowell.

Davies, Stanley P., with Katharine G. Ecob. 1959. *The Mentally Retarded in Society.* New York: Columbia University Press.

Davis, Katharine Bement. 1906a. "Moral Imbeciles." In National Prison Association, *Proceedings, 1906,* pp. 345-50.

———. 1906b. "Treatment of the Female Offender." In New York State Conference of Charities, *Proceedings, 1906.* In NYSBC, *Annual Report, 1906,* pp. 1:785-90.

———. 1912. "Feeble-minded Women in Reformatory Institutions." *The Survey* 27 (Mar. 2): 1849-51.

———. 1913-14. "A Plan of Rational Treatment for Women Offenders." *JCLC* 4:402-8.

———. 1916. Introduction. In Jean Weidensall, *The Mentality of the Criminal Woman,* ix-xiv. Baltimore: Warwick and York.

———. 1919-20. "Some Institutional Problems in Dealing with Psychopathic Delinquents." *JCLC* 10:385-408.

———. 1920. "The Laboratory and the Woman's Reformatory." In American Prison Association, *Proceedings, 1920,* pp. 105-8.

———. 1921. "Plan for the Rational Treatment of Women Offenders (1917) Convicted in the Courts of the County of New York (or City)." In Burdette G. Lewis, *The Offender and His Relations to Law and Society,* appendix 7, pp. 358-71. New York: Harper and Brothers.

———. [1923] 1969. Introduction. In Edith R. Spaulding, *An Experimental Study of Psychopathic Delinquent Women,* xiii-xvi. Repr. Montclair, N.J.: Patterson Smith.

Dechert, Henry M. 1892. "Address of Henry M. Dechert." In AMO, *Proceedings, 1892,* pp. 363-65.

Degler, Carl N. 1991. *In Search of Human Nature.* New York: Oxford University Press.

D'Emilio, John, and Estelle B. Freedman. 1988. *Intimate Matters: A History of Sexuality in America*. New York: Harper and Row.

de Forest, Robert W., Joseph H. Choate, William R. Stewart, et al. 1905. "In Memorium: Josephine Shaw Lowell." *Charities and the Commons* 15:309-35.

Deiser, George F. 1919-20. "Classification of Criminals." *JCLC* 10:601-12.

Deutsch, Albert. 1949. *The Mentally Ill in America: A History of Their Care and Treatment from Colonial Times*. 2d ed., rev. New York: Columbia University Press.

Devine, Edward T. 1905. "Mrs. Lowell's Services to the State." *Charities and the Commons* 15:319-22.

Diefendorf, A. Ross. 1907. *Clinical Psychiatry*. Abstracted and adapted from the 7th German ed. of Kraepelin's *Lehrbuch der Psychiatrie*. New York: Macmillan.

Dix, Dorothea L. [1844] 1971. *Memorial. To the Honorable the Legislature of the State of New-York*. Repr. in Dorothea L. Dix, *On Behalf of the Insane Poor, Selected Reports*. New York: Arno/New York Times.

Dodd, Donald B., comp. 1993. *Historical Statistics of the States of the United States: Two Centuries of the Census*. Westport, Conn.: Greenwood.

Doll, Edgar A., ed. 1932. *Twenty-five Years: A Memorial Volume in Commemoration of the Twenty-fifth Anniversary of the Vineland Laboratory, 1906-1931*. Vineland, N.J.: The Training School, Department of Research.

Dooley, Lucile. 1924. "The Psychopathic Woman." In "The Psychopathic Individual: A Symposium," ed. Ben Karpman, 192-96. *Mental Hygiene* 8:174-201.

Dowbiggin, Ian. 1991. *Inheriting Madness: Professionalization and Psychiatric Knowledge in Nineteenth-Century France*. Berkeley: University of California Press.

Drähms, August. [1900] 1971. *The Criminal: His Personnel and Environment—A Scientific Study*. Repr. Montclair, N.J.: Patterson Smith.

Dreifus, Claudia. 1995. "Present Shock: Alvin and Heidi Toffler, Futurists . . ." *New York Times Magazine* (June 11): 46-50.

Dugdale, Richard L. 1874. "A Report of Special Visits to County Jails for 1874." In PANY, *Annual Report, 1874*, pp. 129-92. New York Sen. doc. no. 78, 1875.

———. 1877. *"The Jukes": A Study in Crime, Pauperism, Disease and Heredity; also Further Studies of Criminals*. New York: Putnam's.

Duster, Troy. 1990. *Backdoor to Eugenics*. New York: Routledge.

Dwyer, Ellen. 1987. *Homes for the Mad: Life inside Two Nineteenth-Century Insane Asylums*. New Brunswick, N.J.: Rutgers University Press.

———. 1992. "Stories of Epilepsy, 1880-1930." In *Framing Disease: Studies in Cultural History*, ed. Charles E. Rosenberg and Janet Golden, 248-72. New Brunswick, N.J.: Rutgers University Press.

Editors, The. 1914-15. "Proceedings of the Sixth Annual Meeting of the

American Institute of Criminal Law and Criminology." *JCLC* 5:744–48.

Ehrenreich, John H. 1985. *The Altruistic Imagination: A History of Social Work and Social Policy in the United States*. Ithaca, N.Y.: Cornell University Press.

Eisenstein, Zillah R. 1988. *The Female Body and the Law*. Berkeley: University of California Press.

Ellis, Havelock. 1890. *The Criminal*. London: Walter Scott.

———. 1891. Preface. In Alexander Winter, *The New York State Reformatory at Elmira*, iii–viii. London: Swan Sonnenschein.

Ellwood, Charles A. 1910. "Notes on Current and Recent Events. Coordination of Correctional Institutions." *JCLC* 1 (July): 98–99.

Emerick, E. J. 1914. "The Defective Delinquent in Ohio." *JP-A* 19:19–21.

Estabrook, Arthur H. 1916. *The Jukes in 1915*. Washington, D.C.: Carnegie Institution of Washington.

Farnell, Frederic J. 1920–21. "The Defective vs. the Psychopath." *JCLC* 11:198–208.

Farnham, Eliza B. 1846. Introductory Preface. In M. B. Sampson, *Rationale of Crime*, xiii–xxi. New York: D. Appleton.

Farrell, Malcolm J., and John Ogonik Jr. 1955. "The Present Status of Defective Delinquency in Massachusetts." *American Journal of Mental Deficiency* 59:439–44.

Fausto-Sterling, Ann. 1992. *Myths of Gender: Biological Theories about Women and Men*. 2d ed. New York: Basic.

Fee, Elizabeth. 1979. "Nineteenth-Century Craniology: The Study of the Female Skull." *Bulletin of the History of Medicine* 53:415–33.

Ferguson, Philip. 1994. *Abandoned to Their Fate: Social Policy and Practice toward Severely Retarded People in America, 1820–1920*. Philadelphia: Temple University Press.

Fernald, Guy G. 1912a. "The Defective Delinquent Class Differentiating Tests." *American Journal of Insanity* 68:523–94.

———. 1912b. "The Recidivist." *JCLC* 3:866–75.

———. 1916–17. "The Mental Examination of Reformatory Prisoners." *JCLC* 7:393–404.

———. 1917. "The Psychopathic Clinic at Massachusetts Reformatory." *JP-A* 21:73–81.

———. 1918. "Character as an Integral Mentality Function." *Mental Hygiene* 2:448–62.

Fernald, Mabel R. 1916–17. "Practical Applications of Psychology to the Problems of a Clearing House." *JCLC* 7:722–31.

Fernald, Mabel Ruth, Mary Holmes Stevens Hayes, and Almena Dawley. 1920. *A Study of Women Delinquents in New York State*. New York: Century.

Fernald, Walter E. 1893. "The History of the Treatment of the Feeble-minded." In NCCC, *Proceedings, 1893*, pp. 203–21.

———. 1909–10. "The Imbecile with Criminal Instincts." *JP-A* 14:16–36.

————. 1912. "The Burden of Feeble-Mindedness." *JP-A* 17:87–99.

————. 1917a. "The Growth of Provision for the Feeble-Minded in the United States." *Mental Hygiene* 1:34–59.

————. 1917b. "Standardized Fields of Inquiry for Clinical Studies of Borderline Defectives." *Mental Hygiene* 1:211–34.

————. 1918–19. Remarks. *JP-A* 23:98–99.

"F.G." 1911–12. "Criminals and Defectives in Massachusetts." *JCLC* 2:404–6.

Fink, Arthur E. [1938] 1962. *Causes of Crime: Biological Theories in the United States, 1800–1915*. Repr. New York: A. S. Barnes.

Fish, William B. 1887. "Institution Discipline." In AMO, *Proceedings, 1887*, pp. 45–48.

————. 1891. "Custodial Care of Adult Idiots." In AMO, *Proceedings, 1891*, pp. 203–11.

————. 1892. "The Colony Plan." In NCCC, *Proceedings, 1892*, pp. 161–65.

Fitzpatrick, Ellen. 1990. *Endless Crusade: Women Social Scientists and Progressive Reform*. New York: Oxford University Press.

Fort, Samuel J. 1892. "Case of Moral Imbecility." In AMO, *Proceedings, 1892*, pp. 326–30.

————. 1894. "Psychical Epilepsy." In AMO, *Proceedings, 1894*, pp. 400–405.

Foucault, Michel. 1972. *The Archeology of Knowledge*. New York: Pantheon.

————. 1988. "The Dangerous Individual." In *Michel Foucault: Politics, Philosophy, Culture—Interviews and Other Writings, 1977–1984*, ed. Lawrence D. Kritzman, 125–51. New York: Routledge.

Frankenberg, Ruth. 1993. *White Women, Race Matters: The Social Construction of Whiteness*. Minneapolis: University of Minnesota Press.

Freedman, Estelle B. 1981. *Their Sisters' Keepers: Women's Prison Reform in America, 1830–1930*. Ann Arbor: University of Michigan Press.

————. 1987. " 'Uncontrolled Desires': The Response to the Sexual Psychopath, 1920–1960." *Journal of American History* 74:83–106.

Gafni, Miriam L., and Barney B. Welsh. 1967. "Post Conviction Problems and the Defective Delinquent." *Villanova Law Review* 12:545–602.

Gallagher, Catherine, and Thomas Laqueur. 1987. *The Making of the Modern Body: Sexuality and Society in the Nineteenth Century*. Berkeley: University of California Press.

Galton, Francis. [1869] 1952. *Hereditary Genius: An Inquiry into Its Laws and Consequences*. Repr. New York: Horizon.

————. [1883] 1973. *Inquiries into Human Faculty and Its Development*. Repr. New York: AMS.

Garber, Marjorie. 1992. *Vested Interests: Cross-Dressing and Cultural Anxiety*. New York: Routledge.

Garfinkel, Harold. 1956. "Conditions of Successful Degradation Ceremonies." *American Journal of Sociology* 61:420–24.

Garland, David. 1985. *Punishment and Welfare: A History of Penal Strategies*. Brookfield, Vt.: Gower.

Gault, Robert H. 1911–12a. "The Feeble-Minded Delinquent." *JCLC* 2:925–27.

———. 1911–12b. "Sentimentalism and Crime." *JCLC* 2:790–91.

——— [as "R.H.G."]. 1911–12c. Summary of "The Feeble-Minded Delinquent," by O. F. Lewis. *JCLC* 2:925–27.

———. 1914–15a. "Clinical Criminology." *JCLC* 5:3–5.

———. 1914–15b. "The Degenerate at Large." *JCLC* 2:819–22.

———. 1914–15c. "The Laboratory in the Criminal Court." *JCLC* 5:167–69.

———. 1914–15d. "Preventing the Development of Criminals." *JCLC* 5:640–42.

———. 1914–15e. "Reformatory Results in New York." *JCLC* 5:1–3.

———. 1923. "Psycho-Social Aspects of Crime." In Ernest Bryant Hoag and Edward Huntington Williams, *Crime, Abnormal Minds and the Law,* 21–56. Indianapolis: Bobbs-Merrill.

Gemmill, William N. 1914–15. "The Criminal, Who Is He, and What Shall We Do with Him?" *JCLC* 5:170–92.

G.E.S. 1894. "Isaac N. Kerlin, M.D." *Journal of Mental Science* 40:172–74.

Gettleman, Marvin E. 1963. "Charity and Social Classes in the United States, 1874–1900," parts 1 and 2. *American Journal of Economics and Sociology* 22:313–29, 417–26.

———. 1975. "Philanthropy as Social Control in Late Nineteenth-Century America: Some Hypotheses and Data on the Rise of Social Work." *Societas* 5:49–59.

Gibson, Mary. 1982. "The 'Female Offender' and the Italian School of Criminal Anthropology." *Journal of European Studies* 12:155–65.

———. 1990. "On the Insensitivity of Women: Science and the Woman Question in Liberal Italy, 1890–1910." *Journal of Women's History* 2:11–41.

Gilbert, James B. 1977. "Anthropometrics in the U.S. Bureau of Education: The Case of Arthur MacDonald's 'Laboratory.'" *History of Education Quarterly* 2:169–95.

Glueck, Bernard. 1916. *Studies in Forensic Psychiatry.* Boston: Little, Brown.

———. 1917a. "Psychiatric Clinic." In New York State, Sing Sing Prison, *Annual Report, 1917,* pp. 95–104.

———. 1917b. "Types of Delinquent Careers." *Mental Hygiene* 1:171–95.

———. 1918a. "Concerning Prisoners." *Mental Hygiene* 2 (2):177–218.

———. 1918b. "A Study of 608 Admissions to Sing Sing Prison." *Mental Hygiene* 2:85–151.

———. 1919. Review of *Die Psychopathischen Verbrecher* (The psychopathic criminal), by Karl Birnbaum. *Mental Hygiene* 3:157–66.

Glueck, Sheldon S. 1925. *Mental Disorder and the Criminal Law.* Boston: Little, Brown.

Glueck, Sheldon S., and Eleanor T. Glueck. 1934. *Five Hundred Delinquent Women.* New York: Knopf.

Goddard, Henry Herbert. 1907–8. "Psychological Work among the Feeble-Minded." *JP-A* 12:18–30.

———. 1909–10. "Suggestions for a Prognostical Classification of Mental
    Defectives." *JP-A* 14:48–52.
———. 1910. "Four Hundred Feeble-Minded Children Classified by the Binet
    Method." *JP-A* 15:17–30.
———. 1911. "Heredity of Feeble-Mindedness." *The Eugenics Review*
    3:46–60.
———. [1912] 1923. *The Kallikak Family: A Study in the Heredity of
    Feeblemindedness.* New York: Macmillan.
———. 1912–13. "The Responsibility of Children in the Juvenile Court."
    JCLC 3:365–75.
———. 1914a. "The Binet Measuring Scale of Intelligence: What It Is and
    How It Is to Be Used." *The Training School Bulletin* 11:86–91.
———. 1914b. *Feeble-Mindedness: Its Causes and Consequences.* New York:
    Macmillan.
———. [1915] 1922. *The Criminal Imbecile: An Analysis of Three Remarkable
    Murder Cases.* New York: Macmillan.
———. 1920–21. "In the Light of Recent Developments: What Should Be
    Our Policy in Dealing with the Delinquents—Juvenile and Adult."
    JCLC 11:426–32.
———. 1921. *Juvenile Delinquency.* New York: Dodd, Mead.
Godding, W. W. 1883. "In Memoriam—Hervey Backus Wilbur." *Journal of
    Nervous and Mental Disease* 10:658–62.
Goffman, Erving. 1961. *Asylums: Essays on the Social Situation of Men-
    tal Patients and Other Inmates.* Garden City, N.Y.: Anchor
    Books/Doubleday.
Gordon, Efrem A., and Lewis Harris. 1950. "An Investigation and Critique of
    the Defective Delinquent Statute in Massachusetts." *Boston University
    Law Review* 30:459–501.
Gordon, Linda. 1977. *Women's Body, Women's Right: Birth Control in
    America.* New York: Penguin.
Goring, Charles. [1913] 1972. *The English Convict: A Statistical Study.* Repr.
    Montclair, N.J.: Patterson Smith.
Gould, Stephen Jay. 1981. *The Mismeasure of Man.* New York: Norton.
Graney, Bernard John. 1979. "Hervey Backus Wilbur and the Evolution of
    Policies and Practices toward Mentally Retarded People." Ph.D. diss.,
    Syracuse University.
Green, David. 1985. "Veins of Resemblance: Photography and Eugenics."
    Oxford Art Review 7 (2): 3–16.
Grob, Gerald N. 1973. *Mental Institutions in America: Social Policy to 1875.*
    New York: Free Press.
———. 1983. *Mental Illness and American Society, 1875–1940.* Princeton, N.J.:
    Princeton University Press.
Groneman, Carol. 1994. "Nymphomania: The Historical Construction of
    Female Sexuality." *Signs* 19:337–67.
Grosskurth, Phyllis. 1985. *Havelock Ellis: A Biography.* New York: New York
    University Press.

Grupp, Stanley E. 1959. "Criminal Anthropological Overtones: New York State Reformatory at Elmira, 1876–1907." *Correction* 24:9–17.

Haber, Samuel. 1964. *Efficiency and Uplift: Scientific Management in the Progressive Era, 1890–1920.* Chicago: University of Chicago Press.

Hahn, Nicolas F. [Nicole F. Rafter]. 1978. "The Defective Delinquency Movement." Ph.D diss., State University of New York at Albany.

———. 1980. "Too Dumb to Know Better: Cacogenic Family Studies and the Criminology of Women." *Criminology* 18:3–25.

Haller, John S., Jr. and Robin M. Haller. 1974. *The Physician and Sexuality in Victorian America.* Urbana: University of Illinois Press.

Haller, Mark H. 1963. *Eugenics: Hereditarian Attitudes in American Thought.* New Brunswick, N.J.: Rutgers University Press.

Halstead, T. H. 1892. "Adenoids and Their Relation to Feeble-Minded Children." In AMO, *Proceedings, 1892,* pp. 286–91.

Hansen, Bert. 1992. "American Physicians' 'Discovery' of Homosexuals, 1880–1900: A New Diagnosis in a Changing Society." In *Framing Disease: Studies in Cultural History,* ed. Charles E. Rosenberg and Janet Golden, 104–33. New Brunswick, N.J.: Rutgers University Press.

Harding, Sandra. 1986. *The Science Question in Feminism.* Ithaca, N.Y.: Cornell University Press.

Hart, Hastings H. 1912. "Extinction of the Defective Delinquent: A Working Program." In American Prison Association, *Proceedings, 1912,* pp. 205–25.

Haskell, Thomas. 1977. *The Emergence of Professional Social Science.* Urbana: University of Illinois Press.

Hassian, Marouf A., Jr. 1996. *The Rhetoric of Eugenics in Anglo-American Thought.* Athens: University of Georgia Press.

Heale, M. J. 1975. "The Formative Years of the New York Prison Association, 1844–1862: A Case Study in Antebellum Reform." *The New-York Historical Quarterly* 59:320–47.

Healy, William. 1911–12. Summary of *Report of the Commission to Investigate the Question of the Increase of Criminals, Mental Defectives, Epileptics and Degenerates.* [Boston, Jan. 1911]. *JCLC* 2:307–8.

———. 1915. *The Individual Delinquent: A Text-Book of Diagnosis and Prognosis for All Concerned in Understanding Offenders.* Boston: Little, Brown.

———. 1922. "Psychiatry, Psychology, Psychologists, Psychiatrists." *Mental Hygiene* 6:248–56.

Henderson, Charles R. 1893. *An Introduction to the Study of the Dependent, Defective and Delinquent Classes.* Boston: D. C. Heath.

———. 1899. "The Relation of Philanthropy to Social Order and Progress." In NCCC, *Proceedings, 1899,* pp. 1–15.

———. 1900. "Prison Laboratories." *American Journal of Sociology* 6:316–23.

Herrnstein, Richard J., and Charles Murray. 1994. *The Bell Curve: Intelligence and Class Structure in American Life.* New York: Free Press.

Hickson, William J. 1914. "The Defective Delinquent." *JCLC* 5:397–403.

Hoag, Ernest Bryant, and Edward Huntington Williams. 1923. *Crime, Abnormal Minds and the Law*. Indianapolis: Bobbs-Merrill.

Hodder, Jessie D. 1918. "The Next Step in the Treatment of Girl and Women Offenders." *Mental Hygiene* 2:443–47.

———. 1920. "Disciplinary Measures in the Management of the Psychopathic Delinquent Woman." *Mental Hygiene* 4:611–25.

Hofstadter, Richard. 1955. *Social Darwinism in American Thought*. Rev. ed. Boston: Beacon.

Holstein, James A., and Gale Miller, eds. 1993. *Reconsidering Constructionism: Debates in Social Problems Theory*. New York: Aldine de Gruyter.

Hooton, Earnest A. 1939a. *The American Criminal: An Anthropological Study*. Cambridge, Mass.: Harvard University Press.

———. 1939b. *Crime and the Man*. Cambridge, Mass.: Harvard University Press.

Howe, Samuel Gridley. 1848. *Report of the Commissioners under the Resolve of April 11, 1846, to Inquire into the Condition of the Idiots of the Commonwealth*. Mass. Sen. doc. no. 51 for 1848.

———. 1850. *Report on Training and Teaching Idiots under the Resolves of May 8, 1848*. Mass. Sen. doc. no. 38.

Hoyt, Charles S. 1876. "The Causes of Pauperism." In NYSBC, *Annual Report, 1876*, pp. 95–331.

Hrdlička, Aleš. 1898. "Anthropological Studies." *JP-A* 3:47–75.

Hurd, Henry M. 1887. "The Colony System as Proposed in Michigan." In NCCC, *Proceedings, 1887*, pp. 215–20.

Jastrow, Joseph. 1886. "A Theory of Criminality." *Science* 8:20–22.

Jenkins, Philip. 1982. "The Radicals and the Rehabilitative Ideal, 1890–1930." *Criminology* 20:347–72.

———. 1984. "Eugenics, Crime and Ideology: The Case of Progressive Pennsylvania." *Pennsylvania History* 51:64–78.

———. 1994. *Using Murder: The Social Construction of Serial Homicide*. New York: Aldine de Gruyter.

Johnson, John M. 1989. "Horror Stories and the Construction of Child Abuse." In *Images of Issues: Typifying Contemporary Social Problems*, ed. Joel Best, 5–19. New York: Aldine de Gruyter.

Johnstone, E. R. 1909–10. "The Summer School for Teachers of Backward Children." *JP-A* 14 (1–4): 122–28.

Jones, Kathleen W. 1986. "Healy, William." In *Biographical Dictionary of Social Welfare in America*, ed. Walter I. Trattner, 364–69. New York: Greenwood.

Kanner, Leo. 1964. *A History of the Care and Study of the Mentally Retarded*. Springfield, Ill.: Charles C. Thomas.

Karpas, Morris J. 1913. "Psychic Constitutional Inferiority." N~ ~ *Medical Journal* 47:594–98.

———. 1916. "Constitutional Inferiority." *Journal of the Association* 67:1831–34.

Karpman, Ben., ed. 1924. "The Psychopathic Individual: A Symposium."
    Mental Hygiene 8:174–201.
Kaye, Howard L. 1986. *The Social Meaning of Modern Biology: From Social
    Darwinism to Sociobiology.* New Haven, Conn.: Yale University Press.
Keller, E. I. 1918. "Psychopathic Laboratory at Police Headquarters, New
    York City." *Journal of Applied Psychology* 2:84–88.
Kellor, Frances A. 1901. *Experimental Sociology. Descriptive and Analytical.
    Delinquents.* New York: Macmillan.
Keniston, J. M. 1910. "Defectives and Degenerates: A Menace to the
    Community." *Yale Medical Journal* 17:1–7.
Kennedy, John S. 1920. "Report to the Governor Relative to the Investigation
    and Inquiry into Allegations of Cruelty to Prisoners in the New York
    State Reformatory for Women, Bedford Hills." In New York State
    Commission of Prisons, *Annual Report, 1920,* pp. 67–99.
Kentucky Institution for the Education and Training of Feeble-Minded
    Children. 1897. *Report.* Leg. doc. no. 2, October 1.
Kerlin, Isaac N. [1858] 1975. "Our Household Pets." In *The History of Mental
    Retardation: Collected Papers,* vol. 1, ed. Marvin Rosen, Gerald R.
    Clark, and Martin S. Kivitz, 283–91. Baltimore: University Park Press.
———. 1877. "The Organization of Establishments for the Idiotic and
    Imbecile Classes." In AMO, *Proceedings, 1877,* pp. 19–24.
———. 1879. "Juvenile Insanity." In AMO, *Proceedings, 1879,* pp. 86–94.
———. 1880. "Etiology of Idiocy." In AMO, *Proceedings, 1880,* pp. 150–62.
———. 1881. "The Epileptic Change and Its Appearance among Feeble-
    Minded Children. In AMO, *Proceedings, 1881,* pp. 202–11.
———. 1884. "Provision for Idiotic and Feeble-Minded Children." In
    NCCC, *Proceedings, 1884,* pp. 246–63.
———. 1885. "Report of Standing Committee on Provision for Idiots." In
    NCCC, *Proceedings, 1885,* pp. 158–74.
———. 1886. "Report of the Committee on Provision for Idiotic and
    Feeble-minded Persons." In NCCC, *Proceedings, 1886,* pp. 288–302.
———. 1887. "Moral Imbecility." In AMO, *Proceedings, 1887,* pp. 32–37.
———. 1892. "President's Annual Address." In AMO, *Proceedings, 1892,* pp.
    274–85.
Kevles, Daniel J. 1985. *In the Name of Eugenics: Genetics and the Uses of
    Human Heredity.* New York: Knopf.
Kiernan, James G. 1884. "Moral Insanity—What Is It?" *Journal of Nervous
    and Mental Disease* 11:549–75.
Kirchwey, George W. 1918–19. "Proceedings of Tenth Annual Meeting of the
    American Institute of Criminal Law and Criminology: The President's
    Address." *JCLC* 9:327–40.
Kite, Elizabeth S. 1912. "Method and Aim of Field Work at the Vineland
    Training School." *The Training School* 9:81–87.
———. N.d. *The Binet-Simon Measuring Scale for Intelligence: What It Is;
    What It Does; How It Does It; With a Brief Biography of Its Authors,*

Alfred Binet and Dr. Thomas [sic] Simon. Philadelphia: The Committee on Provision for the Feeble-Minded.

Klein, Philip. 1915. Review of *The Individual Delinquent,* by William Healy. *The Delinquent* 5:8–10.

———. 1920. *Prison Methods in New York State.* New York: Columbia University.

Knight, George H. 1892. "The Colony Plan for All Grades of Feeble-Minded." In NCCC, *Proceedings, 1892,* pp. 155–60.

———. 1894. "The Feeble-minded." In AMO, *Proceedings, 1894,* pp. 559–63.

Kraepelin, Emil. [1912] 1917. *Lectures on Clinical Psychiatry.* 3d English ed., rev. and ed. Thomas Johnstone. Repr. New York: William Wood.

Krafft-Ebing, Richard von. [1879] 1904. *Text-Book of Insanity.* Trans. from the 1903 German ed. Philadelphia: F. A. Davis.

Kraft, Ivor. 1961. "Edouard Seguin and 19th Century Moral Treatment of Idiots." *Bulletin of the History of Medicine* 35:393–418.

Kuhlmann, Frederick. 1911. "Binet and Simon's System for Measuring the Intelligence of Children." *JP-A* 15:77–92.

———. 1912. Review of "Two Thousand Normal Children Measured by the Binet Measuring Scale of Intelligence," by H. H. Goddard. *JP-A* 16:144–46.

———. 1914–15. "The Mental Examination of Reformatory Cases." *JCLC* 5:666–74.

———. 1916. "Part Played by the State Institutions in the Care of the Feeble-Minded." *JP-A* 21:3–24.

Kuhn, Thomas S. 1970. *The Structure of Scientific Revolutions.* 2d ed., enl. Chicago: University of Chicago Press.

Lamb, Robert Brockway. 1901. "The Imbecile Criminal." In National Prison Association, *Proceedings, 1901,* pp. 143–50.

———. 1906. "Mental Defect and Crime." In NYSBC, *Annual Report, 1906,* vol. 1, pp. 822–30.

Lane, Harland. 1976. *The Wild Boy of Aveyron.* Cambridge, Mass.: Harvard University Press.

Lane, James B. 1973. "Jacob A. Riis and Scientific Philanthropy during the Progressive Era." *Social Service Review* 47:32–48.

Larson, Edward J. 1991. "Belated Progress: The Enactment of Eugenic Legislation in Georgia." *Journal of the History of Medicine and Allied Sciences* 46:44–64.

———. 1995. *Sex, Race, and Science: Eugenics in the Deep South.* Baltimore: Johns Hopkins University Press.

Lebensohn, Zigmond M. 1973. "In Memorium: Bernard Glueck, Sr. 1884–1972." *American Journal of Psychiatry* 130:326.

Leiby, James. 1967. *Charity and Correction in New Jersey: A History of State Welfare Institutions.* New Brunswick, N.J.: Rutgers University Press.

Lejins, Peter P. 1977. "The Patuxent Experiment." *Bulletin of the American Academy of Psychiatry and the Law* 5:116–33.

Lekkerkerker, Eugenia Cornelia. 1931. *Reformatories for Women in the United States*. The Hague: Bij J. B. Wolters Uitgeversmaatschappij.

Lewis, Burdette G. 1921. *The Offender and His Relations to Society*. 2d ed. New York: Harper and Brothers.

Lewis, David Levering. 1984. "Parallels and Divergences: Assimilationist Strategies of Afro-American and Jewish Elites from 1910 to the Early 1930s." *Journal of American History* 71:543–64.

Lewis, O[rlando] F. 1911a. "The Feeble-Minded Delinquent." In New York State Conference of Charities, *Proceedings, 1911*, pp. 190–95. In NYSBC, *Annual Report, 1991*, vol. 1, appendix 1.

———. 1911b. "Lawbreakers." In NCCC, *Proceedings, 1911*, pp. 43–52.

———. 1912. "The Feeble-Minded Delinquent." *JCLC* 3:10–11.

———. 1916. Review of *Studies in Forensic Psychiatry*, by Bernard Glueck. *The Delinquent* 6:12–13.

———. 1922. *The Development of American Prisons and Prison Customs, 1776–1845*. Albany: Prison Association of New York.

Lombroso, Cesare. 1893. Introduction. In Arthur MacDonald, *Criminology*, vii–x. New York: Funk and Wagnalls.

———. 1895. "Criminal Anthropology: Its Origin and Application." *Forum* 20:33–49.

———. [1900] 1971. "Introductory." In August Drähms, *The Criminal*, xxvii–xxviii. Repr. Montclair, N.J.: Patterson Smith.

———. [1911] 1918. *Crime: Its Causes and Remedies*. Boston: Little, Brown.

———. 1912. "Crime and Insanity in the Twenty-first Century." *JCLC* 3:57–61.

Lombroso, Cesare, and William Ferrero. [1895] 1915. *The Female Offender*. New York: D. Appleton.

Lombroso-Ferrero, Gina. [1911] 1972. *Criminal Man according to the Classification of Cesare Lombroso*. Repr. Montclair, N.J.: Patterson Smith.

Longino, Helen. 1990. *Science as Social Knowledge*. Princeton, N.J.: Princeton University Press.

Lorber, Judith. 1993. "Believing Is Seeing: Biology as Ideology." *Gender and Society* 7:568–81.

Love, Albert G., and Charles B. Davenport. 1919. *Physical Examination of the First Million Draft Recruits: Methods and Results*. U. S. War Department, Office of the Surgeon General, Bulletin no. 11. Washington, D.C.: Government Printing Office.

———. 1920. *Defects Found in Drafted Men*. Washington, D.C.: Government Printing Office.

Lowell, Josephine Shaw. 1879a. "One Means of Preventing Pauperism." In NCCC, *Proceedings, 1879*, pp. 189–200.

———. 1879b. "Reformatories for Women." In NYSBC, *Annual Report, 1879*, pp. 173–80.

Lubove, Roy. 1962. "The Progressive and the Prostitute." *Historian* 24:308–30.

———. 1965. *The Professional Altruist: The Emergence of Social Work as a Career, 1880-1930*. Cambridge, Mass.: Harvard University Press.

Ludmerer, Kenneth M. 1972. *Genetics and American Society*. Baltimore: Johns Hopkins University Press.

Lunbeck, Elizabeth. 1994. *The Psychiatric Persuasion: Knowledge, Gender, and Power in Modern America*. Princeton, N.J.: Princeton University Press.

Lydston, G. Frank. 1896. "Some General Considerations of Criminology." In National Prison Association, *Proceedings, 1896*, pp. 347-63.

———. [1904] 1905. *The Diseases of Society*. Philadelphia: J. B. Lippincott.

Lyon, F. Emory. 1914-15. Review of *Sixty-Eighth Annual Report of the Prison Association of New York, 1912*. *JCLC* 5:313-14.

MacCurdy, John T. 1921a. "Psychiatry and 'Scientific Psychology.'" *Mental Hygiene* 5:239-65.

———. 1921b. Review of *The Psychology of Functional Neuroses*, by H. L. Hollingworth. *Mental Hygiene* 5:181-89.

MacDonald, Arthur. 1893. *Criminology*. 2d ed. Intro. Dr. Cesare Lombroso. New York: Funk and Wagnalls.

MacKenzie, Donald A. 1981. *Statistics in Britain, 1865-1930: The Social Construction of Scientific Knowledge*. Edinburgh: Edinburgh University Press.

Marks, Jonathan. 1995. *Human Biodiversity: Genes, Race, and History*. New York: Aldine de Gruyter.

Massachusetts. 1911. *Report of the Commission to Investigate the Question of the Increase of Criminals, Mental Defectives, Epileptics and Degenerates*. Boston: Wright and Potter.

Massachusetts School for Idiotic and Feeble-Minded Youth (Massachusetts School for the Feeble-Minded at Waltham). 1854-1913. *Annual Reports*.

Maudsley, Henry. [1874] 1876. *Responsibility in Mental Disease*. New York: D. Appleton.

Maughs, Sydney. 1941. "A Concept of Psychopathy and Psychopathic Personality: Its Evolution and Historical Development." *Journal of Clinical and Experimental Psychopathology and Quarterly Review of Psychiatry and Neurology* 2:329-56 (part 1); 2:465-99 (part 2).

McCord, Clinton P. 1915-16. "One Hundred Female Offenders: A Study of the Mentality of Prostitutes and 'Wayward' Girls." *JCLC* 6:385-407.

———. 1917. "The Psychopathic Laboratory." *National Humane Review* 5:186-87.

———. 1924. "A Survey of the Albany County Jail and Penitentiary from Social, Physical, and Psychiatric Viewpoints." *JCLC* 15:42-67.

McKelvey, Blake. [1936] 1972. *American Prisons: A Study in American Social History prior to 1915*. Repr. Montclair, N.J.: Patterson Smith.

McKim, W. Duncan. 1900. *Heredity and Human Progress*. New York: Putnam's/Knickerbocker.

Mednick, Sarnoff A., Terrie E. Moffitt, and Susan A. Stack. 1987. *The

Causes of Crime: New Biological Approaches. Cambridge: Cambridge University Press.

Meyer, Adolf. [1905] 1951. "Suggestions concerning a Grouping of Facts according to Cases." In *Psychiatry*, 140–46, vol. 2 of *The Collected Papers of Adolf Meyer.* Baltimore: Johns Hopkins University Press.

———. [1907] 1952. "Modern Psychiatry: Its Possibilities and Responsibilities." In *Mental Hygiene*, 149–72, vol. 4 of *The Collected Papers of Adolf Meyer.* Baltimore: Johns Hopkins University Press.

———. [1916] 1952. "The Psychopathic Hospital Laboratory of Social Hygiene." In *Mental Hygiene*, 130–31, vol. 4 of *The Collected Papers of Adolf Meyer.* Baltimore: Johns Hopkins University Press.

———. 1957. *Psychobiology: A Science of Man.* Springfield, Ill.: Charles C. Thomas.

Miller, A. M. 1895. "The Study of Abnormal Psychology as an Aid in Training the Feeble-minded." In AMO, *Proceedings, 1895*, pp. 532–39.

Miner, James Burt. 1918. *Deficiency and Delinquency: An Interpretation of Mental Testing.* Baltimore: Warwick and York.

Missouri Association for Criminal Justice. 1926. *The Missouri Crime Survey.* New York: Macmillan.

Mitchinson, Wendy. 1985. "Medical Perceptions of Female Sexuality: A Late Nineteenth Century Case." *Scientia Canadensis* 9:67–81.

———. 1991. *The Nature of Their Bodies: Women and Their Doctors in Victorian Canada.* Toronto: University of Toronto Press.

Mohr, James C. 1993. *Doctors and the Law: Medical Jurisprudence in Nineteenth-Century America.* New York: Oxford University Press.

Monroe, Will S. 1894. "Feeble-Minded Children in the Public Schools." In AMO, *Proceedings, 1894*, pp. 430–33.

Montague, Helen. 1919. "Psychopathic Clinic of the Children's Court of the City of New York. Second Annual Report." *Mental Hygiene* 3:650–69.

Moore, Anne. 1911. *The Feeble Minded in New York.* A report prepared for the Public Education Association of New York. New York: State Charities Aid Association, Special Committee on Provision for the Feeble-Minded.

Murchison, Carl. 1926. *Criminal Intelligence.* Worcester, Mass.: Clark University.

Murray, J. H., and Sydney Kuh. 1917–18. "A Psychiatric Clinic at the Chicago House of Correction." *JCLC* 8:837–43.

National Conference of Charities and Correction. 1874–1916. *Proceedings.*

National Prison Association. 1874–1901. *Proceedings.*

Neff, Joseph S., Samuel Laughlin, and Walter S. Cornell. 1910. *The Degenerate Children of Feeble-Minded Women.* Philadelphia: Department of Public Health and Charities.

New York City Police Department. 1915. "Psychopathic Laboratory." In New York City Police Department, *Annual Report, 1915*, pp. xvii–xix.

———. 1916. "Seeking out Defectives." In New York City Police Department, *Annual Report, 1916,* pp. xxvii–xxviii.

———. 1917. "Psychopathic Laboratory." In New York City Police Department, *Annual Report, 1914–17* [*sic*], pp. 82–84.

New York Committee on Feeblemindedness. N.d. [1917?]. *First Annual Report.*

New York County Superintendents of Poor. 1888–90. *Proceedings.*

New York Foundation. N.d. *Forty Year Report, 1909–49.* New York: New York Foundation.

New York State Asylum for Idiots (Syracuse). 1851–1890. *Annual Reports.*

New York State Board of Charities. 1867–1921. *Annual Reports.*

———. 1894. *Report and Proceedings of the State Board of Charities Relative to the Management of the State Reformatory at Elmira.* New York State Ass. doc. 89 (Mar. 19).

New York State Charities Aid Association. 1918. *The Year's Work in Mental Hygiene in New York State.* New York: the Association.

New York State Commission for Mental Defectives. 1919–26. *Annual Reports.*

New York State Commission of Prisons. 1921–26. *Annual Reports.*

———. 1918. *Report of a Special Committee Appointed to Investigate the Matter of Mental Disease and Delinquency.* Ossining: Sing Sing Prison.

———. 1925. *Special Report on the Psychopathic Delinquent.* N.p.: State Commission of Prisons.

New York State Commission to Investigate Provision for the Mentally Deficient. 1915. *Report.* New York Sen. doc. no. 42.

New York State Commissioner of Correction. 1928–42. *Annual Reports.*

New York State Conference of Charities and Correction. 1900–1904. *Proceedings.*

New York State Custodial Asylum for Feeble-Minded Women (Newark Custodial Asylum). 1885–1900. *Annual Reports.*

———. 1893. *Dedication Services, Newark, New York, June 10, 1890.* Newark, N.Y.: W. C. and F. D. Burgess, 1893.

New York State Department of Correction. 1943–63. *Annual Reports.*

———. N.d. [1949?] *Westfield State Farm, Bedford Hills, N.Y.: Its History, Purpose, Makeup and Program.* Albany: Department of Correction.

———. 1949a. *Albion State Training School, Albion, N.Y.: Its History, Purpose, Makeup and Program.* Albany: Department of Correction.

———. 1949b. *Institution for Male Defective Delinquents, Napanoch, N.Y.: Its History, Purpose, Makeup and Program.* Albany: Department of Correction.

———. 1949c. *Woodbourne Institution for Defective Delinquents, Woodbourne, N.Y.: Its History, Purpose, Makeup and Program.* Albany: Department of Correction.

New York State Institution for Defective Delinquents at Napanoch. 1922–26. *Annual Reports.*

New York State Lunatic Asylum, Utica. 1845. *Annual Report.*

New York State Prison Survey Committee. 1920. *Report of the Prison Survey Committee.* Albany: J. B. Lyon.

New York State Probation Commission. 1911. *Annual Report.*

New York State Reformatory at Elmira. 1877–1926. *Annual Reports.*

New York State Reformatory for Women at Bedford Hills. 1901–26. *Annual Reports.*

Noel, Patricia S., and Eric T. Carlson. 1970. "Origins of the Word 'Phrenology.'" *American Journal of Psychiatry* 127:694–97.

———. 1973. "The Faculty Psychology of Benjamin Rush." *Journal of the History of the Behavioral Sciences* 9:369–77.

Noll, Steven. 1991. "Southern Strategies for Handling the Black Feeble-minded: From Social Control to Profound Indifference." *Journal of Policy History* 3:131–51.

———. 1994. " 'Incapable of Living a Clean and Proper Life': The Case of Willie Mallory and Eugenic Sterilization in Virginia before *Buck*." Paper presented at the annual meeting of the Organization of American Historians, Atlanta.

———. 1995a. *Feeble-Minded in Our Midst: Institutions for the Mentally Retarded in the South, 1900–1940.* Chapel Hill: University of North Carolina Press.

———. 1995b. "Under a Double Burden: Florida's Black Feeble-Minded, 1920–1957." In *The African American Heritage of Florida*, ed. David R. Colburn and Jane L. Landers, 275–97. Gainesville: University of Florida Press.

Notes and Abstracts. 1917–18. "Report of the New York Psychiatrical Society Re Clinic Psychologists." *JCLC* 8:266–67.

Noyes, William. 1888. "The Criminal Type." *American Journal of Social Science* 24:31–42.

Nye, Robert A. 1984. *Crime, Madness, and Politics in Modern France: The Medical Concept of National Decline.* Princeton, N.J.: Princeton University Press.

Olsen, Frances. 1984. "Statutory Rape: A Feminist Critique of Rights Analysis." *Texas Law Review* 63:387–432.

Olson, Harry. 1915–16. "The Psychopathic Laboratory Idea." *JCLC* 6:59–64.

Osborne, A. E. 1891. "The Founding of a Great Institution and Some of Its Problems." In AMO, *Proceedings, 1891,* pp. 173–85.

———. 1894. "President's Annual Address." In AMO, *Proceedings, 1894,* pp. 385–99.

Overholser, Winfred. 1935. "The Briggs Law of Massachusetts: A Review and an Appraisal." *JCLC* 35:859–83.

Parker, George. 1911. "Mentally Defective Delinquents." In New York State Probation Commission, *Annual Report, 1911,* pp. 342–47.

Parmelee, Maurice. [1911] 1918. Introduction. In Cesare Lombroso, *Crime: Its Causes and Remedies*, xi–xxxii. Boston: Little, Brown.

Parsons, Philip A. 1909. *Responsibility for Crime*. New York: Columbia University/Longmans, Green.

———. 1924. *Introduction to Modern Social Problems*. New York: Knopf.

———. 1926. *Crime and the Criminal: An Introduction to Criminology*. New York: Knopf.

Peiss, Kathy. 1986. *Cheap Amusements: Working Women and Leisure in Turn-of-the-Century New York*. Philadelphia: Temple University Press.

Peyton, David C. 1913–14. Review of *Prostitution, Its Nature and Cure*, by the Penal Reform League of London. *JCLC* 4:466–68.

———. 1915–16. "Material of a Clinical Research in the Field of Criminology." *JCLC* 6:230–39.

Pick, Daniel. 1989. *Faces of Degeneration: A European Disorder, c. 1848– c. 1918*. Cambridge: Cambridge University Press.

Pickens, Donald K. 1968. *Eugenics and the Progressives*. Nashville: Vanderbilt University Press.

Pinel, Philippe. [1801] 1962. *A Treatise on Insanity*. New York: Hafner.

Pisciotta, Alexander W. 1983. "Scientific Reform: The 'New Penology' at Elmira, 1876–1900." *Crime and Delinquency* 29:613–30.

———. 1994. *Benevolent Repression: Social Control and the American Reformatory-Prison Movement*. New York: New York University Press.

Pivar, David J. 1973. *Purity Crusade: Sexual Morality and Social Control, 1868–1900*. Westport, Conn.: Greenwood.

Pollack, Horatio M. 1921. "Eugenics as a Factor in the Prevention of Mental Disease." *Mental Hygiene* 5:807–12.

Pollock, Herman I. 1951. "The Mentally Ill in Pennsylvania Criminal Law and Administration." *University of Pittsburgh Law Review* 12:587–602.

Prichard, James Cowles. [1837] 1973. *A Treatise on Insanity and Other Disorders Affecting the Mind*. New York: Arno.

Prison Association of New York. 1844–1921. *Annual Reports*.

———. 1912. *Facts Showing the Vital Need of a State Custodial Asylum for Feeble-Minded Male Delinquents*. New York: Prison Association of New York.

Proctor, Robert N. 1991. "Eugenics among the Social Sciences: Hereditarian Thought in Germany and the United States." In *The Estate of Social Knowledge*, ed. JoAnne Brown and David K. van Keuren, 175–208. Baltimore: Johns Hopkins University Press.

Public Education Association of New York. 1913. *Work with Mentally Defective Children in New York City*. Bulletin no. 8. New York: Public Education Association.

Radford, John P. 1991. "Sterilization versus Segregation: Control of the 'Feebleminded,' 1900–1938." *Social Science and Medicine* 33:449–58.

Rafter, Nicole H., ed. 1988. *White Trash: The Eugenic Family Studies, 1877–1919*. Boston: Northeastern University Press.

———. 1990a. *Partial Justice: Women, Prisons, and Social Control*. New Brunswick, N.J.: Transaction.

————. 1990b. "The Social Construction of Crime and Crime Control." *Journal of Research in Crime and Delinquency* 27:376-89.

————. 1992a. "Claims-making and Socio-Cultural Context in the First U.S. Eugenics Campaign." *Social Problems* 39:17-34.

————. 1992b. "Criminal Anthropology in the United States." *Criminology* 30:525-45.

————. 1992c. "Some Consequences of Strict Constructionism." *Social Problems* 39:38-39.

————. 1994. "Eugenics, Class, and the Professionalization of Social Control." In *Inequality, Crime, and Social Control,* ed. George Bridges and Martha Myers, 214-27. Boulder, Colo.: Westview.

Ray, Isaac. [1838] 1983. *A Treatise on the Medical Jurisprudence of Insanity.* Repr. New York: Da Capo.

————. 1861-62. "An Examination of the Objections to the Doctrine of Moral Insanity." *American Journal of Insanity* 18:112-38.

Reilly, Philip R. 1991. *The Surgical Solution: A History of Involuntary Sterilization in the United States.* Baltimore: Johns Hopkins University Press.

Rennie, Ysabel. 1978. *The Search for Criminal Man: A Conceptual History of the Dangerous Offender.* Lexington, Mass.: Lexington.

Reynolds, Amos. 1879. "The Prevention of Pauperism." In NCCC, *Proceedings, 1879,* pp. 210-16.

Ricker, Charles Sherwood. 1934. "A Critique of the Defective Delinquent Law." *Law Society Journal* 6:94-111.

Robinson, Louis N. 1933. "Institutions for Defective Delinquents." *JCLC* 24:352-99.

Rockefeller, John D., Jr. 1913. Introduction. In George J. Kneeland, *Commercialized Prostitution in New York City,* vii-xii. New York: Century.

Rogers, A. C. 1892. "Report of Five Cases of Mental and Moral Aberration." In AMO, *Proceedings, 1892,* pp. 318-25.

Rosanoff, Aaron J., ed. 1927. *Manual of Psychiatry.* 6th ed., rev. and enl. New York: John Wiley and Sons.

Rosen, Ruth. 1982. *The Lost Sisterhood: Prostitution in America, 1900-1918.* Baltimore: Johns Hopkins University Press.

Rosenberg, Charles E. 1968. *The Trial of the Assassin Guiteau: Psychiatry and Law in the Gilded Age.* Chicago: University of Chicago Press.

————. 1976. *No Other Gods: On Science and American Social Thought.* Baltimore: Johns Hopkins University Press.

Ross, Dorothy. 1972. *G. Stanley Hall: The Psychologist As Prophet.* Chicago: University of Chicago Press.

————. 1979. "The Development of the Social Sciences." In *The Organization of Knowledge in Modern America, 1860-1920,* ed. A. Oleson and J. Voss, 107-38. Baltimore: Johns Hopkins University Press.

————. 1991. *The Origins of American Social Science.* New York: Cambridge University Press.

Rossy, C. S. 1915. "Second Note on a Psychological Study of the Criminals at the Massachusetts State Prison." *Massachusetts State Board of Insanity Bulletin*, no. 16:14-20.

Rothman, David J. 1978. "The State as Parent: Social Policy in the Progressive Era." In Williard Gaylin, Ira Glasser, Steven Marcus, and David J. Rothman, *Doing Good: The Limits of Benevolence*, 67-95. New York: Pantheon.

———. 1980. *Conscience and Convenience: The Asylum and Its Alternatives in Progressive America*. Boston: Little Brown.

Rowe, David C., and D. Wayne Osgood. 1984. "Heredity and Sociological Theories of Delinquency: A Reconsideration." *American Sociological Review* 49:526-40.

Ruggles-Brise, Evelyn. 1911-12. "An English View of the American Penal System." *JCLC* 2:356-69.

Rush, Benjamin. [1786] 1815. "An Inquiry into the Influence of Physical Causes upon the Moral Faculty." In Benjamin Rush, *Medical Inquiries and Observations*, 4th ed., vol. 1, pp. 93-124. Philadelphia: M. Corey.

———. 1812. "Of Derangement in the Moral Faculties." In Benjamin Rush, *Medical Inquiries and Observations, upon the Diseases of the Mind*, 357-67. Philadelphia: Kimber and Richardson.

Salisbury, Albert. 1891. "The Education of the Feeble-Minded." In AMO, *Proceedings, 1891*, pp. 219-33.

Salmon, Thomas W. 1917. "The Prisoner Himself. Part II." In *The Prison and the Prisoner*, ed. Julia K. Jaffray, 29-45. Boston: Little, Brown.

———. 1919-20. "Some New Problems for Psychiatric Research in Delinquency." *JCLC* 10:375-84.

Sampson, M[armaduke] B. 1846. *Rationale of Crime*. New York: D. Appleton.

Sanborn, Franklin B. 1871. "How Far Is the Irish Prison System Applicable to American Prisons?" In *Transactions of the National Congress on Penitentiary and Reformatory Discipline*, ed. E. C. Wines, 406-14. Albany, N.Y.: Weed, Parsons.

———. 1900a. *The Development of Reformatory Discipline*. Papers in Penology. Elmira, N.Y.: New York State Reformatory.

———. 1900b. "The Elmira Reformatory." In *The Reformatory System in the United States*, ed. Samuel J. Barrows, 28-47. Washington: Government Printing Office.

Sarason, Seymour B., and John Doris. 1969. *Psychological Problems in Mental Deficiency*. 4th ed. New York: Harper and Row.

Saveth, Edward N. 1980. "Patrician Philanthropy in America: The Late Nineteenth and Early Twentieth Centuries." *Social Service Review* 54:76-91.

Savitz, Leonard D. 1972. Introduction. In Gina Lombroso-Ferrero, *Criminal Man*, v-xx. Montclair, N.J.: Patterson Smith.

Savitz, Leonard D., Stanley H. Turner, and Toby Dickman. 1977. "The Origin of Scientific Criminology: Franz Joseph Gall as the First Criminologist." In *Theory in Criminology: Contemporary Views*, ed. Robert F. Meier, 41-56. Beverly Hills, Calif.: Sage.

Scheerenberger, R.C. 1983. *A History of Mental Retardation*. Baltimore: Paul H. Brookes.

Schlossman, Steven L., and Stephanie Wallach. 1978. "The Crime of Precocious Sexuality: Female Juvenile Delinquency in the Progressive Era." *Harvard Educational Review* 48:65–95.

Schneider, David M., and Albert Deutsch. [1941] 1969. *The History of Public Welfare in New York State, 1867–1940*. Repr. Montclair, N.J.: Patterson Smith.

Schneider, Joseph W. 1985. "Social Problems Theory: The Constructionist View." *Annual Review of Sociology* 11:209–29.

Scott, Augusta. 1922. "Three Hundred Psychiatric Examinations Made at the Women's Day Court, New York City." *Mental Hygiene* 6:343–69.

Seguin, Edward [Edouard Séguin]. 1846. *Traitement moral, hygiène et éducation des idiots et des autres enfants arriérés ou retardés dans leur développement*. Paris: J. B. Bailière.

———. [1866] 1971. *Idiocy and Its Treatment by the Physiological Method*. Repr. New York: Augustus M. Kelley.

Sekula, Allan. 1986. "The Body and the Archive." *October* 39:3–64.

Sheldon, William H., Emil M. Hartl, and Eugene McDermott. 1949. *Varieties of Delinquent Youth*. New York: Harper and Brothers.

Sheldon, William H., and S. S. Stevens. 1942. *The Varieties of Temperament: A Psychology of Constitutional Differences*. New York: Harper and Brothers.

Sheldon, William H., S. S. Stevens, and W. B. Tucker. 1940. *The Varieties of Human Physique: An Introduction to Constitutional Psychology*. New York: Harper and Brothers.

Simmons, Harvey G. 1978. "Explaining Social Policy: The English Mental Deficiency Act of 1913." *Journal of Social History* 11:387–403.

Smart, Carol. 1989. *Feminism and the Power of Law*. New York: Routledge.

Smith, J. David. 1985. *Minds Made Feeble: The Myth and Legacy of the Kallikaks*. Rockville, Md.: Aspen Systems.

Smith, Samuel G. 1896. "Relation of Crime to Economics." In National Prison Association, *Proceedings, 1896*, pp. 254–65.

Smithers, William W. 1911–12. "The 1910 Meeting of the International Union of Penal Law." *JCLC* 2:381–85.

Southard, E. E. 1916. "Psychopathic Delinquents." In NCCC, *Proceedings, 1916*, pp. 529–38.

———. 1917. "Alienists and Psychiatrists: Notes on Divisions and Nomenclature of Mental Hygiene." *Mental Hygiene* 1:567–71.

Spaulding, Edith R. 1914–15. "The Results of Mental and Physical Examinations of Four Hundred Women Offenders—with Particular Reference to Their Treatment during Commitment." *JCLC* 5:704–17.

———. 1916. "The New Psychopathic Hospital, New York State Reformatory for Women, Bedford Hills." *The Delinquent* 6:5–7.

———. [1923] 1969. *An Experimental Study of Psychopathic Delinquent Women*. Montclair, N.J.: Patterson Smith.

———. 1925. *Report of a Mental Health Survey of Staten Island*. New York: National Committee for Mental Hygiene.

Spector, Malcolm, and John I. Kituse. 1987. *Constructing Social Problems*. New York: Aldine de Gruyter.

Spurzheim, J. G. [1847] 1883. *Education: Its Elementary Principles, Founded on the Nature of Man*. 12th American ed. New York: Fowler and Wells.

Starr, Paul. 1982. *The Social Transformation of American Medicine*. New York: Basic.

———. 1987. "The Sociology of Official Statistics." In *The Politics of Numbers*, ed. William Alonso and Paul Starr, 57. New York: Russell Sage Foundation.

Stearns, A. Warren. 1916. "A Survey of Defective Delinquents under the Care of the Massachusetts State Board of Insanity." *American Journal of Insanity* 72:427-37.

———. 1918-19. "The Detection of the Potential Criminal." *JCLC* 9:514-19.

Stepan, Nancy Leys. 1991. *"The Hour of Eugenics": Race, Gender, and Nation in Latin America*. Ithaca, N.Y.: Cornell University Press.

Stevens, Herman C. 1915-16. Review of *The Individual Delinquent*, by William Healy. *JCLC* 6:849-59.

Stewart, William Rhinelander. 1911. *The Philanthropic Work of Josephine Shaw Lowell*. New York: Macmillan.

Storer, Mary. 1914. "The Defective Delinquent Girl." *JP-A* 19:23-30.

Strecker, Edward A. 1921. "Mal-behavior Viewed as an Outpatient Mental and Nervous Clinic Problem." *Mental Hygiene* 5:225-38.

Strong, Gurney S. 1894. *Early Landmarks of Syracuse*. Syracuse, N.Y.: Times.

Taft, Jessie. 1918. "Supervision of the Feebleminded in the Community." *Mental Hygiene* 2:434-42.

Talbot, Eugene S. 1898. *Degeneracy: Its Causes, Signs, and Results*. London: Walter Scott.

Taylor, Lloyd C., Jr. 1963. "Josephine Shaw Lowell and American Philanthropy." *New York History* 44:336-64.

Tenney, Charles W., Jr. 1962. "Sex, Sanity and Stupidity in Massachusetts." *Boston University Law Review* 42:1-31.

Terman, Lewis M. 1912. "The Binet-Simon Scale for Measuring Intelligence. Impressions Gained by Its Application upon Four Hundred Non-Selected Children." *JP-A* 16:103-12.

———. 1913. "Psychological Principles Underlying the Binet-Simon Scale and Some Practical Considerations for Its Correct Use." *JP-A* 18:93-104.

———. 1914. "The Significance of Intelligence Tests for Mental Hygiene." *JP-A* 18:119-27.

———. 1916-17. "The Binet Scale and the Diagnosis of Feeble-Mindedness." *JCLC* 7:530-43.

Terry, Jennifer, and Jacqueline Urla, eds. 1995. *Deviant Bodies: Critical Perspectives on Difference in Science and Popular Culture*. Bloomington: Indiana University Press.

Thayer, Walter N., Jr. 1925. "The Criminal and the Napanoch Plan." *JCLC* 16:278–89.

Thomson, J. Bruce. 1870. "The Psychology of Criminals." *Journal of Mental Science* 17:321–50.

Town, Clara H. 1913. "The Psychological Clinic as a Eugenic Agency." *Institution Quarterly* 4:51–54.

Towne, Arthur W. 1911–12a. "Joint Conference on Legislation Needed in New York State." *JCLC* 2:918–19.

———. 1911–12b. "New York State Conference of Magistrates." *JCLC* 2:921–24.

Tredgold, A. F. 1916. *Mental Deficiency (Amentia)*. 2d ed. New York: William Wood.

Trent, James W., Jr. 1982. "Reasoning about Mental Retardation: A Study of the American Association on Mental Deficiency." Ph.D. diss., Brandeis University.

———. 1986. "Bernstein, Charles." In *Biographical Dictionary of Social Welfare in America,* ed. Walter I. Trattner, 83–86. New York: Greenwood.

———. 1993. "To Cut and Control: Institutional Preservation and the Sterilization of Mentally Retarded People in the United States, 1892–1947." *Journal of Historical Sociology* 6:56–73.

———. 1994. *Inventing the Feeble Mind: A History of Mental Retardation in the United States.* Berkeley: University of California Press.

Tyor, Peter. 1977. " 'Denied the Power to Choose the Good': Sexuality and Mental Defect in American Medical Practice, 1850–1920." *Journal of Social History* 10:472–89.

Tyor, Peter, and Leland V. Bell. 1984. *Caring for the Retarded in America: A History.* Westport, Conn.: Greenwood.

United States Bureau of the Census. 1936. *Crime and Mental Disease or Deficiency, 1933.* Washington: Government Printing Office.

United States Department of Commerce and Labor, Bureau of the Census. 1906. *Insane and Feeble-Minded in Hospitals and Institutions. 1904.* Washington: Government Printing Office.

United States Department of the Interior, Census Office. 1883. *Statistics of the Population of the United States at the Tenth Census (June 1, 1880).* Washington: Government Printing Office.

United States War Department, Office of the Provost Marshal General. 1918. *Physical Examination for Entrance into the Army of the United States by Voluntary Enlistment or by Induction under the Selective Service Law.* Special regulations no. 65. Washington: Government Printing Office.

Vaughan, Victor C. 1914. "Race Betterment." *JP-A* 18:128–38.

Visher, John W. 1922. "A Study in Constitutional Psychopathic Inferiority." *Mental Hygiene* 6:729–45.

Wallack, Walter M., Glenn M. Kendall, and Howard L. Briggs. 1939. *Education within Prison Walls.* New York: Bureau of Publications, Teachers College, Columbia University.

Wallin, J. E. Wallace. 1915–16. "Who Is Feeble-Minded?" *JCLC* 6:706–16.

Walter, Richard D. 1956. "What Became of the Degenerate? A Brief History of a Concept." *Journal of the History of Medicine and Allied Sciences* 11:422–29.

Wattenberg, Ben. 1987. *The Birth Dearth*. New York: Pharos/Ballantine.

Weidensall, Jean. 1916. *The Mentality of the Criminal Woman*. Baltimore: Warwick and York.

Welter, Barbara. 1966. "The Cult of True Womanhood: 1820–1860." *American Quarterly* 18:151–74.

Werlinder, Henry. 1978. *Psychopathy: A History of the Concept*. Stockholm: Almquist and Wiksell.

Westwell, Arthur E. 1951. "The Defective Delinquent." *American Journal of Mental Deficiency* 56:283–89.

Wey, Hamilton D. 1888. "A Plea for Physical Training of Youthful Criminals." In National Prison Association, *Proceedings, 1888*, pp. 181–93.

———. 1890. "Criminal Anthropology." In National Prison Association, *Proceedings, 1890*, pp. 274–90.

White, William A. 1917. "Underlying Concepts in Mental Hygiene." *Mental Hygiene* 1:7–15.

Wickersham, George W. 1922. Foreword. In O. F. Lewis, *The Development of American Prisons and Prison Customs, 1776–1845*. Albany: Prison Association of New York.

Wiebe, Robert. 1967. *The Search for Order 1877–1930*. New York: Hill and Wang.

Wilbur, Hervey B. 1872. *Materialism in Its Relations to the Causes, Conditions, and Treatment of Insanity*. New York: D. Appleton. Repr. from the *Journal of Psychological Medicine* (Jan. 1872).

———. 1876. "Governmental Supervision of the Insane." In [National] Conference of Charities, *Proceedings, 1876*, pp. 72–90.

———. 1877. "Buildings for the Management and Treatment of the Insane." In National Conference of Charities, *Proceedings, 1877*, pp. 134–58.

———. 1880. "Instinct not Predominant in Idiocy." In AMO, *Proceedings, 1880*, pp. 135–44.

———. [1881a] 1964. "Remark by Dr. H. B. Wilbur." In "In Memory of Edouard Seguin, M.D.," separately paginated memorial inset after p. 176 in Association of Medical Officers of American Institutions for Idiotic and Feeble-Minded Persons, *Proceedings 1876–1886*, 27–36. New York: Johnson Reprint.

———. 1881b. *"Chemical Restraint" in the Management of the Insane*. New York: Putnam's. Repr. from the *Archives of Medicine* (Dec. 1881).

Williams, Frankwood E., and V. V. Anderson. 1924. *Report of a Mental Hygiene Survey of New York County Jails and Penitentiaries*. New York: National Committee for Mental Hygiene.

Wilmarth, A. W. 1885. "Notes on the Anatomy of the Idiot Brain." In AMO, *Proceedings, 1885*, pp. 323–28.

———. 1886. "Notes on the Pathology of Idiocy." In AMO, *Proceedings, 1886*, pp. 428–41.

———. 1888. "Mongolian Idiocy." In AMO, *Proceedings, 1888*, pp. 59–61.

———. 1890. "Report on the Examination of One Hundred Brains of Feeble-Minded Children." In AMO, *Proceedings, 1890*, pp. 138–48.

———. 1895. "President's Annual Address." In AMO, *Proceedings, 1895*, pp. 513–21.

Wilson, James Q., and Richard J. Herrnstein. 1985. *Crime and Human Nature*. New York: Simon and Schuster.

Wines, E. C., ed. 1871. *Transactions of the National Congress on Penitentiary and Reformatory Discipline, 1870*. Albany: Weed, Parsons.

Wines, E. C., and Theodore W. Dwight. 1867. *Report on the Prisons and Reformatories of the United States and Canada*. Albany: van Benthuysen and Sons.

Wines, Frederick Howard. 1888. *Report on the Defective, Dependent, and Delinquent Classes of the Population of the United States as Returned at the Tenth Census (June 21, 1880)*. Washington: Government Printing Office.

———. 1895. *Punishment and Reformation*. New York: Thomas Y. Crowell.

———. 1919. *Punishment and Reformation: A Study of the Penitentiary System*. New ed., rev. and enl. by Winthrop D. Lane. New York: Thomas Y. Crowell.

Winter, Alexander. 1891. *The New York State Reformatory in Elmira*. London: Swan Sonnenschein.

Wolfgang, Marvin. 1972. "Cesare Lombroso." In *Pioneers in Criminology*, ed. Hermann Mannheim, 2d ed., 232–91. Montclair, N.J.: Patterson Smith.

Woodbridge, Frederick. 1939. "Physical and Mental Infancy in the Criminal Law." *University of Pennsylvania Law Review* 87:426–54.

Woods, Arthur. 1918. *Crime Prevention*. Princeton, N.J.: Princeton University Press.

Woolgar, Steve, and Dorothy Pawluch. 1985. "Ontological Gerrymandering: The Anatomy of Social Problems Explanations." *Social Problems* 32:214–27.

Yerkes, Robert M. 1916–17. "Mental Examination of Police and Court Cases." *JCLC* 7:366–72.

Zeman, Thomas Edward. 1981. "Order, Crime, and Punishment: The American Criminological Tradition." Ph.D. diss., University of California, Santa Cruz.

Zenderland, Leila. 1987. "The Debate over Diagnosis: Henry Herbert Goddard and the Medical Acceptance of Intelligence Testing." In *Psychological Testing and American Society, 1890–1930*, ed. Michael M. Sokal, 46–74. New Brunswick, N.J.: Rutgers University Press.

Index

AAIF (Association of American Institutions for the Feeble-Minded), 135–37

Abbott, Andrew, 28

Albion (New York) State Training School, 3, 222–23

Alexander, Mrs. George D. (Caroline Wittpen), 193

Allen, Garland E., 163 n. 34

Altruism, 89–90, 210, 240

American Institute of Criminal Law and Criminology, 115

American Prison Association, 196

AMO (Association of Medical Officers of American Institutions for Idiotic and Feeble-Minded Persons), 57–59, 68, 82–86. *See also* AAIF; Kerlin, Isaac N.: influence of, on AMO; Kerlin, Isaac N.: and protégés; Superintendents of institutions for the mentally retarded

Antiprostitution campaigns, 160

Association of Medical Superintendents of American Institutions for the Insane, 29, 58

Auburn (New York) State Prison, 217–18, 220

Autopsies, 61

Backus, Frederick F., 19, 26

Bailey, Pearce, 202–4

Barr, Martin W., 59, 60, 64; Lombroso's influence on, 106; on moral imbecility/moral paranoia, 56, 83–86, 139; relationship with Kerlin, 61; terminology used by, 84–85, 139

Barre (Massachusetts) Institution for the Education of Idiots, Imbeciles and Children of Retarded Mental Development of Mind, 18–19, 31 n. 9, 62, 67

Barrows, Isabel, 56
Baxtrom v. Herold, 221–22, 226
Bedford Hills (New York) Reformatory
for Women, 150; and clearinghouse
plan, 152–54, 194; and defective delinquent legislation, 154–55, 202–4;
Division for Mentally Defective Delinquent Women at, 155, 202–4, 222–23;
and Laboratory of Social Hygiene,
154–55, 179, 181; mental testing at, 12,
153–55; prisoner disturbances at, 154–
55; Psychopathic Hospital at, 179–82,
197; significance of, to eugenic criminology, 12, 150; mentioned, 151, 174.
See also Rockefeller, John D., Jr.
Bell Curve, The, 11, 13, 211, 238, 239
Benedikt, Moriz, 101, 113–14, 116
Bernstein, Charles, 231; attitudes toward
defective delinquents, 192–93; and
campaign for defective delinquent
legislation, 191–92, 200, 213; leader in
community care for mentally retarded,
191; and Napanoch Institution for
Defective Delinquents, 213–15
Bertillon method of criminal identification, 101–2
Best, Joel, 25
Binet, Alfred, 12, 136
Biological theories of crime. *See* Born-
criminal theory
Blackmar, Frank W., 127
Boies, Henry M., 112, 116, 117, 123–24;
Prisoners and Paupers, 117, 118–19,
121, 122, 123, 127–28; *Science of Penology*, 102, 117, 124. *See also* Criminal
anthropologists, American
Born-criminal concept, 72; ambiguous
referents of, 86–87, 119, 183; binaristic
nature of, 11, 87–88, 210; chameleon-
like quality of, 8; definitional approach
to, 9–10, 14–15 n. 15; metaphorical
nature of, 8, 10; terminological issues
relating to, 8. *See also* Born criminals;
Born-criminal theory
Born criminals: feebleminded women
as, 35–50, 159–61; infantilization of,
in work of Henry H. Goddard, 140;
as metaphors, 10, 86–89; nature of,
generically, 13; synonyms for, 8, 14

n. 13, 139, 190. *See also* Born-criminal
theory; Eugenic criminology; Whipple,
Fenix; *specific types and theorists*
Born-criminal theory: and AMO, 55–69;
development of, 4, 6, 10–13, 73–90,
167–68; as discourse on normality, 8,
49–50, 118–19, 122–23, 238; end of
medical monopoly over, 146; metaphorical nature of, 8, 10, 86–89, 237;
recent versions of, 13, 211, 237; somatic
content of, 94, 176, 180; terminology
of, 8, 167. *See also* Born criminal concept; Born criminals; Eugenic criminology; *names of specific producers,
production sites, types of theory, and
criminal types*
Boston, Charles A., 161
Branham, V. C., 215, 223
Bridgewater (Massachusetts) State Farm,
199, 224–26
Bridgewater (Massachusetts) Treatment
Center, 226
Brigham, Amariah, 24, 28, 29
Brockway, Zebulon R.: as born-criminal
theorist, 94–96, 97, 102–5, 106 n. 3; as
a "criminologist" 111, 125; and cruelty
to prisoners, 103–4; and degeneration
theory, 94–96, 100–106; and Eastern New York Reformatory, 212; and
eugenics, 11, 107 n. 4; hereditarian
elements in thinking of, 94–95; and
photography, 126; and professional-
ization of prison administration, 94,
97; reputation of, 97, 99, 105; role at
National Congress on Penitentiary and
Reformatory Discipline, 97; significance of, 94, 96, 97, 98; mentioned,
61, 188, 230. *See also* Elmira (New
York) Reformatory
Broomall, John M., 83–85
Brown, Catharine W., 67–68
Brown, JoAnne, 8, 86–87
Buck, Carrie, 153
Bureau of Social Hygiene, 154–55
Burnham, Edwin K., 43
Burton, Robert, 37
Butler, Fred O., 227

Calvin, John, 74

Carnegie, Andrew, 193

Carson, James C., 84

Centralization of New York State prison system: and plans to establish institutions for defective delinquents, 189, 195–98; role of Sing Sing prison in, 175, 194, 196, 198

Charity Organization Society, 152, 196

Christian, Frank L., 3, 156, 157, 158, 172, 192, 200; and Fenix Whipple, 228

Classification of prisons, 97, 195, 196–98

Clearinghouse plan, 152, 198

Clearinghouses, 172, 193; at Bedford Hills Reformatory, 152–54; at Sing Sing, 174–75, 194, 198

Clemens, Samuel, 99

Clinton Farms. See New Jersey Reformatory for Women at Clinton Farms

Colony plan: Bernstein's model of, 191; and education, 64; and eugenics, 63–65, 151, 191; and farming, 63–64; "funnel" model of, 191; imperialistic nature of, 55, 63–64, 191; Kerlin's model of, 63–64, 68, 191; practicality of, 64; Wilbur's model of, 191

Columbia University Teachers College, 218

Connecticut Commissioners on Idiocy, 24, 25, 27

Cooter, Roger, 77

Cowan, Ruth Schwartz, 89

Criminal anthropologists, American: on born criminals, 120; on crime causation, 11, 118–24; and criminal typologies, 121–23; and criminology, 110, 111–12; departures from Lombroso's doctrines, 11, 120–21, 123–24; and determinism, 111–12, 124; and eugenics, 123–24; goals of, 116; major works of, 116–17; professional identities of, 117–18; sources of information of, 113–16. See also Criminal anthropology; names of specific theorists

Criminal anthropology, 94, 101, 106, 110, 112; American receptivity to, 102, 105–6, 125–28; basic works on, and their dissemination, 113–25; and construction of the professional middle class, 119; the criminal class in, 118–

19; criminal types in, 120–23; as discourse on normality, 118–19, 122–23; at Elmira Reformatory, 94–95, 101–3, 106 n. 3; and eugenics, 123–24; and phrenology, 125; representations of the body in, 7, 12, 104, 112, 113, 119, 120, 140; resistance to, in United States, 124–25; and sentences for criminals, 123–24; size of criminal class in, 119; and social class, 119–23; views of heredity in, 104, 121–24; waning of, 133, 137, 140. See also Autopsies; Criminal anthropologists, American; Degeneration theory: criminal anthropology's influence on; Evolution, influence of theory of: on criminal anthropology; names of specific theorists

Criminal imbeciles, 11, 137–46

Criminal responsibility, 82, 85, 95, 222; criminal anthropologists on, 125, 140; 1870 prison congress reformers' views on, 95–97, 140; Henry H. Goddard on, 140–41, 143–44; Henry Maudsley on, 81; recent scholarly literature on, 7

Cult of curability, 26–27, 169

Custodialism: and eugenics, 62–68; and institutional size, 62–68; at mental hospitals, 169; scientific, 62–66; Wilbur's resistance to, 21, 29–30. See also Colony plan

Dangerousness, criminal: as a condition, 5, 47, 140, 158, 183, 228; and gender, 47; and heredity, 36, 104, 120–21, 158; history of ideas about, 4–5, 104; invisibility of, 56; and psychopathy, 168, 175, 183; and recidivism, 5; redefined by Baxstrom, 222

Darwin, Charles, 37, 38, 56, 124, 126, 127

Davenport, Charles B., 141, 143, 170, 192

Davies, Stanley P., 227

Davis, Katharine Bement: and Bureau of Social Hygiene, 154–55; on causes of crime, 150; and clearinghouse plan, 152–54; and defective delinquent legislation, 154–55, 200; and eugenic sentencing, 151–55; impact of, on eugenic criminology, 12, 150; and intelligence testing of criminals, 12, 153–54; on

Davis, Katharine Bement (*continued*)
moral imbeciles, 150-51; as New York
City's commissioner of correction,
154; on psychopaths, 181-82; and
Rockefeller, John D., Jr., 12, 154-55;
mentioned, 192, 197, 231
Day, Jane, 153
Declaration of Principles. See National
Congress on Penitentiary and Reformatory Discipline: *Declaration of
Principles*
Defective delinquency movement: and
antiprostitution, 160; waning of, 173,
176, 177. *See also* Defective delinquency theory: popularity of, resistance to; *Defective delinquents*; Defective delinquents; Defective delinquents,
institutions for; Eugenic criminology;
names of specific leaders and institutions
Defective delinquency theory, 156-62;
popularity of, 156, 161; replaced by
psychopathy theory, 4, 162; resistance
to, 161-62
Defective delinquent legislation, 149,
188-204, 213-16, 222-23, 224-28; at
Bedford Hills Reformatory, 154-55,
202-4; factors encouraging, 189-98,
203; as liberal cause, 203-4; in Massachusetts, 189, 198-99, 224-26; as
moral crusade, 203; for Napanoch,
202-4; in New York State, 154-55,
200-204; overlooked by historians
and legal theorists, 226; timing of,
188-89. *See also* Clearinghouse plan;
Sentencing: eugenic
Defective delinquents, 146, 149, 156-61;
effectiveness of term, 190; origins of
term, 156, 199; synonyms for, 8, 14
n. 13
Defective delinquents, 210-31; castration
of, in Kansas, 235 n. 85; defined, 156-
57, 198, 213, 228; female, 159-61;
fertility of, 160; as institutional problems, 158, 213, 216; male, 156-59;
number of prisoners so designated, in
New York State, 223; and race, 218,
220; stereopticon presentation on,
200. *See also* Whipple, Fenix; *names of
specific institutions*
Defective delinquents, institutions for,

159, 212-30; in California, 227; and
commitment restrictions, 212-16, 218;
in Maryland, 228; in Massachusetts,
199, 224-26; and medical model of
criminality, 2, 212; in New York, 212-
24, 228-30, 232 n. 23; in Pennsylvania,
226-27; in Virginia, 227
Degeneracy: causes of, 36; and dangerousness, 47; defined, 36, 57, 93, 100;
protean nature of, 37, 100; synonyms
for, 51 n. 15. *See also* Degeneration
theory
Degenerates, 80-89, 93; at Elmira Reformatory, 93-96, 98, 99-105
Degeneration theory, 94, 104, 228; criminal anthropology's influence on, 103,
116, 120-21, 125-26; in early twentieth century, 142-43; and eugenics, 38,
57, 83; and evolution theory, 37-38;
and image of society as body, 38, 127-
28, 133-34; influence of, today, 211;
and psychopathy, influence on the concept of, 174-75, 177-79, 180-81, 182;
sources of, 80. *See also* Degeneracy;
Degenerates; Heredity: in degeneration theory; Lamarck's theory of
inheritance of acquired characteristics;
Phrenology: and degeneration theory;
names of specific theorists
Deterioration, American, 127-28
Detroit House of Correction, 97
Deutsch, Albert, 26
Dix, Dorothea L., 25, 27, 30
Drähms, August, 111, 114, 117, 119, 121-
22. *See also* Criminal anthropologists,
American
Dugdale, Richard L., 81; as a degenera-
tionist, 38-39, 94; *"Jukes," The,* 38-39,
41, 81, 200
—influence of: on criminal anthropology,
125, 126; on eugenics movement, 38;
on family studies, 51 n. 13, 141, 142;
on Kerlin, 83; on Lombroso, 126; on
Lowell and New York's State Board of
Charities, 38-39, 41
Duster, Troy, 239
Dwight, Theodore W., 96

Eisenstein, Zillah R., 9, 10
Ellis, Havelock, 102, 115, 116

Elmira (New York) Reformatory, 94, 96; cruelty to prisoners at, 103–4; intelligence testing at, 201; investigations of mismanagement at, 103–4; prisoner rehabilitation at, 98–103; production of degenerates at, 101–4; sentencing at, 98; significance of, 11, 94; mentioned, 2, 3, 115, 116, 192, 200, 212, 228. *See also* Brockway, Zebulon R.; Christian, Frank L.; Wey, Hamilton; Whipple, Fenix: at Elmira Reformatory

Elwyn School. *See* Pennsylvania Training School

Estabrook, Arthur H., 165 n. 46, 200

Eugenic criminology: achievements of, 188, 210, 212–31; binarisms of, 49–50, 87–88, 122–23; on causes of crime, 55, 74; and construction of professional middle class, 50, 87–90, 119, 122–23, 178–79, 183, 212; defined, 6, 74; as discourse on normality, 49–50, 87–88, 118–19, 122–23, 238; financing of, 163 n. 34, 174, 175, 176, 179, 193–96; low-visibility effects of, 227–28; in mid-twentieth century, 210–11; neglect of, by scholars, ix, 6–7; producers of, 82–90; and professionalization, 28, 68–69, 83, 87–90, 94, 113, 168–73, 183, 210; race and racism in, 50; on reproduction of criminals, 158, 160; respectability of, in Progressive Era, 155; and social class, 48–50, 57, 87–90, 119, 122–23, 183; and solutions to crime, 64, 66; waning of, 4, 168, 176, 180, 182, 210. *See also* Eugenics theory; Sentencing: eugenic; *names of specific producers, production sites, criminal types, and theories*

Eugenic field-workers, 142, 153, 193; police officers as, 195; as "psychiatrists" 170

Eugenics: avoided as a term by eugenicists, 150, 176; becomes familiar as a term to U.S. audiences, 6; coined as a term, 6, 14 n. 8; meaning of, 1–2; unfamiliar as a term in nineteenth-century America, 6, 56

Eugenics movement: financing of, 163 n. 34, 174, 175, 176, 179, 193–96; and gender, 47–50, 159–61; and jurisdictional claims, 28; and Progressive movement, 133–34, 153, 210; and race, 50; as reform movement, 155; rhetoric of, 86–90, 239; and social class, 48–50. *See also* Eugenic criminology: and social class; Eugenics theory; *names of specific eugenicists and eugenic institutions*

Eugenics Record Office, 141, 153, 170, 192, 195, 200

Eugenics theory: before 1850, 37; changes in, over time, 6; decline in vitality of, 173, 180; effects of, on professionalization of social control, 90; Mendelian versions of, 141–42; in Nazi Germany, 7, 13; today, 237, 239; and view of society as a body, 12, 38, 124, 127–28, 133–34. *See also* Eugenic criminology

Evolution, influence of theory of: on criminal anthropology, 106, 110, 120, 126–27; on criminal imbecile theory, 138; on degeneration theory, 37, 81, 82; on eugenics movement, 56–57

Family studies, 51 n. 13, 127, 141–45, 148 nn. 40, 42, 200

Farm colonies. *See* Colony plan: and eugenics

Fausto-Sterling, Anne, 8

Feebleminded, institutions for the: attitudes toward, on part of inmates' families, 45; in California, 56, 62, 68, 227; and changes in title of, 65; discipline at, 67; as dumping grounds for defective delinquents, 227; education at, 28, 64; eugenicization of, 55–69; as fashionable cause, 56; as generators of deviance, 66–67; and growth of system of, 68; hierarchy in staff at, 67; in Kentucky, 67; in Minnesota, 64, 66; in Nebraska, 63; in New Jersey, 56; private, 67–68; size of, 58, 62–68; and social class of inmates, 64–65. *See also* Colony plan; Custodialism; Defective delinquents, institutions for; Idiot education; *names of specific institutions and superintendents*

Feeble-Minded Club, The, 135

Feebleminded criminals: representations of, 140, 179. *See also* Born criminals;

Feebleminded criminals (*continued*)
  Criminal anthropologists, American:
  and departures from Lombroso's doctrines; *names of specific theorists and
  criminal types*
Feeblemindedness: as criminal defense,
  144, 161; definitions of, 65; and terminological issues, 65. *See also* Defective
  delinquents; Goddard, Henry H.;
  Moral imbecility
Feebleminded women: as born criminals,
  36, 159–61; contradictory discourses
  about, 53 n. 53; in poorhouses, 40, 43;
  as sex degenerates, 45, 49, 159–61
Fels, Samuel, 135, 142, 148 n. 39
Fernald, Guy G., 156, 157, 158, 172; as
  "psychiatrist," 170
Fernald, Mabel R., 161
Fernald, Walter E.: and defective delinquent legislation, 198–99; and
  diagnostic dispute with Goddard, 170;
  on moral (criminal) imbeciles, 66, 139–
  40, 156, 159, 160; as "psychiatrist,"
  170; revision of position on criminality
  of the feebleminded, 173, 190, 210;
  and term *defective delinquent*, 156, 199;
  mentioned, 65, 141, 143, 192, 230
Feuchtersleben, Ernst von, 173
Fink, Arthur E., 6
Fish, William B., 64, 67, 85, 106
Fitzpatrick, Ellen, 150
Flower, Roswell, 103
Fort, Samuel J., 83, 84
Fosdick, Raymond B., 193
Foucault, Michel, x, 4, 5, 6, 104
Fowler, E. P., 114
Frankenberg, Ruth, 50

Gall, Franz Joseph, 76, 113
Galton, Francis, 89, 101, 116; coins the
  term *eugenics*, 14 n. 8; and family
  studies, 51 n. 13, 141, 142
Garber, Marjorie, 110
Garfinkel, Harold, 5
Gault, Robert H., 149
Gemmill, William N., 161
Gender: and defective delinquency,
  159–61; and degeneracy, 47–50; and
  psychopathy, 177–82
Genealogical research. *See* Family studies

Glueck, Bernard, 174–76, 182; degenerationist themes in work of, 175, 182;
  and eugenics, 176, 185 nn. 45, 47; as
  leader in psychiatric criminology, 168,
  174; on psychopathy, 167, 175–76; and
  work of, at Sing Sing, 174–76, 196;
  mentioned, 177, 179, 181, 197
Glueck, Eleanor T., 176, 211
Glueck, Sheldon S., 176, 211, 225
Goddard, Henry Herbert, 135; and classification of the mentally retarded,
  138; concept of intelligence, as static,
  142; *The Criminal Imbecile*, 143–45;
  degenerationist concepts in work of,
  142–43; diagnostic dispute with W. E.
  Fernald, 171; and eugenics, 137–46,
  143–45; and family studies, 141–45;
  *Feeble-mindedness: Its Causes and Con-
  sequences*, 139–40, 142; on fertility of
  the feebleminded, 160; and intelligence
  testing, 12, 135–40, 153; introduces
  Binet method, 136; *The Kallikak Family*,
  143–45; and "moron" category, 137–39;
  significance of, to field of psychology,
  12, 135–38, 146; mentioned, 150, 152,
  161, 189, 190, 192, 200, 231
—as criminologist, 146, 158; defines
  criminal imbeciles, 138–40; discredits
  criminal anthropology, 140
Godding, W. W., 29, 30
Goffman, Erving, 299–30
Goring, Charles, 88
Gray, John P., 29, 30
Green, David, 112
Grob, Gerald, 169
Guggenheim, Daniel, 193

Hall, G. Stanley, 135
Haller, Mark H., ix, 120–21, 210
Hart, Hastings H., 158, 160, 192,
Hassian, Marouf A., 239, 240
Hayes, Rutherford B., 97
Healy, William, 176–79; degenerationist
  themes in work of, 177–79; influence
  of, on psychiatric criminology, 172,
  177, 186 n. 48; as "psychiatrist," 170;
  on psychic constitutional inferiority
  (psychopathy), 177–79; mentioned,
  168, 174, 181
Hebberd, Robert W., 192–93, 201

Hebberd Commission (New York State Commission to Investigate Provision for the Mentally Deficient), 192–93, 204

Henderson, Charles Richmond, 116, 117, 119, 120, 155. *See also* Criminal anthropologists, American

Heredity: in Brockway's thought, 94–95, 97, 102, 104; in criminal anthropology, 118–24; in degeneration theory, 36–39, 61–62, 94–95, 100; in eugenic criminology, 83, 141–45; and feeble-minded women, 159–61; in Goddard's work, 141–45; in *The "Jukes,"* 38–39, 126; Lamarckian view of, 85, 94–95, 134, 141; Mendelian formula for, 141–42, 173; and pauperism, 38–39; and psychopathy, 168, 173, 174, 175–76, 177, 180, 182. *See also* Family studies; Howe, Samuel Gridley: on inheritance of idiocy

Heredity charts. *See* Family studies

Herrnstein, Richard J., 11, 211, 238, 239

Hickson, William J., 157

Hodder, Jessie D., 181–82

Homosexuality, 12, 175, 178–79, 181–82

Hooton, Earnest A., 211

Horton, Henry P., 114

Howe, Samuel Gridley: on classification of idiots, 24; degenerationist themes in work of, 79; and idiot education, 19, 20, 26; on inheritance of idiocy, 79; on moral idiocy, 78–79; and phrenology, 79; position in development of born-criminal theory, 78–79; as a professional, 29; survey of Massachusetts idiots, 19, 24, 31 n. 9, 79; mentioned, 19, 25, 27, 75,

Hoyt, Charles S., 39, 40, 41, 45

Hrdlička, Alešander, 44–45

Idiocy: confused with insanity, 23–24; definitions of, 23, 65; and terminological issues, 24. *See also* Howe, Samuel Gridley: on inheritance of idiocy; Idiots; Mentally retarded persons; Mental retardation; Syracuse Asylum

Idiots: education of, 17–27; statistics on, 24; status of, relative to insane, 26;

treatment of, 17–18, 24–27. *See also* Wilbur, Hervey B.; *names of specific institutions*

Immigration, 57, 127

Incorrigibles. *See* Criminal imbeciles; Defective delinquents; Degenerates

Indiana State Reformatory, 153

Inheritance of acquired characteristics. *See* Lamarck's theory of inheritance of acquired characteristics

Inheritance of feeblemindedness in early twentieth-century eugenics, 141–43

Intelligence: of born criminals, 120, 122; as caste mark, 50, 122–23, 212; Goddard's concept of, as static, 142; and heredity, in work of H. H. Goddard, 141–42; Wilbur's understanding of, as elastic, 23

Intelligence testing: and Binet method, 12, 136–37; and clearinghouse plan, 152; and criminal law, 144, 161; effects of, on born-criminal theory, 12; at Elmira Reformatory, 201; and eugenics, 137–46; improvements in, at New York State prisons, 218; by New York City Police Department, 193–94; professional struggles over, 170–73; and Progressive Era concerns, 12. *See also* Bedford Hills: mental testing at; Goddard, Henry H.: and intelligence testing

Involuntary commitment, 21, 42, 45

Jackson v. Indiana, 226, 222, 226

James, Walter B., 202

Jastrow, Joseph, 115

Johnson, Alexander, 69 n. 15

Johnstone, Edward R., 134–35

"Jukes," The. See Dugdale, Richard L.

Jurisdiction, professional, 28, 94; and criminality, 170–73, 183; and eugenics, 28

Juvenile Psychopathic Institute, Chicago, 153, 177

Keller, Helen, 135

Kellor, Frances A., 118

Kentucky Institution for the Education and Training of Feeble-Minded Children, 67

Kerlin, Isaac N., 59–62, 67; on causes of
mental retardation, 61–62; and custodialism, 62–68; and degeneration
theory, 61–62, 94; and eugenics, 55,
60–68; influence of, on AMO, 58, 59,
60, 68, 83; influences on, 61, 62, 105;
on moral imbecility, 55, 65–66, 83–85;
and protégés, 61, 70 n. 32; relationship
with Hervey B. Wilbur, 60; repression
of inmates, 66; scientific bent of, 61–
62; and sterilization, 61; mentioned,
10, 93, 106, 230. *See also* Colony plan:
Kerlin's model of
Kirchwey, George W., 206 n. 40, 209
n. 89
Kirkbride, Thomas Story, 26
Knight, George H., 66, 106
Kraepelin, Emil, 173, 178
Krafft-Ebing, Richard von, 173, 176
Kuhlmann, Frederick, 137, 161

Laboratory of Social Hygiene, 154–55
Lamarck's theory of inheritance of ac-
quired characteristics, 85, 94–95, 134,
141
Laura Spelman Rockefeller Memorial,
196
Laurelton (Pennsylvania) State Village,
227
Leavenworth, Elias W., 21–22
Letchworth Village, 2
Lewis, O. F.: consultant to Hebberd
commission, 192–93; finds Dugdale's
manuscript, 200; general secretary to
PANY, 188, 195–97; leader of defective
delinquency campaign in New York
State, 195–97, 200–201; and term
defective delinquent, 156; mentioned,
231
Lewisohn, Adolph, 197
Lombroso, Cesare, 118; *Crime: Its Causes
and Remedies,* 114, 123; on criminal
anthropology as a science, 111; on
criminal inheritance, 120; *Criminal
Man,* 114, 115, 120, 123; and degeneration theory, 120; Dugdale's influence
on, 126; and eugenics, 11, 123; *The
Female Offender,* 114; influence of, in
United States, 115; introductions and
articles in English, 114; and sentences

for crimes, 123; translations of work
of, 114; mentioned, 81, 83, 101, 102,
104, 110, 112, 113, 115, 116, 118, 120,
121, 124, 125, 134, 140, 177
Lowell, Charles Russell, 36
Lowell, Josephine Shaw, 105; and Bedford Hills Reformatory, 150; commissioner of New York State Board
of Charities, 34; efforts to identify
Newark commitments, 44; and eugenics, 38; founder of institutions,
generally; founder of Newark Custodial Asylum, 34–43, 47–50; personal circumstances of, 36, 49–50;
philanthropy, influence on, 36; and
social control, 36; and social purity
movement, 48; mentioned, 38, 47, 55,
56, 159, 211, 230. *See also* Dugdale,
Richard L.: influence of, on Lowell
Lydston, G. Frank, 117, 125; and criminal anthropology, 110, 111, 116, 117;
and eugenics, 124. *See also* Criminal
anthropologists, American

MacDonald, Arthur, 106, 117, 118;
Criminology, 112, 114, 116, 117. *See also*
Criminal anthropologists, American
Manie sans délire, 75, 77, 78
Marks, Jonathan, 239
Maryland Institution for Defective De-
linquents. *See* Patuxent (Maryland)
Institution for Defective Delinquents
Massachusetts Board of Insanity, 158
Massachusetts Commission to Investigate
the Question of the Increase of Crimi-
nals, Mental Defectives, Epileptics
and Degenerates, 156, 159, 164 n. 38,
198–99
Massachusetts defective delinquent
legislation. *See* Defective delinquent
legislation: in Massachusetts
Massachusetts Reformatory at Concord,
156, 225
Massachusetts Reformatory for Women
at Framingham, 179–80, 225
Massachusetts School for Idiotic and
Feeble-Minded Youth (School for the
Feeble-Minded), 66, 78
Maudsley, Henry, 1, 210; as born-
criminal theorist, 81, 126; on criminal

responsibility, 81; degenerationist themes in work of, 81; on moral imbecility, 80, 81; mentioned, 9, 80, 83

Maughs, Sydney, 6

McKim, W. Duncan, 117, 128; and criminal anthropology, 117, 120; and eugenics, 124. *See also* Criminal anthropologists, American

Medical model of criminality as disease, 77, 85, 95, 97, 105, 107 n. 6, 153, 171, 172, 228; and institutions for defective delinquents, 2, 188, 197, 212

Mendel, Gregor, 141–42

Mendelian formula of inheritance, 141–42

Mental hospitals, 29, 42, 63

Mental hygiene movement, 168, 170, 171. *See also* National Committee on Mental Hygiene

Mentally retarded persons: classifications of, 137–38, 147 n. 28; defined as a social problem, 25–27; shifts in attitudes toward, 189–93. *See also* Feebleminded, institutions for the; Feebleminded women; Idiots; Mental retardation

Mental retardation: attitudes toward, in mid-nineteenth century, 17–18, 23–27; status of, relative to insanity, 7; terminology of, 13–14 n. 2, 24, 32–33 n. 33, 33 n. 35, 137–38, 147 n. 24, 184 n. 17, 190–91. *See also* Feeblemindedness; Idiocy; Ray, Isaac: on idiocy and imbecility

Metaphor. *See* Born-criminal concept: metaphorical nature of; Born criminals: as metaphors

Meyer, Adolf, 171, 185 n. 32

Miller, Nathan L., 204

Moral derangement, 77–78

Moral idiocy. *See* Defective delinquency; Howe, Samuel Gridley: on moral idiocy; Moral imbecility

Moral imbeciles: as born criminals, 66, 81, 84–85, 105–6, 150–51; female, 151; as good workers, 66, 191. *See also* Moral imbecility: defined; Criminal imbeciles

Moral imbecility, 80, 81; AMO's work on, 82–86; defined, 55–56, 65–66, 72 n. 66; and eugenics theory, 66, 69; synonyms for, 7, 83–86, 101, 138–39; theory of, overlooked by historians, 7. *See also* Criminal imbeciles; Moral imbeciles; *names of specific theorists*

Moral insanity, 7, 56, 75–77

Moral treatment, 23, 25

"Moron" category, 137–39

Murray, Charles, 11, 211, 238

Napanoch (New York) Institution for Male Defective Delinquents, 13, 188, 192, 212–22, 223, 228; architecture of, 213; board of managers of, 202, 213; closing of, 222; commitments to, 212–18; establishing legislation, 202–4; institutional nature of, 2, 213; means of release from, 221; and prisoner characteristics, 216–20; significance of, 2; time served at, 220–21. *See also* Whipple, Fenix

NAPIPI (National Association for the Protection of the Insane and Prevention of Insanity), 30, 169–70

National Committee on Mental Hygiene, 175, 176, 193

National Committee on Prisons and Prison Labor, 197

National Conference of Charities and Correction, 105

National Congress on Penitentiary and Reformatory Discipline, 96–98, 188, 195; *Declaration of Principles*, 97–98

National Prison Association, 102, 107 n. 11, 115–16

Newark, New York, 42–43

Newark (New York) Custodial Asylum: attitudes toward, of inmates' families, 45; campaign for, 39–42, 47–50; and commitment sources, 43–46; compared to Syracuse Asylum, 46; conditions at, 46–47; establishment of, 41–43; eugenical purpose of, 46; inmates of, 44–47; investigations of, 43, 46–47; involuntary commitment at, 45; significance of, 10, 35; mentioned, 55, 56, 63, 150, 151, 154

New Jersey Reformatory for Women at Clinton Farms, 227–28

New Jersey Training School for Feeble-
minded Boys and Girls. *See* Vineland
(New Jersey) Training School for
Feeble-minded Boys and Girls
New York City Police Department's
Psychopathic Laboratory, 193–95
New York Committee on Feeble-
mindedness, 195, 197, 201–2, 204
New York Foundation, 153
New York Prison Association. *See* PANY
(Prison Association of New York)
New York Psychiatrical Society, 171
New York Public Education Association,
153
New York School of Philanthropy, 153
New-York State Asylum for Idiots at
Albany, 19–21
New York State Asylum for Idiots at
Syracuse. *See* Syracuse Asylum
New York State Board of Charities, 103,
203, 204; and founding of Newark
Custodial Asylum, 41. *See also* Heb-
berd, Robert W.; Hebberd Com-
mission; Hoyt, Charles S.; Lowell,
Josephine Shaw
New York State Charities Aid Associa-
tion, 202, 204
New York State Commission for Mental
Defectives, 201–2, 213
New York State Commission of Prisons,
213, 216; Special Committee on Mental
Disease and Delinquency, 194, 204
New York State Commission on the
Feeble-minded. *See* New York State
Commission for Mental Defectives
New York State Commission to In-
vestigate Provision for the Mentally
Deficient. *See* Hebberd Commission
New York State Conference of Charities,
200
New York State Conference of Magis-
trates, 200
New York State Custodial Asylum for
Feeble-minded Women at Newark. *See*
Newark (New York) Custodial Asylum
New York State Custodial Asylum
(Training School) at Rome. *See* Rome
State School
New York State Department of Correc-
tion, 213, 221, 222, 223

New York State Eastern Reformatory
at Napanoch, 202. *See also* Napa-
noch (New York) Institution for Male
Defective Delinquents
New York State Hospital Development
Commission, 204
New York State Institution for Defec-
tive Delinquents at Woodbourne. *See*
Woodbourne (New York) Institution
for Defective Delinquents
New York State Institution for Male
Defective Delinquents. *See* Napa-
noch (New York) Institution for Male
Defective Delinquents
New York State institutions for defective
delinquents, proportion of all New
York state prisoners at, from 1922 to
1956, 223–24
New York State Lunatic Asylum at Utica,
22, 29, 42
New York State Mental Deficiency Law
of 1919, 202
New York State Prison at Auburn. *See*
Auburn (New York) State Prison
New York State Prison Survey Commit-
tee, 197–98, 204
New York State Reformatory at Elmira.
See Elmira (New York) Reformatory
New York State Reformatory for Women
at Bedford Hills. *See* Bedford Hills
(New York) Reformatory for Women
New York State, Sing Sing Prison. *See*
Sing Sing (New York) State Prison
New York State Training School at
Albion. *See* Albion (New York) State
Training School
Noyes, William, 115

Olson, Harry, 159
Original sin, 1, 74
Osborne, A. E., 59, 62, 63, 65

PANY (Prison Association of New York),
105, 188–89; bureau of inspection
and research, 196; committee on defective delinquents, 200; financing
of, 163 n. 34, 164 n. 36; as leader of
defective delinquency movement, 195–
97, 200–201, 203, 204. *See also*
Lewis, O. F.

Parker, George M., 200–201
Parrish, Joseph, 59
Parsons, Philip A., 116, 117, 121, 122; and eugenics, 123–24. *See also* Criminal anthropologists, American
Patuxent (Maryland) Institution for Defective Delinquents, 228
Pauperism, 39
Pedigree studies. *See* Family studies
Peirson, Silas S., 43–44
Pennsylvania Institution for Defective Delinquents, 227
Pennsylvania plan. *See* Colony plan: Kerlin's model of
Pennsylvania Training School, 58, 59–68; sterilization at, 61
Penology, professionalization of, 94, 96–98
Perkins, Eliza C., 43
Pick, Daniel, 113
Pinel, Philippe, 23, 75, 77, 78
Philanthropy: Jewish, 164 n. 34; and Josephine Shaw Lowell, 36; nineteenth-century, compared to twentieth-century, 36. *See also* Eugenics movement: financing of; *names of specific donors and organizations*
Photography: in criminal anthropology, 112–13, 126, 145; and criminological science, 106; as rhetoric, 113
Phrenology, 6, 56, 75, 76–77, 78, 79, 113; and causes of crime, 94; and criminal anthropology, 125; and degeneration theory, 77
Poorhouses: idiots in, 25, 27; state takeovers of, 27
Positivism, 111–13, 115, 125–26
Prichard, James Cowles, 75–76, 77, 79, 83
Probation, 151
Professionalization: and altruism, 89–90; and care of mentally retarded, 19, 55–69, 83–90; and criminological theory, 113, 168, 183, 210; and eugenics, 57, 62–66, 87–90; and jurisdictional issues, 12, 28–30, 94; of prison administration, 94, 96–98, 99; of psychiatry, 12, 168–73, 183; of psychology, 12, 138, 168, 170–73, 183; and social problems movements, 28; and specialized

knowledge, 59, 68–69, 83–90
Professional middle class. *See* Eugenic criminology: and construction of professional middle class
Prostitutes: at Bedford Hills reformatory, 181; intelligence of, 153–54, 160
Psychiatric criminology, 168–83
Psychiatrist, 34 n. 54; meanings of term, 170; qualifications and criteria for use of the term, 170, 172
Psychiatrists, 74; and clearinghouse plan, 152; and eugenics, 168, 176, 179, 180, 182; and professional struggles with psychologists, 12, 168–73, 183. *See also* Psychiatry
Psychiatry: doldrums of, in late nineteenth century, 169; professionalization of, 168–73, 183; and Progressive movement, 170. *See also* Psychiatrists
Psychology, field of: before intelligence testing, 135; Goddard's contributions to, 12, 135–38, 146; and opposition to defective delinquency theory, 161–62; and professional struggles with psychiatry, 12, 168–73, 183
Psychopathic Hospital. *See* Bedford Hills (New York) Reformatory for Women: Psychopathic Hospital at
Psychopathic Laboratory. *See* New York City Police Department's Psychopathic Laboratory
Psychopaths: at Bedford Hills Reformatory, 179–82; definitions of category, 12, 168, 173–76, 177, 182–83; and eugenics, 168, 176; gender differences among, 177–82; homosexual tendencies of, 12, 178–79; as institutional troublemakers, 176, 179–82; intellectual capacity of, 12, 173, 175; at Massachusetts Reformatory for Women, 179–80; at Sing Sing, 174–76. *See also* Psychopaths, sexual; Psychopathy theory
Psychopaths, sexual, 185 n. 40, 226
Psychopathy theory, 167, 173–83; constitutional elements in, 12, 168, 174, 175, 176, 177; critiques of, 183; and defective delinquency theory, 161–62; and homosexuality, 12, 175, 178–79, 181; and the professionalization of

Psychopathy theory (*continued*)
  psychiatry, 168–73, 183. *See also* Degeneration theory: and psychopathy, influence on the concept of; Heredity: and psychopathy; *names of specific theorists*
Purity crusades. *See* Social purity movement

Race. *See* Defective delinquents: and race; Eugenic criminology: race and racism in
Ray, Isaac: and born-criminal theory, 80, 91 n. 28; on criminal responsibility, 80, 81, 82; on idiocy and imbecility, 24, 80; and phrenology, 80, 91 n. 28; mentioned, 79–80, 94
Recidivists, identification of, 132
Reformatory plan. *See* Reformatory prisons for adults
Reformatory prisons for adults, 93, 96–98. *See also* Bedford Hills (New York) Reformatory; Elmira (New York) Reformatory
Rehabilitation theory, 93, 95, 96–103; and eugenics, 93–94
Rhetoric, 25, 26, 40–41, 86–90, 194
Rockefeller, John D., Jr., 12, 154–55, 174, 175, 176, 179, 193, 196
Rockefeller, John D., Sr., 196
Rockefeller, William, 193
Rogers, A. C., 67, 84
Rome (New York) State School (Custodial Asylum), 200, 216; colony placements from, 191; commitments to Napanoch, 213–15; defective delinquents at, 192, 202
Roosevelt, Theodore, 103
Rosenberg, Charles E., 48, 56
Rowland, Eleanor, 153
Rush, Benjamin, 75, 79, 80, 83, 169; on moral derangement, 77–78; and phrenology, 77–78; as proto-degenerationist, 78
Russell Sage Foundation, 158, 193; and traveling eugenics exhibit, 201

Salmon, Thomas W., 171, 193, 197
Sanborn, Franklin B., 96, 97, 98, 99, 101, 102

Savitz, Leonard D., 115
Schiff, Jacob, 163 n. 26
Schiff, Mortimer, 163 n. 26, 193, 196
Scientific criminology, 111, 112, 125–26
Scientific penology, 94, 112, 153
Seguin, Edward, 18, 59, 67; and Hervey B. Wilbur, 18, 22–23; and idiot education, 18, 20, 22–23, 25, 33 n. 43, 66
Sekula, Allan, 101, 119
Sentencing: eugenic, 3, 123–24, 146, 149, 151–55, 176, 198, 203, 212, 220–21; indefinite, 3, 95, 98, 105, 123, 149, 151–53, 176, 180, 190, 211, 212, 221, 224, 225, 227, 228; indeterminate, 11, 95, 97–99, 123; under New York's fourth felony law, 217
Sharp, H. C., 153
Sheldon, William H., 211
Simon, Théodore, 136
Sing Sing (New York) State Prison, 220; clearinghouse at, 174–75, 194, 196, 198; psychiatric clinic at, 174–75; research on psychopathy at, 174–76; role of, in centralization of New York State prison system, 175
Social Darwinism, 37
Social purity movement, 48
Sonoma (California) State Home, 227
Spaulding, Edith R., 168, 179–82; absense of degenerationist themes in work of, 180–82; at Bedford Hills Psychopathic Hospital, 179–82; on Massachusetts defective delinquent legislation, 199; at Massachusetts Reformatory for Women, 179; on psychopathy, 174, 179–81
Spencer, Herbert, 37, 126
Spurzheim, Johann Gaspar, 77
Statistical record keeping, 24, 39, 82
Sterilization, 83, 124, 152–53; in California, 227; eugenicists' attitudes toward, 61, 67; at Indiana State Reformatory, 153; Kerlin's endorsement of, 61; at New Jersey Reformatory for Women, 227–28; in New York State, 152–53; opposition to, 70 n. 38, 161; in Virginia, 153
Storer, Mary, 159, 160
Superintendents of institutions for the mentally retarded: client definitions

of, 28–29, 65–66, 69; and eugenics,
55–69, 82–90; and jurisdiction, 28–
30, 65–67, 69; professionalization of,
55–69, 83–90. *See also* AMO; *specific
names*
Syracuse (New York) Asylum for Idiots:
and colony plan, 71 n. 48, 191; compared to Newark Custodial Asylum,
46; custodialism at, 30, 46; donors
to, 21–22; founding of, 21–22; initial
purpose of, 27; inmates of, in Union
Army, 65; original building of, 22;
significance of, 10; mentioned, 41, 62,
63. *See also* Seguin, Edward; Wilbur,
Hervey B.
Syracuse, New York, 21–22

Talbot, Eugene S., 116, 117, 118, 120.
See also Criminal anthropologists,
American
Terman, Lewis M., 137, 143, 171; objec-
tions to initial Binet scale, 137
Terry, Jennifer, 238
Thayer, Walter N., Jr., 215, 216, 219
Thomson, J. Bruce, 80, 102; and criminal
anthropology, 81, 125, 126; and crimi-
nal statistics, 82; influence of, 61, 62,
81, 83; on moral imbecility, 80
Thorndike, Edward L., 193
Toffler, Alvin and Heidi, 211
Trent, James W., Jr., 190

United States Supreme Court, 153, 220,
221–22
University of Chicago, 150
Urla, Jacqueline, 238
Utica Lunatic Asylum. *See* New York
State Lunatic Asylum at Utica

Vanderbilt, F. W., 193
Victor of Aveyron, 26
Vineland (New Jersey) Training School
for Feeble-minded Boys and Girls, 56,
153, 157, 200; and criminal imbecile
theory, 134; and intelligence testing,
136–37; research at, 135–40, 142. *See
also* Goddard, Henry H.
Virginia State Farm, 227

Wallin, J. E. Wallace, 161,

Weidensall, Jean, 153
Weismann, August, 141, 142
Werlinder, Henry, 6
Wey, Hamilton D., 93, 104, 105; influence of, 102, 106, 125; and Lombroso,
101, 116; and photography, 102, 126;
and physical training of prisoners,
100–102; place in the development of
criminology, 116, 125–26; and studies
in criminal anthropology, 101–2, 108
n. 49, 111, 115–16, 124
Whipple, Fenix: and bestiality, 4; death
of, 4, 230–31; at Elmira Reformatory,
3, 228; family of, 3; and Frank Christian, 3–4, 228; habeas corpus petitions
by, 229; intelligence test results of, 3,
229; later years of, 230–31; at Napanoch, 2–4, 228–31; offenses of, 2–3,
4; paroles of, 4, 230; sentence of, 2, 3,
220; mentioned, 9
White, William A., 169, 183
Wilbur, Harry Aguiro, 30
Wilbur, Hervey Backus, 18; anti-eugeni-
cism of, 42–43; and colony plan, 191;
and concept of intelligence as elastic,
23; on curability of idiocy, 27; and custodialism, 21, 29–30, 42; and disputes
with psychiatrists, 29–30; and dispute
with Kerlin, 60; as father of retarded
son, 30; as first president of NAPIPI,
30, 169–70; as founder of farm colony,
71 n. 48; as founder of first institution for education of idiots, 17–19; as
founder of Syracuse Asylum for Idiots,
21–22; historical significance of, 19;
and jurisdiction, attitudes toward, 28–
30; and Newark Custodial Asylum,
41–44; personal traits of, 18, 30, 34
n. 62; provisions of will of, 30; terminological obduracy of, 24, 32–33 n. 33;
mentioned, 25, 26, 29, 40, 45, 55, 68.
See also Seguin, Edward: and Hervey B.
Wilbur
Wilmarth, Alfred W., 61, 64, 67
Wines, Enoch C., 96, 97, 195, 196
Wines, Frederick Howard, 124, 156
Wilson, James Q., 239
Women, 47–48; and double standard, 49;
and eugenics propaganda, 160; institutionalization rates of, 160–61; testing

Women (*continued*)
of social control innovations on, 54
n. 66. *See also* Feebleminded women;
Gender; Sterilization
Woodbourne (New York) Institution for
Defective Delinquents, 223

Woods, Arthur, 188, 193–94

Yerkes, Robert M., 171

Zeman, Thomas E., 122
Zenderland, Leila, 138

Nicole Hahn Rafter is a professor at Northeastern University. Her books include *Partial Justice: Women, Prisons and Social Control, White Trash: The Eugenic Family Studies, 1877-1919,* and, most recently, *International Feminist Perspectives in Criminology: Engendering a Discipline* (with Frances Heidensohn). She is working on a book on crime films and a study of mobbing, the phenomenon of psychological terror in the workplace.